Comparative Physiology of Desert Animals

FRONTISPIECE: *Dasycercus cristicauda*, a desert marsupial insectivore that lives in deep burrows. One of its Aboriginal names is Mulgara. (Photograph W. V. Macfarlane.)

SYMPOSIA OF THE ZOOLOGICAL SOCIETY OF LONDON
NUMBER 31

Comparative Physiology of Desert Animals

(The Proceedings of a Symposium held at The Zoological Society of London on 15 and 16 July, 1971)

Edited by

G. M. O. MALOIY

Department of Animal Physiology, University of Nairobi, Nairobi, Kenya

Published for

THE ZOOLOGICAL SOCIETY OF LONDON

by

ACADEMIC PRESS

1972

ACADEMIC PRESS INC. (LONDON) LTD.
24/28 Oval Road
London NW1

U.S. Edition published by
ACADEMIC PRESS INC.
111 Fifth Avenue,
New York, New York 10003

Library of Congress Catalog Card Number: 70-189935

ISBN: 0-12-613331-X

PRINTED IN GREAT BRITAIN BY
J. W. ARROWSMITH LTD., BRISTOL

CONTRIBUTORS

BORUT, A., *Department of Zoology, University of Tel-Aviv, Israel** (p. 175)

BLIGH, J., *ARC Institute of Animal Physiology, Babraham, Cambridge, England* (p. 357)

BRADLEY, S. R., *Section of Ecology and Systematics, Division of Biological Sciences, Cornell University, Ithaca, New York, 14850, U.S.A.* (p. 191)

CASTEL, M., *Department of Zoology, Hebrew University, Jerusalem, Israel* (p. 175)

CHOSHNIAK, J., *Department of Zoology, University of Tel-Aviv, Israel* (p. 229)

CLOUDSLEY-THOMPSON, J. L., *Department of Zoology, Birkbeck College, University of London, London, England* (p. 39)

DAWSON, T. J., *School of Zoology, University of New South Wales, Kensington, New South Wales, Australia* (p. 133)

DEAVERS, D. R., *Section of Ecology and Systematics, Division of Biological Sciences, Cornell University, Ithaca, New York, 14850, U.S.A.* (p. 191)

FINCH, V. A., *Department of Animal Physiology, University of Nairobi, P.O. Box 30197, Nairobi, Kenya* (p. 315)

HOROWITZ, M., *Department of Zoology, Hebrew University, Jerusalem, Israel* (p. 175)

HOWARD, B., *Department of Animal Physiology, Waite Agricultural Research Institute, University of Adelaide, South Australia, 5064* (p. 261)

HUDSON, J. W., *Section of Ecology and Systematics, Division of Biological Sciences, Cornell University, Ithaca, New York, 14850, U.S.A.* (p. 191)

IGGO, A., *Department of Veterinary Physiology, Royal (Dick) School of Veterinary Studies, University of Edinburgh, Summerhall, Edinburgh, Scotland* (p. 327)

LOUW, G. N., *Zoological Institute, University of Stellenbosch, Stellenbosch, South Africa* (p. 297)

MCEWAN JENKINSON, D., *Department of Physiology, The Hannah Research Institute, Ayr, Scotland* (p. 345)

* Address: Department of Zoology, Hebrew University, Jerusalem, Israel.

MACFARLANE, W. V., *Department of Animal Physiology, Waite Agricultural Research Institute, University of Adelaide, South Australia, 5064* (p. 261)

MACMILLEN, R. E., *Department of Population and Environmental Biology, University of California, Irvine, California, 92664, U.S.A.* (p. 147)

MALOIY, G. M. O., *Animal Physiology Division, East African Veterinary Research Organization, Muguga, Kabete, Kenya** (p. 243)

SCHMIDT-NIELSEN, K., *Department of Zoology, Duke University, Durham, North Carolina, 27706, U.S.A.* (p. 1, p. 371)

SHAW, J., *Department of Zoology, University of Newcastle upon Tyne, Newcastle upon Tyne, England* (p. 15)

SHKOLNIK, A., *Department of Zoology, University of Tel-Aviv, Israel* (p. 1, p. 229)

SKADHAUGE, E., *Institute of Medical Physiology A, University of Copenhagen, Denmark* (p. 113)

STOBBART, R. H., *Department of Zoology, University of Newcastle upon Tyne, Newcastle upon Tyne, England* (p. 15)

TAYLOR, C. R., *Museum of Comparative Zoology, Harvard University, Cambridge, Massachusetts, 01730, U.S.A.* (p. 1, p. 215)

TEMPLETON, J. R., *Department of Zoology, University of Montana, Missoula, Montana, 59801, U.S.A.* (p. 61)

WARBURG, M. R., *Israel Institute for Biological Research, Ness Ziona, Israel* (p. 79)

*Present adress: Department of Animal Physiology, University of Nairobi, P.O. Box 30197, Nairobi, Kenya.

ORGANIZER AND CHAIRMEN

ORGANIZER

G. M. O. Maloiy, *Department of Animal Physiology, University of Nairobi, Nairobi, Kenya*

CHAIRMEN OF SESSIONS

S. E. Dicker, *Department of Physiology, Chelsea College of Science and Technology, London, England*

L. E. Mount, *ARC Institute of Animal Physiology, Babraham, Cambridge, England*

A. T. Phillipson, *School of Veterinary Medicine, University of Cambridge, Cambridge, England*

S. Thomas, *Department of Physiology, University of Manchester, Manchester, England*

PREFACE

The arid fifth of the earth provides habitats for a surprisingly wide range of animals. The hot and the cold deserts represent the furthest extremes to which originally aquatic animals have moved in radiation to dry land. Analysis of the structural, functional and behavioural aspects of this wayout fringe of physiology has proceeded steadily over the past decade. It is becoming clear that not only methods of rejecting heat at the surface but also of generating less heat internally have evolved for the desert. Intermittent food supplies and the concentration of salts in desert water have been met by fat storage and salt tolerance. Water independence and low rates of water turnover have evolved in desert animals, in association with low rates of energy metabolism. The evolution of behavioural patterns for seeking shelter from the environmental forces has linked with the development of high resistance to electrolyte, osmotic, or biochemical stress applied to cells during drought or dehydration.

The present Symposium was conceived as a way of bringing together current thinking on animals of many phyla and at the same time for formulating principles of regulation in the hot dry environment. It has become apparent also that the desert is not free from invasion by less adequately adapted animals than the truly desert forms. Pressures driving migrants into the desert are always present and a non-adapted form may often survive many years in severe conditions until locally eliminated. The species has the opportunity to re-invade from favourable environments.

This book has been shaped on the basis of reviews and synthesis of current physiological understanding of animals, from molluscs and insects, through birds and mammals, investigated in the last few years. Not only have samples of the phyla been covered but also the continents so that African, Asian, Australian and American animals have been included in the pattern. Some attention is given to the cold deserts of the arctic region.

The exponential increase in human population and an even greater increment in means of transport has meant that the desert has become increasingly accessable to exploiters and tourists. Understanding of the animals living in these regions is increasingly necessary as these environments are threatened by further pastoralism, fire and mineral search. Desert animals are probably more susceptible to human interference than most because of the slender margin of resources, so that any understanding of their needs and responses is important in the planning of conservation methods and in the setting aside of areas protected against human incursions.

Increasingly, the studies of animals in their normal environment has become possible as techniques have developed. There are, therefore, in this report of the Symposium, pictures both of desert animals in the laboratory or experimental situation, and of the animals in the niches and habitats where, it may be hoped, they may be permitted to survive. Fortunately, the defences of the desert are formidable and it is important that they be maintained.

June, 1972 G. M. O. Maloiy

FOREWORD

My experience of desert life amounts to one visit to Khartoum. This is a great deal less than I could have wished, but at least the visit left me with the imprint of a memorable conversation. I was talking to a Sudanese lady who had spent three years at Cambridge working for her Ph.D. They were, she told me, the most wonderful years of her life. This I could well understand, but (betraying, perhaps, a certain note of prejudice) I could not resist asking if there had not been at least some disadvantages in Cambridge life: the wind, for example, the rain, and all those fens! She unhesitatingly replied that, that was all part of the attraction. "I can assure you", she said, "that I used to get up early in the morning, walk out into the Cambridge drizzle, and say to myself 'this is how I have always wanted to be—WET' ".

We are in no position to say whether or not the animals discussed in this Symposium actually *want* to be wet. But it is certain that in almost completely depriving themselves of the opportunity for this, and with no prospect of rehydrating themselves at the University of Cambridge, they are stretching almost to breaking-point the Hendersonian concept of *The Fitness of the Environment*. In so doing, they are providing zoologists with an immense range of adaptational problems to investigate; problems that, as we shall see, involve a correspondingly wide range of techniques, extending from classical procedures of whole-animal respiration studies to electron microscopical investigations of the structure of capillary endothelia.

One result of recent physiological investigations has been to enlarge our understanding of the evolutionary status of groups of animals which have been interpreted in the past in too simplified a way. A marsupial, for example, was at one time presented to students as a placental *manqué*, imperfect in its organization and in its achievement. Of course, there is a sense in which this is true. After all, this Symposium has been organized by placental mammals, not by marsupials, and this must presumably mean something. But today we are much better informed of the complexities of marsupial organization, and of the many remarkable convergences that have developed between them and placentals. Indeed, we shall learn in this Symposium that their lower metabolic rate has proved of positive advantage in their exploitation of desert conditions. Much of this new knowledge comes to us from the brilliant studies of Australian biologists, and it is thus a particular pleasure to have two representations in this Symposium from them.

The reptiles are another group which we have tended to over-simplify in physiological analysis, especially in our interpretation of their poikilothermy. True, we have known for some time that behavioural responses enable these animals to maintain a much more constant body temperature than was formerly appreciated. But we shall learn in this Symposium that behaviour is not all, for they achieve physiological thermoregulation by controlling metabolic heat production, by thermal adjustment and acclimation, and by evaporative cooling. In fact, one contributor has gone right out along a limb, and from that exposed position presented us with the challenging view that reptiles, apart from their lack of feathers, hair and sweat glands, possess in some form or other all of the aspects of thermal control found in homeotherms.

Cherished physiological principles will also come under investigation; the belief, for example, that the metabolic rate of homeotherms is an exponential function of surface area, and that there has been no evolutionary adaptation of this relationship except in hibernators. This dogma has been undermined (appropriately enough) by the ground squirrels. In these animals a reduction in basal metabolism, with a concomitant reduction in the amount of heat to be dissipated, proves to be highly adaptive for desert life, just as in marsupials. This illustrates the way in which we may misleadingly and unwittingly strengthen a proposition by our failure to study a sufficiently wide range of species and of their habitats. And let me emphasize the need to study the habitats, for purely laboratory studies will not always serve. For example, it is less easy than it might appear to match the conditions within controlled climatic chambers with those obtaining in the world outside them. We are going to see that failure to simulate solar radiation may result in a thermal stimulus activating the wrong receptors.

It is certainly encouraging to find upon what a broad front investigations of desert life are now being mounted. These investigations, however, will not necessarily tell us how the animals concerned came to exploit such conditions in the first place. What, we may ask, could have induced a species of pulmonate snail to start exposing itself to maximum sun and heat upon the surface of the desert? The demonstration that it has water reserves for several years' survival in heat dormancy does not lessen in any way our wonder that the situation should exist at all. Perhaps competition, natural selection and a measure of pre-adaptation are adequate to account for this exploitation of life at the limits of survival. Certainly there will be implications of the importance of preadaptation in our discussion of the water economy of ruminants, as well as of ground squirrels. But we should not, I suggest, overlook the importance of the elements of exploration and choice in determining animal distribution. Sir Alister Hardy has drawn attention to this, quoting Elton's reminder that we should take into account the selection of the environment by the animal as well as the natural selection of the animal by the environment.

I write as a Zoologist, who finds in this programme the promise of abundant matter of exceptional interest. But I write also as Chairman of the London Zoological Society's Publications Committee, which is responsible for the series of Symposia volumes in which we have come to take great pride, and of which your contributions are a part. I recall that in my undergraduate days we were all greatly stimulated by Buxton's *Animal Life in Deserts*, and I look forward with the greatest confidence to your own volume taking a distinguished place beside that classic work.

E. J. W. Barrington
Department of Zoology
The University of Nottingham, England

ACKNOWLEDGEMENT

The Editor would like to thank Professor W. V. Macfarlane for his editorial assistance and preparation of the indexes.

CONTENTS

Temperature Regulation in Desert Reptiles

J. L. CLOUDSLEY-THOMPSON

Salt and Water Balance in Desert Lizards

J. R. TEMPLETON

Water Economy and Thermal Balance of Israeli and Australian Amphibia from Xeric Habitats

M. R. WARBURG

Salt and Water Excretion in Xerophilic Birds

ERIK SKADHAUGE

Thermoregulation in Australian Desert Kangaroos

TERENCE J. DAWSON

Water Economy of Nocturnal Desert Rodents

RICHARD E. MACMILLEN

Blood Volume Regulation in the Spiny Mouse: Capillary Permeability Changes due to Dehydration

A. BORUT, M. HOROWITZ and M. CASTEL

A Comparative Study of Temperature Regulation in Ground Squirrels with Special Reference to the Desert Species

J. W. HUDSON, D. R. DEAVERS and S. R. BRADLEY

The Desert Gazelle: A Paradox Resolved

C. RICHARD TAYLOR

Water Economy of the Beduin Goat

A. SHKOLNIK, A. BORUT and J. CHOSHNIAK

Renal Salt and Water Excretion in the Camel (*Camelus dromedarius*)

G. M. O. MALOIY

Comparative Water and Energy Economy of Wild and Domestic Mammals

W. V. MACFARLANE and BETH HOWARD

The Role of Advective Fog in the Water Economy of Certain Namib Desert Animals

GIDEON N. LOUW

Energy Exchanges with the Environment of Two East African Antelopes, the Eland and the Hartebeest

VIRGINIA A. FINCH

Cutaneous Thermoreceptors

A. IGGO

Evaporative Temperature Regulation in Domestic Animals

D. MCEWAN JENKINSON

Evaporative Heat Loss in Hot Arid Environments

JOHN BLIGH

Recent Advances in the Comparative Physiology of Desert Animals

KNUT SCHMIDT-NIELSEN

Knut Schmidt-Nielsen

DEDICATION

Knut Schmidt-Nielsen

This volume on the Comparative Physiology of Desert Animals is dedicated to Professor Knut Schmidt-Nielsen. More than any other individual, he has defined the physiological problems of animal life in the desert, and through his work has helped understanding of the physiological mechanisms which allow animals to exist in dry regions. The extent of his contributions to this field is clearly evident in this Symposium. Nearly all the papers either refer to his work or are stimulated by the clear definition of problems laid out in his reviews and in his book on desert animals. In a sense, all of the contributors to the Symposium felt that they were students who had learned from Professor Schmidt-Nielsen. It was a spontaneous decision of the contributors to acknowledge their debt by dedicating this volume to him.

His seminal studies have always been marked by a rare clarity and originality. His study of the Kangaroo rat demonstrated that this animal could survive in hot deserts without drinking, which, at that time, was a provocative finding. Moving from desert rats to camels, Professor Schmidt-Nielsen pointed to the role of body size in determining functional options in the desert environment. He emphasized the advantage of a labile body temperature in adjusting to the heat of the desert: until that time a labile temperature was considered a sign of primitive or imprecise regulation rather than an adaptation. Jack rabbits he found could vasoconstrict to minimize heat gain from a hot environment, as well as to minimize heat loss in a cold environment. Recently, he has pointed out and illustrated a counter-current heat exchanger in the nasal passageways of the kangaroo rat and in many other mammals and birds. With this exchanger an animal cools the exhaled air, which thus dissipates less water.

This dedication is not made only in appreciation of past work, but also in anticipation of Professor Schmidt-Nielsen's continued contribution and stimulation to the field of physiology of desert animals.

G. M. O. MALOIY

Symp. zool. Soc. Lond. (1972) No. 31, 1–13

DESERT SNAILS: PROBLEMS OF SURVIVAL

KNUT SCHMIDT-NIELSEN, C. RICHARD TAYLOR* and AMIRAM SHKOLNIK§

Department of Zoology,
Duke University, Durham, North Carolina, U.S.A.

SYNOPSIS

The pulmonate snails, *Sphincterochila boissieri* and *Helicella seetzeni* are common in deserts of the Near East. Live specimens of *Sphincterochila*, dormant and withdrawn into the shell, can be found on the desert surface in the summer, fully exposed to sun and heat. *Helicella* is frequently found dormant and attached to the lower parts of shrubs and other vegetation.

The severe habitat to which these snails are exposed poses several problems of survival:

1. exposure to high temperatures and the threat of thermal death;
2. lack of water during most of the year and death from desiccation; and
3. lack of suitable food except during the short rainy season.

These three problems were studied in the laboratory and in the field. It was found that the lethal temperature of *Sphincterochila* is between 50 and 55°C, depending on the duration of the exposure. The lethal temperature of *Helicella* is slightly higher. In the field the temperature of the dormant animal within the shell does not reach the lethal level, although the temperature of the surrounding soil surface in summer exceeds this temperature. The rate of water loss from dormant snails of both species was about 0·5 mg/day. A single snail contains about 1400 mg of water, and if the observed rate of water loss of 0·5 mg/day were to be sustained throughout the year, the water reserves would still suffice for several years' survival. This is in accord with observations. Determinations of the metabolic rate of dormant *Sphincterochila* show very low rates of oxygen consumption. The stores of fat and carbohydrate (glycogen) in this snail are small, but the body tissues could suffice to sustain the very low metabolic rate of dormant animals for several years' survival.

It can be concluded that desert snails should be able to survive in the dormant state, even if periods of drought should extend for more than one year.

INTRODUCTION

Explaining how an animal can withstand the environmental extremes of deserts often taxes the ingenuity of biologists. One such instance is desert snails. White snails dot the desert surface in many areas of the Near East. During the hot summer many of these animals are found

* Present address: Museum of Comparative Zoology, Harvard University, Cambridge, Massachusetts, U.S.A.

§ Present address: Department of Zoology, University of Tel-Aviv, Israel.

fully exposed to the sun and heat; alive, although dormant. They remain in their shells during the summer and emerge after rains, which usually occur irregularly during a few winter months. Such a severe habitat poses three seemingly insurmountable problems regarding these snails: 1. thermal death; 2. desiccation; and 3. death from starvation.

We spent one summer in the central Negev desert trying to understand how desert snails are adapted to meet these three hazards. In this area four types of mineral surfaces are common: (a) a firmly packed powdery soil (loess); (b) limestone rock and pebbles with a granular, disintegrating surface; (c) broken-up black flint; and (d) sand. Snails were found on all of these surfaces, except the sand. We were interested in the differences between the various substrates in terms of the thermal conditions they presented to a snail resting on their surface.

Snails are also found in a number of micro-climates which are less severe than the barren exposed surface: (a) in shade under shrubs; (b) attached to branches of shrubs; (c) buried a few cm below the surface; and (d) in the shade of or under rocks. We were interested in knowing the relative advantages to the snail of the different habitats in terms of heat, water, and nutrients.

Two snails are particularly common in the area where we worked: *Sphincterochila boissieri* and *Helicella seetzeni*. *Sphincterochila* is common on loess and limestone, but is also found, although much less commonly, on flint. *Sphincterochila* is a mud eater. After rain it comes out and ingests large quantities of the loess and also the surface material of limestone rocks and pebbles. *Sphincterochila* shows no interest in the higher plants, even though it may be found in the shade of a bush or be attached to lower branches. *Helicella*, on the other hand, eats the higher plants and when dormant is most frequently found attached to the branches of these plants.

Both *Sphincterochila* and *Helicella* are fairly small snails. They are chalky white in colour and weigh 2–4 g. Although they are superficially quite similar in appearance, they are easily distinguished once one has gained some experience. Most of the *Sphincterochila* are found on the surface of or buried beneath the soil, while most of the *Helicella* are attached to the vegetation in the area. Yom-tov (1970) has provided more detailed information about the ecology of desert snails.

In a recent paper (Schmidt-Nielsen, Taylor & Shkolnik, 1971) we discussed an extreme ecological situation: *Sphincterochila* resting on a loess surface. We should now like to review this extreme case, contrast it with other situations in which the snails occur, and finally compare *Sphincterochila* with *Helicella*.

THERMAL MEASUREMENTS ON SNAILS

Outside the laboratory at the Midrasha Sde Bokher in the central Negev we constructed a quadrant in order to investigate the effect of different substrates on the heat balance of snails (see Fig. 1). This quadrant contained four substrates common to the mid-eastern deserts: loess, sand, limestone, and flint. Each substrate surface was flush with the surrounding area, occupied approximately 1 m^2, and was about

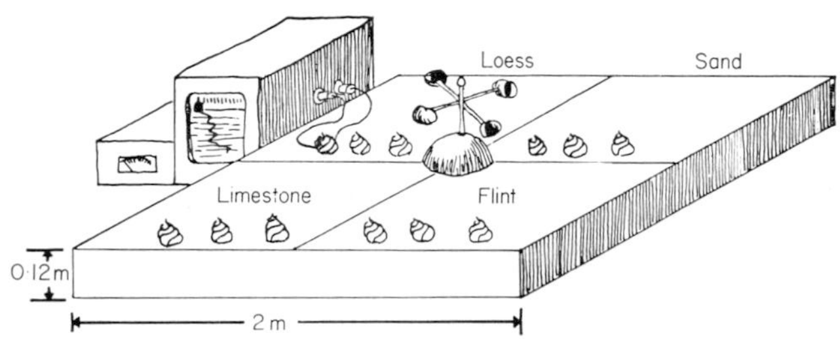

FIG. 1. Quadrant arrangement of the four common desert surface materials, arranged to permit exposure of snails to uniform conditions of solar radiation, wind, etc. The top surface was level with the surrounding soil area.

12 cm deep. On this quadrant, snails could be exposed to nearly identical solar radiation, wind and ambient temperature conditions; thus establishing the effect of different substrates. On each substrate we placed snails equipped with fine thermocouples for measuring their temperatures. Copper-constantan thermocouples were made from nylon-insulated wire of 0·125 mm or 0·025 mm diam. and were calibrated against mercury thermometers of known calibration (U.S. National Bureau of Standards). The accuracy of the thermocouples was $\pm$ 0·2°C. For soil surface temperatures butt-soldered thermocouples and several cm of the leads were placed in direct contact with the surface. Thermocouples made from 0·25 mm diam. or smaller wire give the actual surface temperature within a few tenths of a degree, provided that the thermocouple as well as the leads are placed within the thin stagnant boundary layer of air at the surface (Molnar & Rosenbaum, 1963). Temperatures inside the snails were measured with thermocouples inserted through minute holes drilled in the shell with a high-speed needle-point steel drill and cemented in place with epoxy cement. Air temperatures were measured with thermocouples placed in the center of a reflecting aluminum-foil cylinder of 10 mm diam. and 30 mm length, thus excluding solar radiation and most extraneous radiation from the environment. The readings were independent of changes in air

flow rate through the cylinder and can thus be assumed to represent actual air temperature.

Figure 2 compares temperature measurements from *Sphincterochila* on the four substrates. We measured temperatures of:

1. soil surface in the sun;

2. soil under the snail;

3. air space in the large whorl;

4. the live snail (which occupies the second and smaller whorls); and the air (at the same height above the surface as the middle of the snail).

It can be seen that of the different substrates, the sand surface reached the highest temperature (nearly 65°C), followed by loess (about 60°C), flint (about 57°C), and limestone surface (about 48°C). Sand under a snail (shaded from the sun) was much cooler than loess under a snail.

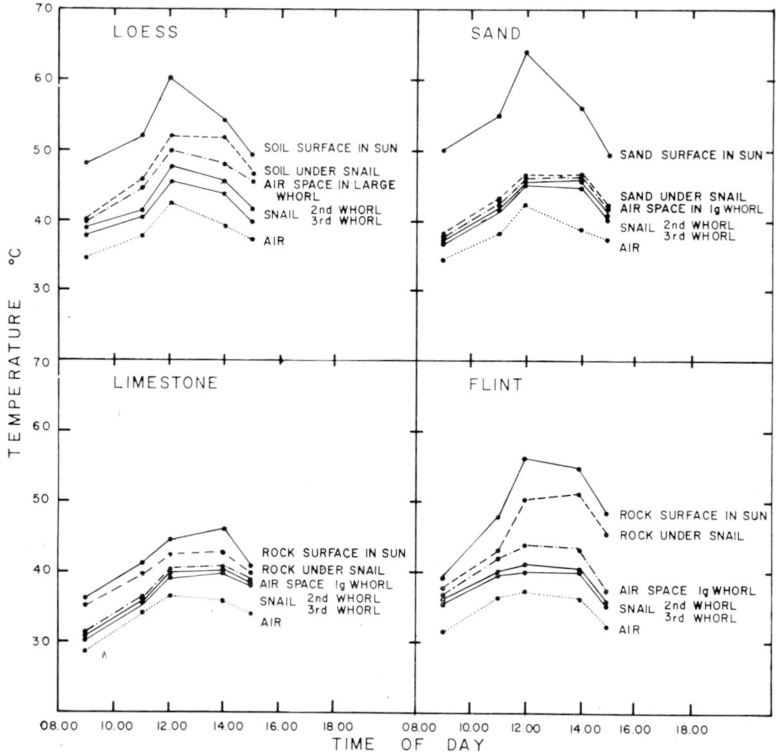

FIG. 2. Temperature measurements in and around dormant *Sphincterochila* on four different substrates.

This supposedly is due to the larger particle size of sand compared to loess and the larger amounts of air trapped between individual sand particles.

The bottom (largest) whorl of the snail contains air. The air space within this whorl reached 51°C on the loess, compared with 46°C on the sand, 42°C on the flint, and 40°C on the limestone. The low temperature on the flint and limestone can be explained by the relatively small area of contact between the rough hard surface of the rock and the curved surface of the snail shell. Often there is merely point contact between the hard rock surface and a snail shell, and the air space in between is easily seen from the side.

The live snail itself is withdrawn into the smaller (upper) whorls, where it reaches a maximum temperature of between 45 and 47°C on loess, nearly the same temperature on sand, while it is more than 5°C cooler (between 39 and 40°C) on limestone and flint.

It is obvious that *Sphincterochila* encounter the most severe thermal habitat on loess or sand surfaces, rather than on limestone or flint. However, *Spincterochila* do not naturally occur on sand and, when non-dormant, are unable to move more than a few cm on this substrate before they fall over and end up moving in circles while churning up the sand.

In formulating an explanation for the heat balance of a *Sphincterochila* on loess, one is immediately struck with the fact that the bottom of the snail is warmer than the top. Let us consider the record with the highest temperatures met in the field (July 9, 1969, Fig. 3). The peak surface temperature of the loess was about 65°C, the surface under the snail about 60°C, the air space in the large whorl was 56°C, and the animal itself was 50°C. This temperature distribution establishes that heat was flowing from the surrounding soil surface to the soil underneath the snail; through the air space under the shell; up into the air space within the large whorl; from the large whorl to the smaller whorls (the live snail) and then to the surrounding air, which was at 43°C.

Since the snail is much cooler than the surrounding soil surface, it must be reflecting most of the solar radiation impinging on it. Dr. W. J, Hamilton, III, using a Beckman DK-2 reflectance spectrophotometer. measured the reflectance of *Sphincterochila*. He found that within the visible part of the solar spectrum, the reflectance was about 90%. In the near infra-red (up to 1350 nm) the reflectance was similar to that of magnesium oxide and was estimated to be 95%. In the range of the solar spectrum, therefore, it seems justified to say that the snails reflect well over 90% of the total incident radiant energy.

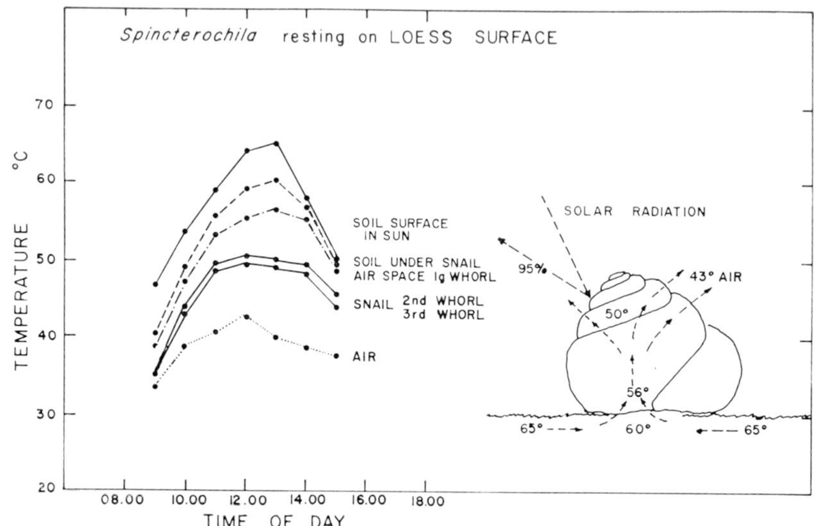

FIG. 3. The temperature in a dormant *Sphincterochila*, on 9 July, 1969. This graph is selected as the highest temperature recorded during 40 days of observation during July and early August 1969.

Two factors appear important in preventing the snail from attaining the same high temperature as the soil surface:

1. the high reflectance of solar radiation and
2. the pocket of air in the large whorl which effectively insulates the snail from the hot soil surface.

In order to demonstrate the significance of this air space as a thermal insulator, we filled the space in several snails with water (after reinforcing the epiphragm with epoxy cement). Figure 4 shows the results of comparing a normal snail with intact air space and one with the air space filled with water. When the large whorl was filled with water the live snail (in the second and third whorls) was about 5°C warmer than when the large whorl contained air. This 5°C could readily mean the difference between thermal death and survival. It is extremely important then, that when the snail withdraws it does not fill the shell but leaves the largest whorl filled with air. This cushion of insulating air, together with the high reflectivity of the shell, explains how the snail remains appreciably cooler than the desert surface.

In some measurements made in Wadi Zohar we tried to determine the relative thermal advantage to a snail of choosing different habitats (Fig. 5). The thermally most severe habitat was that of the snail (1) on

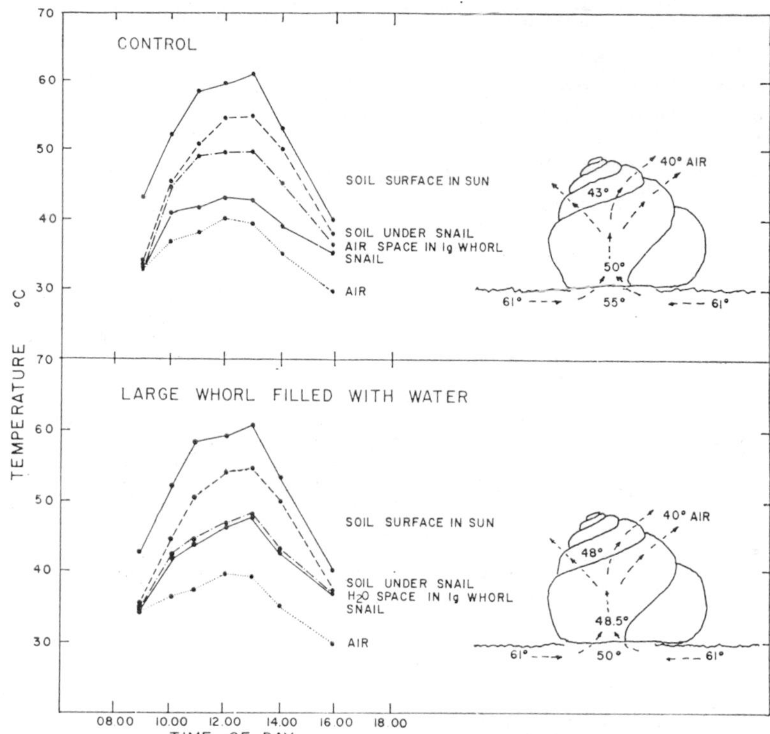

FIG. 4. Experiment to show the insulation value of the air within the shell of *Sphincterochila*. When the air space in the large whorl was filled with water, the temperature of the snail itself reached 48°C, or 5° higher than in a control snail with the air space intact (43°C).

loess, (2) buried 2 cm beneath the loess surface, (3) under a bush and the coolest being that of the snail (4) on the limestone.

How do the temperatures attained by *Sphincterochila* compare with those of *Helicella* in the same situation? Figure 6 illustrates the fact that when *Sphincterochila* and *Helicella* rest on the loess surface, the live animal within the *Helicella* shell reaches a temperature almost 3° higher than the *Sphincterochila*. This apparently is because of the spatial configuration of the shells. The *Helicella* shell is vertically more flattened, and thus the air space in the large whorl provides less insulation between the live snail and the substrate.

When both *Helicella* and *Sphincterochila* were placed 2 cm above the loess (on small wooden dowels about 1 mm in diam.), the temperature was the same in both—about 10–15°C lower than in snails resting on the loess surface. Thus *Helicella*, which normally is found attached to the lower parts of bushes above the surface of the ground, selects a less severe habitat than that in which *Sphincterochila* is commonly found.

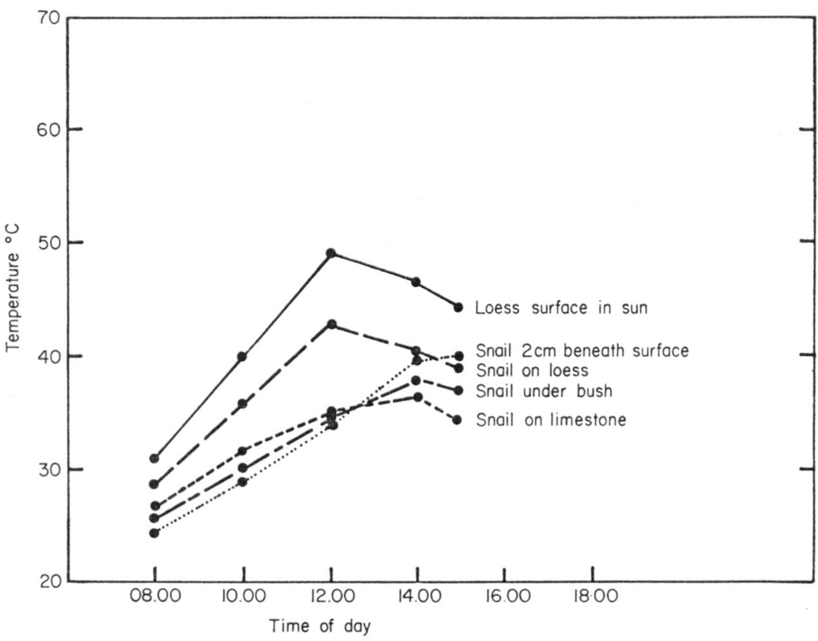

FIG. 5. Temperatures measured in dormant snails placed on different substrates. Top curve, temperature of soil (loess) surface; the four broken curves, snails placed as indicated for each curve.

LETHAL TEMPERATURES

We now have some idea of the temperatures snails may encounter in their natural desert habitat. The next question is the maximum temperature they can tolerate? This was determined by observing survival of snails which were placed in individual water-tight containers and immersed in constant temperature baths at 50, 55, and 60°C. To monitor the temperature actually attained by the animals, one additional snail equipped with a thermocouple was included in each group of 20. Exposure time was recorded, beginning when this snail was within 1°C of the water bath. Table I shows the results of these heat tolerance experiments. Snails heated to 60°C for one-half hour invariably died. At 55°C *Helicella* survived longer than *Sphincterochila*. For example,

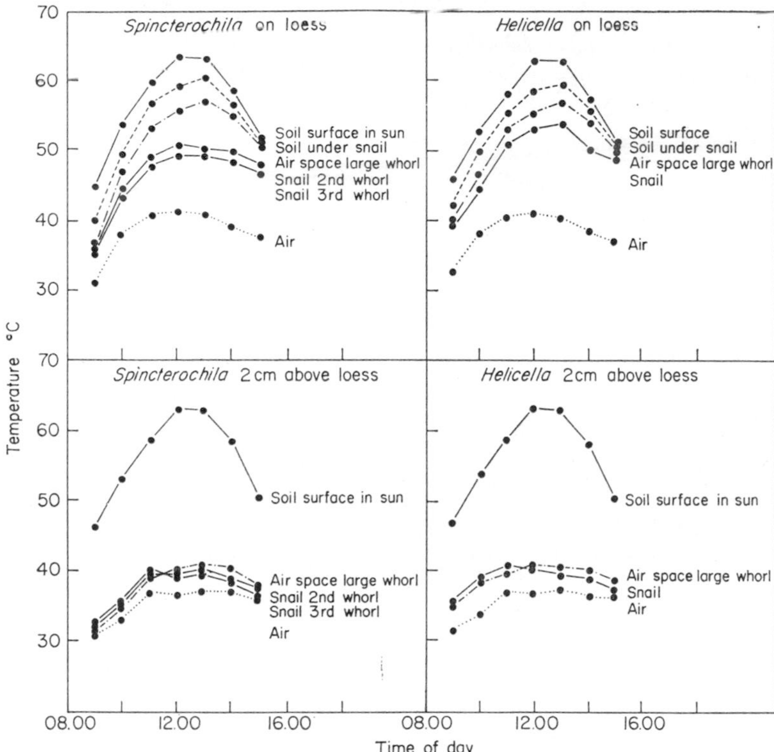

FIG. 6. Comparison of temperatures in dormant *Sphincterochila* and *Helicella*, placed on soil (loess) surface, and on sticks 2 cm above surface (the latter because *Helicella* is often found above ground, attached to the lower parts of small shrubs).

85% of the *Helicella* survived 2 h at 55°C, compared to 30% for *Sphincterochila*. It seems safe to conclude, however, that 55°C is nearly lethal to dormant *Sphincterochila* or *Helicella* if the exposure lasts for longer than 4 h. At 50°C, all individuals of both species could survive 8-h exposures. Since the peak temperature of a desert day usually occurs during a few hours in the early afternoon, the snails are not likely to be exposed to high temperatures for many hours, and experiments of more than 8 h are, therefore, of minor interest in the evaluation of heat exposure in nature. The slightly higher tolerance of *Helicella* at 55°C corresponds with the higher temperature which the snail would reach because of its flattened air space. It seems likely, therefore, that both *Sphincterochila* and *Helicella* could survive thermally on the desert floor.

TABLE I

Temperature tolerance of the snails Sphincterochila boissieri *and* Helicella seetzeni. (*Percent survival after indicated time. Sample size* 20 *individuals of each species for each exposure*)

Hours	0·5	1	2	4	8
50°C					
Helicella	—	—	100	100	100
Sphincterochila	—	—	100	100	100
55°C					
Helicella	100	85	85	20	0
Sphincterochila	95	80	30	5	0
60°C					
Helicella	0	—	—	—	—
Sphincterochila	0	—	—	—	—

WATER LOSS

Do snails have enough water available to sustain losses during periods when no external water supply is available? In nature rain normally falls each winter, but at times more than one year may pass between rains. To determine the use of water in summer we measured the rate of water loss from dormant snails exposed to the sun in a number of different habitats. The rates determined in summer presumably are maximal, for during the cooler parts of the year the vapour pressure deficit is smaller and the rate of water loss probably lower.

Ten *Sphincterochila* were weighed and placed on an area of loess, fully exposed to sun during the day. They were weighed daily before sunrise, between 04.30 and 05.00 h, and again in the evening between 16.00 and 18.00 h. We assumed that weight change was primarily due to water loss or gain. During a 5 day period of being weighed twice daily, 3 snails became active and departed. The remaining 7 snails all showed a similar pattern of weight gain at night and loss during the day. A representative record is given (Fig. 7) which shows a nightly gain from a few mg up to 20 mg. Interestingly, similarly exposed empty shells gained weight at night at approximately the same rate. During the day all the snails lost weight again. The shells of dead snails lost almost exactly the amount that they gained during the preceding night; by evening they had returned to within a fraction of a mg of their weight of 24 h earlier. The live snails, on the other hand, lost during the day slightly more than they had gained during the preceding night. A live snail, therefore, showed a day-to-day decline in weight. In Fig. 7 the average decline over 5 days was 1·72 mg/day. The conclusion that live snails achieve no net advantage from nightly weight gain is clear from comparison with control animals kept indoors. Such snails showed no gain of weight during the night, and their 24-h loss was similar to that of snails kept outdoors. Since empty shells gain as much weight as live snails when outdoors, and snails indoors show no gain, we conclude that water is absorbed on the outside of the shell and evaporates again during the day.

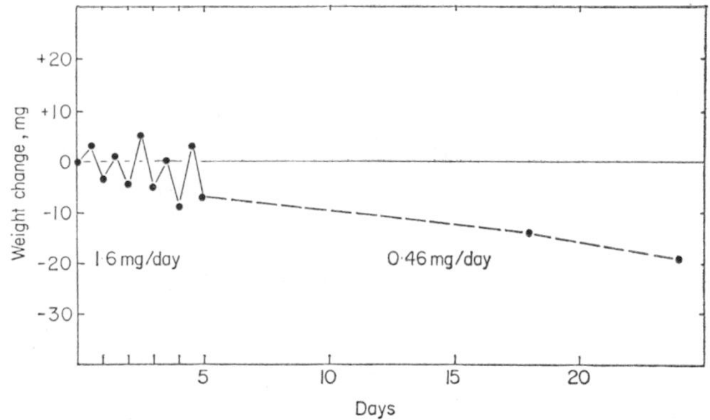

FIG. 7. Weight changes of dormant *Sphincterochila*, placed on the desert surface, fully exposed to sun. Weighed twice daily during days 1 to 5, subsequently weighed on days 18 and 24 only. The daily weight loss was smaller when the snail was left completely undisturbed.

The question of whether dew can be utilized by the snails remains open. In summer, on nights when visible dew is formed on the shell, no net weight gain was achieved. The excess water evaporated shortly after sunrise and the total daily weight loss was the same as if no dew had occurred. If the snails broke the epiphragm and became active, they lost some 50–150 mg, even on nights with dew. Conditions in winter may be different, and after rain when the soil is moist, nights with dew may be important to active snails when they are feeding. There is no information available as to whether feeding activity in winter may be supported by dew in the absence of rain.

It has previously been established that even minor disturbances of a dormant snail, such as a slight knock or being placed on the pan of a balance, increases water loss (Machin, 1965). We therefore discontinued daily weighings and left the snails completely undisturbed for longer periods of time. The average daily weight loss now decreased and during 13 days the snail (Fig. 7) lost 5·9 mg, or an average of 0·45 mg/day. Five live snails remained inactive during the 13 day period at a mean weight loss of 0·66 mg/day (range 0·45–0·92).

Table II compares the rates of water loss from snails left undisturbed for 20 days in different habitats. The water loss was remarkably similar, whether the snails were kept on the loess surface, on a branch at the base of a bush, on limestone, or on flint. Those buried 2 cm below the loess surface lost slightly (but significantly) less water than the others. There was no significant difference in the evaporation from groups of *Helicella* and groups of *Sphincterochila*.

TABLE II

Rate of water loss from the snail Sphincterochila *under different conditions in the desert. Mean of measurements on* 10 *snails left undisturbed from* 18 *July to* 8 *August*, 1969, *at Avdat*

	mg wt change/day ± SE(N)
Exposed to sun on loess	−0·63 ± 0·05 (10)
c. 2 cm below loess surface	−0·43 ± 0·04 (10)
On branch at base of bush	−0·60 ± 0·06 (10)
On flint	−0·64 ± 0·04 (10)
On limestone	−0·58 ± 0·03 (10)

The water content of living *Sphincterochila* is about 80% (i.e. 80 g water/100 g live animal, excluding weight of shell). This water content remains nearly unchanged throughout the year, and there is no noticeable decrease in water content during the summer months. Thus, there is no indication of a gradual depletion of water reserves during the long dry season (Schmidt-Nielsen *et al.*, 1971).

The animal itself, removed from a specimen weighing 4 g with the shell, weighs 1·8 g, and with 80% water, it contains a total of 1·44 g water. If we assume a continued water loss throughout the seasons as high as that measured in summer (0·5 mg/day), a year would give a total loss of less than 200 mg water. If there were no loss of dry matter, the animal would now be reduced to a weight of 1·6 g. The water content after a year (still assuming no loss of solid matter) would then be 76%.

Since there would always be some loss of solid matter due to metabolism, and the estimated water loss was based on the presumably high summer value, the actual water percentage after a year without water could be expected to be higher than the estimated 76%. In other words, the water loss observed to take place from snails in their natural habitat in summer should be barely noticeable as a decrease in the water percentage of summer animals, and thus there is agreement between independently determined water loss from animals in nature and the water content of their tissues.

In summary, we can say that the snails in the deserts of the Near East have successfully met the physiological problems of the most apparent threats posed by the environmental heat and aridity. (The metabolic rate of *Sphincterochila* and the apparent lack of food reserves in the snails has been discussed in a previous paper by Schmidt-Nielsen *et al.*, 1971.)

Acknowledgements

The field studies were financed by a research grant from the National Geographic Society. Additional support was provided by NIH Research Grant HE-02228 and by NIH Research Career Award 1-K6-GM-21,522 to Schmidt-Nielsen.

We wish to acknowledge the hospitality provided by Midrasha Sde Bokher and its Director, Avriham Tsivion, who arranged for excellent working facilities and living accommodation.

References

Machin, J. (1965). Cutaneous regulation of evaporative water loss in the common garden snail *Helix aspersa*. *Naturwissenschaften* **52** : 18.

Molnar, G. W. & Rosenbaum, J. C. (1963). Surface temperature measurement with thermocouples. In *Temperature, its measurement and control in Science and industry* **3**: *Part 3, Biology and medicine*: 3–11. J. D. Hardy, (ed.). New York: Reinhold.

Schmidt-Nielsen, K., Taylor, C. R. & Shkolnik, A. (1971). Desert snails: problems of heat, water, and food. *J. exp. Biol.* **55**: 385–398.

Yom-Tov, Y. (1970). The effect of predation on population densities of some desert snails. *Ecology* **51**: 907–911.

Symp. zool. Soc. Lond. (1972) No. 31, 15–38.

THE WATER BALANCE AND OSMOREGULATORY PHYSIOLOGY OF THE DESERT LOCUST (*SCHISTOCERCA GREGARIA*) AND OTHER DESERT AND XERIC ARTHROPODS

J. SHAW and R. H. STOBBART

Department of Zoology,
University of Newcastle upon Tyne, Newcastle upon Tyne, England

INTRODUCTION

The vast majority of terrestrial arthropods are small, or very small, and so have a large ratio of surface area to volume. Consequently terrestrial arthropods, unless they inhabit very moist environments, must be well adapted to resist water losses. So far, the physiology of only a few true desert arthropods has been examined, but the evidence already clearly suggests that the desert dwellers exhibit no particular physiological adaptations not found in other xeric species (Edney, 1967). Indeed it seems likely that many xeric insects and arachnids live under conditions which are physiologically as stringent as those besetting the desert vertebrates.

Xeric arthropods have been extensively studied from the point of view of water conservation (see Bursell, 1964; Edney, 1967) but often their excretory physiology has not. The desert locust, *Schistocerca gregaria*, although not a true desert species, has the advantage that many aspects of its physiology are well known and it is a useful animal in which to attempt to bring together our knowledge of water balance and osmoregulatory mechanisms. Other desert and xeric arthropods may be compared where possible. The desert cockroach, *Arenivaga*, recently studied by Edney (1966, 1968) is particularly valuable in this respect, especially as it is not too remote from *Periplaneta*, an inhabitant of urban deserts, and another favourite with insect physiologists.

The major problem facing these animals is one of continual water loss. This is a result of transpiration through the general cuticular surface, transpiration associated with respiratory exchanges and water loss in the excreta. Total water loss is restricted by the possession of a highly impermeable cuticle and by measures to reduce respiratory losses and faecal water loss. It may be offset by the ingestion of water, the production of metabolic water and by the uptake of water vapour from sub-saturated atmospheres, although the latter is known in only a few species. In common with other animals, desert arthropods also regulate the composition of their body fluids within species specific limits.

CUTICULAR WATER LOSS

Loss through the general body surface

In view of their small size, a low rate of cuticular water loss seems essential to the water economy and osmotic regulation of desert and xeric arthropods. In freshly-moulted unhandled *Schistocerca* the rate of cuticular transpiration is very low (Fig. 1)—in the order of 0·04 mg/animal/mm Hg saturation deficit (SD)/h at 30°C—comparable with that

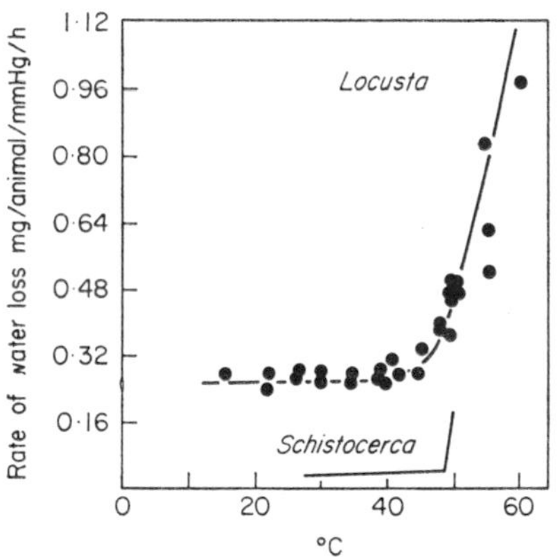

Fig. 1. The relationship between cuticular transpiration and temperature in *Locusta* (Loveridge, 1968a) and *Schistocerca* (Beament, 1959).

in *Rhodnius* nymphs and *Tenebrio* larvae (Beament, 1959). The rate is lower (Fig. 1) than that found in *Locusta migratoria* (Loveridge, 1968a), but the higher figure found by Church (1960) for *Schistocerca* (7 mg/animal/h at 30°C and 40% rh, = 0·35% body weight/h) is more comparable and is probably nearer to the rate of loss in field or laboratory conditions during post-moult adult life. It is also comparable with that obtained by Beament in his initial experiments on specimens of *Schistocerca* which were not specially selected. Edney (1968) found no marked difference in cuticular permeability between the xeric and desert cockroaches, *Periplaneta* and *Arenivaga*. Desert tenebrionid beetles, as might be expected, have almost impermeable cuticles (Ahearn, 1970) and show a water loss of about 0·1–0·15% body wt/h in dry air at 30°C

(Fig. 2). In these beetles the abdominal spiracles open into the sub-elytral space which functions effectively to reduce transpiration (Ahearn & Hadley, 1969). Various desert scorpions and the solfugid, *Galeodes arabs* show an appreciably lower loss of 0·03–0·09% body wt/h (Cloudesley-Thompson, 1961; Hadley, 1970). This may, however, be due to a lower ratio of surface area to volume. Variations in this ratio must vitiate many inter-specific comparisons of transpiration rates, but their low values illustrate clearly the importance of low cuticular permeability for the terrestrial arthropods.

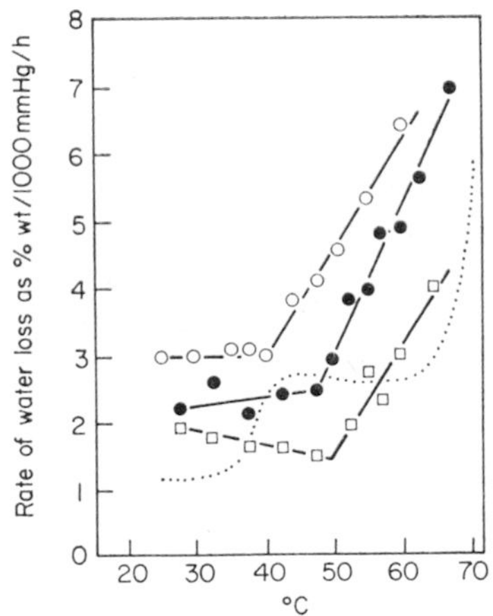

Fig. 2. The relationship between cuticular transpiration and temperature in (A) desert tenebrionid beetles: ○, *Eleodes armata*; ● *entrioptera muricata*; □, *Cryptoglossa* verrucosa (Ahearn, 1970) and (B) desert scorpion: .... *Hadrurus arizonensis* (Hadley, 1970).

In most insects cuticular permeabilities are greatly increased at certain characteristic transition temperatures (Figs 1, 2), usually well above the ecological temperatures. This is attributed to the thermal disorientation of a waterproofing wax monolayer in the epicuticle (Beament, 1958, 1959). In adult *Schistocerca* and *Locusta* the transition temperature is about 48°C (Beament, 1959; Loveridge, 1968a). Values between 40 and 50°C are shown by desert tenebrionid beetles (Ahearn, 1970); but the desert scorpion *Hadrurus arizonensis* (Fig. 2) shows two transitions (Hadley, 1970). Beament (1959) found this also in *Pieris* and *Tenebrio* pupae and interprets it as evidence for the presence of two wax monolayers in the epicuticle.

Loss through the spiracles

In living insects spiracular or respiratory water loss may be considerable. It may be estimated either by subtracting values obtained for the general cuticular surface from the total loss rate (excluding faecal loss), or from a knowledge of the ventilation rate, assuming the air in the tracheoles has equilibrated with the haemolymph and has a rh of 99%. In resting *Schistocerca* the ventilation in the tracheal system caused by abdominal pumping is 42 l/kg/h (Weis-Fogh, 1967). Assuming the air becomes 99% saturated, a locust breathing air at 20% rh and 30°C will lose water at a rate of 2·1 mg/2 g locust/h (Hamilton, 1964). Adding this to the estimated cuticular loss of 7 mg/locust/h gives a total cuticular loss of 9·1 mg/locust/h, the respiratory loss comprising 23% of the total. This may not be constant since spiracle opening is subject to physiological control (Miller, 1960a, b, c). In *Locusta* the

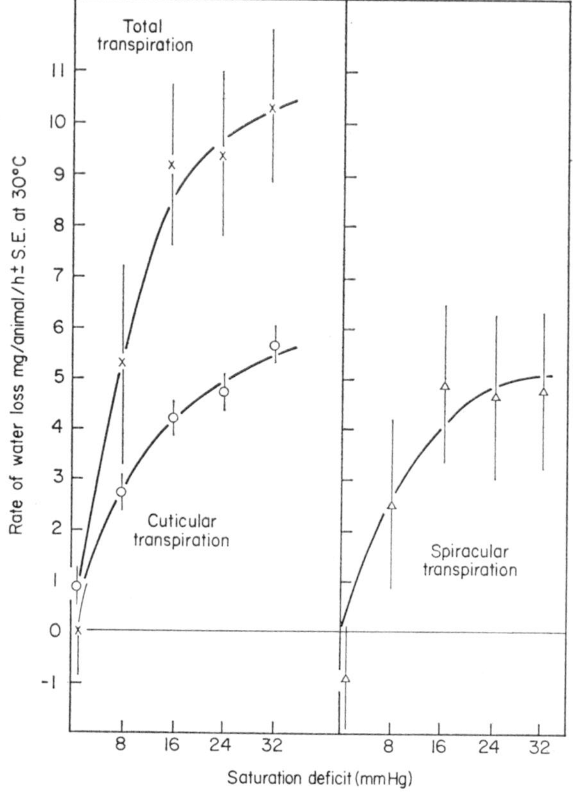

FIG. 3. The relationship between total, cuticular, and spiracular transpiration and saturation deficit in *Locusta* at 30°C (Loveridge, 1968a, b).

spiracular loss at 30°C is about half the total loss. For a SD of 8 mm Hg a value of 2·5 mg/1·6 g locust/h was obtained (Fig. 3; Loveridge, 1968a, b) and this only increased to 5 mg/h for a SD of 30 mm Hg. Proportionally less water is lost from the spiracles at higher SDs. Control is brought about by a reduction in the rate and amplitude of ventilatory movements and an increased incidence of discontinuities is found. This seems to be more important than the control of the spiracles.

At increased temperatures (above 40°C at 0% rh) the ventilatory movements are greatly increased (Fig. 4a) and this is associated with

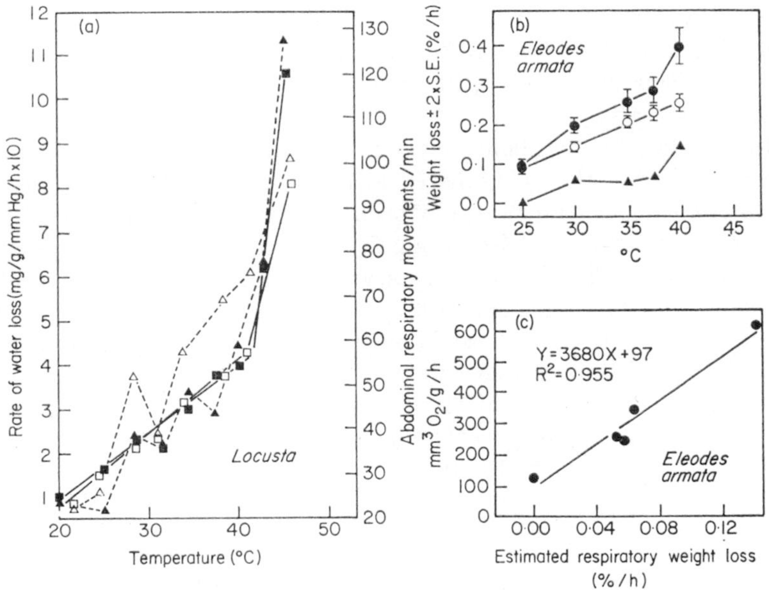

FIG. 4. (a) Effect of temperature on respiratory rate and total transpiration in *Locusta*: ■——■, water loss; ▲---▲, respiratory rate, animal 1; □——□, △---△, ditto animal 2. (b) Effect of temperature on total, cuticular, and respiratory transpiration in *Eleodes armata*: ●, total loss; ○, cuticular loss; ▲, estimated respiratory loss. (c) Relationship between O_2 consumption and estimated respiratory transpiration in *Eleodes armata*. (a) Loveridge (1968b); (b) and (c) Ahearn (1970).

an abrupt increase in water loss (Loveridge, 1968b). Similar temperature effects have been observed in desert tenebrionid beetles (Fig. 4b, c) and the scorpion *Hadrurus* (Ahearn, 1970; Hadley, 1970). In the former the respiratory water loss is directly proportional to O_2 consumption. It would appear that regulation of the metabolic rate breaks down at the higher temperatures possibly due to stress in the CNS, since in *Schistocerca* the ventilatory movements vary with the degree of excitement and the CNS is the system primarily supplied with air by them (Miller, 1960b; Weis-Fogh, 1967).

THE IMPORTANCE OF METABOLIC WATER

Water produced by the oxidation of foodstuffs, and of food reserves within the body, enters the general metabolic pool and to this extent contributes to the water economy of an animal. If the rate of water loss is low enough this source of water may be adequate, and this is indeed the case in some of the most water-thrifty species, for example larvae of the mealworm *Tenebrio molitor* and the flour moth *Ephestia kühniella* amongst the insects (Buxton, 1930; Mellanby, 1932; Fraenkel & Blewett, 1944).

In *Schistocerca* metabolic water is not sufficient to maintain water balance, except in the flying insect, at least when the ambient rh is low. The total cuticular water loss has been estimated at 9·1 mg/locust/h for a rh $< 40\%$ at 30°C. Now the resting O_2 consumption at this temperature is about 0·7 l/kg/h, and the respiratory quotient is 0·82 (Krogh & Weis-Fogh, 1951; Weis-Fogh, 1967). From these the calculated rate of production of metabolic water is only 0·93 mg/2 g locust/h, and hence is about 10% of the total cuticular loss rate. It follows, therefore, that *Schistocerca* must obtain most of its water from its diet. There are records of *Locusta*, at any rate, chewing crops and leaves for the sake of the moisture (Uvarov, 1928).

WATER BALANCE DURING FLIGHT

In *Schistocerca* at rest abdominal movements ventilate the tracheal system. These movements (which vary greatly with the degree of excitement) show no simple relationship to O_2 demand, and although they are much increased during flight the unidirectional air flow they cause remains constant at ~ 30 l air/kg/h. The much greater rates of ventilation necessary for flight are caused by the pumping action of the thorax (Weis-Fogh, 1967). Water loss is consequently much increased during flight to about 1·05% body wt/h for a locust flying in air of 40% rh at 30°C (calculated from Church (1960) for a 2·0 g locust). As the rate of production of water from the combustion of fat during flight amounts to only 0·8% body wt/h (Weis-Fogh, 1967), it follows that a locust flying in dry air must eventually deplete itself of water. At higher rh's however a water balance may be struck, and Weis-Fogh (1967) has computed curves showing the relationship between air temperature, rh, and the temperature of the thorax, for this to occur. For flying locusts to be in water balance at 30°C a rh of 55–75% is required whereas at 25°C (the minimum temperature for extended flight) 30–50% rh suffices. It seems therefore that in true desert conditions it may be advantageous for the locusts to fly in the higher, cooler air.

Similarly *Aphis fabae* may achieve a water balance during flight in atmospheres of suitable rh (Cockbain, 1961) and a comparable situation exists in tsetse flies (Bursell, 1964).

UPTAKE OF WATER VAPOUR FROM SUBSATURATED ATMOSPHERES

In general the osmotic pressures (OP) of the haemolymphs of terrestrial arthropods are such that they are in equilibrium with air of approximately 99% rh. A few species (listed by Noble-Nesbitt, 1969, 1970) are unique in possessing the ability to take up water vapour from air of rh less than the equilibrium value. This ability (which is lacking in *Schistocerca*, but present in nymphs of the grasshopper *Chortophaga viridifasciata* (Ludwig, 1937)) has so far been found in only one truly desert species, namely in the nymphs and females of the cockroach *Arenivaga* (Edney, 1966). Not surprisingly however the habitats of the other species in which it occurs are generally xeric in the sense that liquid water may be difficult to obtain.

In ticks, uptake following dehydration is interrupted while experimental damage to the integument is made good (Lees, 1947), while in *Arenivaga* moulting interrupts the process for 1–2 days (Edney, 1966). This type of result led to the suggestion that the cuticle and epidermis of the general body surface were involved in the process (see reviews by Beament, 1961, 1964 and 1965).

Generally, uptake is possible only from high rh's, 70% or greater (Shaw & Stobbart, 1963) but the firebrat *Thermobia domestica* can take up from a rh of only 63% (Noble-Nesbitt, 1969). The uptake in this species is interesting in that its control is good and that it appears to take place through the rectum (Noble-Nesbitt, 1969, 1970).

Beament (1964, 1965) suggested mechanisms for vapour uptake on the assumption that it occurs through the general body surface. But if rectal vapour uptake should prove to be the rule (cf. section on osmotic balance, p. 30) these suggestions will clearly need to be reconsidered in the light of the considerable information available concerning uptake (i.e. reabsorption) of liquid water by the rectum (Phillips, 1964a,b,c; Irvine & Phillips, 1971; Wall, Oschman & Schmidt-Nielsen, 1969; Wall & Oschman, 1970).

THE REGULATION OF HAEMOLYMPH OSMOTIC PRESSURE UNDER DEHYDRATING CONDITIONS

Osmotic regulation has been studied in a few xeric or desert insects by keeping them in a subsaturated atmosphere, and either depriving them of liquid water or providing a hyperosmotic saline to drink. The atmospheric rh in equilibrium with water in the haemolymph is about 99% and the ability to absorb water vapour is rarely found (Noble-Nesbitt, 1969, 1970), so an insect without water and at an atmospheric rh $< 99\%$ will steadily lose water. Osmotic regulation can thus only achieve a slowing down of the increase in concentration which must inevitably follow this water loss. The time course of this process seems not to have been determined yet in any arthropod. With hyperosmotic saline available a steady state can be achieved if osmotically-free water can be obtained from it. A hyperosmotic saline has been used to maintain the haemolymph volume during dehydration in *Schistocerca* (Phillips, 1964a,b,c; Stobbart, 1968).

In *Schistocerca* osmotic regulation is effective. Hydrated animals maintain a haemolymph OP equivalent to $\Delta = 0{\cdot}75°C$, while in a rh of $<75\%$ and with hyperosmotic saline the OP was only $\Delta\ 0{\cdot}95°C$ (Phillips, 1964a,b,c; Stobbart, 1968). In this context it is instructive to note that saturated NaCl is in equilibrium with 75% rh. Similarly the Australian locust *Chortoicetes terminifera* shows only a small rise in haemolymph OP (from $\Delta\ 0{\cdot}80°C$ to $\Delta\ 0{\cdot}88°C$) after 24 h dehydration at 0% rh (Djajakusumah & Miles, 1966). Comparable degrees of regulation are found in larvae and adults of the mealworm *Tenebrio molitor* (Marcuzzi, 1955, 1956) in nymphs of the sand-burrowing American desert cockroach *Arenivaga* (Edney, 1966) and in nymphs and adults of *Periplaneta americana* (Edney, 1968; Wall, 1970).

Upon rehydration with water vapour or pure water the haemolymph OP becomes lower than normal in *Arenivaga* and *Chortoicetes* and in the latter there is evidence that the contribution of amino acids to the haemolymph OP is increased. These results suggest that salts are lost during dehydration, and this, as we shall see later, seems from our knowledge of the excretory system to be very likely.

Although the haemolymph OP is well regulated during dehydration the haemolymph volume drops markedly. This seems to be very general, and the difficulty of obtaining haemolymph from dehydrated insects has often been commented upon (e.g. Phillips, 1964a; Edney, 1968). Mellanby (1939) suggested that the haemolymph might function as a water reservoir for the tissues, and Lee's (1961) data for *Schistocerca* support this, although it would be more correct to regard the haemolymph as buffering the tissue water against the large reductions which would otherwise occur. In *Arenivaga* and *Periplaneta* nymphs this is less obvious (Edney, 1966, 1968). Hydration increases the haemolymph volume in *Schistocerca* and the volume is maintained when drinking a hyperosmotic saline under dehydrating conditions (Lee, 1961; Stobbart, 1968). Volume changes of ±20% are also caused by dehydration and rehydration in *Chortoicetes* (Djajakusumah & Miles, 1966).

THE MECHANISM OF OSMOTIC REGULATION DURING DEHYDRATION

In the previous section it was shown that in xeric and desert insects so far studied, regulation of the haemolymph OP is apparent during dehydration despite a large reduction in haemolymph volume. The importance of the excretory system in the control of haemolymph composition is now well established: the Malpighian tubules produce a fluid of relatively constant composition and this fluid flowing into the rectum is subjected to differential reabsorption of water and solutes. It is finally ejected together with faecal matter derived from the midgut (Ramsay, 1955; Shaw & Stobbart, 1963; Phillips, 1964c). As far as osmotic regulation is concerned the Malpighian tubules play a minor role since, as shown in many species including *Schistocerca*, the fluid is always virtually isosmotic with the haemolymph whatever its OP (Ramsay, 1953; Shaw & Stobbart, 1963; Berridge, 1968; Maddrell, 1969; Phillips, 1964b). Phillips also found only small changes in composition of this fluid from hydrated animals compared with that from animals given a hypertonic saline to drink (Table I). The composition is similar to that of other insects and is characterized by the high K

TABLE I

The composition of the haemolymph and the hindgut fluid is Schistocerca gregaria *(from Phillips, 1964c)*

Solution available for drinking	Haemolymph				Hindgut fluid (derived from Malpighian tubules)			
	Na	K	Cl	△°C	Na	K	Cl	△°C
Tap water	108	11	115	0·75	20	139	93	0·78
Hyperosmotic saline	158	19	163	0·95	67	186	192	—

(concentrations in m-mole/1)

concentration. The rate at which this fluid is produced may be appreciable. In hydrated *Schistocerca* the rate is about 8 ml/h (0·4% body weight/h) and this is not significantly reduced in saline-fed animals (Phillips, 1964c). In *Carausius* the rate is even greater—some 0·75% body weight/h in feeding animals (Ramsay, 1955). There is evidence, however, that the rate may be appreciably reduced during dehydration. Mordue's (1969) studies of the effect of an antidiuretic hormone from the corpora cardiaca in *Schistocerca* suggest this; and in *Carausius* the rate of fluid production in fasting animals is about half the normal rate (Ramsay, 1955; Pilcher, 1970). Similarly in *Periplaneta*, where both diuretic and antidiuretic hormones may be produced, the dehydrated level is low (Wall & Ralph, 1964; Mills, 1967).

Phillips (1969), observed an increased urine production in dehydrated *Calliphora* caused by injection into the haemolymph of either hypo- or hyper-osmotic solutions, and suggested that the rate of production is a function of the haemolymph volume rather than the osmotic pressure.

A decrease in volume flow is further enhanced by differential water uptake in the rectum. In *Schistocerca* water can be reabsorbed at the same rate whether there is simultaneous solute reabsorption or not and this will raise the osmotic pressure of the rectal contents to a level where the uptake rate is balanced by the osmotic withdrawal of water from the haemolymph across the rectal wall. The rate of water uptake, and hence the final osmotic pressure in the rectum, depends on prevailing conditions, being lower in hydrated animals. In experiments where the haemolymph OP ranged from $\Delta = 0{\cdot}7°C–1{\cdot}0°C$ the rectal osmotic pressure was found to be linearly related (Fig. 5) (Phillips, 1964a). The rate of water uptake in the rectum also appears to be hormonally controlled (Mordue, 1969). Measurements of rectal fluid osmotic pressure in hydrated and dehydrated *Periplaneta* leave little doubt that a similar situation is to be found in this insect except that the rectal fluid may be significantly hypo-osmotic in hydrated animals (Table II), and here too there seems to be hormonal control of rectal water uptake (Wall, 1967).

The first problem is to attempt to assess the contribution which the Malpighian tubule-rectal system could make to the regulation of haemolymph osmotic pressure during dehydration. Obviously the system has the potential for a degree of isosmotic solute removal with some retrieval of the water in which the solute is initially carried—a necessary requirement for osmotic regulation when the haemolymph volume is decreasing. It may be noted at this point that the haemolymph volume, itself, comprises rather a small proportion of the total body weight,

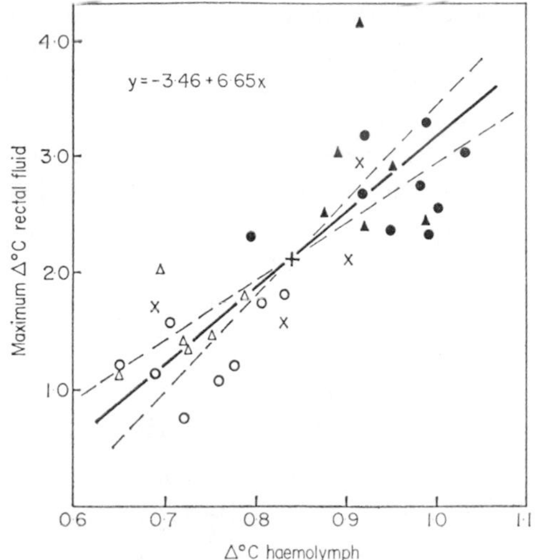

Fig. 5. The relationship between the osmotic pressure of *Schistocerca* haemolymph and the maximum osmotic pressure developed in the rectal fluid following injection of hypertonic trehalose solution (circles) or saline (triangles) into the ligated rectum. Open symbols = locusts fed on tap water; solid symbols = locusts fed on hypertonic saline; X = miscellaneous observations. The solid line is the best straight line calculated by the method of least squares, while broken lines represent 95 % confidence limits for the slope of the calculated line (Phillips, 1964a).

Table II

Osmotic concentrations of haemolymph and rectal lumen contents in dehydrated and hydrated Periplaneta *adults (from Wall & Oschman,* 1970)

Condition	Haemolymph	Rectum	
		Ant. lumen	Post. lumen
Dehydrated	436	572	972
Hydrated	379	275	275
	(concentrations in m-osmole/kg H_2O)		

much of the total water being present in the tissues. In normally feeding *Schistocerca* the relative proportions are: haemolymph water about 15% of the body weight and tissue water about 50% (Lee, 1961; Fayadh, 1969) although the haemolymph volume may increase to 25% in hydrated animals (Stobbart, 1968; Fayadh, 1969). Very similar proportions are found in normally feeding *Periplaneta* and *Arenivaga* nymphs (Edney, 1968) and in *Carausius* (Ramsay, 1955).

The functional importance of the Malpighian tubule-rectum system can be examined by considering the rates of flow of water and solutes through the system, the rate of cuticular water loss and the movement of water from tissues to haemolymph assuming that they are in osmotic equilibrium, all of which can be expressed quantitatively.

The appropriate equations, the derivation of which is given in the Appendix, show how the haemolymph osmotic pressure, haemolymph volume and tissue water volume may be expected to change with time after the onset of dehydration. The results of some calculations which use the available data for *Schistocerca* are shown in Fig. 6.

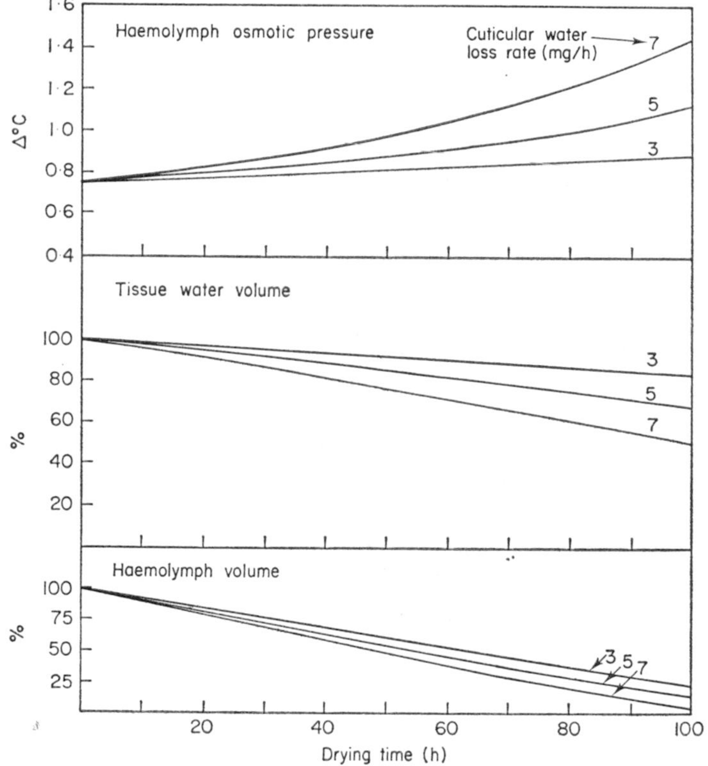

FIG. 6. Predicted changes in haemolymph osmotic pressure, tissue water volume and haemolymph volume with time after the start of dehydration for cuticular water loss rates from 3–7 mg/h. For a 2 g locust the starting values were taken as: haemolymph OP, $\Delta = 0{\cdot}75$°C; tissue water volume, 1000 mg; haemolymph volume, 300 mg.

It is evident that this model reproduces the important events occurring during dehydration. The haemolymph volume falls steadily and to a low level, whereas tissue water declines to a lesser extent.

Osmotic control is effective particularly at low cuticular loss rates: control is less effective as the haemolymph volume falls but the osmotic pressure is always well below that expected from the change in volume. Quantitatively the predictions can be compared with experimental results obtained for *Periplaneta* and *Arenivaga* nymphs (Edney, 1968). The basic parameters for *Periplaneta* and *Schistocerca* are very similar on a unit weight basis although the time scale is different because of the lower cuticular water loss rates and Malpighian tubule fluid rate in *Periplaneta*. Edney (1968) found that in *Periplaneta* when the haemolymph volume had fallen to 67% of its initial value the tissue water was 82·6% and the osmotic pressure had risen from $\Delta = 0{\cdot}75°C$ to $0{\cdot}85°C$. These values correspond very closely to those predicted for a situation where the cuticular water loss and the Malpighian tubule production are initially at about the same rate.

The tempting conclusion that our existing knowledge of the insect excretory system is adequate to explain osmotic changes during dehydration would be premature. The above treatment is based on the assumption that solute output through the system can be maintained at a constant level, i.e. if the tubule fluid production rate falls, the degree of solute reabsorption also decreases. This assumption is not unreasonable (see below). But a reduction of reabsorption from a tubule fluid with K as the major cation must mean that K becomes the major component of the excreted solute, as indeed was found to be the case in fasting *Carausius* (Ramsay, 1955). This would lead to a rapid depletion of the limited reservoir of haemolymph K and would be ineffective as an osmotic control mechanism. In fact in fasting *Carausius* the haemolymph K is maintained (Ramsay, 1955). A possible explanation is that the K output is sustained by the release of K from the tissues. If the released K is exchanged for Na (or another cation) then the conditions for osmotic control will be maintained. A low sodium output during dehydration has been observed in *Periplaneta* (Wall, 1970).

IONIC REGULATION AND SOLUTE REABSORPTION

The regulation of total osmotic pressure cannot be considered adequately without regard to the nature of the solutes. There is indeed evidence that the marked ability at osmotic regulation shown by these insects is reflected in a close control over the concentration of individual ions. *Schistocerca* may be mentioned in this respect. Table I shows that there are relatively small differences in haemolymph concentrations of

Na, K and Cl despite large differences in intake (tap-water, compared with a saline containing NaCl 300 m-mole/l and KCl, 150 m-mole/l). Fayadh (1969) also found little change in ionic concentrations in *Schistocerca* given a variety of different fluids to drink. In *Periplaneta* and *Arenivaga* nymphs the haemolymph Cl changes little on dehydration (Edney, 1968) and the same is true for Na and K in *Periplaneta* adults (Wall & Oschman, 1970). Also *Periplaneta* appears unresponsive to attempts to shift ion concentrations by providing a variety of diets and water regimes (Pichon, 1970).

This marked ability at ionic regulation must also depend largely on the properties of the rectum. Malpighian tubules do respond to large changes in the ionic composition of their bathing medium by changing the rate of secretion of particular ions (Ramsay, 1955; Shaw & Stobbart, 1963; Berridge, 1968; Maddrell, 1969); but in the intact animal the variations in ion concentrations even under extreme conditions are relatively small and hence changes in Malpighian tubule secretory rates would not be expected to be great. The values given in Table I for *Schistocerca* hind gut fluid are evidence of this. The tubule output may thus vary to some degree in both volume and composition and hence present a changing load to the rectum, but major changes in the composition of this fluid are brought about by the activity of the rectal epithelium. In hydrated *Schistocerca* the major ions, Na, K and Cl are almost completely removed from the fluid; whereas in saline-fed animals the concentrations of all three ions exceeds those in the original tubule fluid. Reabsorption can be rapid and each ion actively transported out of the rectum if the need arises (Phillips, 1964b). The rate of reabsorption is much reduced in the saline-fed animals and is clearly under physiological control. A special feature, illustrated in Fig. 7, is that when the rate of absorption is high (in hydrated animals) it is almost linearly dependent on rectal concentration. In contrast, when the rate is low, it is virtually independent of concentration above a critical value. This suggests a control of rectal wall permeability rather than a regulation of the active transport rate (Phillips, 1964c).

It would seem that regulation of the rate of uptake of Na and K also occurs in the rectum of *Periplaneta*. Here again, the rectal concentration of these ions is relatively low in hydrated animals and higher (particularly in K) in dehydrated ones (Wall & Oschman, 1970). There is some support for the view that the reabsorption of each ion may be regulated independently of the others, as it appears to be true in *Carausius* (Ramsay, 1955). Fayadh (1969) measured the haemolymph and rectal fluid Na and K concentrations in *Schistocerca* with a variety of fluids available for drinking. Table III shows that, with regard to the

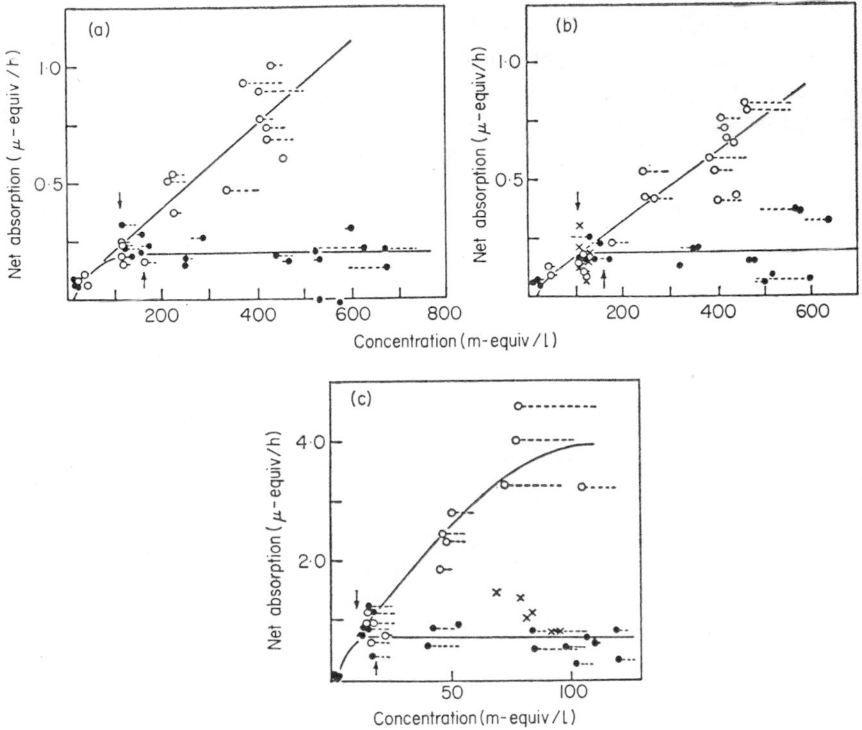

Fig. 7. The relationship between the mean rectal fluid concentration and net rate of absorption of (a) chloride, (b) sodium, (c) potassium from the ligated rectum of *Schistocerca*. Tap water-fed (open circles) and saline-fed (solid circles) locusts at 28 ± 1°C. Broken horizontal lines extend from the mean to the initial concentration. Arrows indicate mean concentrations in the haemolymph (Phillips, 1964b).

Table III

Sodium and potassium concentrations in the haemolymph and rectum of Schistocerca *under differing conditions* (**from Phillips*, 1964*b*; *†from Fayadh*, 1969)

Fluid available for drinking	Haemolymph		Rectal fluid	
	Na	K	Na	K
200 KCl	117	17	90	492
200 NaCl	150	10	587	126
100 NaCl †100 KCl	142	12	354	349
*Tap water	108	11	1	22
*300 NaCl †150 KCl	158	19	405	241

(concentrations in m-mole/l)

relative proportions of Na and K, there is a good correlation between the composition of the rectal fluid and that of the fluid available for drinking. In general, too, the higher the haemolymph Na concentration, the higher is its concentration in the rectal fluid. The same is true for K. It is possible, therefore, that the rate at which an ion is reabsorbed from the rectum is a function of the concentration of the ion in the haemolymph. This would certainly provide a very effective mechanism for ion regulation, but still requires a rigorous test to establish it. The main point, however, that an increase in overall ion concentration and hence of total osmotic pressure, leads to a reduction in solute readsorption seems well established.

OSMOTIC BALANCE DURING FEEDING

The next problem is to attempt to assess the potentiality of the excretory system for maintaining osmotic balance in xeric and desert insects on a dry diet or with a hyperosmotic solution available (the two situations are comparable as the ion content of the food will produce a hyperosmotic solution in its available water). Osmotic balance implies a steady-state with regard to both solutes and water, so that the water intake must equal the total water loss and the solute output must match the solute input.

Our present knowledge of the physiology of the midgut is limited, but it seems that ions are readily absorbed and probably accompanied by an osmotic uptake of water (Shaw & Stobbart, 1963; O'Riordan, 1969). If we assume that this is so, let us see what would happen to the haemolymph OP of an insect like *Schistocerca* ingesting sufficient food to maintain water balance.

Suppose that the rate of water absorption from the midgut $= v_3$ and that the osmotic concentration of the absorbed fluid $= C_g$. Using the same symbols as before (see Appendix) for cuticular water loss (v_1), tubule fluid rate (v_2), the degree of solute reabsorption (α) and the haemolymph and rectal fluid OP, C and C_r respectively.

Then for water balance,

$$v_3 = v_1 + v_2(1-\alpha)\frac{C}{C_r} \tag{1}$$

and for solute balance

$$v_3 C_g = v_2(1-\alpha)C \tag{2}$$

$$\therefore \quad v_3 = v_1 + v_3 C_g/C_r \quad \text{and} \quad C_r = v_3 C_g/v_3 - v_1.$$

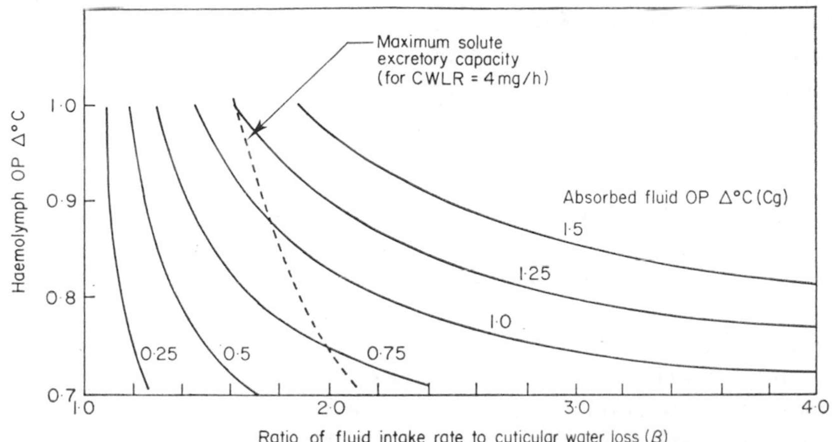

FIG. 8. The relationship between the steady-state haemolymph osmotic pressure and the ratio of fluid intake to cuticular water loss (β) for various concentrations of absorbed fluid. The maximum solute excretory capacity is calculated for a ratio of Malpighian tubule fluid output to cuticular water loss = 2 (see text).

Writing the ratio of water intake to cuticular water loss $(v_3/v_1) = \beta$, then

$$C_r = C_g\beta/\beta - 1. \tag{3}$$

But C_r is a function of C (see Fig. 5). For *Schistocerca* $C_r = 6{\cdot}65\,C - 3{\cdot}46$. Therefore C, the steady-state haemolymph OP, can be calculated in terms of C_g and β.

Figure 8 shows calculated values of C in relation to the relative rate of fluid intake (β) for a variety of absorbed fluid concentrations (C_g) and is applicable to *Schistocerca*. An apparently impressive feature is that effective osmotic regulation can be achieved with hyperosmotic solutions providing the fluid intake is large enough. Stabilization at a high osmotic pressure only occurs if the water uptake rate is less than twice the cuticular water loss rate. It must be noted, however, that in this calculation no restriction is placed on the rate of Malpighian tubule fluid production and hence on the solute excretory capacity of the system. In practice, of course, this will be limited by the maximum rate at which this fluid can be produced.

From (2) above

$$v_3C_g = \beta v_1C_g = v_2(1-\alpha)C.$$

If we take the most favourable situation where there is no rectal solute reabsorption ($\alpha = 0$) and hence a maximum solute output per unit volume of tubule fluid, then

$$v_2 = \beta v_1C_g/C.$$

If one applies the restriction that v_2 must not exceed the maximum tubule fluid rate ($\bar{v}_2$), about 8 mg/h for fully hydrated *Schistocerca* (Phillips, 1964c), then

$$\beta v_1 C_g / C \leqslant 8,$$

and in the case where $v_1 = 4$ mg/h, the limiting condition is when $\beta C_g = 2C$ or, more generally, $= \bar{v}_2 C / v_1$. Combining this with the previous Equation 3 and eliminating C (as C_r is a function of C), the limiting values of β for particular values of C_g can be determined. This curve is also shown in Fig. 8 and represents the maximum solute excretory capacity of the system for these conditions. With this imposed, osmotic balance is only possible to the left of the curve (Fig. 8). The curve, itself, will move further to the left if v_1 is larger, if v_2 is smaller, or if a degree of specific solute reabsorption is necessary to maintain a balance in the relative proportions of haemolymph ions. This limitation in the solute excretory capacity of the tubules means that the full potential of the system cannot be realized. In practice, even at a moderate atmospheric rh the absorption from the midgut of a hyperosmotic solution would push the haemolymph OP to a high level. Even with an isosmotic solution ($\Delta = 0{\cdot}75°$C) regulation of the haemolymph OP at a normal level can only take place if the absorbed solution approximates in composition to the tubule fluid, i.e. no specific reabsorption is necessary in order to maintain haemolymph ratios. If the absorbed solution departs much from the tubule fluid in composition (for example, if the Na concentration is higher) then it must be hypo-osmotic and absorbed at a rate not much greater than the cuticular water loss rate.

This means that if *Schistocerca* used a midgut absorption–tubule output–rectal reabsorption system for regulating its haemolymph osmotic pressure it would be limited to a diet with free water available or to a diet of high water content. Fresh grass and leaves are very suitable. The water content is high (about 90% of the fresh weight) and the cation contents of fresh rye grass, for example, (Na, 2·8; K, 63·9; Ca, 79·3; Mg, 8·8 m-equiv/100 mg dry wt) indicate that the fluid ingested would be hypo-osmotic even if all the ions were absorbed. The K/Na ratio is also favourably high.

The same will apply to *Periplaneta*. The rate of tubule fluid production is high in hydrated animals or after the application of a diuretic hormone from the terminal abdominal ganglion (Mills, 1967), but it is still not greater than the normal cuticular water loss rate under dry conditions.

The point has been made in detail because it leads to an important conclusion. If, under conditions of survival on a dry diet, the ingested material forms a hyperosmotic fluid in the gut, the route taken by the ingested solutes and water cannot be the one previously envisaged, unless the haemolymph OP is allowed to rise markedly. Possible alternative routes would have to be considered including extra-renal secretion. On the whole the most likely mechanism is that solute absorption through the midgut wall would be greatly reduced, and hence parallel to the reduction of solute absorption from the rectum under the same conditions. Since there is no evidence of solute-independent water transport against a gradient in the midgut, water uptake would also be reduced.

The net result would be that the midgut contents, relatively unchanged in water and ions, would be passed on to the rectum where osmotically-free water could be withdrawn, as from the Malpighian tubule fluid. This would use the full potential of rectal water-absorbing mechanisms while relieving the Malpighian tubules from maintaining a high solute output under dehydrating conditions.

Previously we saw that in the absence of food there is a problem in maintaining an appropriate solute output. With food of low water content the problem becomes more acute. The solution, by restricting midgut absorption, assigns a major role to this organ in the overall homeostatic mechanism and it must be stressed such a role has yet to be demonstrated experimentally. It emphasizes our lack of detailed knowledge of solute turnover in the animal as a whole.

Clearly the driest diet for *Schistocerca* and *Periplaneta* is one where the equivalent OP of its non-metabolizable solutes and water is less than a $\Delta = 2$–$3°C$ which can be achieved in the rectum. The larva of *Tenebrio* is better in this respect. In the posterior region of the rectum water is reabsorbed as a vapour and a faecal pellet is produced with an equilibrium rh of about 90% (Ramsay, 1964). Water reabsorption is assisted by the cryptonephridial arrangement in which the OP of the distal regions of the tubules, which are closely associated with the rectum and enclosed within the perirectal space, is raised by the inward secretion of K from the haemolymph by highly specialized tubule cells, called leptophragmata (Ramsay, 1964; Grimstone, Mullinger & Ramsay, 1968). This greatly reduces the gradient against which water must be reabsorbed across the rectal wall.

The uptake of water vapour in the rectum provides a possible explanation of the ability of this larva to absorb water vapour from its environment providing the rh of the latter exceeds 88% (Mellanby, 1932). Support for this view comes from the recent demonstration that uptake of water vapour by dehydrated fire-brats, *Thermobia domestica*, which occurs from rh's $\geqslant 63\%$ is prevented by occlusion of the anus (Noble-Nesbitt, 1970).

CONCLUSIONS

The mechanisms of water conservation and the routes of water loss in xeric and desert arthropods are now well understood and are well demonstrated by *Schistocerca*. In view of their small size, cuticular waterproofing is probably essential to all terrestrial arthropods, nevertheless cuticular losses are always a major component of the total loss, and are not conspicuously lower in true desert insects. Tracheal losses are minimized by appropriate control of ventilation, and by closure of the spiracles. Faecal water losses are greatly reduced by solute-independent reabsorption of water by the rectum. Only rarely do we find that the overall rate of water loss is sufficiently low to be balanced by the production of metabolic water, and intake of fluids is therefore necessary. This is probably a consequence of small size. In some flying insects however (including *Schistocerca*) the metabolic rate is raised sufficiently for such a balance to be possible. In a few species water vapour is taken up. The mechanism of this process has hitherto proved to be elusive, but if this process is proved to be a function of the rectum, the remaining problem concerning the exchanges of water with the atmosphere will be resolved.

The mode of operation of the excretory system can explain the regulation of the ionic composition and osmotic pressure under most conditions. During dehydration in the absence of food, however, additional mechanisms, perhaps involving tissue-haemolymph exchanges, may be necessary to maintain the solute output required for osmotic control. In the presence of food the main problem is the way in which the available water is extracted. If the water is absorbed in the midgut along with ingested salts, then the solute excretory capacity of the Malpighian tubules may be exceeded and a marked rise in haemolymph OP result. As the capacity of the Malpighian tubules will be maximally exploited if the absorbed fluid approximates in composition to the tubule fluid, it is possible that correlations between the composition of the latter and that of the diet would be found. In recent results obtained with *Rhodnius*, Maddrell (1969) suggests that such correlations may in fact exist. It is also possible that the flexibility of the excretory system may be greatly increased if the rate of solute uptake by the midgut is regulated. In dehydrating situations ingested material would pass through to the rectum and the water would be absorbed there. There is at present no experimental evidence for this suggestion, but whether valid or not it is abundantly clear that the rectum is a highly (and possibly the most) important regulatory element in the excretory system.

References

Ahearn, G. A. (1970). The control of water loss in desert tenebrionid beetles. *J. exp. Biol.* **53**: 573–595.

Ahearn, G. A. & Hadley, N. F. (1969). The effects of temperature and humidity on water loss in two desert tenebrionid beetles, *Eleodes armata* and *Cryptoglossa verrucosa*. *Comp. Biochem. Physiol.* **30**: 739–749.

Beament, J. W. L. (1958). The effect of temperature on the water-proofing mechanism of an insect. *J. exp. Biol.* **35**: 494–519.

Beament, J. W. L. (1959). The waterproofing mechanism of arthropods. I. The effect of temperature on cuticle permeability in terrestrial insects and ticks. *J. exp. Biol.* **36**: 391–422.

Beament, J. W. L. (1961). The water relations of insect cuticle. *Biol. Rev.* **36**: 281–320.

Beament, J. W. L. (1964). The active transport and passive movement of water in insects. *Adv. Insect Physiol.* **2**: 67–129.

Beament, J. W. L. (1965). The active transport of water: evidence, models and mechanisms. *Symp. Soc. exp. Biol.* **19**: 273–298.

Berridge, M. J. (1968). Urine formation by the Malpighian tubules of *Calliphora*. I. Cations. *J. exp. Biol.* **48**: 159–174.

Bursell, E. (1964). Environmental aspects: Humidity. In *The physiology of Insecta* **1**: Chapter 8. Rockstein, M. (ed.). New York & London: Academic Press.

Buxton, P. A. (1930). Evaporation from the meal-worm (Tenebrio: Coleoptera) and atmospheric humidity. *Proc. R. Soc.* (*B.*) **106**: 560–577.

Church, N. S. (1960). Heat loss and the body temperature of flying insects. I. Heat loss by evaporation of water from the body. *J. exp. Biol.* **37**: 171–185.

Cloudesley-Thompson, J. L. (1961). Some aspects of the physiology and behaviour of *Galeodes arabs*. *Ent. exp. appl.* **4**: 257–263.

Cockbain, A. J. (1961). Water relationships of *Aphis fabae* Scop. during tethered flight. *J. exp. Biol.* **38**: 175–180.

Djajakusumah, T. & Miles, P. W. (1966). Changes in the relative amounts of soluble protein and amino acid in the haemolymph of the locust *Chortoicetes terminifera* Walker (Orthoptera: Acrididae), in relation to dehydration and subsequent hydration. *Aust. J. biol. Sci.* **19**: 1081–1094.

Edney, E. B. (1966). Absorption of water vapour from unsaturated air by *Arenivaga* sp. (Polyphagidae, Dictyoptera). *Comp. Biochem. Physiol.* **19**: 387–408

Edney, E. B. (1967). Water balance in desert arthropods. *Science, N.Y.* **156**: 1059–1066.

Edney, E. B. (1968). The effect of water loss on the haemolymph of *Arenivaga* sp. and *Periplaneta americana*. *Comp. Biochem. Physiol.* **25**: 149–158.

Fayadh, L. (1969). *Salt and water balance in the desert locust Schistocerca gregaria Forskål*. M.Sc. Thesis, University of Newcastle upon Tyne.

Fraenkel, G. & Blewett, M. (1944). The utilization of metabolic water in insects. *Bull. ent. Res.* **35**: 127–137.

Grimstone, A. V., Mullinger, A. M. & Ramsay, J. A. (1968). Further studies on the rectal complex of the mealworm, *Tenebrio molitor* L. (Coleoptera, Tenebrionidae). *Phil. Trans. R. Soc.* (*B.*) **253**: 343–382.

Hadley, N. F. (1970). Water relations of the desert scorpion *Hadrurus arizonensis*. *J. exp. Biol.* **53**: 547–558.

Hamilton, A. G. (1964). Occurrence of periodic or continuous discharge of carbon dioxide by male desert locusts (*Schistocerca gregaria* Forskål). *Proc. R. Soc.* (*B.*) **160**: 373–395.

Irvine, H. B. & Phillips, J. E. (1971). Effects of respiratory inhibitors and ouabain on water transport by isolated locust rectum. *J. Insect Physiol.* **17**: 381–383.

Krogh, A. & Weis-Fogh, T. (1951). Respiratory exchange of the desert locust (*Schistocerca gregaria*) before, during and after flight. *J. exp. Biol.* **28**: 344–357.

Lee, R. M. (1961). The variation of blood volume with age in the desert locust (*Schistocerca gregaria* Forskål.). *J. Insect Physiol.* **6**: 36–51.

Lees, A. D. (1947). Transpiration and the structure of the epicuticle in ticks. *J. exp. Biol.* **23**: 379–410.

Loveridge, J. P. (1968a). The control of water loss in *Locusta migratoria migratorioides* R. & F. I. Cuticular water loss. *J. exp. Biol.* **49**: 1–13.

Loveridge, J. P. (1968b). The control of water loss in *Locusta migratoria migratorioides* R. & F. II. Water loss through the spiracles. *J. exp. Biol.* **49**: 15–29.

Ludwig, D. (1937). The effect of different relative humidities on respiratory metabolism and survival of the grasshopper *Chortophaga viridifasciata* de Geer. *Physiol. Zoöl.* **10**: 342–351.

Maddrell, S. H. P. (1969). Secretion by the Malpighian tubules of *Rhodnius*. The movements of ions and water. *J. exp. Biol.* **51**: 71–97.

Marcuzzi, G. (1955). Osservazioni fisico-chimiche sul sangue dei Coleotteri Tenebrionidi.–I. La pressione osmotica nel *Tenebrio molitor* L. *Atti accad. naz. Lincei Rc.* (Classe sci. fis. mat. e nat.) **18**: 654–662.

Marcuzzi, G. (1956). L'osmoregolazione nel *Tenebrio molitor* L. *Atti accad. naz. Lincei Rc.* (Classe sci. fis. mat. e nat.) **20**: 492–500.

Mellanby, K. (1932). The effect of atmospheric humidity on the metabolism of the fasting mealworm (*Tenebrio molitor* L., Coleoptera). *Proc. R. Soc.*, (*B.*) **111**: 376–390.

Mellanby, K. (1939). The functions of insect blood. *Biol. Rev.* **14**: 243–260.

Miller, P. L. (1960a). Respiration in the desert locust. I. The control of ventilation. *J. exp. Biol.* **37**: 224–236.

Miller, P. L. (1960b). Respiration in the desert locust. II. The control of the spiracles. *J. exp. Biol.* **37**: 237–263.

Miller, P. L. (1960c). Respiration in the desert locust. III. Ventilation and the spiracles during flight. *J. exp. Biol.* **37**: 264–278.

Mills, R. R. (1967). Hormonal control of excretion in the American cockroach. I. Release of a diuretic hormone from the terminal abdominal ganglion. *J. exp. Biol.* **46**: 35–41.

Mordue, W. (1969). Hormonal control of Malpighian tube and rectal function in the desert locust *Schistocerca gregaria*. *J. Insect Physiol.* **15**: 273–285.

Noble-Nesbitt, J. (1969). Water balance in the firebrat *Thermobia domestica* (Packard). Exchanges of water with the atmosphere. *J. exp. Biol.* **50**: 745–769.

Noble-Nesbitt, J. (1970). Water balance in the firebrat *Thermobia domestica* (Packard). The site of water uptake from the atmosphere. *J. exp. Biol.* **52**: 193–200.

O'Riordan, A. M. (1969). Electrolyte movement in the isolated midgut of the cockroach (*Periplaneta americana* L.). *J. exp. Biol.* **51**: 699–714.

Phillips, J. E. (1964a). Rectal absorption in the desert locust *Schistocerca gregaria* Forskål. I. Water. *J. exp. Biol.* **41**: 15–38.

Phillips, J. E. (1964b). Rectal absorption in the desert locust *Schistocerca gregaria* Forskål. II. Sodium potassium and chloride. *J. exp. Biol.* **41**: 39–67.

Phillips, J. E. (1964c). Rectal absorption in the desert locust *Schistocerca gregaria* Forskål. III. The nature of the excretory process. *J. exp. Biol.* **41**: 69–80.

Phillips, J. E. (1969). Osmotic regulation and rectal absorption in the blowfly, *Calliphora erythrocephala*. *Can. J. Zool.* **47**: 851–863.

Pichon, Y. (1970). Ionic content of the haemolymph in the cockroach *Periplaneta americana*. A critical analysis. *J. exp. Biol.* **53**: 195–209.

Pilcher, D. E. M. (1970). Hormonal control of the Malpighian tubules of the stick insect *Carausius morosus*. *J. exp. Biol.* **52**: 653–665.

Ramsay, J. A. (1953). Active transport of potassium by the Malpighian tubules of insects. *J. exp. Biol.* **30**: 358–369.

Ramsay, J. A. (1955). The excretory system of the stick insect *Dixippus morosus* (Orthoptera; Phasmidae). *J. exp. Biol.* **32**: 183–199.

Ramsay, J. A. (1964). The rectal complex of the mealworm *Tenebrio molitor* L. (Coleoptera, Tenebrionidae). *Phil. Trans. R. Soc.* (*B*.) **248**: 279–314.

Shaw, J. & Stobbart, R. H. (1963). Osmotic and ionic regulation in insects. *Adv. Insect Physiol.* **1**: 315–399.

Stobbart, R. H. (1968). Ion movements and water transport in the rectum of the locust *Schistocerca gregaria*. *J. Insect Physiol.* **14**: 269–275.

Stobbart, R. H. & Shaw, J. (1964). Salt and water balance: excretion. In *The physiology of Insecta*. **3**: Chapter 4. Rockstein, M. (ed.). New York & London: Academic Press.

Uvarov, B. P. (1928). *Locusts and Grasshoppers. A handbook for their study and control*. London, Beccles: W. Clowes & Sons.

Wall, B. J. (1967). Evidence for antidiuretic control of rectal water absorption in the cockroach *Periplaneta americana* L. *J. Insect Physiol.* **13**: 565–578.

Wall, B. J. (1970). Effects of dehydration and rehydration on *Periplaneta americana*. *J. Insect. Physiol.* **16**: 1027–1042.

Wall, B. J. & Oschman, J. L. (1970). Water and solute uptake by rectal pads of *Periplaneta americana*. *Am. J. Physiol.* **218**: 1208–1215.

Wall, B. J., Oschman, J. L. & Schmidt-Nielsen, B. (1969). Fluid transport: concentration of the intercellular compartment. *Science, N.Y.* **167**: 1497–1498.

Wall, B. J. & Ralph, C. L. (1964). Evidence for hormonal regulation of Malpighian tubule excretion in the insect *Periplaneta americana* L. *Gen. comp. Endocr.* **4**: 452–456.

Weis-Fogh, T. (1952). Fat combustion and metabolic rate of flying locusts (*Schistocerca gregaria* Forskål). *Phil. Trans. R. Soc.* (*B*.) **237**: 1–36.

Weis-Fogh, T. (1967). Respiration and tracheal ventilation in locusts and other flying insects. *J. exp. Biol.* **47**: 561–587.

Appendix

The time course of osmotic and volume changes during dehydration.

The problem is to find how the haemolymph OP, haemolymph volume and tissue water volume change with time after the start of dehydration.

Let the haemolymph volume $= V$ and its concentration (OP) $= C$.

Let the tissue water volume $= V'$ and its concentration also $= C$ (and hence assume that the two fluids are in osmotic equilibrium). Assume also that there is no net solute exchange between the two fluids, then $V'C$ is constant and on differentiating,

$$V'\,\mathrm{d}C/\mathrm{d}t + C\,\mathrm{d}V'/\mathrm{d}t = 0, \text{ hence } \mathrm{d}V'/\mathrm{d}t = -\frac{V'}{C}\cdot \mathrm{d}C/\mathrm{d}t. \tag{1}$$

The total solute in the haemolymph $= VC = n$.

$V\,\mathrm{d}C/\mathrm{d}t + C\,\mathrm{d}V/\mathrm{d}t = \mathrm{d}n/\mathrm{d}t =$ the rate of solute flow.

Let the rate of Malpighian tubule fluid production $= v_2$ and the degree of reabsorption of solute from this fluid $= \alpha$. Since the fluid is isosmotic with the haemolymph the rate of solute loss $= v_2(1-\alpha)C$.

Hence

$$V\,\mathrm{d}C/\mathrm{d}t + C\,\mathrm{d}V/\mathrm{d}t = -v_2(1-\alpha)C$$

and

$$\mathrm{d}C/\mathrm{d}t = -\frac{C}{V}(v_2(1-\alpha) + \mathrm{d}V/\mathrm{d}t). \tag{2}$$

The rate at which fluid is lost through the excretory system $= v_2(1-\alpha)\,C/C_r$ where $C_r =$ the OP of the rectal fluid.

The rate of haemolymph volume change,

$$\mathrm{d}V/\mathrm{d}t = -(v_1 + v_2(1-\alpha)C/C_r) - \mathrm{d}V'/\mathrm{d}t \tag{3}$$

where v_1 is the rate of water loss through cuticle. Combining Equations 1, 2 and 3 gives,

$$\mathrm{d}C/\mathrm{d}t = \frac{C}{V+V'}\,(v_1 + v_2(1-\alpha)C/C_r - v_2(1-\alpha)) \tag{4}$$

Equations 1, 3 and 4 must now be solved simultaneously to give C, V and V' in relation to t. v_1, $v_2(1-\alpha)$ and C_r must be known.

For *Schistocerca* v_1 varies with ambient rh and a range of values between 3 and 7 mg/h are used. v_2 is taken initially to be at its maximum rate (8 mg/h, Phillips, 1964c) and α given a nominal value of 0·75 to allow for the reabsorption of K. $v_2(1-\alpha)$ is assumed to remain constant throughout the period. $C_r = 6{\cdot}65C - 3{\cdot}46$ over a range of haemolymph OP's for $\Delta = 0{\cdot}7°\text{C}–1{\cdot}0°\text{C}$ (Phillips, 1964a). The starting values for a 2 g locust were taken at $C = 0{\cdot}75°\text{C}$ (Phillips, 1964a), $V = 300$ mg and $V' = 1000$ mg (Lee, 1961). The equations were solved by a numerical method.

Symp. zool. Soc. Lond. (1972) No. 31, 39–59.

TEMPERATURE REGULATION IN DESERT REPTILES

J. L. CLOUDSLEY-THOMPSON

Department of Zoology,
Birckbeck College, University of London, London, England

SYNOPSIS

Although it has long been known that reptiles are ectothermal and regulate their body temperatures chiefly by behavioural means, the significance of physiological thermoregulation has only recently become apparent. Behavioural thermoregulation is achieved mainly by sun basking or moving into shade, and by making bodily contact with a thermally favourable substratum. Diurnal and seasonal rhythms of activity, although overtly behavioural, have a physiological basis and link the two methods of temperature regulation. Physiological thermoregulation is achieved also by metabolic heat production, cardiovascular adjustments, evaporative cooling and changes in albedo. Reptiles lack feathers, hair and sweat glands. Apart from this, all aspects of thermal control found in homeotherms are present in some form or another. Thus desert reptiles do not differ greatly from birds and mammals in regard to their temperature and water relations especially when differences in size and shape are taken into account.

INTRODUCTION

Most higher animals show some degree of thermal adjustment. Apart from birds and mammals, however, only the Arthropoda and reptiles, whose integuments are comparatively impervious, are able to maintain an internal temperature consistently higher than that of the environment. Evaporation from a moist body surface in other terrestrial poikilotherms precludes the attainment of temperatures comparable with those of homeothermic mammals and birds.

Large animals have a relatively smaller surface area in proportion to their mass than do small animals. Heat exchange with the environment by radiation, conduction and convection, like transpiration, is therefore correspondingly reduced in larger forms. The size of the big sauropod dinosaurs of the Mesozoic period was so great that these animals must almost certainly have been homeothermic (Colbert, 1962). So, too, were the pterosaurs, fossils of which show a hairy covering (Bramwell, 1970). Homeothermy is metabolically expensive even to smaller birds and mammals on account of their relatively large surface areas. In the case of small reptiles, whose surface areas are enhanced by their elongated shape, behavioural control of temperature is naturally both more efficient and more important than physiological thermoregulation although the two are, in fact, intimately related.

Among recent reptiles, metabolic heat production reaches significant proportions only in large forms, such as pythons and boas. Smaller species are ectothermal and achieve thermal control by behavioural rather than by physiological mechanisms which, as already mentioned, are extravagant when the surface to volume ratio is high. Since they do not transpire rapidly, desert reptiles are not restricted to nocturnal habits except when day temperatures become excessive. They are of particular interest because thermoregulation is better developed in them than among species from temperate latitudes (Schmidt-Nielsen & Dawson, 1964).

Thermoregulation by sun basking and the avoidance of excessive heat (Fig. 1), supplemented by more subtle parameters of behaviour, is closely associated with rhythmical activity. An endogenous periodicity is responsible for emergence at dawn or dusk, independently of cyclical environmental changes in temperature or light intensity. But for this, desert reptiles would be unable to make full use of their burrows and other retreats without losing valuable time at the commencement of their normal activity. Finally, reptiles show true physiological thermoregulation analogous to, but less effective than, that found in homeothermic birds and mammals, except that they have not evolved a protective coat of feathers or fur (Fry, 1967).

BEHAVIOURAL THERMOREGULATION

Cowles & Bogert (1944) were among the first to point out that behaviour plays a major role in the thermoregulation of ectothermal animals. Since their initial studies, many other workers have accumulated data on body temperature and various other aspects of reptilian thermoregulation. This work has been summarized in recent reviews by Bellairs (1969), Brattstrom (1965), Cloudsley-Thompson (1971), Mayhew (1968) and Templeton (1970). The effectiveness of behavioural thermoregulation is illustrated by the fact that Burns (1970) did not detect any significant difference in the body temperatures of *Sceloporus jarrovi* at elevations from 2000–3600 m in the Pinaleño Mountains of south-eastern Arizona. Strel'nikov (1944) measured an excess of 29·2°C in the body temperature of *Lacerta agelis* above the ambient temperature at an altitude of 4100 m in the Caucasus, and Pearson (1954) observed *Liolaemus multiformis* at high altitudes in southern Peru warming its

FIG. 1. Agamid lizard, in the Red Sea hills, sheltering in a rock crevice from the excessive mid-day heat.

body to above 30°C by the absorption of solar radiation, even though nearby shade temperatures were below freezing.

Sun basking

When they are cold, reptiles crawl into the sun and warm themselves by basking. Some lizards climb to the tops of bushes to obtain maximum exposure, crawling back into shade or down to their burrows when they have achieved a satisfactory body temperature (Bellairs, 1969; Cloudsley-Thompson, 1971). It has been suggested that the function of the huge, sail-like crest of vertical spines in certain Permian pelycosaurs such as *Dimetrodon* and *Edaphosaurus* may have been to absorb solar radiation (Rodbard, 1949).

Regulation of body temperature by basking in the sun has been recorded in a large number of terrestrial tortoises, lizards and snakes. *Testudo sulcata*, like other desert tortoises, basks in the morning sunshine but avoids the heat of the day in its burrow. The response has been shown experimentally to be mediated by heat rather than light, and the avoidance of high temperature is direct and not achieved by negative phototaxis (Cloudsley-Thompson, 1970a).

Thermoregulation by sun basking is employed by most day-active species of lizards and snakes, especially in deserts where intense solar radiation undiminished by cloud cover is available throughout most of the year. Bogert (1949) attributed to this fact that more than 25 species of lizard inhabit the North American deserts where the number of clear days exceeds 180 annually. There is a correlation between body size and habitat selection in Teiidae of the genus *Cnemidophorus* in the western deserts of North America. Small size is apparently related to a desert physiogamy, and the larger species are associated with the densest vegetation. Larger lizards also spend more time in the shade than do smaller animals, but they maintain similar body temperatures (Asplund, 1968).

Bartlett & Gates (1967) determined the absorption of heat, surface area, body temperatures and convection coefficients, and estimated metabolic and evaporative energy exchanges for a representative *Sceloporus barbatus*. They then related these to the environmental properties of a particular tree trunk in Florida on a day in June and predicted the postures that the lizard would assume to maintain its body temperature within the range characteristic of the population in that habitat. Their predictions were confirmed by field observations. They calculated that a change of 10% in the absorptivity of the lizard to direct sunlight would alter the gain in energy by 1·3 cal/min, or by about 4%. Doubling the production of metabolic heat would increase the total gain in this particular example by only 1·2% (see below).

Orientation of the body

More subtle parameters of sun basking and retreat into shade include arboreal behaviour, orientation of the body to the rays of the sun, flattening of the body or raising on the toes. These show parallels with the behaviour of insects and other arthropods (Cloudsley-Thompson, 1970b), and of homeotherms.

When they are cold, reptiles orientate their bodies at right angles to the rays of the sun, sometimes making use of sloping surfaces to align themselves. Tortoises are known to tilt their bodies against rocks and other objects in order to catch the sun better (Bellairs, 1969).

When relatively cool, *Dipsosaurus dorsalis* orients itself so that its body is nearly perpendicular to the rays of the sun. As the temperature of the lizard nears the range employed for activity, the body is realigned so that the long axis becomes parallel to the rays of the sun. The amount of solar radiation absorbed can also be influenced by the amount of body surface exposed, the ventral surface being shielded or otherwise by postural adjustments. Once the animal has warmed to a suitable level, it tends to control body temperature by dividing its time between the sun and the shade (De Witt, 1967; Schmidt-Nielsen & Dawson, 1964).

Likewise, *Phrynosoma m'calli* usually faces the sun when it has achieved its preferred body temperature, and this places the relatively broad expanse of the back out of the direct rays of the sun. At such times the animals are most often to be seen with their bodies raised well above the hot substrata (see below) (Norris, 1949). Regular alterations in shape and contour of the body occur in species of *Amphibolurus* according to Bradshaw & Main (1968). These probably control the absorption of radiant heat by the basking animals.

Amblyrhynchus cristatus, the marine iguana of the Galapagos Islands, is able to keep its body temperature below 40°C without resorting to shade, although black bulb temperatures may exceed 50°C. This remarkable feat is achieved on bare lava flows exposed to the intense radiation of the equatorial sun. When sun basking at high temperatures, marine iguanas orient their bodies so that they face directly towards the sun. Much of the back and hind quarters is therefore shaded by the head, neck and shoulders which are held high in the air. At the same time the front legs are extended so that the anterior part of the body is well clear of the substratum. Shortly after sunrise, however, or when returning cold from the sea, *A. cristatus* basks in a prostrate posture with its body oriented at right angles to the rays of the sun. In this way a maximum amount of solar radiation is intercepted. Not until the body temperature has reached 39–40°C is the elevated, basking position adopted (Bartholomew, 1966).

Contact with the substratum

Contact with the substrate may be used both for warming and for cooling the body. After they have been heated by the sun, lizards and snakes often dig their bodies into the cooler layers beneath the surface of the soil. When running across a hot, sandy surface, *Dipsosaurus dorsalis* may stop suddenly, press its abdomen close to the sand and wriggle its body rapidly from side to side. In this way it comes into contact with the cooler sand underneath. At other times it flexes its toes and elevates its tail from the hot sand surfaces (Norris, 1953). Under experimental conditions, *Mabuya quinquetaeniatus* does not avoid high sand temperatures until the body temperature has begun to approach lethal limits, when the skink sometimes attempts to burrow (Cloudsley-Thompson, 1965).

McGinnis & Dickson (1967) showed that extensive thermoregulatory behaviour occurs in the burrows of *D. dorsalis* before the lizards' morning emergence by means of temperature-sensitive radio-transmitters implanted in their bodies. This is achieved by selecting the warmest segments of the burrow near to the surface. Such behaviour is highly adaptive, since it enables the iguana to attain the optimum body temperature for surface activity before emerging from its burrow.

Responses to warm substrates are probably as important in the thermoregulation of nocturnal desert reptiles as is sun basking to day-active species. It probably accounts for the large numbers of rattlesnakes and other reptiles found at night on the roads of the American deserts (Brattstrom, 1965).

Figure 2 summarizes the inter-relations of temperature-regulating behaviour in *Phrynosoma coronatum*. Initiation of activity in the morning is independent of temperature, at least when the lizards are warm enough to move. The body temperature is then elevated by sun basking and associated behaviour until the normal range for activity is attained. At temperatures above the maximum tolerated voluntarily, other behavioural and physiological temperature control mechanisms are invoked (Heath, 1965).

RHYTHMIC BEHAVIOUR

Diurnal and seasonal rhythms of activity in reptiles, although overtly behavioural, have a physiological basis. They thereby

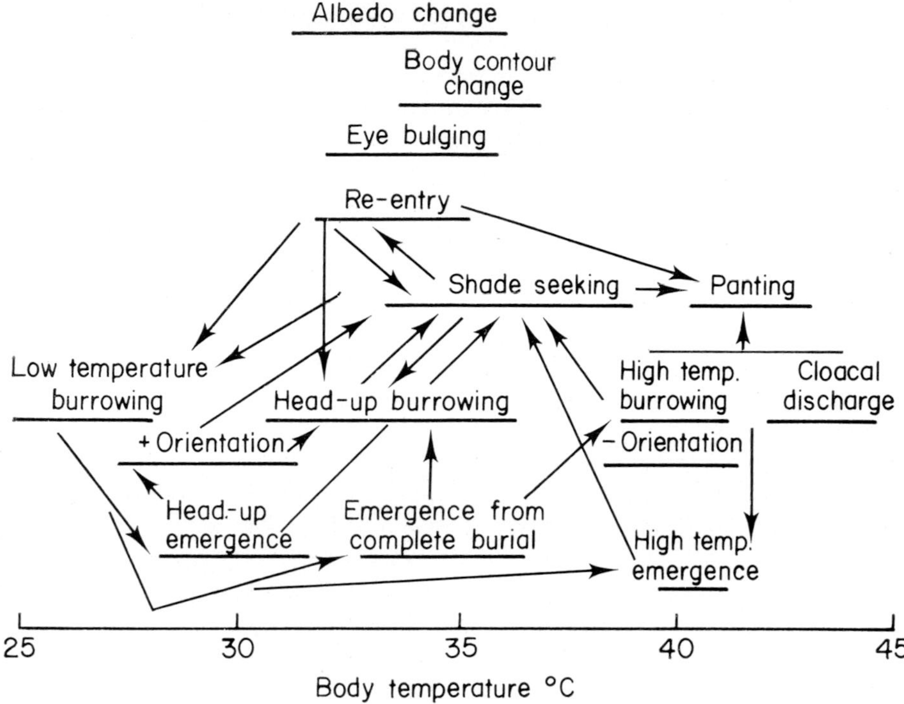

Fig. 2. The inter-relations of temperature regulating behaviour in *Phrynosoma coronatum*. The range of body temperature for each pattern is given. (From Cloudsley-Thompson, 1971 after Heath, 1965.)

provide a link between behavioural and physiological thermoregulation.

Diurnal rhythms

Temperature regulation by behavioural means is intimately related to diurnal rhythms of activity. Although the period of a rhythm is virtually independent of environmental variables within their natural range, several factors may alter its phase setting. In addition, short-term exogenous factors may influence the expression of the rhythm. For example, both *Ameiva quadrilineata* and *Basiliscus vittatus* are diurnal, heliophilic lizards: their cycles of activity are dominated and controlled by thermoregulatory needs and are interrupted by periods of rain (Hirth, 1963).

An investigation of the relationship between morning emergence and body temperature of horned lizards of the genus *Phrynosoma* has demonstrated an endogenous rhythmic anticipation of conditions favourable for normal activity (Fig. 2). Initiation of activity in the morning is independent of temperature, at least when the animals are warm enough to move. By this means, ectothermic reptiles can use safe nocturnal shelters without loss of time for feeding and other activities (Heath, 1962, 1965).

By means of aktograph experiments, Bustard (1970) found that the activity of the nocturnal gecko *Hemidactylus frenatus* is not restricted by temperature, although this is still a major factor during the first few hours after night fall. The endogenous component of the rhythm is more marked than in *Diplodactylus vittatus* where exogenous factors play a greater part. *D. vittatus* shows a pattern of activity which is initiated by sunset, provided that the temperature lies within a prescribed range. Activity is inhibited by temperatures below 17°C and 13°C in southern and northern Australian populations respectively, and by temperatures above 25–26°C. Between these ranges, however, the activity of *D. vittatus* may continue until dawn (Bustard, 1968) whereas that of *Gehyra variegata* is appreciably reduced by midnight, even on warm nights (Bustard, 1967). During the day these geckoes thermoregulate actively by moving about beneath the bark of tree stumps where they live, pressing their bodies to the inner surface of the bark where it is heated by the sun.

From an extensive survey of the reptiles of California, Klauber (1939) has shown that strenuous high temperature conditions in deserts lead to a change from diurnality to nocturnality in coastal species which have invaded the desert. He lists several day-active snakes which are apparently limited to the coastal region by their inability to assume a nocturnal pattern of activity.

Diurnal emergence from nocturnal retreats is accomplished differently by different species of reptiles. Some burrowing forms, such as *Dipsosaurus dorsalis*, become active in their burrows for as long as two hours before conditions above ground are suitable for emergence (De Witt, 1962). This iguanid heats up rapidly upon leaving its burrow, but remains near the entrance until it has reached an optimum temperature of 38–40°C before moving away to forage or seek a mate (Mayhew, 1968).

Lizards that submerge themselves in sand often expose only their heads for several minutes before emergence. Such behaviour suggests that blood is warmed in the head region and released slowly to other parts of the body so that the animals are capable of rapid movement before they are endangered by coming into the open (Mayhew, 1968). This may also explain the ecological significance of blood shunting. The

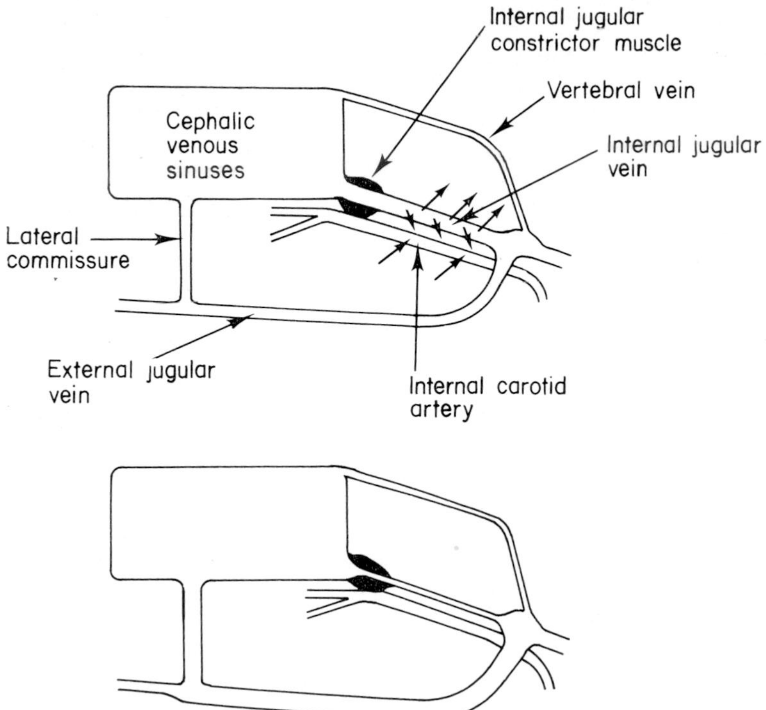

FIG. 3. Diagram showing the relations of the major vessels in the head *Phrynosoma coronatum*. The venous spaces of the head are abstracted to a single space. *Above*: Internal jugular vein is open. Arrows indicate heat exchange between internal jugular veins, internal carotid artery and tissues of the neck. *Below*: Closure of the internal jugular constrictor muscle causes collapse of the internal jugular vein. Venous blood returns through a shunt to the external jugular vein. Cool blood, warmed only by the neck tissue, enters the head, while warm blood flows through the external jugular vein to the body. (From Cloudsley-Thompson, 1971 after Heath, 1966.)

temperature of the head of *Phrynosoma coronatum* is regulated by opening lateral shunt vessels from the cephalic sinuses to the external jugular veins, thus by-passing a counter-current heat exchange between the internal jugular veins and the internal carotid arteries (Fig. 3) (Heath, 1966). The subject of jugular shunts and head-body temperatures is discussed in detail by Templeton (1970).

Seasonal rhythms

Comparatively little research has been carried out on seasonal rhythms in relation to temperature regulation in desert reptiles. *Gopherus agassizii*, like other species of reptile, may, however, hibernate in deep dens during the winter, thereby evading cold weather (Woodbury & Hardy, 1948). Seasonal changes in the activity patterns of desert lizards and snakes are often less marked. Gauthier (1967), however, found that the time of activity of certain reptiles of the north-western Sahara varies according to the season. Snakes, such as *Natrix maura*, *Spalerosophis diadema* and *Malpolon moilensis* are nocturnal in summer but day-active in spring, autumn and winter. On the other hand, apart from a few exceptions, such as *Scincus scincus* and *Chalcides ocellatus*, the lizards of that region do not change their times of activity at different seasons of the year.

Mayhew (1964) showed that in species of the genus *Uma* in America, there may be two peaks of activity in summer when it is very hot at midday, but only one in the spring and autumn months. The activity pattern of *Tiliqua rugosa* also changes during the year, activity in mid-summer being restricted to short periods in the early morning and late afternoon (Warburg, 1965).

Seasonal changes in preferred body temperature have been observed in a number of reptile species. In some instances, these have been related to alterations in the photoperiod. A mechanism by which a reptile could predict the onset of cooler or warmer weather would be of selective value in adjusting the preferred temperature to utilize the mechanism of acclimation. Ballinger, Hawker & Sexton (1969) determined the preferred temperatures of *Sceloporus undulatus* acclimated to 20°C under 12-h and 6-h photoperiods. They found that the longer photoperiod increased the preferred temperatures of lizards collected in May, while the shorter photoperiod decreased the preferred temperature of lizards collected in July. But short photoperiod in May did not result in a decrease in the preferred temperature, nor did longer photoperiod increase the preferred temperature of lizards collected in July.

PHYSIOLOGICAL THERMOREGULATION

Reptiles are extremely heterogeneous with respect to temperature regulation. Day-active lizards may have mean temperature ranges of 33–42°C when active, while nocturnal species living in the same desert habitat have comparatively low activity temperatures of 27–31°C (Cowles & Bogert, 1944). Saint Girons & Saint Girons (1956) recorded body temperatures of 32–34°C in the nocturnal Saharan viper *Aspis cerastes*. Day-active species are usually heliothermic and obtain most of their heat from the rays of the sun, but nocturnal species tend to obtain their warmth from the substrate.

Although physiological thermoregulation is of less importance to desert ectotherms than it is to birds and mammals, it is still of some significance in the regulation of their body temperatures. Metabolic heating and evaporative cooling both occur to some extent, and various physiological processes have been evolved which prolong the time at which body temperatures are suitable for activity in the field.

Metabolic heat production

The rate of metabolic heat production per m^2 of body surface is usually at least five times greater in homeotherms than in reptiles (Benedict, 1938). Galvo, Tarasantchi & Guertzanstein (1965) measured heat production in tropical snakes in relation to weight and surface area of the body. They found that metabolism was in no way proportional to body surface: only in large species, with small surface areas in proportion to their mass, can the production of metabolic heat be of much thermal significance. Indeed, thermoregulation by means of metabolic heat production appears to be better developed in large snakes than in any other living reptile.

It has long been known that *Python molurus*, coiled about its eggs, produces metabolic heat as an aid to incubation. Hutchison, Dowling & Vinegar (1966) showed that, during the brooding period, this reptile can regulate its body temperature by physiological means analogous to those of endotherms. Ambient temperatures below 33°C result in spasmodic contractions of the body musculature with a consequent increase in metabolism and body temperature (Fig. 4). In this way, the body temperature can be elevated 7·3°C above the ambient temperature.

Unlike *P. molurus*, lizards do not appear to increase endogenous heat as the ambient temperature is lowered. In this respect, therefore, pythons resemble mammals more closely than they do lizards. Although the large varanid *Amphibolurus barbatus* heats up faster than it cools, due, in part to the production of metabolic heat, it cannot produce a body temperature appreciably higher than that of the ambient air. If heat production were taken to be 0·05 cal/g/min, which represents the highest oxygen consumption recorded in this species, the excess temperature of the body over the ambient temperature would be only 1·2°C (Bartholomew, Tucker & Lee, 1965).

The metabolic rate of a reptile at any particular temperature depends to some extent on the previous thermal history of the individual: that is, on its previous acclimation. Thus, Dawson & Bartholomew (1956) found that *Sceloporus occidentalis* shows a lower metabolic rate if it has been maintained at a relatively high temperature than if it has been maintained at a low one. Similarly, Buikema & Armitage (1969) found

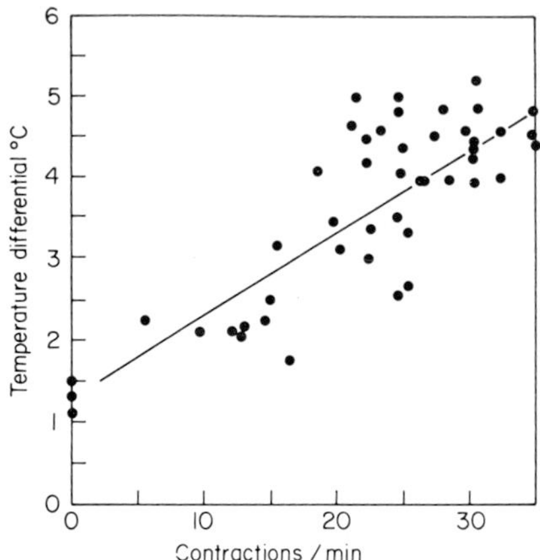

FIG. 4. Correlation of rate of contraction with temperature differential = 0·1 contr./min + 1·3 in a brooding *Python molurus*. (From Cloudsley-Thompson, 1971 after Hutchison *et al.*, 1966.)

in *Diadophis punctatus* that the Q_{10} was higher at high temperatures for warm-acclimated than for cold-acclimated snakes in a range of temperatures above 20°C.

Cardio-vascular adjustments

The importance of blood shunting from superficial to deep tissues as a means of heat conservation has probably evolved from the cutaneous respiratory system of Amphibia. This later became modified as a heat collector and dispenser, and finally developed into an essential temperature-regulating system in endotherms (Cowles, 1958). Thermoregulation, therefore, presumably originated among the large Permian Labyrinthodontia. These probably evolved costal breathing and, correlated with this, a dry and relatively impervious skin.

The temperature range at which the ventricles of lizards develop maximum tension *in vitro*, in response to widely-spaced electrical stimuli, is correlated with the eccritic body temperature. For example, Dawson & Bartholomew (1958) found that maximum tension is developed between 28–33°C in the excised heart of *Dipsosaurus dorsalis*. This species is active in nature at body temperatures around 42°C in summer. In contrast, maximum tension is developed between 16–26°C in *Eumeces obsoletes* according to Dawson (1960), a species normally active at body temperatures averaging 33°C.

Skinks, agamid and varanid lizards have the ability to modify the rate of change of their body temperatures. They can thereby increase the length of time at which they remain at, or near, the eccritic level (Bartholomew & Tucker, 1963, 1964; Bartholomew *et al.*, 1965).

When exposed to a new temperature, reptiles heat up faster than they cool. This differential is probably associated partly with the production of metabolic heat and also with changes in the heart rate, so that there is a circulatory adjustment (Bartholomew & Tucker, 1963; Bartholomew *et al.*, 1965). In addition, when the ambient temperature drops, blood may be shunted from the appendages to the centre of the body. Thus the shallow and deeper muscles of the legs and tail of *Varanus varius* drop from 45°C to 10°C within 15 min while the core takes up to 7 h to reach the new ambient temperature (Brattstrom, 1968). Likewise, local cutaneous vascular responses in *Amblyrhynchus cristatus* to variations in ambient temperature explain differences in rates of heating and cooling and help to maintain thermal stability (Morgareidge & White, 1969).

Skin colour and reflectivity

Although chromatic changes in reptiles are concerned more with concealment or display than with thermoregulation, Cole (1943) and others have shown that dark-coloured reptiles are more readily overheated by the absorption of radiation than are pale ones. When the body temperature rises to a level which can barely be tolerated, the skin turns lighter. In general, the colour of the body represents a compromise between the requirements of crypsis and the advantages of thermoregulation. When the two effects are contradictory, the one possessing the greater survival value is probably selected and, through evolutionary development, becomes the controlling factor (Norris & Lowe, 1964; Norris, 1967).

The ability to reflect light is more marked in desert species than in other lizards. Hutchison & Larimer (1960) determined skin albedo in various lizards and found that this decreased on both dorsal and ventral surfaces from American desert species, through those of semi-desert, plains, eastern and southern pine, deciduous forests, European temperate forests and tropical rain-forests. Calculated average heat gain was correlated with reflectivity, and it was concluded that concealment and thermoregulation are largely synergistic.

Correlations in the literature between diurnal habits, the presence of internal pigments and the inferred decrease in the transmission of light have been confirmed spectrophotometrically by Porter (1967) and by Porter & Norris (1969). Although transmission of light is a function of the thickness of the body wall and the amount of melanin in it, the latter factor is by far the more important. A black or pigmented peritoneum occurs when skin and inter-muscular deposits of melanin are poorly developed or absent. It is not significant in thermoregulation, nor does it shield the internal organs from heat; but it probably protects the tissues from ultra-violet light that might otherwise induce mutations.

Evaporative cooling

The integument of desert reptiles is relatively impermeable (Chew, 1961) and water loss through transpiration at equivalent body temperatures is much lower than it is in birds or mammals of comparable size (Schmidt-Nielsen & Dawson, 1964). Evaporative cooling is, therefore, more restricted so that desert reptiles, more than homeotherms, must depend upon their behaviour to avoid heat stress. Reichling (1957) found that European *Lacerta* sp. transpired from the lungs, skin and eyes. In the case of *L. agilis*, 25–36%, depending upon the temperature, was lost through the lungs: for *L. vivipara*, which inhabits drier environments, 7–16%, depending on temperature. The eyes accounted for 20% of the loss from *L. agilis* at 3°C, the skin for 47% and the lungs for 33%.

Respiratory cooling

Although not all lizards pant when exposed to high temperatures, genera such as *Varanus* and *Uromastix* use panting as an effective means of cooling the body (Langlois, 1902). The skink *Eumeces obsolitus* does not pant even at the highest temperatures that it can tolerate (Dawson, 1960) and the same is true of *Mabuya quinquetaeniatus* also (Cloudsley-Thompson, 1965).

The advantageous effect of panting at high body temperatures has been studied in *Crotaphytus collaris* by Dawson & Templeton (1963) and in *Dipsosaurus dorsalis* by Templeton (1960). In both species, the water evaporated in this way can dissipate all metabolic heat produced as well as a small amount of heat gained from the environment.* Panting has also been noted in other Iguanidae, such as *Sauromalus obesus* by Dill (1938). Its absence in the skinks, mentioned above, indicates qualitative as well as quantitative differences between heat-sensitive and heat-resistant lizards.

Panting in *S. obesus* and other thermophilic lizards entails fast, shallow breathing through gaping mouth and over a partly extruded,

* Dr. C. B. De Witt informs me that in unpublished work he has found that *D. dorsalis* can, by panting, lower its body temperature considerably more than was found to be the case by Templeton (1960). Differences in experimental results can be attributed to variations in the amount of air circulated and in its relative humidity.

blood-engorged tongue (Dawson & Bartholomew, 1958). At temperatures exceeding 38°C, the cordylid *Gerrhonotus multicarinatus* opens its mouth as if to pant, but the breathing rates and movements accompanying this activity are lower and more limited than those of panting iguanid lizards and only 66% of the metabolic heat produced is dissipated by evaporation (Dawson & Templeton, 1966). In contrast, Warburg (1965) reported that the large *Amphibolurus barbatus* and, to a lesser extent, the smaller *Tiliqua rugosa* can lower their body temperatures several °C by means of transpiration.

Evaporation via the lungs is more efficient and economical of water than is sweating from the surface of the body. This is because the differential between ambient and skin temperature is increased when the latter is cooled by evaporation. Consequently the absorption of heat from the environment is increased. Licking of the lips and the spectacle of the eye precedes panting in some lizards, especially geckoes, of the

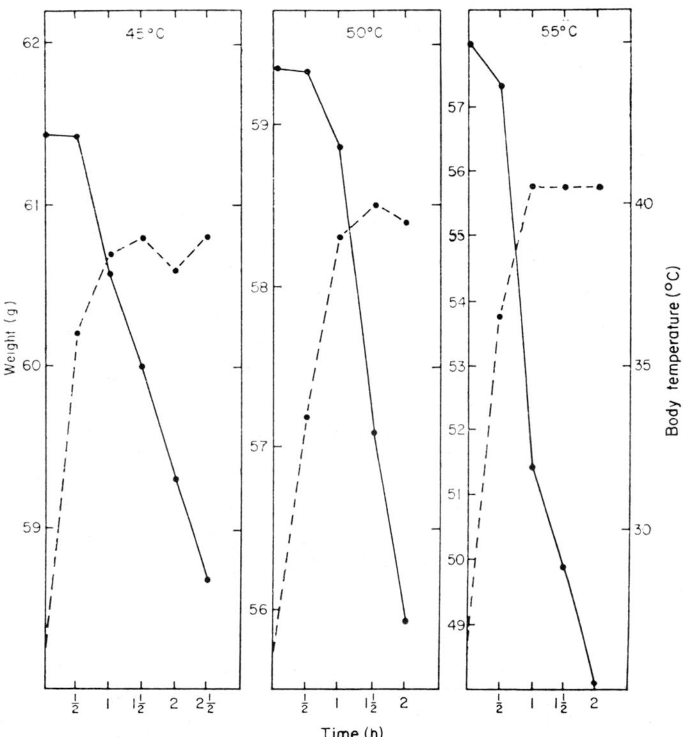

Fig. 5. Loss in weight and increase in body temperature during consecutive exposures of 30 min in dry air at various high air temperatures in *Testudo sulcata*. Weight (—); body temperature (– – – –). (After Cloudsley-Thompson, 1970a.)

Namib desert. This moistening of the head may possibly result in evaporative cooling with less loss of liquid than in the case of panting, and thus achieves economy of water (Brain, 1962).

Salivation

It has been found experimentally that if the body temperature of *Testudo sulcata* should rise above 40–41°C, copious salivation takes place through the mouth and nostrils, wetting the head, neck and front legs. This is clearly a thermoregulatory mechanism because the evaporative cooling which results from it prevents any further rise in body temperature (Fig. 5, Cloudsley-Thompson, 1970a). In *Terrapene ornata*, both salivary frothing and urination take place when the cloacal temperature reaches 32–41°C, and both assist in thermoregulation. Whereas heart rate is directly dependent upon body temperature, salivation may be triggered both by the temperature of the body and of the brain. It is probable that a function of the enlarged bladder of desert tortoises and terrapins may be to store urine for emergency thermoregulation (Riedesel, Cloudsley-Thompson & Cloudsley-Thompson, 1971). It is also a defence against predators. Heath (1965) likewise found that, when maintained at elevated temperatures, *Phrynosoma* spp. produced a copious flow of clear cloacal fluid which moistened the vent and base of the tail, possibly serving to cool the animal (Fig. 2). Thermoregulatory salivation has been confirmed in *Gopherus agassizii* by McGinnis & Voigt (1971).

DISCUSSION

Thermal homeostasis in desert reptiles is achieved by a combination of behavioural responses, cyclical processes and physiological reactions. Homeostasis, however, implies more than just the maintenance of a constant internal medium. By means of its cicadian rhythms, the organism mirrors internally, or even preadapts to, diurnal changes in the external environment. At the same time, the cicadian rhythm is, itself, constantly modified by seasonal changes in the photoperiod, ambient temperature and so on. There is thus an intimate relationship between behavioural and physiological thermoregulation in reptiles.

It is significant that only relatively large mammals can afford to regulate their body temperatures by means of cutaneous evaporation. Small forms would lose too much water if this method were employed. In any case, sweating is a far less efficient method than panting for cooling the body. As already pointed out, when the skin is cooled by transpiration, the gradient of temperature from the environment becomes greater, thus increasing the amount of heat absorbed by conduction and convection. The insulation provided by hair must also be reduced for sweating to be effective. In addition, this method of cooling the body results in the excretion of valuable electrolytes which are not lost in respiratory evaporation.

Whereas endotherms appear to regulate their body temperatures around a single set point, ectotherms have both high and low points, separated by several degrees Celsius. They commonly undergo fluctuations in body temperature, even though these are less than those that occur in the ambient environment, and cannot rely upon a rigid internal receptor or receptors.

Behavioural control of body temperature implies the existence of an absolute sense of temperature, otherwise adaptation would result in a steady drift in the eccritic temperature. Virtually nothing is known of the mechanism on which this sense depends, although it apparently lies in the hypothalamus or the pituitary. It is acted upon both by afferent impulses from temperature receptors at the periphery of the body and by small changes in the temperature of the blood. By this means, the regulation of body temperature is correlated with blood pressure, respiration, endogenous rhythms of activity, sexual cycle and the control of metabolic and endocrine functions (Rodbard, 1948). Heath, Gasdorf & Northcutt (1968) localized a thermosensitive area specifically in the anterior hypothalamus.

Riedesel *et al.* (1971) showed that, whereas the heart rate of *Terrapene ornata* is correlated with the temperature of the body rather than with that of the head, thermoregulatory salivation may depend upon both. Hammel, Caldwell & Abrams (1967) found that heating the brain stem of *Tiliqua scincoides* to 41°C caused the lizard to move from a hot environment at a cloacal temperature 1–2°C lower than normal. Conversely, cooling the brain to 25°C delayed movement from a hot environment to a cooler one. Neither heating nor cooling the brain stem alone produced the response. The lizards only responded after the cloacal and skin temperatures had also increased or decreased. Consequently, behavioural thermoregulation in *T. scincoides* appears to be activated by a combination of hypothalamic and other body temperatures. De Witt (1967) suggested that control of body temperature in *Dipsosaurus dorsalis* might be located in the head, but the evidence for this was slight. Studies of the heating rates of *Phrynosoma coronatum* during burial likewise suggest that emergence from the sand during hours of normal activity may be dependent upon a high head temperature and independent of that of the body (Heath, 1964).

Temperature regulation in reptiles is, therefore, part of a complex physiological homeostatic mechanism, and the differences between desert reptiles and homeothermic birds and mammals are perhaps related more to their smaller sizes and elongated shapes than to a completely dissimilar physiology.

References

Asplund, K. K. (1968). Evolution of body size and habitat selection in whiptail lizards. *Diss. Abstr.* **29**: 2236B.

Ballinger, R. F., Hawker, J. & Sexton, O. J. (1969). The effect of photoperiod acclimation on the thermoregulation of the lizard *Sceleporus undulatus*. *J. exp. Zool.* **171**: 43–47.

Bartholomew, G. A. (1966). A field study of temperature relations in the Galápagos marine iguana. *Copeia* **1966**: 241–250.

Bartholomew, G. A. & Tucker, V. A. (1963). Control of changes in body temperature, metabolism and circulation by the agamid lizard, *Amphibolurus barbatus*. *Physiol. Zoöl.* **36**: 199–218.

Bartholomew, G. A. & Tucker, V. A. (1964). Size, body temperature, thermal conductance, oxygen consumption and heart rate in Australian varanid lizards. *Physiol. Zoöl.* **37**: 341–354.

Bartholomew, G. A., Tucker, V. A. & Lee, A. K. (1965). Oxygen consumption, thermal conductance, and heart rate in the Australian skink, *Tiliqua scincoides*. *Copeia* **1965**: 169–173.

Bartlett, P. N. & Gates, D. M. (1967). The energy budget of a lizard on a tree trunk. *Ecology* **48**: 315–322.

Bellairs, A. (1969). *The life of reptiles.* London: Weidenfeld & Nicolson.

Benedict, F. G. (1938). Vital energetics: a study in comparative basal metabolism. *Publs Carneg. Instn* No. 520: 1–215.

Bogert, C. M. (1949). Thermoregulation and eccritic body temperatures in Mexican lizards of the genus *Sceloporus*. *An. Inst. Biol. Univ. N. Mex.* **20**: 415–426.

Bradshaw, S. D. & Main, A. R. (1968). Behavioural attitudes and regulation of temperature in *Amphibolurus* lizards. *J. Zool., Lond.* **154**: 193–221.

Brain, C. K. (1962). Observations on the temperature tolerance of lizards of the central Namib desert, South West Africa. *Cimbebasia* No. **4**: 1–5.

Bramwell, C. D. (1970). The first hot-blooded flapper. *Spectrum* No. 69: 12–14.

Brattstrom. B. H. (1965). Body temperatures of reptiles. *Am. Midl. Nat.* **73**: 376–422.

Brattstrom, B. H. (1968). Heat retention by large Australian monitor lizards, *Varanus varius*. *Am. Zool.* **8**: 766.

Buikema, A. L. Jr. & Armitage, K. B. (1969). The effect of temperature on the metabolism of the prairie ringneck snake, *Diadophis punctatus arnyi* Kennicott. *Herpetologica* **25**: 194–206.

Burns, T. A. (1970). Temperature of Yarrow's spiny lizard, *Sceloporus jarrovi* at high altitudes. *Herpetologica* **26**: 9–16.

Bustard, H. R. (1967). Activity cycle and thermoregulation in the Australian gecko *Gehyra variegata*. *Copeia* **1967**: 753–758.

Bustard, H. R. (1968). Temperature dependent activity in the Australian gecko *Diplodactylus vittatus*. *Copeia* **1968**: 606–612.

Bustard, H. R. (1970). Activity cycle of the tropical house gecko, *Hemidactylus frenatus*. *Copeia* **1970**: 173–176.

Chew, R. M. (1961). Water metabolism of desert-inhabiting vertebrates. *Biol. Rev.* **36**: 1–31.

Cloudsley-Thompson, J. L. (1965). Rhythmic activity, temperature-tolerance, water relations and mechanism of heat death in a tropical skink and gecko. *J. Zool., Lond.* **146**: 55–69.

Cloudsley-Thompson, J. L. (1970a). On the biology of the desert tortoise *Testudo sulcata* in Sudan. *J. Zool., Lond.* **160**: 17–33.

Cloudsley-Thompson, J. L. (1970b). Terrestrial invertebrates. In *Comparative physiology of thermoregulation*. **1**: 55–77. Whittow, G. C. (ed.). New York and London: Academic Press.

Cloudsley-Thompson, J. L. (1971). *The temperature and water relations of reptiles.* Watford: Merrow Publ. Co.

Colbert, E. H. (1962). *Dinosaurs. Their discovery and their world.* London: Hutchinson.

Cole, L. C. (1943). Experiments in toleration of high temperature in lizards with reference to adaptive coloration. *Ecology* **24**: 94–108.

Cowles, R. B. (1958). Possible origin of dermal temperature regulation. *Evolution* **12**: 347–357.

Cowles, R. B. & Bogert, C. M. (1944). A preliminary study of thermal requirements of desert reptiles. *Bull. Am. Mus. nat. Hist.* **83**: 265–296.

Dawson, W. R. (1960). Physiological responses to temperature in the lizard, *Eumeces obsoletus*. *Physiol. Zoöl.* **33**: 87–103.

Dawson, W. R. & Bartholomew, G. A. (1956). Relation of oxygen consumption to body weight, temperature and temperature acclimation in lizards *Uta stansburiana* and *Sceloporus occidentalis*. *Physiol. Zoöl.* **29**: 40–51.

Dawson, W. R. & Bartholomew, G. A. (1958). Metabolic and cardiac responses to temperature in the lizard *Dipsosaurus dorsalis*. *Physiol. Zoöl.* **31**: 100–111.

Dawson, W. R. & Templeton, J. R. (1963). Physiological responses to temperature in the lizard *Crotaphytus collaris*. *Physiol. Zoöl.* **36**: 219–236.

Dawson, W. R. & Templeton, J. R. (1966). Physiological responses to temperature in the alligator lizard, *Gerrhonotus multicarinatus*. *Ecology* **47**: 759–765.

De Witt, C. B. (1962). Effects of body size and wind speed on rates of cooling of lizards. *Am. Zool.* **2**: 517–518.

De Witt, C. B. (1967). Behavioural thermoregulation in the desert iguana. *Science, N.Y.* **158**: 809–810.

Dill, D. B. (1938). *Life, heat and altitude: Physiological effects of hot climates and great height.* Cambridge, Mass.: Harvard University Press.

Fry, F. E. J. (1967). Responses of vertebrate poikilotherms to temperature. In *Thermobiology*: 375–409. Rose, A. H. (ed.). London and New York: Academic Press.

Galvo, P. E., Tarasantchi, J. & Guertzanstein, P. (1965). Heat production in tropical snakes in relation to body weight and body surface. *Am. J. Physiol.* **209**: 501–506.

Gauthier, R. (1967). Ecologie et ethologie des reptiles du Sahara nord-occidental (Région de Beni-Abbès). *Annls Mus. r. Afr. cent.* (*Zool.*) No. 155: 1–83.

Hammel, H. T., Caldwell, F. T. & Abrams, R. M. (1967). Regulation of body temperature in the blue-tongued lizard. *Science, N.Y.* **156**: 1260–1262.

Heath, J. E. (1962). Temperature-independent morning emergence in lizards of the genus *Phrynosoma*. *Science, N.Y.* **146**: 784–785.

Heath, J. E. (1964). Head-body temperature differences in horned lizards. *Physiol. Zoöl.* **37**: 273–279.

Heath, J. E. (1965). Temperature regulation and diurnal activity in horned lizards. *Univ. Calif. Publs Zool.* **64**: 97–136.

Heath, J. E. (1966). Venous shunts in the cephalic sinuses of horned lizards. *Physiol. Zoöl.* **39**: 30–35.

Heath, J. E., Gasdorf, E. & Northcutt, R. G. (1968). Effect of thermal stimulation of anterior hypothalamus on blood pressure in the turtle. *Comp. Biochem. Physiol.* **26**: 509–518.

Hirth, H. F. (1963). The ecology of two lizards on a tropical beach. *Ecol. Monogr.* **33**: 83–112.

Hutchison, V. H., Dowling, H. G. & Vinegar, A. (1966). Thermoregulation in a brooding female Indian python, *Python molorus bivittatus*. *Science, N.Y.* **151**: 694–696.

Hutchison, V. H. & Larimer, J. L. (1960). Reflectivity of the integuments of some lizards from different habitats. *Ecology* **41**: 199–209.

Klauber, L. M. (1939). Studies of reptile life in the arid southwest. *Bull. zool. Soc. S. Diego* **14**: 1–100.

Langlois, J. (1902). La régulation thermique chez les poikilothermes. *J. Physiol. Path. gén.* **4**: 249–256.

McGinnis, S. M. & Dickson, L. L. (1967). Behavioural thermoregulation in the desert iguana *Dipsosaurus dorsalis*. *Science, N.Y.* **156**: 1757–1759.

McGinnis, S. M. & Voigt, W. G. (1971). Thermoregulation in the desert tortoise, *Gopherus agassizii*. *Comp. Biochem. Physiol.* **40**A: 119–126.

Mayhew, W. W. (1964). Photoperiodic responses in three species of the lizard genus *Uma*. *Herpetologica* **20**: 95–113.

Mayhew, W. W. (1968). Biology of desert amphibians and reptiles. In *Desert biology* **1**: 195–421. Brown, G. W., jnr. (ed.). New York & London: Academic Press.

Morgareidge, K. R. & White, F. N. (1969). Cutaneous vascular changes during heating and cooling in the Galapagos marine iguana. *Nature, Lond.* **223**: 587–591.

Norris, K. S. (1949). Observations on the habits of the horned lizard *Phrynosoma m'callii*. *Copeia* **1949**: 176–180.

Norris, K. S. (1953). The ecology of the desert iguana, *Dipsosaurus dorsalis*. *Ecology* **34**: 265–287.

Norris, K. S. (1967). Color adaptation in desert reptiles and its thermal relationship. In *Lizard ecology*: A Symposium: 162–299. Milstead, W. W. (ed.). Columbia: University Missouri Press.

Norris, K. S. & Lowe, C. H. (1964). An analysis of background color-matching in amphibians and reptiles. *Ecology* **45**: 565–580.

Pearson, P. P. (1954). Habits of the lizard, *Liolaemus multiformis* at high altitudes in southern Peru. *Copeia* **1954**: 111–116.

Porter, W. P. (1967). Solar radiation through the living body wall of vertebrates with emphasis on desert reptiles. *Ecol. Monogr.* **39**: 227–244.

Porter, W. P. & Norris, K. S. (1969). Lizard reflectivity change and its effect on light transmission through body wall. *Science, N.Y.* **163**: 482–484.

Reichling, H. (1957). Transpiration und Vorzugstemperatur mitteleuropäischer Reptilien und Amphibien. *Zool. Jb.* (Zool.) **67**: 1–64.

Riedesel, M. L., Cloudsley-Thompson, J. L. & Cloudsley-Thompson, J. A. (1971). Evaporative thermoregulation in turtles. *Physiol. Zoöl.* **44**: 28–32.

Rodbard, S. (1948). Body temperature, blood pressure and hypothalamus. *Science, N.Y.* **108**: 413–415.

Rodbard, S. (1949). On the dorsal sail of *Dimetrodon*. *Copeia* **1949**: 224.

Saint Girons, H. & Saint Girons, M. C. (1956). Cycle d'activité et thermorégulation chez les reptiles (lézards et serpents). *Vie Milieu* **7**: 133–226.

Schmidt-Nielsen, K. & Dawson, W. R. (1964). Terrestrial animals in dry heat: desert reptiles. In *Handbook of Physiology*. Section 4: *Adaptation to the Environment*: 467–480. Dill, D. B. (ed.). Washington, D.C.: American Physiological Society.

Strel'nikov, I. (1944). [Importance of solar radiation in the ecology of high mountain reptiles.] *Zool. Zh.* **23**: 250–257 [In Russian].

Templeton, J. R. (1960). Respiration and water loss at the higher temperatures in the desert iguana, *Dipsosaurus dorsalis*. *Physiol. Zoöl.* **33**: 136–145.

Templeton, J. R. (1970). Reptiles. In *The comparative physiology of thermoregulation*. **1**: 167–221 Whittow, G. C. (ed.). New York and London: Academic Press.

Warburg, M. R. (1965). The influence of ambient temperature and humidity on the body temperature and water loss from two Australian lizards: *Tiliqua rugosa* (Gray) (Scincidae), and *Amphibolurus barbatus* Ceevier (Agamidae). *Aust. J. Zool.* **13**: 331–350.

Woodbury, A. M. & Hardy, R. (1948). Studies of the desert tortoise, *Gopherus agassizii*. *Ecol. Monogr.* **18**: 145–200.

Symp. zool. Soc. Lond. (1972) No. 31, 61–77.

SALT AND WATER BALANCE IN DESERT LIZARDS

J. R. TEMPLETON

Department of Zoology, University of Montana, Missoula, Montana, U.S.A.

SYNOPSIS

Lizards are the most abundant vertebrates on hot deserts and are found where drinking water is usually not available. Although the skin of desert lizards is permeable to water they lose less cutaneous water than other lizards. By excreting salts and nitrogenous wastes as insoluble urates they lose little water. The colloid osmotic pressure of the plasma assists water absorption from the cloaca, leaving the excreta to be voided as moist pellets of mixed urates and faeces. Active transport may also move NaCl and thus water from the cloaca. Some families of lizard possess a nasal gland which secretes Cl and HCO_3 as Na and K salts with little loss of water. These reptiles are mostly herbivorous and can remain in salt and water balance without drinking, utilizing only dietary and metabolic water sources. They excrete the excess dietary K as nasal secretion and as mono-potassium urate. They also store water as extracellular fluid when sufficient dietary water is available. When it is not, they excrete Na from the extracellular fluid and use the water retained. Some species without salt glands tolerate salt or water imbalance when water is scarce and correct it when water becomes available. Aldosterone increases the K/Na ratio of urine and nasal fluid in the desert iguana thereby removing excess K and retaining valuable Na. Aldosterone conserves nasal Na even during hypernatraemia or if the lizards are adrenalectomized. Untreated adrenalectomized lizards greatly increase nasal Na output. Cortisol and deoxycorticosterone also act to retain nasal Na.

INTRODUCTION

The most abundant vertebrates in deserts are lizards and the different species occupy nearly every habitat conceivable (Mayhew, 1968). The extensive data on the complex behavioural and physiological responses to temperature by desert lizards have been reviewed by Schmidt-Nielsen & Dawson (1964), and more recently by Dawson (1967), Mayhew (1968), and Templeton (1970). The adaptations of desert lizards to water scarcity are complex, and the mechanisms to remove salt and nitrogenous wastes with little loss of water appear as complex as those shown for homeotherms.

INTAKE OF WATER

The desert iguana, *Dipsosaurus dorsalis* may drink water if it is available (Minnich & Shoemaker, 1970) but it can remain in salt and water balance (Minnich, 1970a) with only dietary and metabolic water (Fig. 1). The chuckwallas, *Sauromalus* spp., found on hot American deserts probably have little access to drinking water. They store the

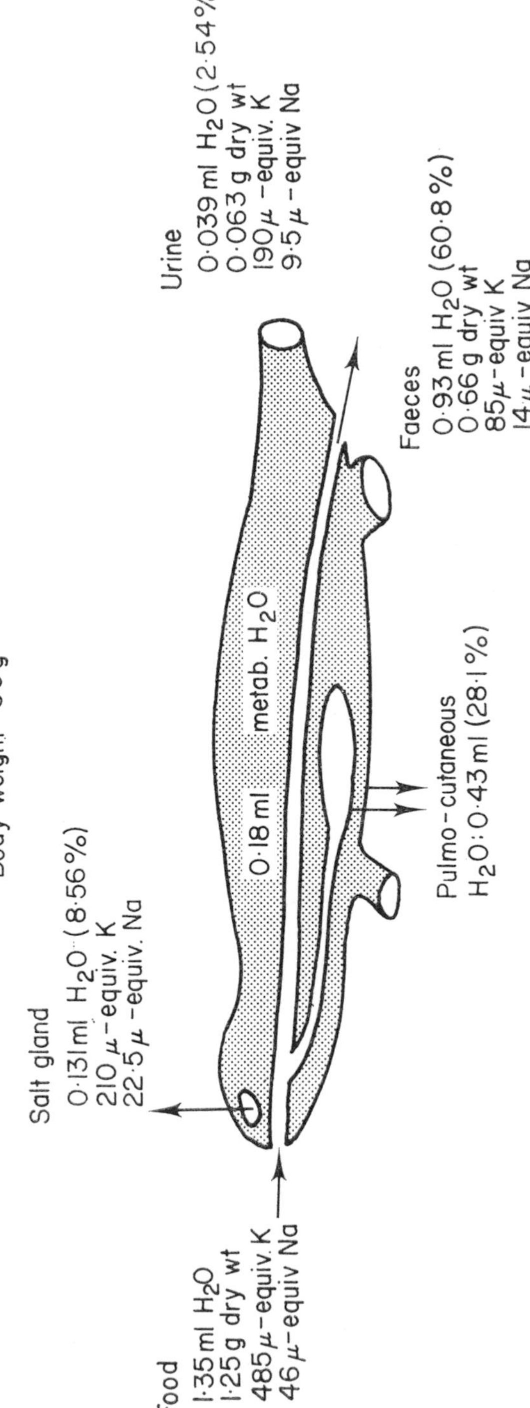

Fig. 1. Daily salt and water turnover in a desert iguana weighing 50 g. The lizard gains as much salt and water as it loses. The proportion of nasal K to nasal water lost may be somewhat high. Data calculated from Minnich (1970a).

water from succulent plants during moist periods in discrete lateral and gular lymph sacs and utilize this extracellular water when dietary water is insufficient to maintain water balance (Norris & Dawson, 1964). *Amphibolurus ornatus* tolerates salt and water imbalances when there is insufficient water, and restores such imbalances by drinking when there is water available (Bradshaw & Shoemaker, 1967). *Phrynosoma m'calli* (Mayhew, 1965) probably never drinks either in the field or in captivity. Dew is rarely available to many species because it is evaporated by the morning sun before the lizards are active (Schmidt-Nielsen & Dawson, 1964). The lizard, *Moloch horridus* may collect dew or rain on its skin and pass this water by capillarity to its mouth where it is absorbed by mucous glands to be swallowed as mucous plus the collected water (Bentley & Blumer, 1962). Yet Mayhew & Wright (1971) showed that *Phrynosoma m'calli*, a lizard of similar habits, does not possess this ability.

Can desert lizards absorb water from wet skin like amphibians? This question remains unanswered. Mayhew (1968), after reviewing the literature, concluded that if a lizard possessed such a hygroscopic skin any water absorbed would soon be lost to the desert environment. He later showed that *Phrynosoma m'calli* does not gain weight when immersed in water (Mayhew & Wright, 1971). Conversely, the nocturnal gecko, *Coleonyx variegatus*, transferred where cool to a warm moist environment (a simulated burrow) gained weight from the water which condensed on its skin (Lasiewski & Bartholomew, 1969). They concluded that such condensation on the skin might provide physiologically useful water to nocturnal forms, not only by absorption but by licking (drinking) the condensed water from another lizard. The skin of most, if not all, desert lizards is permeable to water. Some of any water in the liquid phase on the lizards skin should move inward, and for a desert lizard any gain of water is advantageous. Although possession of a hygroscopic skin would be disadvantageous (Mayhew, 1968) this does not preclude desert lizards absorbing water across a skin wetted by condensation or scattered showers.

We can assume that most desert lizards either remain in salt and water balance with only dietary water (Fig. 1), or tolerate temporary dehydration and salt imbalance during times of inadequate water availability (Bentley, 1959; Bradshaw & Shoemaker, 1967).

SALT AND WATER BALANCE

Evaporative water loss

It has long been held that the skin of terrestrial reptiles is essentially impermeable to water (see Chew & Dammon, 1961). This view was challenged by Schmidt-Nielsen (1964) because he thought the evaporative water loss of the desert iguana (Templeton, 1960) was too high to represent only respiratory water loss. Bentley & Schmidt-Nielsen in 1966 discovered that 44% of the water evaporated by the desert iguanid, *Sauromalus obesus* at a body temperature of 40°C was cutaneous in origin. They also found that cutaneous water loss decreased with aridity of habitat. The tropical lizard, *Iguana iguana*, a close taxonomic relative to *Sauromalus* lost appreciably more water via the skin than did *Sauromalus*. Dawson, Shoemaker & Licht (1966) also showed that though cutaneous water loss is appreciable in desert lizards it increases significantly in less xerophyllic forms. Claussen (1967) confirmed this concept with two American iguanids, *Uta* and *Anolis*. Even so, desert lizards lose about half the evaporative water via the skin. Minnich (1970b) calculated that the adult desert iguana lost 0·86% of its body weight each day through evaporation which represents about 28% of daily water turnover (Fig. 1). Furthermore, the rate of loss increases with activity. It is of interest to note at this time that the desert iguana spends only 3 h abroad each day and stays underground in humid burrows for the remainder of the time (Minnich & Shoemaker, 1970). Nevertheless, it cannot entirely replace evaporative water loss with water metabolically produced (Minnich, 1970b), and it must eat to remain in water balance.

The role of the kidney

Reptiles became successful on land in part because they developed uricotelism. This long accepted view considered mainly uric acid, and largely ignored the fact that urates could be a major vehicle in removing excess Na and K (Fig. 1) with little loss of water (see Minnich, 1970a, Templeton, Murrish, Randall & Mugaas, 1972a). The pH of the ureteral urine (7·15–7·28) of *Dipsosaurus* indicates that the urate is voided predominantly as the mono-urate salt (Minnich, 1970a). Seshadri (1956) showed that allantoin is also voided in appreciable quantities by the house lizard, *Hemidactylus*, and by *Varanus monitor* (Seshadri, 1959).

The reptilian kidney lacks the loops of Henle possessed by birds and mammals. Although the gecko kidney (*Hemydactylus*) can form a ureteral urine hypotonic to the blood (Roberts & Schmidt-Nielsen, 1966), the typical lizard kidney has not been shown to produce a hypertonic ureteral urine. This evidence can be misleading in terms of the final voided product because the cloaca plays a role in determining urine concentration.

The rates of urine flow and amount of glomerular fluid filtered increases with temperature in water loaded *Tiliqua* (Shoemaker, Licht

& Dawson, 1966), especially at lower body temperatures. They suggested that glomerular filtration rate may be dependent upon arterial pressure since carotid pressure also increases with body temperature (Templeton, 1964a). The role of the respective tubules in determining water and electrolyte composition remains unclear in desert reptiles. About 6% of the uric acid voided was filtered by the glomerulus in *Iguana* while 94% was secreted by the renal tubules (Marshall, 1932). The uric acid descends the ureters as a cloudy suspension or as precipitated threads to the cloaca.

The roles of the gut and cloaca

Khalil & Abdel-Messeih (1954) found that the water content of the tissues of the alimentary canal of *Uromastix aegyptia* increased in a caudal direction with the cloacal tissues possessing the most water of all. They concluded that the cloaca absorbed water from the urine and faeces at high rates. Murrish & Schmidt-Nielsen (1970) showed that colloid osmotic pressure of the plasma provided sufficient force to absorb water from the urine and faeces within the cloaca. The final pellet produced by dehydrated animals contained about 45% water. The capillary spaces in the urate and faecal pellets still retained some water. The amount of water in the voided pellets would be proportionate to their mass. These authors do not, however, exclude the possibility that ions could be actively pumped from the cloaca, drawing water passively with them. Although such transport has been demonstrated in the bladder and cloaca of other reptiles little is accurately known about the respective roles of the renal tubules, the cloaca and the gut of lizards in the regulation of ionic composition. The K/Na ratio in the faeces and urine of *Dipsosaurus* does not necessarily reflect that of the diet, which suggests that the gut or cloaca can regulate ion exchange across their walls (Templeton *et al.*, 1972a).

The ability of *Dipsosaurus* to remove cations as urates with little loss of water rivals the urine concentrating mechanism of xerophyllic mammals. Desert iguanas in the field (Minnich, 1970a) can remove about 4900 m-equiv of K for each liter of urine water lost (see also Fig. 1). Removal of anions by the urine of desert lizards is apparently less efficient than that of mammals. The Cl level in *Dipsosaurus* urine is lower than that of the plasma (Minnich, 1970a). Desert lizards living on plant and animal foods high in Cl or those living near the sea might face special problems in Cl removal. Some lizard families have developed the lateral nasal gland into an efficient device to remove the chlorides of Na and K with little loss of water.

The role of the nasal salt gland

The lateral nasal gland (Fig. 2) and associated structures in lizards have been adequately described for most lizards (Malan, 1940; Pratt, 1948; Bellairs, 1949; Oelrich, 1956). These authors either did not assign the gland a function or they called it a mucus secreting gland. Schmidt-Nielsen & Fange (1958) using the marine iguana, *Amblyrhynchus cristatus*, first demonstrated that this gland secretes a concentrated saline fluid. Templeton (1963, 1964b) found that the crystals deposited around the nostrils of the desert lizard, *Sauromalus obesus* and the false iguana, *Ctenosaura pectinata* were secreted as the salts of K and Na at high concentration. At this time, Schmidt-Nielsen, Borut, Lee & Crawford (1963) showed that the desert iguana, the tropical iguana, *Iguana iguana*, and the agamid, *Uromastix aegyptius* possessed functional salt glands. The dried salt contained the bicarbonates and chlorides of K and Na. Norris & Dawson (1964) confirmed that the nasal secretion in *Sauromalus hispidus* and *S. obesus* contained these four particular salts. Templeton (1967) analysed the proportion of these salts in uncontaminated and unevaporated nasal fluid in *Ctenosaura pectinata* (Fig. 3). Later, Grenot (1968) demonstrated that *Uromastix acanthinurus* possessed a functional nasal salt gland. With the exception of the marine iguana, the gland of these iguanids and agamids functions mainly to remove K and, if necessary, Cl with little loss of water and even the marine iguana relies on the gland to remove ingested K (Dunson, 1969).

The branched tubular glands are bilateral (Fig. 2) encased in cartilage, and in iguanids at least are nourished by the postnarial artery and innervated by a branch of the lateral ethmoidal nerve (Oelrich, 1956). The histology and ultrastructure of the gland of iguanids (Philpott & Templeton, 1964) resembles that of the agamids (van Lennep & Komnick, 1970) possessing the general characteristics of salt-secreting glands of other vertebrates. The main duct is relatively short and placing an indwelling cannula therein is exceedingly difficult. Templeton (1964b) succeeded in placing the end of a precurved glass capillary tube over the exposed duct thereby removing unevaporated fluid by capillarity and siphon action. The flow rate of fluid is intermittent and less than that of the salt gland of marine birds. Nevertheless, the high concentration of K in the fluid could theoretically clear all of the K from the plasma of *Sauromalus* in less than 1 h if the gland secreted continuously (Table I). In summary the salt gland has especially evolved in the herbivorous iguanid and agamid lizards to remove K ingested in relatively high quantities in the plant food. It supplements

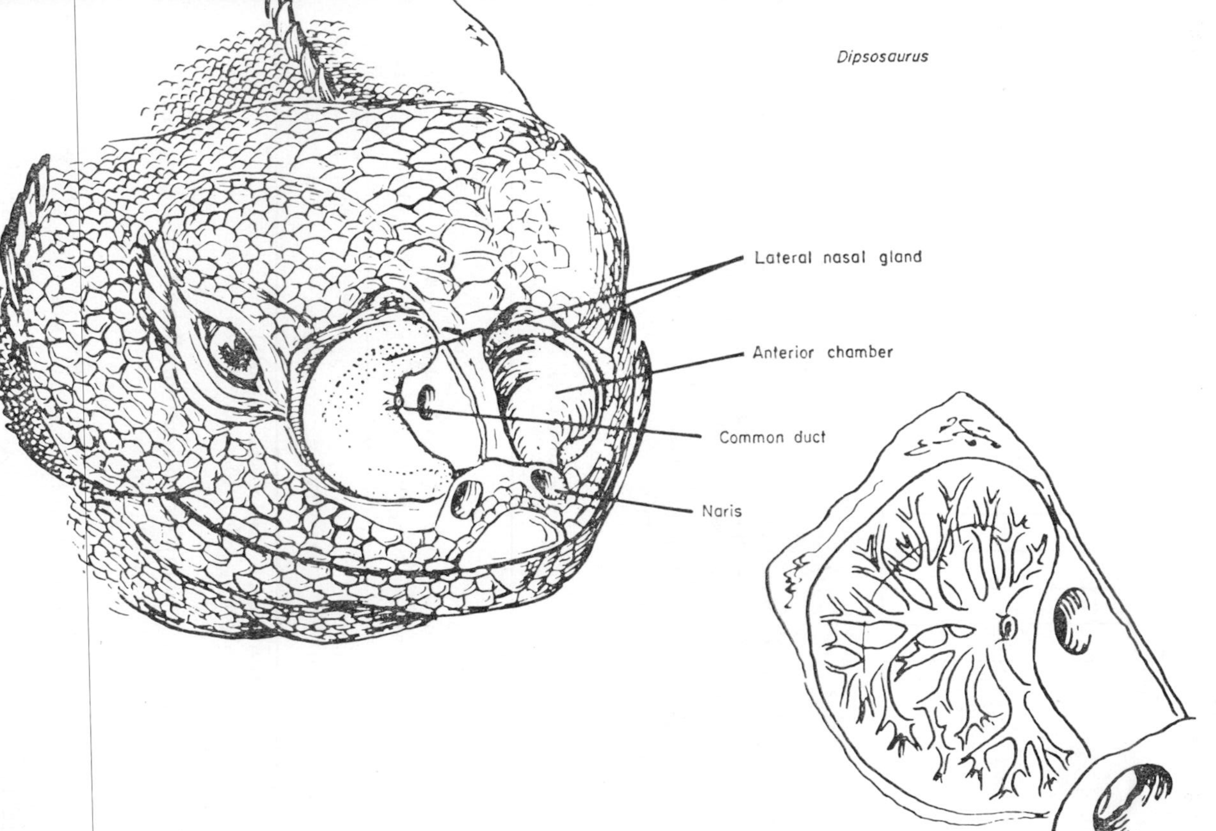

FIG. 2. A drawing of the head of *Dipsosaurus* showing the exposed nasal region and the nasal salt gland. The diagram at the right illustrates the gross morphology of the duct system of the gland (J. R. Templeton, unpubl. data).

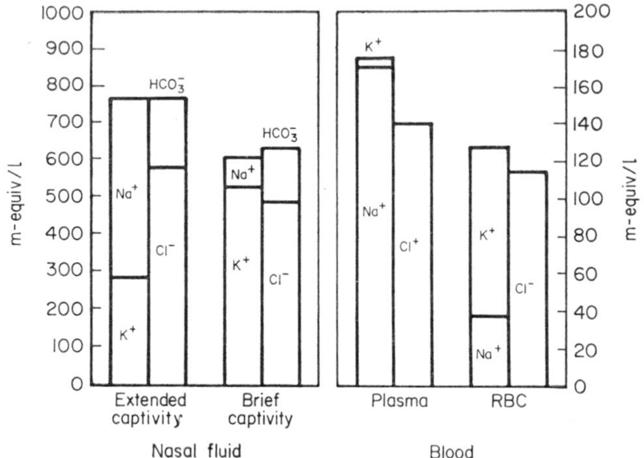

Fig. 3. The electrolyte composition of the nasal fluid, plasma, and red blood cells of a false iguana, *Ctenosaura* held captive for 12 weeks (extended captivity) on a diet relatively high in Na, and the composition of the nasal fluid only of another false iguana held captive for one week (brief captivity) on a diet high in K. The proportions of K to Na in the respective nasal fluids reflect these dietary differences (J. R. Templeton, unpubl. data; see also Templeton, 1967).

Table I

*Maximal secretory activity for one hour or less of both nasal salt glands**

Species	Nasal flow ml/h	K m-equiv/liter	K m-equiv/kg/h	Plasma clearance of K ml/h	% plasma† cleared of K/h
Sauromalus	0·077	611	311	10·5	139
Ctenosaura	0·193	535	94	15·0	27

* Data taken from Templeton (1964b).
† Total plasma calculated as 5% of body weight.

the kidney–cloaca–gut complex to remove Cl, and like the complex, it removes salts with little loss of water.

WATER AND SALT IMBALANCES

Imbalances of salt and water have been reported for desert lizards in nature and many experiments of salt and water loading and of dehydration have been carried out in the laboratory.

Water imbalances

Dehydration depressed urine flow only moderately in the gecko, *Hemidactylus* sp. Water loading increased urine flow in this lizard almost 10 fold (Roberts & Schmidt-Nielsen, 1966) and to a maximum of 50 fold in *Tiliqua* (Bentley, 1959). Conversely, dehydration suppressed urine flow in the horned lizard, *Phyrnosoma cornutum*, and the Galapagos lizard, *Tropidurus* sp., whereas, water-loading had little effect (Roberts & Schmidt-Nielsen, 1966). Similarly, dehydrated desert iguanas depress urine secretion, and rehydrating animals with water available continue to suppress urine formation (Templeton *et al.*, 1972a) retaining water (Table II) and K and removing Na (Table III). *Dipsosaurus* during dehydration probably removed Na stored in the lateral and gular lymph sacs (Norris & Dawson, 1964) and utilized the fluid therein. They also excreted K and utilized intracellular fluid. During rehydration on a lettuce diet with a K/Na ratio of almost 7 they favoured K over Na

TABLE II

Water relationships of food to excreta in 50 g Dipsosaurus

		Field*	Well hydrated†	Rehydrating†
Water content (ml/g dry wt)	Food	1·04	5·12	5·12
	Faeces	1·41	7·35	3·65
	Urine	0·62	59·7	2·80
Dry weight (mg)	Food	1250	250	250
	Faeces	660	22·0	52·0
	Urine	63·0	12·0	20·0
Water gained (ml)	Food	1·35	1·28	1·28
	Metabolism	0·18	0·17	0·17
	Total gained	1·53	1·45	1·45
Water lost (ml)	Faeces	0·93 (60·8)‡	0·16 (11·0)	0·19 (19·8)
	Urine	0·04 (2·6)	0·72 (49·7)	0·20 (20·8)
	Nasal fluid	0·13 (8·5)	0·02 (1·4)	0·02 (2·1)
	Evaporation	0·43 (28·1)	0·55 (37·9)	0·55 (57·3)
	Total lost	1·53	1·45	0·96
Net gain (ml)		0	0	0·49

* Data calculated from Minnich (1970a,b) for lizards in the field.
† Data calculated from Templeton *et al.* (1972a) for lizards in the laboratory.
‡ Numbers in brackets represent the percentage of total water lost.

TABLE III

Daily potassium and sodium exchange in 50 g Dipsosaurus

		Field*	Well hydrated†	Rehydrating†
μ-equiv in food	K	485	109	109
	Na	46·0	16·5	16·5
	K/Na	10·5	6·61	6·61
Total μ-equiv in excreta	K	485	109	18·9
	Na	46·0	16·5	8·33
	K/Na	10·5	6·61	2·26
Net μ-equiv gained	K	0	0	8·02
	Na	0	0	8·17
μ-equiv lost	Faecal K	85·0 (17·5)‡	31·5 (28·9)	5·33 (28·4)
	Urine K	190 (39·2)	63·3 (58·1)	1·27 (6·0)
	Nasal K	210 (43·3)	14·2 (13·0)	12·2 (64·9)
	Faecal Na	14·0 (30·4)	4·00 (24·3)	2·67 (32·0)
	Urine Na	9·50 (20·7)	8·83 (53·5)	1·83 (22·0)
	Nasal Na	22·5 (48·9)	3·67 (22·2)	3·83 (46·0)
	Faecal K/Na	6·07	7·88	2·00
	Urine K/Na	20·0	7·17	0·69
	Nasal K/Na	9·33	3·87	3·19

* Data calculated from Minnich (1970a,b) for lizards in the field.
† Data calculated from Templeton *et al.* (1972a) for lizards in the laboratory.
‡ Numbers in brackets represent the percentage of that total cation lost.

retention (Table III) and thereby restored intracellular fluid more rapidly than extracellular fluid. The fall of K/Na ratio in both urine and faeces (Table III) suggests that there is active regulation of ion movement across the walls of the gut or cloaca of rehydrating lizards. Upon hydration, normal renal function was re-established, and with subsequent excessive hydration the urine flow (Table II) was much greater than that of *Dipsosaurus* in the field.

The laboratory lizards ate lettuce which contained about 5 times more water than the diet of field *Dipsosaurus* (Table II). Furthermore, the dry mass of the food and faeces respectively was about 5 and 30 fold heavier than those of laboratory lizards. The ratio of dry food to dry faeces was about 2 in field lizards and over 10 in laboratory lizards. This suggests either a lower digestive efficiency in field *Dipsosaurus* or the ingestion of excess food as a source of water. Even so, faecal water loss represented 63% of the total lost by field lizards (compared with only 10% in well hydrated lizards) though the faeces of field lizards had one fifth the amount of water (Table II).

Hypernatraemia

Bradshaw & Shoemaker (1967) studied the Australian lizard *Amphibolurus ornatus* which in summer lives almost exclusively on ants rich in NaCl. Lacking sufficient water to remove the Na, they simply retain the Na and conserve the water by expanding the extracellular fluid at the expense of the fluid inside the cells. Occasional summer thunderstorms provide sufficient water to remove the retained ions. Unlike *Uromastix* this agamid lacks an effective salt gland to augment Na removal by the inefficient kidney. The authors did not measure nor mention Cl in the interpretation of their results. It is tempting to add that the kidney and cloaca could possibly remove much of the Na as insoluble urates but without a functional nasal salt gland it could not efficiently remove the Cl and anuria resulted, until sufficient water again became available.

Bentley (1959) reported that the Australian skink, *Tiliqua* (= *Trachysaurus*) *rugosa* tolerated elevated plasma Na levels in the summer presumably because of dehydration. Bradshaw & Shoemaker (1967) suggest that sodium retention by *Tiliqua* might be an alternate interpretation of Bentley's data. Bentley (1959) also induced hypernatraemia in *Tiliqua* by intraperitoneal injection of a hypertonic NaCl solution. Pronounced anuria resulted and mean blood Na was raised from 150 to 228 m-equiv/liter after 7 days. Such toleration may not only have survival value in nature but may serve to retain water as extracelullar fluid.

Induced hypernatremia led to only moderate anuria in *Dipsosaurus* (Templeton, Murrish, Randall & Mugaas, 1972b) and stimulated nasal salt excretion (see also Templeton, 1966). Such stimulation was also observed in the chuckwalla (Templeton, 1964b), and in the false iguana (Templeton, 1964b; Templeton, 1967). The adaptation of the nasal salt gland, which usually secretes mainly K, to Na loading is of interest. The gland responds initially to induced hypernatraemia by removing even more K than before. Within a few days (Fig. 4) the gland begins to favour Na removal (Templeton, 1966, 1967; Templeton *et al.*, 1972b). The concentration of K in the nasal fluid of *Ctenosaura* (Templeton, 1967) decreased after 6 days of hypernatraemia yet the rate of nasal K output of hypernatraemic *Dipsosaurus* remained essentially unchanged (Templeton, 1966; Templeton *et al.*, 1972b) presumably because of increased nasal salt excretion. All of these iguanas are closely related and all are considered herbivorous. However, the sceloporine iguanid, *Sceloporus cyanogenys* which is insectivorous possesses a less functional nasal salt gland which does not adjust to Na loads (Fig. 4)

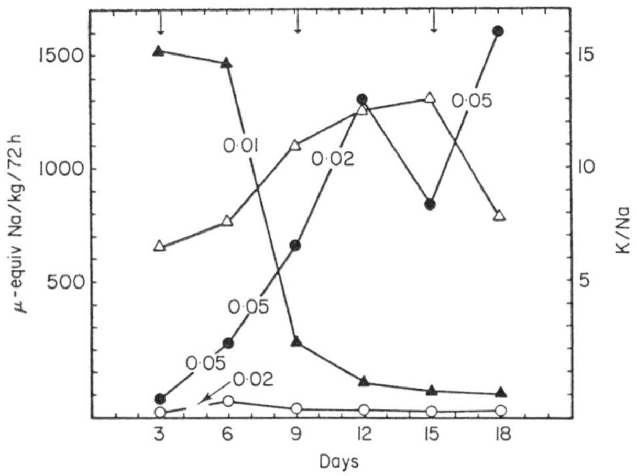

FIG. 4. Comparison of mean nasal Na excretion (circles) and mean K/Na ratios of nasal fluid (triangles) of *Dipsosaurus* (closed symbols) with *Sceloporus* (open symbols). The arrows represent periodic injection of a NaCl solution hypertonic to the plasma. If adjacent connected means differ significantly, the line is interrupted and the *P* value is shown therein. Note that the *Dipsosaurus* gland adjusts to hypernatraemia whereas that of *Sceloporus* does not. Data taken from Templeton (1966).

even after 17 days of hypernatremia (Templeton, 1966). Perhaps these lizards rely more on the kidney and cloaca to remove sodium or they may simply retain it as do *Tiliqua* (Bentley, 1959) and *Amphibolurus* (Bradshaw & Shoemaker, 1967).

Hyperkalemia

Injection of KCl solutions more hypertonic than the plasma caused an immediate increase in K concentration of the nasal fluid of *Ctenosaura*, whereas the concentration of Na remained relatively unchanged (Templeton, 1964b). One hyperkalaemic *Ctenosaura* secreted a fluid containing 950 m-equiv K/litre, the highest concentration recorded for any lizard, and which compares favourably with renal tubular secretion of K in hyperkalaemic dogs and man (Berliner, Kennedy & Hilton, 1950). Similarly, nasal K secretion was immediately enhanced in hyperkalaemic

Dipsosaurus and *Sceloporus* (Templeton, 1966), and nasal Na excretion remained relatively unchanged.

REGULATION OF SALT AND WATER BALANCE

Little is known about neural control of the gut and cloaca in desert lizards. The nasal salt gland (Templeton, 1964), however, is stimulated

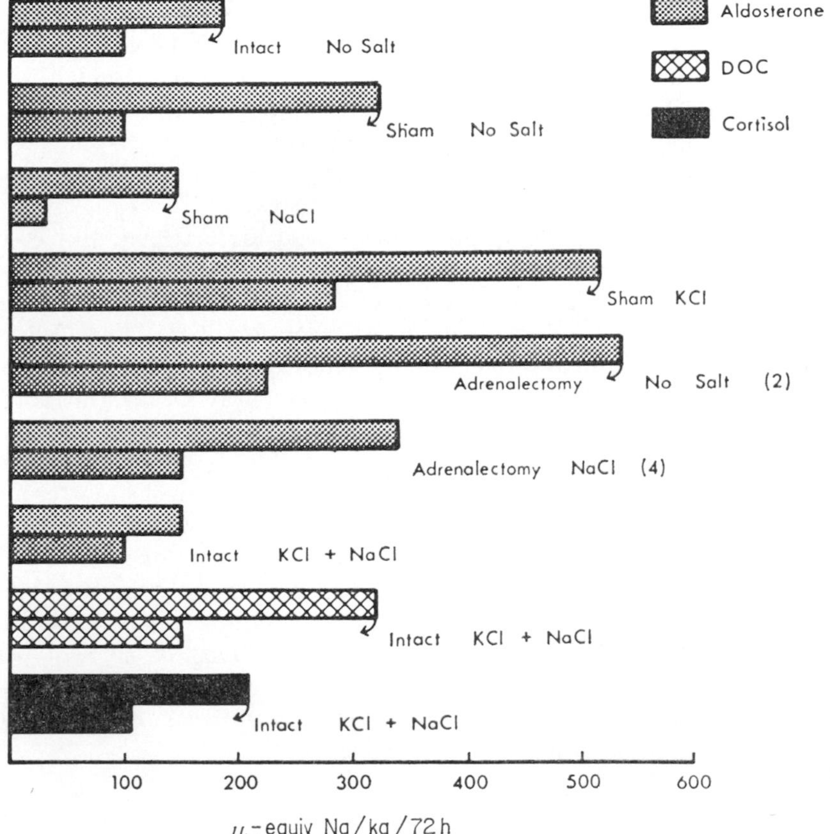

FIG. 5. The effects of aldosterone, DOC, and cortisol on the mean excretion of nasal Na in *Dipsosaurus* for three days before (top bar of each pair) and for three days after experimentation (bottom bar of each pair). Each pair of the nine groups was either left intact, sham adrenalectomized or bilaterally adrenalectomized by cautery. Each pair was also either not salt loaded, or loaded with NaCl, or with KCl, or with equimolar amounts of each. Each pair represents seven to eight lizards except where the no. is in brackets. The arrows represent a significant difference between the means for that particular pair ($P < 0{\cdot}05$ at least). Data for aldosterone, and for DOC and cortisol taken from Templeton *et al.* (1972b) and from unpublished data of these investigators respectively.

by mecholyl, a cholinergic drug and is inhibited by atropine and epinephrine (J. R. Templeton, unpubl. data) which suggest autonomic control via the lateral ethmoidal nerve.

The data presented thus strongly indicate that the composition of nasal fluid, urine and faeces is under hormonal control. Braysher & Green (1970), have demonstrated that arginine vasotocin acts to remove water and Na from the isolated cloaca of the goanna, *Varanus goudii*. Chan, Callard & Chester-Jones (1970) measured body fluid composition of *Dipsosaurus* but not that of the urine or nasal fluid. Their hypophysectomized animals retained body Na and water even though the adrenals had atrophied. Injection of prolactin and corticosterone into hypophysectomized lizards restored salt and water balance. When aldosterone was administered along with these two hormones body Na was retained and K was lost.

Templeton *et al.* (1972b) has shown that aldosterone (injected 12 μg/lizard daily) acts on both the nasal gland and the complex of the kidney, gut and cloaca of *Dipsosaurus* to elevate the K/Na ratio of the nasal fluid and urine. Aldosterone caused retention of Na (Fig. 5), but appears to have no obvious effect on K removal. The elevated ratio of K to Na in the nasal fluid and the retention of nasal Na is induced by aldosterone whether the animals are intact, sham adrenalectomized or bilaterally adrenalectomized by cautery. Inducing hypernatraemia, hyperkalaemia, or hypersalaemia does not essentially affect aldosterone action. Of four *Dipsosaurus* successfully adrenalectomized, two were given aldosterone (see Fig. 5) which caused Na retention; the other two markedly increased nasal output to uncommonly high values (Templeton *et al.*, 1972b). These investigators (unpubl. results) also injected I.M. 0·30 mg of deoxycorticosterone or 0·30 mg of cortisol per animal daily into hypersalaemic *Dipsosaurus* and observed retention of nasal sodium (Fig. 5) and elevation of the nasal K/Na ratio. Removal of nasal K appeared unaffected.

References

Bellairs, A. d'A. (1949). Observations on the snout of *Varanus* and a comparison with that of other lizards and snakes. *J. Anat., Lond.* **83**: 116–146.

Bentley, P. J. (1959). Studies on the water and electrolyte metabolism of the lizard *Trachysaurus rugosus* (Gray). *J. Physiol.* **145**: 37–47.

Bentley, P. J. & Blumer, W. F. C. (1962). Uptake of water by the lizard, *Moloch horridus*. *Nature, Lond.* **194**: 699–700.

Bentley, P. J. & Schmidt-Nielsen, K. (1966). Cutaneous water loss in reptiles. *Science, N.Y.* **151**: 1547–1549.

Berliner, R. W., Kennedy, T. J., Jr. & Hilton, J. G. (1950). Renal mechanisms for excretion of potassium. *Am. J. Physiol.* **162**: 348–367.

Bradshaw, S. D. & Shoemaker, V. H. (1967). Aspects of water and electrolyte changes in a field population of *Amphibolurus* lizards. *Comp. Biochem. Physiol.* **20**: 855–865.

Braysher, M. & Green, B. (1970). Absorption of water and electrolytes from the cloaca of an Australian lizard, *Varanus goudii* (Gray). *Comp. Biochem. Physiol.* **35**: 607–614.

Chan, D. K. O., Callard, I. P. & Chester-Jones, I. (1970). Observations on the water and electrolyte composition of the iguanid lizard, *Dipsosaurus dorsalis* (Baird and Girard), with special reference to the control by the pituitary gland and the adrenal cortex. *Gen. comp. Endocr.* **15**: 374–387.

Chew, R. M. & Dammon, A. E. (1961). Evaporative water loss of small vertebrates, as measured with an infrared analyzer. *Science, N.Y.* **133**: 384–385.

Claussen, D. L. (1967). Studies of water loss in two species of lizards. *Comp. Biochem. Physiol.* **20**: 115–130.

Dawson, W. R. (1967). Inter-specific variation in physiological responses of lizards to temperature. In *Lizard ecology: A Symposium*: 230–257. Milstead, W. W. (ed.). Columbia, Missouri: University of Missouri Press.

Dawson, W. R., Shoemaker, V. H. & Licht, P. (1966). Evaporative water losses of some small Australian lizards. *Ecology* **47**: 589–594.

Dunson, W. A. (1969). Electrolyte excretion by the salt gland of the Galapagos marine iguana. *Am. J. Physiol.* **216**: 995–1002.

Grenot, C. (1968). Sur l'excretion nasale de sels chez le lézard saharien: *Uromastix acanthinurus. C. r. hebd. Séanc. Acad. Sci. Paris* **266**: 1871–1874.

Khalil, F. & Abdel-Messeih, G. (1954). Water content of tissues of some desert reptiles and mammals. *J. exp. Zool.* **125**: 407–414.

Lasiewski, R. C. & Bartholomew, G. A. (1969). Condensation as a mechanism for water gain in nocturnal poikilotherms. *Copeia* **1969**: 405–407.

van Lennep, E. W. & Komnick, K. (1970). Fine structure of the nasal salt gland in the desert lizard *Uromastyx acanthinurus. Cytobiologie* **2**: 47–67.

Malan, M. E. (1940). Cranial anatomy of the genus *Gerrhosaurus. S. Afr. J. Sci.* **37**: 192–217.

Marshall, E. K. Jr. (1932). Kidney secretion in reptiles. *Proc. Soc. exp. Biol. Med.* **29**: 971–973.

Mayhew, W. W. (1965). Hibernation in the horned lizard, *Phrynosoma m'calli. Comp. Biochem. Physiol.* **16**: 103–119.

Mayhew, W. W. (1968). Biology of desert amphibians and reptiles. In *Desert biology*. **1**: 195–356. Brown, G.W. Jr. (ed.). New York and London: Academic Press.

Mayhew, W. W. & Wright, S. J. (1971). Water impermeable skin of the lizard *Phrynosoma m'calli. Herpetologica* **27**: 8–11.

Minnich, J. E. (1970a). Water and electrolyte balance of the desert iguana, *Dipsosaurus dorsalis*, in its natural habitat. *Comp. Biochem. Physiol.* **35**: 921–933.

Minnich, J. E. (1970b). Evaporative water loss from the desert iguana, *Dipsosaurus dorsalis. Copeia* **1970**: 575–578.

Minnich, J. E. & Shoemaker, V. H. (1970). Diet, behavior and water turnover in the desert iguana, *Dipsosaurus dorsalis. Am. Midl. Nat.* **84**: 496–509.

Murrish, D. E. & Schmidt-Nielsen, K. (1970). Water transport in the cloaca of lizards: active or passive? *Science, N.Y.* **170**: 324–326.

Norris, K. S. (1967). Color adaptations in desert reptiles and its thermal relationships. In *Lizard ecology: A Symposium*: 162–229. Milstead, W. W. (ed.). Columbia, Missouri: University of Missouri Press.

Norris, K. S. & Dawson, W. R. (1964). Observations on the water economy and electrolyte excretion of chuckwallas (Lacertilia, *Sauromalus*). *Copeia* **1964**: 638–646.

Oelrich, T. M. (1956). The anatomy of the head of *Ctenosaura pectinata* (Iguanidae). *Misc. Publs Mus. Zool. Univ. Mich.* **94**: 1–122.

Philpott, C. W. & Templeton, J. R. (1964). A comparative study of the histology and fine structure of the nasal salt secreting gland of the lizard, *Dipsosaurus*. *Anat. Rec.* **148**: 394–395.

Pratt, C. W. M. (1948). The morphology of the ethmoidal region of *Sphenodon* and lizards. *Proc. zool. Soc. Lond.* **118**: 171–201.

Roberts, J. S. & Schmidt-Nielsen, B. (1966). Renal ultrastructure and excretion of salt and water by three terrestrial lizards. *Am. J. Physiol.* **211**: 476–486.

Schmidt-Nielsen, K. (1964). *Desert animals*. London, New York: Oxford Univ. Press.

Schmidt-Nielsen, K. & Fange, R. (1958). Salt glands in marine reptiles. *Nature, Lond.* **182**: 783–785.

Schmidt-Nielsen, K. & Dawson, W. R. (1964). Terrestrial animals in dry heat: Desert reptiles. In *Handbook of Physiology*. Section 4: Adaptations to the environment: 467–480. Dill, D. B. (ed.). Washington, D.C.: American Physiological Society.

Schmidt-Nielsen, K., Borut, A., Lee, P. & Crawford, E. (1963). Nasal salt excretion and the possible function of the cloaca in water conservation. *Science, N.Y.* **142**: 1300–1301.

Seshadri, C. (1956). Urinary excretion in the Indian house lizard *Hemidactylus flavirudis* (Rüppell). *J. zool. Soc. India* **8**: 63–78.

Seshadri, C. (1959). Functional morphology of the cloaca of *Varanus monitor* (Linnaeus) in relation to water economy. *Proc. natn. Inst. Sci. India* **25** (B5): 101–106.

Shoemaker, V. H., Licht, P. & Dawson, W. R. (1966). Effects of temperature on kidney function in the lizard *Tiliqua rugosa*. *Physiol. Zoöl.* **39**: 244–252.

Templeton, J. R. (1960). Respiration and water loss at the higher temperatures in the desert iguana, *Dipsosaurus dorsalis*. *Physiol. Zoöl.* **33**: 136–145.

Templeton, J. R. (1963). Nasal salt excretion in terrestrial iguanids. *Am. Zool.* **3**: 530.

Templeton, J. R. (1964a). Cardiovascular response to temperature in the lizard *Sauromalus obesus*. *Physiol. Zoöl.* **37**: 300–306.

Templeton, J. R. (1964b). Nasal salt excretion in terrestrial lizards. *Comp. Biochem. Physiol.* **11**: 223–229.

Templeton, J. R. (1966). Responses of the nasal salt gland to chronic hypersalemia. *Comp. Biochem. Physiol.* **18**: 563–572.

Templeton, J. R. (1967). Nasal salt gland excretion and adjustment to sodium loading in the lizard, *Ctenosaura pectinata*. *Copeia* **1967**: 136–140.

Templeton, J. R. (1970). Reptiles. In *Comparative physiology of thermo-regulation*. **1**: 167–221. Whittow, G. C. (ed.). New York and London: Academic Press.

Templeton, J. R., Murrish, D. E., Randall, E. M. & Mugaas, J. N. (1972a). Salt and water balance in the desert iguana, *Dipsosaurus dorsalis* I. The effect of dehydration, rehydration, and full hydration. *Z. vergl. Physiol.* **76**: 245–254.

Templeton, J. R., Murrish, D. E., Randall, E. M. & Mugaas, J. N. (1972b). Salt and water balance in the desert iguana, *Dipsosaurus dorsalis* II. The effect of aldosterone and adrenalectomy. *Z. vergl. Physiol.* **76**: 255–269.

Symp. zool. Soc. Lond. (1972) No. 31, 79–111.

WATER ECONOMY AND THERMAL BALANCE OF ISRAELI AND AUSTRALIAN AMPHIBIA FROM XERIC HABITATS

M. R. WARBURG

Israel Institute for Biological Research,
Ness Ziona, Israel

SYNOPSIS

The physiological adaptation to water shortage found in amphibians inhabiting xeric habitats involves both reduction of evaporative water loss and an increased rate of water uptake when water becomes available. The main organ involved is the skin. This was studied in the urodele *T. vittatus* and in several anurans: *H. rubella*, *H. caerulea*, and *H. arborea* (Hylidae), *P. syriacus* (Pelobatidae), and *Cyclorana*, *Neobatrachus*, *Limnodynastes* and *Heleioporus* (Leptodactylidae). Another physiological mechanism involves the urinary bladder. The main adaptation is an increased bladder capacity for water storage and the capability during aestivation of reabsorbing the water. This adaptation has been studied in the urodeles; *T. vittatus* and *S. salamandra*, and several anurans of the lepodactylids (*Cyclorana*, *Notaden*), bufonids (*B. cognatus*, *B. viridis*) and pelobatids (*S. couchi*, *P. syriacus*). The kidney of some pelobatids and bufonids enables depression of urinary loss during dehydration, and the concentration of body fluids by storing nitrogenous wastes as urea in the blood during aestivation.

The length of time the amphibian survives exposure to high temperatures was found to be a good criterion for judging its adaptation to xeric environments. Both hylids (*H. rubella*) and leptodactylids (*N. centralis*) show a remarkable capacity for surviving high temperatures in dry air for very long periods.

The mechanisms of Amphibia aiding survival under xeric conditions vary with families, genera and species. Even within a species, metamorphosis shifts the response to water loss or uptake, a shift that probably involves a change in the physiological capacity of some organs. This was shown in *R. ridibunda*, *P. syriacus* and *T. vittatus* in their aquatic and terrestrial phases.

A series of adaptations and some dynamic shift from one type of adaptation to another correlated with the ontogeny of the animal, assists survival under arid conditions.

INTRODUCTION

Amphibia as a group are not normally associated with xeric habitats and certainly not with arid regions. However, there are several genera mainly among the anura, that inhabit such places, and several more that live under xeric conditions during part of the year. The mechanisms that enable their survival under conditions of high temperature, low humidity and shortage of water that prevail in dry habitats, are not well understood.

The amphibia of arid or semi-arid habitats belong mostly to two families: the Bufonidae and the Leptodacylidae, with a few Pelobatidae and Hylidae. The Leptodactylidae are confined to the southern hemisphere in xeric habitats of Australia, southern Africa and South America. The Pelobatidae are found only in the northern hemisphere and inhabit xeric habitats in Asia, Europe, North and Central America. The Hylidae and Bufonidae are cosmopolitan and have a wide distribution in both the northern and southern hemispheres.

Whereas in general the hylids are found mostly in or close to water, the bufonids and pelobatids are terrestrial, ranging into arid habitats. On the other hand the leptodactylids range from aquatic through terrestrial, into extremely arid habitats.

Studies on physiological adaptations of the amphibia to terrestrial habitats have been mostly concerned with their thermal and water balances. Although the water economy of a large number of amphibian species (120) has been studied only a comparatively small number (about 37) of these species live in xeric habitats (Table I).

Table I

Anuran species from xeric habitats in which some aspect of water economy was studied

Species	Family	Author
	Pelobatidae	
Pelobates syriacus		Warburg, 1971b
Scaphiopus hammondi		Thorson & Svihla, 1943; Thorson, 1955; Shoemaker *et al.*, 1969; Ruibal *et al.*, 1969; Lasiewski & Bartholomew, 1969.
S. couchi		Thorson & Svihla, 1943, McClanahan, 1964, 1967; Shoemaker *et al.*, 1969; McClanahan & Baldwin, 1969; Claussen, 1969; Lasiewski & Bartholomew, 1969; Mayhew, 1965.
S. holbrooki		Thorson & Svihla, 1943.
	Bufonidae	
Bufo viridis		Gordon, 1962; Warburg, 1971b;
B. punctatus		McClanahan & Baldwin, 1969; Claussen 1969; Fair, 1970.
B. cognatus		Ruibal, 1962a,b; McClanahan, 1964; Schmid, 1965a; McClanahan & Baldwin, 1969.

TABLE I—(*continued*)

Species	Family	Author
B. regularis		Rey, 1937; Ewer, 1951a,b, 1952; Cloudsley-Thompson, 1967.
B. woodhousi		Spight, 1968.
B. boreas		Thorson & Svihla, 1943; Thorson. 1955; Claussen, 1969; Fair, 1970,
B. debilis		Claussen, 1969; Fair, 1970.
B. marinus		Shoemaker, 1964, 1965; Warburg, 1965a; Spight, 1967c; Krakauer, 1970.
	Hylidae	
Hyla rubella		Main & Bentley, 1964; Warburg, 1965a, 1967.
H. caerulea		Main & Bentley, 1964; Warburg, 1967.
H. latopalmata		Main & Bentley, 1964.
H. moorei		Main & Bentley, 1964.
H. arborea		Overton, 1904; Reichling, 1958; Warburg, 1971b.
	Leptodactylidae	
Cyclorana sp.		Warburg, 1967.
C. platycephalus		Main & Bentley, 1964.
Notaden nichollsi		Main & Bentley, 1964.
Neobatrachus pictus		Warburg, 1965a.
N. centralis		Bentley *et al.*, 1958; Warburg, 1965a.
N. sutor		Bentley *et al.*, 1958.
N. wilsmorei		Bentley *et al.*, 1958.
N. pelobatoides		Bentley *et al.*, 1958.
Heleioporus eyrei		Bentley, 1959; Bentley *et al.*, 1958; Packer, 1963.
H. inornatus		Bentley *et al.*, 1958.
H. psammophilus		Bentley *et al.*, 1958.
H. australiacus		Bentley *et al.*, 1958; Lee, 1968.
H. albopunctatus		Bentley *et al.*, 1958.
H. barycragus		Main, 1968.
Pseudophryne bibroni		Warburg, 1965a.
Limnodynastes ornatus		Warburg, 1965a.
L. dorsalis		Warburg, 1965a; 1967.
Eleuterodactylus portoricensis		Heatwole *et al.*, 1969.
Lepidobatrachus asper		Ruibal, 1962b.
Pleurodema nebulosa		Ruibal, 1962b.
P. tucumana		Ruibal, 1962b.

The thermal response of many amphibians has been studied by Hutchison (1961) and Brattstrom (1963, 1968). These investigations were mainly on critical thermal maximum temperature (CTM). Time-temperature curves of body temperature in field and laboratory conditions have also been obtained (Mellanby, 1941; Warburg, 1965a, 1967; Lillywhite, 1970).

From these studies a pattern of evolution emerges which indicates some general lines of physiological adaptation in the various amphibian genera studied so far. The present paper is concerned with the functions evolved in various amphibian groups to adjust them for life in hot and dry environments.

THE HABITAT

The scope of the study includes amphibia that live not only in arid habitats or deserts but also in semi-arid and xeric habitats. In general the arid regions include areas where the average annual rainfall does not exceed 100 mm whereas in semi-arid habitats the annual rainfall is up to 250 mm. Xeric habitats are not necessarily confined to deserts but are areas where the annual rainfall is concentrated within a short season and during the rest of the year there is no rain or surface water. Temperatures during summer are in general high in both arid and semi-arid habitats. Thus in the Sonoran Desert in the Santa Rita Mountains, Arizona, temperatures may reach 44·5°C in summer on the ground in the shade at an air temperature in the shade of 43°C (Warburg, 1965b). In the Negev desert microclimatic measurements in similar habitats have indicated similar summer temperatures, up to 45°C on the ground and 44°C air temperature both in the shade (Warburg, 1964). A typical pattern of time–temperature curves for the Negev is given in Fig. 1. Microclimatic data indicated a rather similar pattern in maximal temperatures and in temperature ranges (Warburg, 1965c).

In all the three desert areas studied the humidities were rather low during summer in spite of the fact that in the Sonora Desert (Warburg, 1965b) and in Central Australia (Warburg, 1965d) part of the annual rainfall occurs during summer. In other words, the fact that summer rain amounts to almost half of the annual rainfall, does not necessarily imply high air humidities which remain rather low even after rain (Warburg, 1965b). On the other hand moisture in the ground may be higher and thus animals inhabiting the soil will have more moisture available to them than in deserts where there are no summer rains.

Although microclimatic measurements may give some indication of the temperature and humidity within certain desert habitats, their value is restricted to the animals which inhabited the microhabitats at the time when the measurements were taken (Warburg, 1964).

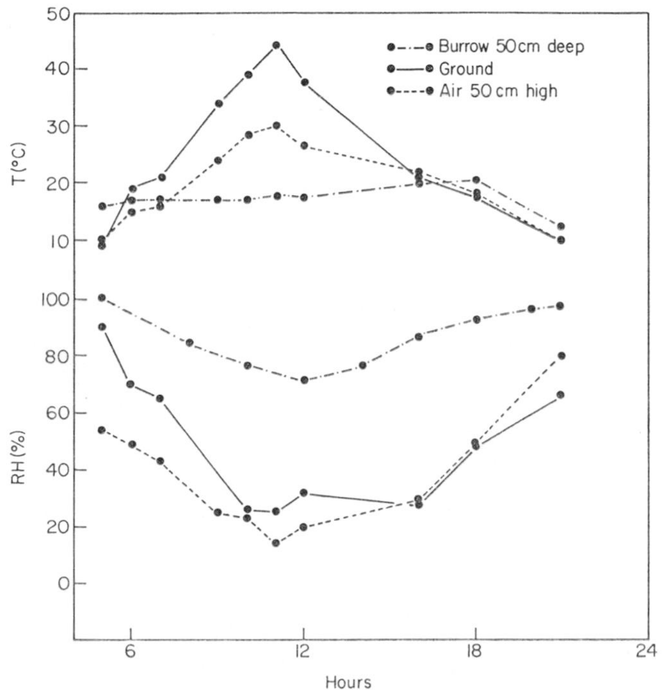

Fig. 1. Time–temperature curves on a summer day taken in a microhabitat of *Bufo viridis* at Revivim, Negev, Israel.

There are, however, few data pertaining to amphibian microhabitats (Licht & Brown, 1967). Some measurements were taken by the author and it can be seen that temperatures under normal conditions can be rather high (Fig. 2).

Thus in microhabitats of *Hyla arenicolar* in Sabino Canyon, Santa Catalina Mountains, Southern Arizona, measurements were taken in summer, 1957. The temperature in the crevices was 31°C as compared with 37·5°C outside. Relative humidity was 10% in the canyon (M. R. Warburg, unpubl. data). Similarly temperature measurements were taken in the microhabitat of *Hyla rubella* and *H. caerulea* in the vicinity of Alice Springs, Northern Territory, Australia, during summer, 1963 (Fig. 2). Thus the rock crevices inhabited by both species were cooler by 6°C than the ambient temperature (38°C). Temperature in shallow burrows of *Limnodynastes ornatus* was 9°C lower than air temperature. It is of interest to note that in burrows of *Notaden nichollsi* and *Glauertia mjöbergi*, Main (1968) found temperatures of 33·6°C whereas adult *Cyclorana cultripes* and *C. platycephalus* were found in pools at 39·2°C.

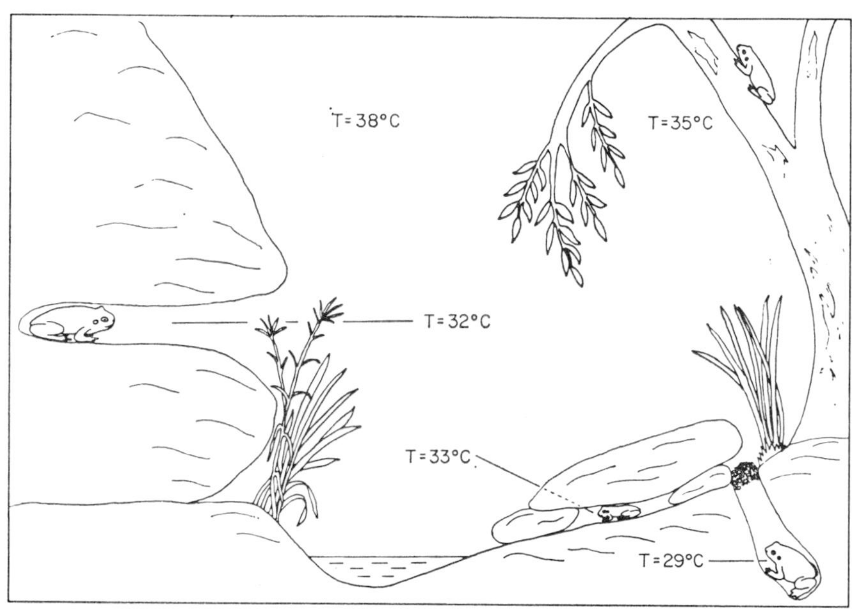

FIG. 2. Temperatures in the microhabitats of *Hyla rubella* (under rock), *H. caerulea* (in crevice and on tree), and *Limnodynastes ornatus* (in burrow), taken on a summer day near Alice Springs, N.T., Australia.

THE WATER BALANCE

Studies on water economy of urodeles

Evaporative water loss

Only a comparatively small part of the voluminous literature on water economy of the amphibia deals with urodeles. Part of the reason for this is that members of this ancient amphibian group do not on the whole show remarkable terrestrial adaptations.

So far 39 species of urodeles have been studied. Most of these (25 species) belong to the Plethodontidae which is a New World family mostly inhabiting forest areas or otherwise definite mesic habitats. Several studies are concerned with Salamandridae which are on the whole a more terrestrial group and include the newts and salamanders.

These studies deal with the rate at which water is lost mostly through evaporation, and the survival under various conditions of dehydration, as well as the rate of water uptake (Hall, 1922; Littleford, Keller & Phillips, 1947; Cohen, 1952; Ray, 1958; Spight, 1967b, 1968; Warburg, 1971a). Most experiments were conducted at room temperature (Spight, 1967a; Ray, 1958; Littleford *et al.*, 1947). Various techniques were used in these studies. Thus the air at which animals were dehydrated ranged from dry air to air at various humidities (Spight, 1968; Warburg, 1971a). The speed at which the air was moving over the animal ranged from still air to 2000 cm/min. Consequently it is difficult to compare the results obtained by these methods (see discussion in Warburg, 1971a). In general, however, most animals showed a high rate of water loss when exposed to dry air even at room temperatures of 20–25°C. In one study the rate of water loss at higher temperatures was measured as well (Warburg, 1971a).

With increasing temperature the evaporation rate from the animals increased greatly. As these studies were conducted in completely dry air the changes in temperature did not alter the humidity and therefore the responses were mostly brought about by temperature.

The few Old World species investigated so far include: *Triturus marmoratus*, *T. cristatus*, *T. alpestris*, *T. vittatus*, *Salamandra salamandra* (or *S. maculosa*), and *S. atra*. Of these species, *T. vittatus* is undoubtedly the most interesting and shows the highest degree of terrestrial adaptation (Warburg, 1971a). This newt can be found several miles from water, and has been excavated from ground where it took refuge during long dry summer months. It has a low rate of water loss at temperatures up to 30°C (Fig. 3). When compared with another terrestrial species (*Salamandra salamandra*) *T. vittatus* shows a remarkable degree of water conservation. *S. salamandra* is found in more mesic habitats than *T. vittatus* but when compared with the various other salamandrids as well as the plethodontids it is definitely a more terrestrial species.

The rate at which *S. salamandra* loses water appears to be less affected by temperature than in *T. vittatus*. Temperatures up to 30°C did not change the response, however, but at higher temperatures (up to 37·5°C) the rate of evaporation increased greatly, especially in *T. vittatus* (Fig. 3). Exposure to dry air for 3 days brought about a similar pattern of water loss, which increased with temperature (Warburg, 1971a).

Rate of water uptake

The rate at which water is absorbed following dehydration can give a good indication of the degree of terrestrial adaptation of the species (Bentley, 1966b). Only in a few studies was this aspect of physiological response examined in urodeles (Rey, 1937; Heatwole & Lim, 1961; Spight, 1967a,b; Warburg, 1971a).

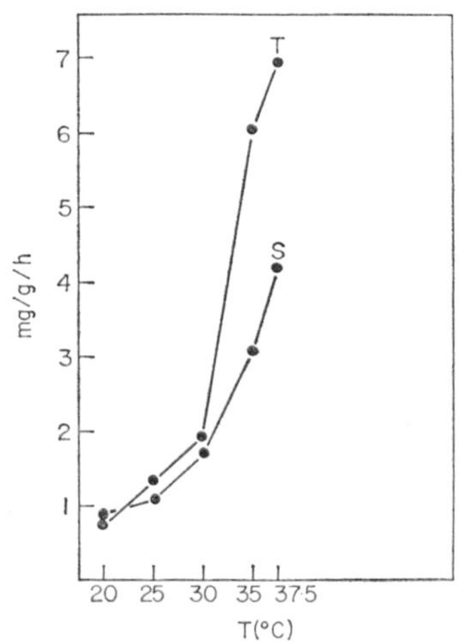

FIG. 3. Evaporative water loss in Israeli urodeles. T, *Triturus vittatus*; S, *Salamandra salamandra*.

Urodeles can absorb water from the soil at a rate depending on soil properties, as well as on body weight and hydration deficit (Spight, 1967a). Thus sand with a water content of 11·9% or more provided water for absorption by the urodele, *Plethodon cinereus* (Heatwole & Lim, 1961). Lower moisture content of soil, however, caused water loss from this and other species (Spight, 1967a).

S. maculosa (= *S. salamandra*) absorbed water at a rate of 17 mg/cm^2/h (Rey, 1937).

Both *T. vittatus* and *S. salamandra* show a remarkably rapid rate of water uptake so that the water deficit can be replaced in 2–3 h (Fig. 4).

Response to neurohypophysial extracts

Response in vivo. Extracts of neurohypophysial hormones or their synthetic derivatives stimulate the absorption of water by amphibia *in vivo*. *In vitro* isolated skin or bladder preparations also respond to pituitary polypeptides (Bentley & Heller, 1964).

In urodeles this response was studied in *Ambystoma tigrinum*, *Triturus alpestris*, *T. cristatus*, (Bentley & Heller, 1964), *Salamandra*

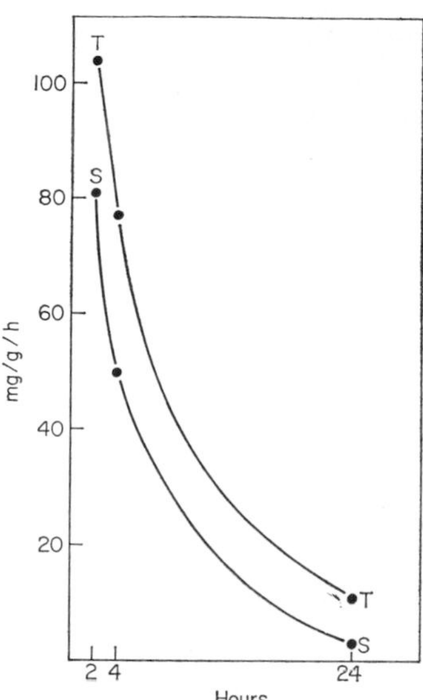

FIG. 4. Rate of water uptake following dehydration. T, *Triturus vittatus*; S, *Salamandra salamandra.*

maculosa (Bentley & Heller, 1965), *A. tigrinum* and *A. gracile* (Alvarado & Johnson, 1965), *T. vittatus* and *S. salamandra* (Warburg, 1971a). Arginine vasotocin was more effective than oxytocin (Figs 5 and 6).

It is of great interest to note that the response of the terrestrial phase of the newt, *T. vittatus*, was comparatively higher than either the aquatic phase of this species or that of *S. salamandra*. Water uptake rates change throughout the life cycle of the urodele. Thus,

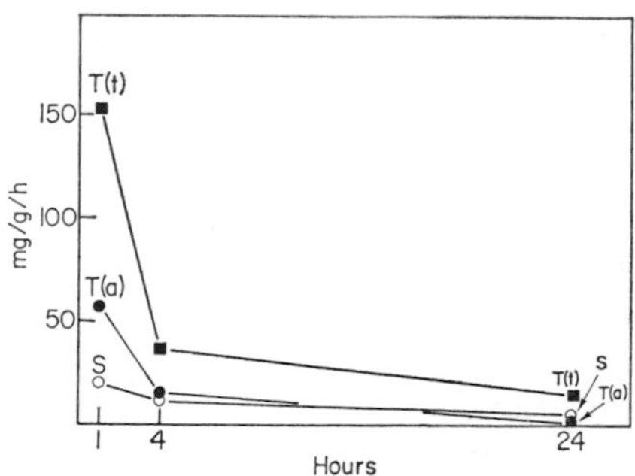

FIG. 5. Response of Israeli urodeles to oxytocin (0·05 mμ-mole/g, *in vivo*). S, *Salamandra salamandra*; T(a), *Triturus vittatus* (aquatic phase); T(t), *Triturus vittatus* (terrestrial phase).

as tadpoles, *S. salamandra* show no response at all to pituitary hormones (Table II). The response to hormones apparently develops only upon completion of metamorphosis.

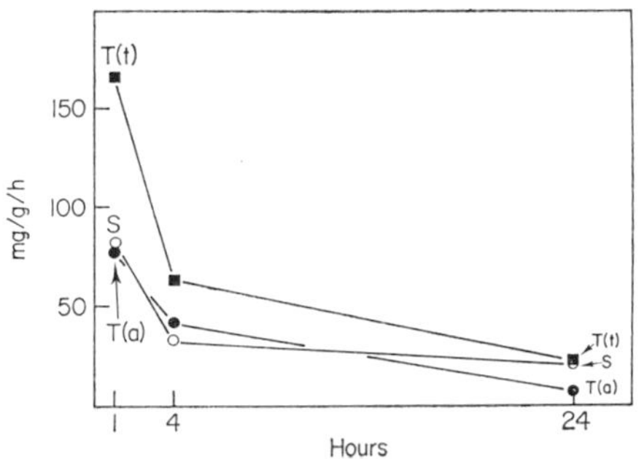

FIG. 6. Response of urodeles to vasotocin (0·05 mμ-mole/g, *in vivo*). Key as in Fig. 5.

TABLE II

The response of Salamandra salamandra *through tadpole, juvenile and adult stages, to treatment* in vivo *with oxytocin*

Hours	1	4	24
Tadpoles (1 g)			
0·01 mμ-mole/g	133·3	26·3	2·0
Control	279·9	34·0	7·0
Juveniles (5–7 g)			
0·05 mμ-mole/g	19·9	12·1	7·5
Control	4·6	3·0	2·2
2nd yr adults (25–50 g)			
0·50 mμ-mole/g	59·6	9·5	3·0
Control	1·2	0·8	0·3

Water uptake in mg/g/h.

Response in vitro. Neurohypophysial hormones act on the skin by increasing the rate of passage of water: on the kidney they are anti-diuretic. Furthermore it acts on the urinary bladder to increase the rate of water reabsorption.

In their study on urodeles, Bentley & Heller (1964, 1965) demonstrated the action of the hormone on the kidney of *Triturus alpestris* and *T. cristatus* where the hormone appears to cause a drop in urinary flow. No indication of any action on the skin could be demonstrated.

However in *Salamandra* there was a marked increase of water passage through the isolated urinary bladder. The response of the bladder of *S. salamandra* is considerable but it is even greater in the aquatic phase of the newt, *T. vittatus* (Warburg, 1971a). The skin of the terrestrial phase of the newt responds readily to the hormone (Fig.7).

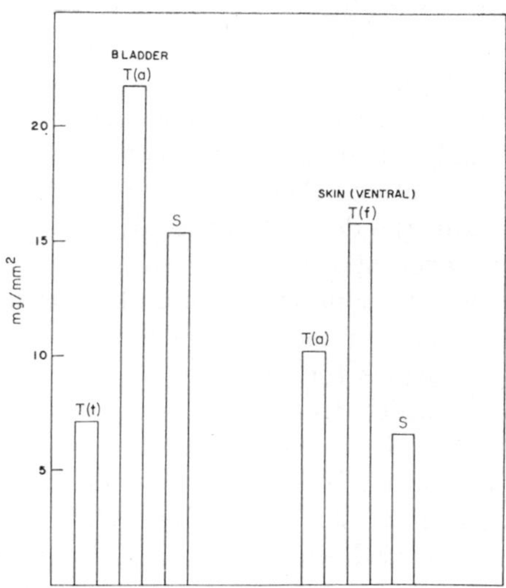

FIG. 7. Response *in vitro* of urodeles to oxytocin. Skin and urinary bladder preparations. Key as in Fig. 5.

Studies on water economy of anurans

About 80 species of Anuran have been studied so far. The four major families: Bufonidae, Hylidae, Ranidae and Leptodactylidae received most attention. Of the Bufonidae and Hylidae 17 species have been studied in each family, of the Ranidae 13 species, whereas of the Leptodactylidae 26 species have been studied. Of the 5 species of Pelobatidae studied the two that received the greatest attention among all the Anura were *Scaphiopus couchi* and *S. hammodi* (Table I).

Evaporative water loss

Effect of ambient conditions. Measurement of evaporative water loss has mostly been conducted at room temperature between 20–25°C (Thorson & Svihla, 1943; Thorson, 1956; Schmid, 1965a; Claussen, 1969; Heatwole, Torres, de Austin & Heatwole, 1969; Bentley, Lee & Main, 1958; Spight, 1967a; Packer, 1963). A few studies were made at lower temperatures (10–20°C—Jameson, 1966), or higher temperatures

(25–40°C—Warburg, 1965a, 1967, 1971b). Humidity varied in these experiments but was mostly low.

The animals were usually exposed to air moving at speeds ranging from 270 cm/min (Claussen, 1969) to 4000 cm/min (Thorson, 1956). Only occasionally were the animals studied in still air (Spight, 1967c; Warburg, 1965a, 1967, 1971b). Differences in technique used by the various authors add to the difficulty of comparing species (see discussion Warburg, 1971b). It is evident, however, that animals exposed to moving air show a higher rate of water loss than those in still air. It has been argued elsewhere that still air normally prevails in anuran microhabitats and only when the ground is wet are the frogs and toads exposed to windy conditions (Warburg, 1967). On the other hand, it is difficult to maintain the desired and controlled humidity conditions when air is moving even at such a low speed as 1 cm/min (Warburg, 1965c). It is for these reasons that I found it preferable to compare responses of frog species under semi-natural conditions by exposing them to still air at various temperatures and humidities.

The humidity at which frogs have been studied varies from dry air (rh 0–5%) to humid air (rh 95–100%) (Bentley *et al.* 1958; Heatwole *et al.*, 1969; Spight, 1967c). In some reports the humidity is not given whereas in others it is doubtful that humidity conditions could be identical with those stated by the authors because of the high air movement in the experimental container which therefore could not be sufficiently dried.

Cloudsley-Thompson (1967) argued that water loss for *Bufo regularis* follows the saturation deficit. An attempt was made to determine whether water loss from an amphibian correlated with the vapour pressure deficit (VPD) rather than with relative humidity (Warburg, 1965a, 1967). In these studies the frogs were exposed to the same VPD (9·2 mm Hg) at different temperatures and the results were compared with the rate of water loss at high (95–100% rh) or low (0–5% rh) humidities at the same temperatures.

From the results it was apparent that in general the rate of water loss was temperature-dependent in both dry and humid conditions. In smaller frogs (*Crinia signifera*) water loss at constant VPD was almost constant per unit time indicating a loss in proportion to the drying power of the air. In larger frogs (*Limnodynastes dorsalis*) evaporation rate did not remain constant when the temperature was varied.

It appears that both temperature (above 30°C) and greater dryness of the air, increase water loss. Small frogs, however, lose more water in proportion to their body weight than larger species. Of the anurans studied, the Australian burrowing frog (*N. centralis*; Warburg, 1965a, 1967) and *P. syriacus* (Table IV) in Israel (Warburg, 1971b) show remarkably low rates of water loss that compare well with the American spade-foot toads, *S. couchi* and *S. hammondi* (see ref. in Table I).

Similarly the rate of water loss of the Australian hylids *H. rubella* and *H. caerulea* compares well with that of *H. arborea* (Table III).

TABLE III

Evaporative water loss (in mg/g/h) of some Australian and Israeli anurans during 4 h exposure to dry air (rh 0–10%)

Temperature (°C)	20	25	30	35	37·5
Cyclorana (*)	0·42	0·99	1·28	2·06	2·20
Pelobates	0·32	0·56	1·06	1·23	1·47
Hyla caerulea (*)	0·08	0·22	0·87	1·18	1·29
H. rubella (NT) (*)	0·84	1·03	1·13	1·23	1·38
H. rubella (WA) (*)	1·18	1·65	2·02	2·20	2·28
H. arborea (G)	0·62	0·83	1·01	1·96	2·21
H. arborea (C)	0·78	1·37	1·69	2·48	3·52

(*) data from Warburg (1967); (NT) Northern Territory, Australia; (WA) Western Australia; (G) Galil Mountains, Israel; (C) Coastal Plain, Israel.

TABLE IV

Water uptake (in mg/g/h) following dehydration in some Australian and Israeli anurans

	Hours		
	0–1	0–2	0–24
Cyclorana sp. (*)	173	109	6
Neobatrachus centralis (*)	120	112	10
Pelobatus syriacus	58	42	6
Limnodynastes ornatus (*)	40	25	8
Hyla caerulea (*)	158	78	8
H. rubella (*)	108	62	10
H. arborea	72	54	10

(*) data for the Australian species from Warburg (1967) and for the Israeli species from Warburg (1971b)

The water loss curve as a function of time. It is evident that the rate of evaporative water loss varies with the period of exposure. Therefore, most animals were studied for short periods up to 1 h. In moving air frogs could not survive longer periods of exposure. In other works long exposures of 4, 8 and 24 h, up to 3 days were used (Cloudsley-Thompson, 1967; Claussen, 1969; Warburg, 1967, 1971b).

In general the greatest water loss took place within the 1–2 h exposure regardless of low or high humidity. The rate of water loss was fairly constant at low temperatures of 22·5–30°C in both small species of toadlets (*P. bibroni*) or hylids (*H. ewingi*), as well as in larger burrowing frogs (*N. pictus* and *L. dorsalis*) (Warburg, 1965a). It was necessary to take the animals out of their container in order to weigh them at intervals. This disturbed ambient conditions in the container. In order to overcome this, remote and continuous weight measurements were taken in some of the smaller species (*Crinia signifera*, *P. bibroni* and *H. rubella*) (Warburg, 1967). The water loss from *Crinia* in dry air was linear. On the other hand at constant VPD these species lost water rapidly during the first hour and then more slowly at temperatures up to 25°C. At higher temperatures there was a curved relationship. In *P. bibroni* this effect of temperature was evident at 30°C and in *H. rubella* at 35°C.

Packer (1963) found that the weight loss of *Heleioporus eyrei* when in dry sand was at a rate of 0·32 g/h, compared with a rate of water loss by *Cyclorana* in moist sand of 0·15 g/h during 10 days (Warburg, 1967).

Water loss as a response to acclimation temperature. In *H. rubella* the effect of acclimation temperature on the rate of water loss was investigated (Warburg, 1967). When exposed to experimental conditions, frogs kept for 2 weeks or more at a high temperature (30°C) lost water at higher rates than frogs previously kept at 20°C or 10°C. The curves for water loss of frogs acclimated at 30°C indicated a high water loss at temperatures up to 35°C but dropping at higher temperatures. It is probable that the frogs responded to the temperatures within the range of their acclimation exposure by evaporating more water. Similar observations were made on *H. arborea* (M. R. Warburg unpubl. data).

Water loss and geographic distribution. Whether anurans of the same species differ in their rate of water loss according to their microhabitat or geographic distribution is of importance in comparing results obtained from different species and localities. As an example, Thorson (1955) studied *S. couchi* and *S. hammondi* in the northern part of their geographic distribution (Washington). It is doubtful whether these data can be compared with those obtained from this species in the arid region of southern California (McClanahan, 1967).

It was found that *H. rubella* from different localities in Australia differ significantly in rate of water loss (Warburg, 1967). Thus frogs from the Northern Territory were best at conserving water, followed by frogs from North Western Australia and the interior of New South Wales. These differences showed especially at high temperatures and it was suggested that they were due in part to the different survival mechanism of frogs living under different climatic conditions. Jameson (1966) found differences in the response of *H. regilla* and *H. californiae* from arid and mesic habitats in different regions of California.

Even such small geographic differences as can be found in Israel between the Coastal Plain and the Galil Mountains are sufficient to produce differences in the rate of water loss of *H. arborea*. Thus a population of this hylid from the Galil Mountains showed a low rate of water loss compared with the Coastal Plain frogs (Table III).

Rate of water uptake

After dehydration most frogs and toads absorb water, even from moist surfaces, and this facilitates replacement of the water lost (Packer, 1963; Fair, 1970; Warburg, 1967).

Packer (1963) found little difference between the rate of hydration of *H. eyrei* in water (1·2 g/h) relative to wet sand (0·85 g/h). Fair (1970) observed that *B. boreas* and *B. punctatus* gained about 40 mg/cm^2/h in moist soil with particles smaller than 0·5 mm. Larger soil particles, up to 1·5 mm diam., caused a decrease in the rate of water uptake.

The rate at which water is absorbed varies with species and was found to be a good criterion of the degree of adaptation to terrestrial conditions. Accordingly the more terrestrial species tend to absorb larger quantities of water at a higher rate than aquatic forms (Rey, 1937; Jørgensen, 1950; Bentley *et al.*, 1958). Thorson (1955) measured the water uptake of frogs (*R. pipiens, R. clamitans, S. hammondi*) after dehydration. Both he and Claussen (1969), however, found no correlation with the terrestrial adaptations of the species studied. On the other hand Bentley *et al.* (1958) found a good relationship between the rate of water uptake and the degree of terrestrial adaptation in some Leptodactylids but not in others. Thus several *Neobatrachus* species showed a good correlation between water uptake and adaptation to xeric environments, whereas in several *Heleioporus* species such correlation was not evident. Various authors (Thorson & Svihla, 1943; Thorson, 1955; Bentley *et al.*, 1958; Warburg, 1965a, 1967, 1971b).

argue that there is a definite inter-specific difference in the rate of water loss or uptake correlated well with the degree of terrestrial adaptation. Other studies (Claussen, 1969) do not support the existence of inter-specific differences or correlation with terrestrial adaptation.

These conflicting findings may be in part due to the use of different techniques, such as ambient conditions in the container, air speed, length of exposure period, or the state of the urinary bladder during the experiment.

The burrowing frogs, *N. centralis* and *N. pictus*, from xeric environments have a high rate of water uptake especially during the first period of 1–4 h, falling off within 24 h (Warburg, 1965a). Similar results with other species of this genus as well as *Cyclorana*, *Notaden* and *Hyla* are given by Main (1968). In the smaller species (*P. bibroni* and *H. ewingi*) the rate of water uptake was low compared with another small form, *C. signifera* which is nevertheless not so terrestrial as *P. bibroni* (Warburg, 1965a).

The rate of water uptake in three desert species (the burrowing toad *Cyclorana* and the two hylids *H. rubella* and *H. caerulea*) followed a similar pattern of high water uptake during the first 2 h. The rate was highest in *Cyclorana* followed by *H. caerulea* and *H. rubella* (Warburg, 1967). These data are compared with water uptake in some Israeli species in Table IV.

McClanahan & Baldwin (1969) found that in *Bufo punctatus* the ventral pelvic integument accounts for 10% of the total surface area and takes up water at a mean rate of 423 mg/cm^2/h, accounting for 70% of the total water uptake. Fair (1970) reported that the rate of water uptake of *B. punctatus* in water was 400 mg/cm^2/h compared with 700 mg/cm^2/h in *B. boreas*, while both had a rate of uptake of 40 mg/cm^2/h in moist soil. Because of its larger surface to volume ratio, *B. punctatus* regained its deficit faster than *B. boreas*.

Response to neurohypophysial extracts

Response in vivo. Steen (1929) showed that anurans do not lose water through urine when on land but reabsorb the urine from the bladder.

It was Brunn (1921) who noted the weight increase in anuran amphibians when in water. This phenomenon, known as the "Brunn" or "Water Balance" effect, was later found also to be correlated with the activity of hypophysial extracts (Heller, 1930). Part of this was due to the antidiuretic response and it was found to be due to increased tubular reabsorption of water (Sawyer, 1957).

On the other hand the rate of water uptake through the skin increased and so did the rate at which water was absorbed from the urinary bladder. The active hormone in the pituitary was found to be arginine vasotocin (Heller & Pickering, 1961). This hormone was known to be active on both skin (Sawyer, 1951) and bladder (Sawyer, 1960). Isolated skin and bladder show an increased rate of water absorption when the serosal side of the membrane is exposed to the neurohypophysial hormone (Bentley, 1958).

Dehydration is known to cause an increase in the rate of water reabsorption from the bladder (Sawyer & Schisgall, 1956), possibly by changing the size of the intercellular spaces in the bladder wall of toads (DiBona & Civan, 1969). A similar effect is caused by neurohypophysial extracts on both bladder wall and skin.

The response of urodeles to these extracts was studied by Bentley & Heller (1964, 1965) and Warburg (1971a). Whereas in *Salamandra*, 100% of the water retained was due to reabsorption from the bladder, in *Bufo marinus* only 50% of the water retained after treatment with oxytocin was reabsorbed from the bladder. Heller & Bentley (1965) and Heller (1965) analysed the three main ways in which the Amphibia respond to neurohypophysial hormones:

1. the frog may respond through the kidney by an antidiuretic response.
2. absorption of water through the epidermis may increase, and
3. reabsorption of water stored in the urinary bladder takes place.

The mechanisms of this response are thought to include:

1. increased permeability of cell membranes to osmotic movement of water in the relevant epithelia in these three organs.
2. Constriction of afferent glomerular arterioles thereby effecting a drop in glomerular filtration rates (Heller & Bentley, 1965).
3. Increase in Na transport across skin and bladder cell membranes (Bentley & Heller, 1964, 1965).

The last two points are of importance in Anura.

Bentley *et al.* (1958) studied the response in several Australian leptodactylids of the genus *Neobatrachus* and *Heleioporus*.

Of the anurans studied by Bentley & Heller (1965), *Hyla hyla* gave a response to vasotocin ten times greater then *Rana esculenta*, *Bufo bufo* and *Pelobates cultripes*. The aquatic anurans *Xenopus* and *Discoglossus* did not respond at all.

In some Israeli anurans the response to oxytocin and vasotocin was found to be different according to the species (Warburg, 1971b). Thus *B. viridis* responded more to vasotocin than to oxytocin (Figs 8 and 9). The response of *H. arborea* was greater in both treatments than of adult *P. syriacus*. However, juveniles of *P. syriacus* showed the highest response found so far among Anurans (Fig. 11), exceeding that of *H. arborea*. This would indicate a change in response to neurohypophysial extracts taking place during the life cycle of the animal. Indeed in tadpoles Howes (1940) did not find any indication of response

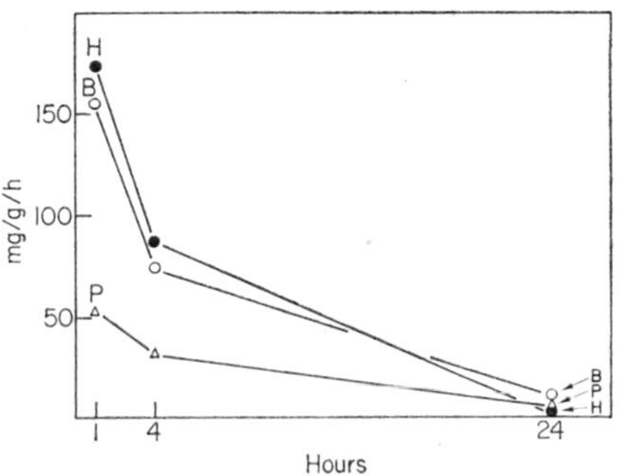

Fig. 8. Response of Israeli anurans to oxytocin *in vivo*. B, *Bufo viridis*; H, *Hyla arborea*; P, *Pelobates syriacus* (adult).

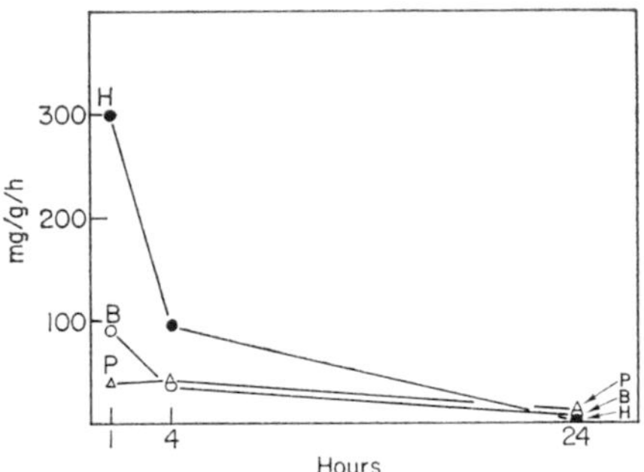

Fig. 9. Response of Israeli anurans to vasotocin *in vivo*. Key as in Fig. 8.

in the toad, *B. bufo*. Similarly, Alvarado & Johnson (1966) studying tadpoles of *R. catesbeiana* found evidence for the action of vasotocin only in older tadpoles. But *H. eyrei* tadpoles at a relatively early stage responded to this treatment (Bentley, 1959), while *P. syriacus* tadpoles did not respond even at a rather late stage. Vasotocin acted only in metamorphosed frogs still with tail stumps (Table V), and similar results were obtained in *Bufo* (Table VI). The response at that stage was much more pronounced than in the adult.

There was a pronounced effect on small juvenile *R. ridibunda* (average body weight 4·4 g) but less in the larger frogs (Fig. 12). Apparently the response did not start immediately upon completion of metamorphosis because the smallest juvenile frogs (averaging 2·5 g), did not show any marked reaction (Fig. 12). In *Hyla* the response increased with the age of the frog (Table VII).

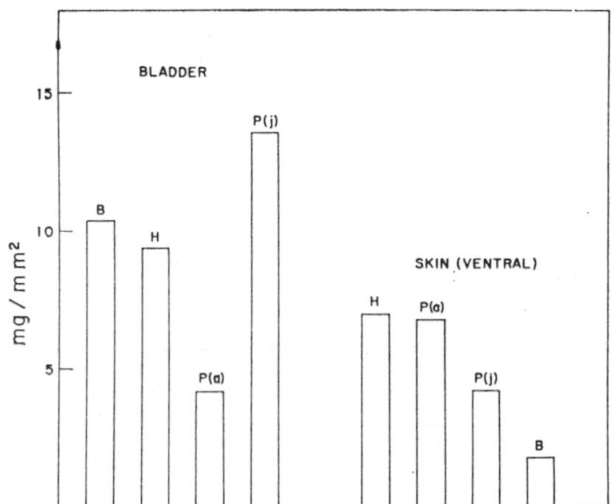

FIG. 10. Response *in vitro* of anurans to oxytocin. Skin and urinary bladder preparations. Key as in Fig. 8.

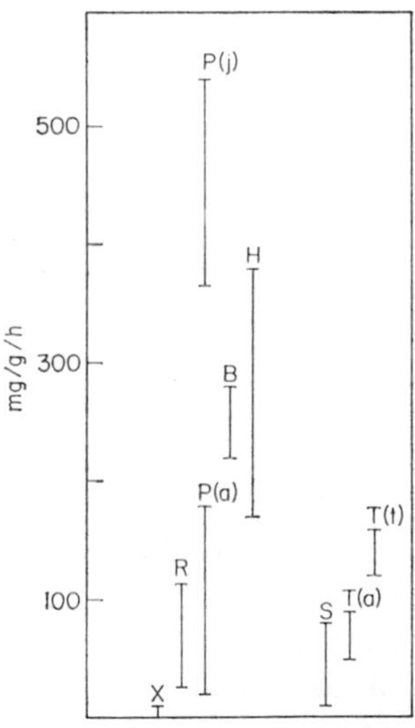

Fig. 11. Summary of responses to oxytocin *in vivo*. X, *Xenopus laevis*; P(a), *Pelobates syriacus* (adult); P(j), *Pelobates syriacus* (juvenile); B, *Bufo viridis*; H, *Hyla arborea*; R, *Rana ridibunda*; S, *Salamandra salamandra*; T(a), *Triturus vittatus* (aquatic phase); T(t), *Triturus vittatus* (terrestrial phase).

Table V

The response of Pelobates syriacus *through tadpole, juvenile and adult stages, to treatment* in vivo *with oxytocin*

Hours	1	4	24
Tadpoles (5–10 g)			
0·05 mμ-mole/g	22·0	11·8	0·8
Control	37·4	23·7	1·4
Juveniles (5–8 g)			
0·05 mμ-mole/g	164·0	44·1	0·2
Control	89·2	8·0	0·2
Adults (25–50 g)			
1·25 mμ-mole/g	52·9	32·4	6·4
Control	12·2	9·0	1·8

Water uptake, mg/g/h.

Table VI

The response of Bufo viridis *to treatment with oxytocin at juvenile and adult stages*

Hours	1	4	24
Juveniles (1–3 g)			
0·05 mμ-mole/g	221·7	191·1	6·0
Control	31·5	25·6	3·7
Adults (17·25 g)			
0·50 mμ-mole/g	121·2	75·2	10·5
Control	124·0	10·7	0·2

Water uptake mg/g/h

Response in vitro. The effect of neurohypophysial hormones was studied also *in vitro* using urinary bladder and isolated skin preparations (Warburg, 1971b). These studies enabled evaluation of the main route of water control. Thus in *B. viridis*, *H. arborea* and juveniles of *P. syriacus* the main response to oxytocin was in the bladder, which increased in capacity for water reabsorption. The adults of *P. syriacus* responded significantly less. On the other hand water passage through the skin of adult *P. syriacus* was greatly enhanced following treatment

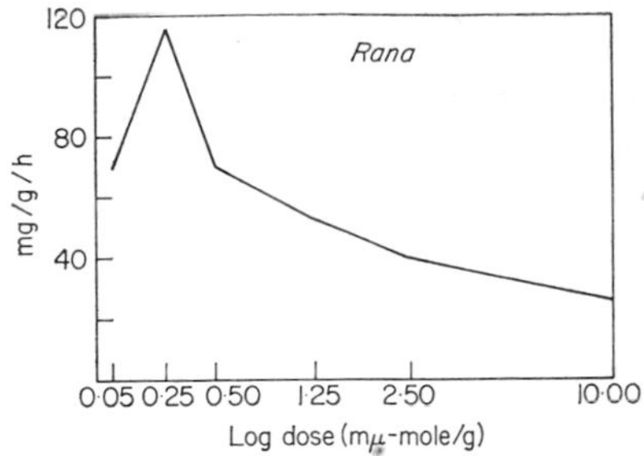

FIG. 12. Ontogeny of response to oxytocin in *Rana ridibunda*.

Average weight	Dose
2·55	0·05 mμ-mole/g
4·43	0·25
12·59	0·50
15·74	1·25
44·34	2·50
123·73	10·00

TABLE VII

The response of Hyla arborea *to treatment with oxytocin at juvenile and adult stages*

Hours	1	4	24
Juveniles (1g)			
0·05 mμ-mole/g	243·7	58·1	1·0
Control	74·4	33·7	1·0
Adults (3–5 g)			
0·25 mμ-mole/g	296·6	87·1	4·1
Control	142·7	11·0	2·3

Water uptake, mg/g/h

and reached the same level as in the skin of *H. arborea*, whereas no response was apparent in *B. viridis* (Fig. 10).

Water conserving mechanisms in urodeles and anurans

From the foregoing discussion it appears that Amphibia evolved different ways to adjust to water shortage. Thus among urodeles from xeric habitats the rate of water loss is low at temperatures up to 30°C. As these newts (*T. vittatus*) are found in the ground during summer they would normally not encounter high temperatures. Furthermore, it can be expected that in their hiding places they would seek, and remain in, the moist subsoil. On the other hand when water becomes available it can be replenished rapidly because of the high rate of water uptake.

The response to neurohypophysial extracts is particularly pronounced in the terrestrial phase of the newt. From the *in vitro* studies it is also evident that these animals can absorb moisture through their skin, as well as reabsorb whatever water is stored in the bladder.

The Anura inhabiting arid or semi-arid regions have evolved mechanisms enabling low evaporative water loss. Another survival mechanism is the rapid replenishment of water through the skin. Both of these were found in most burrowing leptodactylids of the genera *Limnodynastes*, *Neobatrachus* and *Heleioporus*, and in the pelobatid *P. syriacus* as well as in the hylids (*H. arborea*). Some desert hylids (*H. rubella* and *H. caerulea*) also have a high rate of water uptake. Apparently the main mechanism for water conservation is water storage in the bladder particularly in the hylids (*H. arborea*), the pelobatids (*S. couchi*), *P. syriacus* (juveniles) as well as the bufonids (*B. viridis*, *B. cognatus*).

THE THERMAL BALANCE

Body temperature

Mellanby (1941) studied the body temperature of *Rana temporaria* and found that in still air there was a drop of 3·5°C in body temperature which was increased by moving air, according to air speed (300–1900 cm/sec). Body temperature, therefore, dropped as a result of evaporative cooling. The main conclusion was that body temperature of a frog was entirely controlled by external physical conditions and there was no evidence for body temperature regulation. Kirk & Hogben (1946) have shown a correlation between body temperature of a toad and the humidity of the air, because at low humidities the body temperature became lower.

When evaporative cooling was excluded as a factor, the body temperature of a large burrowing frog (*L. dorsalis*) exposed to 37·5°C in humid air, was found to be lower than its skin temperature (Warburg, 1967). There was a time lag of about 20 min between skin and body temperature when the temperature of the skin reached ambient temperature earlier. The small frog, *P. bibroni*, took less time to reach the ambient temperature, and the gradient between skin and body temperature was smaller. As ventilation in the natural microhabitat of amphibians (under rocks, in cracks or underground), is thought to be minimal and evaporation is kept low in these xeric species, it appears that body temperature remains somewhat lower than ambient temperature even when temperatures are high and no evaporative cooling takes place.

Body temperatures of frogs were found to be related to their thermal history. Thus *H. rubella* acclimated to 10°C, had a lower body temperature curve than frogs acclimated to 30°C under the same experimental conditions (Warburg, 1967). The time lag was about 2 h before the frogs acclimated at 10°C reached the same body temperature as those acclimated at 30°C.

Critical thermal maximum (CTM)

This term implies the existence of a high temperature at which activity becomes disorganized but when temperature drops the animal resumes its normal activity.

In Amphibia CTM has been determined in a large number of species. Thus Zweifel (1957), Hutchison (1961) and Selander & West (1969) have described the CTM in urodeles, whereas Brattstrom & Lawrence (1962) and Brattstrom (1963), Heatwole, Mercado & Ortiz (1965) Dunlap (1968) and Mahoney & Hutchison (1969) studied CTM in anurans.

The CTM was found to be directly related to the acclimation temperature of the animals (Table VIII). This was shown first indirectly in animals collected and tested during different seasons of the year (Hutchison, 1961; Schmid, 1965b) and then in the laboratory (Hutchison, 1961; Brattstrom & Lawrence, 1962; Warburg, 1967; Dunlap, 1968). The ability to adjust the lethal temperature (or CTM) by acclimation is found in most amphibians studied so far (Brattstrom, 1963).

TABLE VIII

Critical Thermal Maximum (CTM) in two hylids

Acclimation temperature (°C)	10	30
Hyla arborea	35·8	37·2
Hyla rubella (*)	38·9	40·4

* Data from Warburg (1967).

Animals from different localities have different CTM. This has been shown in *H. rubella* where populations from the Northern Territory had a somewhat higher CTM than those from New South Wales and Western Australia (Warburg, 1967). In anuran species within a limited geographic region the differences in CTM are mostly correlated with altitude rather than latitude (Brattstrom, 1968, 1970). Undoubtedly this thermal adjustment of the CTM in amphibians is related to their thermal history (whether it is seasonal, microclimatic or acclimation temperature). It is one of the main mechanisms helping survival in high temperatures in their habitats.

Survival at high temperatures

This criterion of survival at high temperatures is useful in assessing the degree of adaptation to terrestrial condition. Thus in several Australian anurans survival time at high temperatures was studied in both dry and humid air (Warburg, 1965a). Among the leptodactylids the desert species *N. centralis* survived exposure to dry air at 37·5°C for more than 8 h. The desert hylid, *H. rubella,* survived in dry air at 40°C for more than 8 h. Such temperatures would normally not occur for long periods in their habitats. The other species studied survived exposure to high temperatures better in humid air than in dry air.

To conclude, the main mechanisms evolved in the Amphibia for adapting to high temperatures appear to be their ability to acclimate and adjust the CTM. There is a limited ability to control body temperature depending on both evaporative cooling (Lillywhite, 1970) and the size of the animal (Warburg, 1967).

STRUCTURE AND FUNCTION

The integument

In leptodactylids as in hylids the skin is kept moist, whereas in bufonids the skin is mostly dry. The glands found in the epidermis of the frogs are probably responsible for keeping the skin moist. In *Hyla* Czopek (1955) found 97 glands per mm^2 as compared with only 8 in *Bufo*. The activity of these glands appears to increase with temperature. Another possible source may be the numerous lymphatic sacs capable of storing water; these could be important when the skin dries (Szarski, 1964).

The frog's skin serves as the main organ of respiration (Szarski, 1964). Czopek (1955) has shown that in *Hyla arborea* 70% of respiration takes place through the skin. The skin is kept moist to facilitate better gas exchange. In *H. arborea* which also inhabits dry places Czopek (1955) found the greatest number of skin capillaries (700/mm^2). This indicates the importance of hylid skin for respiration. Furthermore, *H. arborea* was estimated to have the greatest length of capillaries in both skin and lung (46 m/g) as compared with 26 m/g in *Bufo* and 15 m/g in *Pelobates*.

Farquhar & Palade (1964) described the intercellular spaces in the epithelium of *Rana* which form a network in the epidermis. Its function is to facilitate free shifts of K^+ and Na^+ from cell to cell in order to equilibrate their concentrations. The spaces are apparently closed to the exterior.

Taenaka (1963) has shown that the space between the epithelial basal cells increase from 1·2–1·3 μ at 9°C to 1·7–2·7 μ at 22°C. The interesting fact observed by Capraro & Garampi (1956) who found that inflow of water through isolated frog's skin increased with temperature could be related to Taenaka's observation. Other evidence suggests that out of an epidermis 58 μ thick only 21 μ were osmotically active (MacRobbie & Ussing, 1961). Recently Imamura, Takeda & Sasaki (1965) found evidence for accumulation of Na^+ and Ca^{++} in a layer between the papillary and reticular layer in the corium. This layer contains mucopolysaccharides as indicated by histological methods and strongly adsorbs Ca^{++} (Elkan, 1968). In a systematic study of this acellular layer he named it "ground substance" and suggested a correlation between the storage of mucopolysaccharides and Ca^{++} with terrestrial adaptation of the anurans. Through the binding power of Ca^{++}, water can be stored in this layer thereby protecting the Anura against desiccation.

Schmid & Barden (1965) studied permeability of isolated skin bags prepared from hind legs of *Rana septentrionalis*, *Hyla versicolor* and *Bufo hemiophrys*. They found increased permeability of skin in the more terrestrial forms. Thus the skin of *Rana* was less permeable to water (16·5 mg/h/cm^2) than that of *Bufo* (36·6 mg/h/cm^2) and it also contained more lipids. McClanahan & Baldwin (1969) found that the ventral pelvic integument, accounting for 10% of total surface area, takes up water at a rate of 423 mg/cm^2/h, which was 70% of the total water uptake.

The urinary bladder

The capacity of the urinary bladder is greater in arid land species of amphibians. In some Australian leptodactylids (*Notaden*, *Neobatrachus* and *Cyclorana*) the capacity of the bladder was given as 50% of body weight (Main & Bentley, 1964). In some Australian hylids it was only 30% of the body weight. A similar value is given by Ruibal (1962b) for *B. cognatus*, and by McClanahan (1967) for *S. couchi*. In *S. maculosa* bladder capacity was 34% of body weight (Bentley & Heller, 1965), compared to only 2% in *T. cristatus* (Bentley & Heller, 1964). Measurements of bladder capacity in *P. syriacus* were close to 25%, whereas in *T. vittatus* it was about 10% body weight.

Schmid (1969) has shown a remarkable correlation between bladder capacity and terrestrial adaptation in several species of *Rana*. The range was between 9·7% in the aquatic *R. septentrionalis* to 37·7% in *R. cognatus*.

As described earlier the urinary bladder responds to neurohypophysial hormones in both urodeles and anurans (Table IX). Recently there has been some evidence to indicate that the hormone may cause dilation of intercellular spaces of the mucosal epithelium of the bladder (DiBona & Civan, 1969). This does not necessarily imply that the water transport increases through these spaces.

TABLE IX

The main target organs of neurohypophysial hormones involved in water conservation, arranged in order of significance for each species studied

	Skin	Kidney	Bladder
Urodela			
S. salamandra	†	††	†††
T. vittatus (aquatic)	††	††	†††
T. vittatus (terrest.)	†††	†††	†
Anura			
P. syriacus (juv.)	†	†††	†††
P. syriacus (adult)	††	††	†
B. viridis	†	†††	†††
H. arborea	††	†††	††

Summary based on data of studies *in vivo* and *in vitro*.
† = noticeable response; †† = marked response; ††† = strong response.

The kidney

The capacity of frogs to reduce urine flow when in dry conditions was known to Steen (1929). Schmidt-Nielsen & Forster (1954) found that in *Rana clamitans* this was due to reduced filtration rate and increased tubular resorption of water. Even in the aquatic *Xenopus* there was a change in kidney function during dehydration when the animal excreted urea in addition to its normal secretion of ammonia.

Similar results were obtained by Shoemaker (1965) in *B. marinus* when dehydration caused depressed urinary loss. The water loss in *H. eyrei* caused an increase in Na concentration in the plasma and a drop in plasma K (Lee, 1968). In *B. marinus* dilute urine in the bladder helps to maintain the concentration of Na in the plasma at normal levels (Shoemaker, 1964). Dehydrated *S. couchi* upon emergence from aestivation have a high osmotic concentration of 590 m-osmole/litre or 20%, compared with 190 m-osmole/litre or 7% in hydrated spadefoot toads (Mayhew, 1965; McClanahan, 1967).

There are seasonal changes in the level of urea and electrolytes in the plasma of *S. couchi* and *S. hammondi* with a rise during summer and low levels in autumn and spring. The same was found for urea in the urine (Shoemaker, McClanahan & Ruibal, 1969).

S. couchi has a high concentration of body fluids up to 600 m-osmole/litre and urea accounts for approximately half of that concentration. This spadefoot-toad stores nitrogenous wastes and conserves water. It can also store fat (0·13% body wt) and presumably use it as metabolic water source during aestivation.

CONCLUSION

Discussing the adaptation of amphibians to life in deserts, Mayhew (1968) recognized three main categories of adaptations:

1. Behavioural adaptations which include the avoidance of extreme climatic conditions.
2. Physiological adaptations which include mechanisms for water conservation by reducing evaporative and urinary water loss and increasing water uptake through skin and reabsorption from bladder.
3. Tolerance, or the ability to withstand both thermal and osmotic stress.

Further studies are needed in order to clarify behavioural, physiological and anatomical adaptations. It is also essential to know the climatic conditions prevailing in xeric microhabitats. The formation of a cocoon during aestivation in some desert leptodactylids (Lee & Mercer, 1967) and in *S. couchi* (McClanahan, 1967) is probably of great significance. We need to know the real limits of tolerance in each case.

The physiological adaptations include first reducing water loss and increasing the rate of water uptake. Here the main organ involved is the skin. It seems that some urodeles (*T. vittatus*), and several anurans (*S. couchi, P. syriacus, H. arborea*) show a special kind of adaptation involving the skin. More data are needed here to explain the water passage both physiologically and anatomically in these species (rather than concentrating on the aquatic forms of *Rana*). On the other hand the changes in the structure of the skin are not yet sufficiently known.

The second aspect of physiological adaptation involves the storage of water in the urinary bladder, and the capacity to reabsorb the water when dehydrated. Most terrestrial anuran groups have representatives showing this adaptation. It has evolved in several Australian burrowing leptodactylids (*Neobatrachus, Heleioporus, Limnodynastes, Notaden*) some bufonids (*B. cognatus, B. viridis, B. marinus*), pelobatids (*S. couchi* and *P. syriacus*) and to a certain extent the hylids (*H. arborea*). Among the urodeles *S. salamandra* and *T. vittatus* are capable of storing water in the bladder.

The third adaptation involves the kidney. Here most studies are on American desert pelobatids (*S. couchi*) and bufonids (*S. punctatus, B. marinus*), and the leptodactylid *H. eyrei*. All show a remarkable ability to depress urinary loss during dehydration. Concentration of body fluids takes place and urea levels rise in the blood while nitrogenous wastes are stored during aestivation. Recently uric acid has been found in the African Rhacophorid *Chiromantis xerampelina* (Loveridge, 1970). There is some evidence for uric acid also in adult *P. syriacus* during aestivation (M. R. Warburg, unpubl.).

The mechanisms developed in Amphibia to assist survival under dry conditions vary with families, genera and species. Even within a species metamorphosis brings about a shift in the response to water loss or uptake, a shift that probably involves a change in the physiological capacity of some organs (*R. ridibunda, P. syriacus, T. vittatus* aquatic and terrestrial phases).

Survival under arid conditions, involves a series of adaptations, including some dynamic shifts from one type of adaptation to another during the ontogeny of an animal.

References

Alvarado, R. H. & Johnson, S. R. (1965). The effects of arginine vasotocin and oxytocin on sodium and water balance in *Ambystoma*. *Comp. Biochem. Physiol.* **16**: 531–546.

Alvarado, R. H. & Johnson, S. R. (1966). The effects of neurohypophysial hormones on water and sodium balance in larval and adult bullfrogs (*Rana catesbeiana*). *Comp. Biochem. Physiol.* **18**: 549–561.

Bentley, P. J. (1958). The effects of neurohypophysial extracts on water transfer across the wall of the isolated urinary bladder of the toad *Bufo marinus*. *J. Endocr.* **17**: 201–209.

Bentley, P. J. (1959). The effects of neurohypophysial extracts on the tadpole of the frog *Heleioporus eyrei*. *Endocrinology* **64**: 609.

Bentley, P. J. (1966). Adaptations of Amphibia to arid environments. *Science, N.Y.* **152**: 619–623.

Bentley, P. J. & Heller, H. (1964). The action of neurohypophysial hormones on the water and sodium metabolism of urodele amphibians. *J. Physiol., Lond.* **171**: 434–453.

Bentley, P. J. & Heller, H. (1965). The water-retaining action of vasotocin on the fire salamander (*Salamandra maculosa*): the role of the urinary bladder. *J. Physiol., Lond.* **181**: 124–129.

Bentley, P. J., Lee, A. K. & Main, A. R. (1958). Comparison of dehydration and hydration of two genera of frogs (*Heleioporus* and *Neobatrachus*) that live in areas of varying aridity. *J. exp. Biol.* **35**: 677–689.

Brattstrom, B. H. (1963). A preliminary review of the thermal requirements of amphibians. *Ecology* **44**: 238–255.

Brattstrom, B. H. (1968). Thermal acclimation in anuran amphibians as a function of latitude and altitude. *Comp. Biochem. Physiol.* **24**: 93–111.

Brattstrom, B. H. (1970). Thermal acclimation in Australian amphibians. *Comp. Biochem. Physiol.* **35**: 69–103.

Brattstrom, B. H. & Lawrence, P. (1962). The rate of thermal acclimation in anuran amphibians. *Physiol. Zoöl.* **35**: 148–156.

Brunn, F. (1921). Beitrag zur kenntnis der Wirkung von Hypophysenextract auf den Wasserhaushalt des Frosches. *Z. ges. exp. Med.* **25**: 170–175.

Capraro, V. & Garampi, M. L. (1956). Studies on the frog skin. *Mem. Soc. Endocr.* **5**: 60–68.

Claussen, D. L. (1969). Studies on water loss and rehydration in anurans. *Physiol. Zoöl.* **42**: 1–14.

Cloudsley-Thompson, J. L. (1967). Diurnal rhythms, temperature and water relations of the African toad, *Bufo regularis*. *J. Zool., Lond.* **152**: 43–54.

Cohen, N. W. (1952). Comparative rates of dehydration and hydration in some California salamanders. *Ecology* **33**: 462–479.

Czopek, J. (1955). The vascularization of the respiratory surfaces of some salientia. *Zoologica Pol.* **6**: 101–134.

DiBona, D. R. & Civan, M. M. (1969). Toad urinary bladder: Intercellular spaces. *Science, N.Y.* **165**: 503–504.

Dunlap, D. G. (1968). Critical thermal maximum as a function of temperature and acclimation in two species of hylid frogs. *Physiol. Zoöl.* **41**: 432–439.

Elkan, E. (1968). Mucopolysaccharides in the anuran defence against desiccation. *J. Zool., Lond.* **155**: 19–53.

Ewer, R. F. (1951). Water uptake and moulting in *Bufo regularis* Reuss. *J. exp. Biol.* **28**: 369–373.

Ewer, R. F. (1951b). Effect of pitressin and pitocin on water balance in *Bufo regularis* Reuss. *J. exp. Biol.* **28**: 374–404.

Ewer, R. F. (1952). The effect of pituitrin on fluid distribution in *Bufo regularis* Reuss. *J. exp. Biol.* **29**: 173–177.

Fair, J. W. (1970). Comparative rates of rehydration from soil in two species of toads *Bufo boreas* and *Bufo punctatus*. *Comp. Biochem. Physiol.* **34**: 281–287.

Farquhar, M. G. & Palade, G. E. (1964). Functional organization of amphibian skin. *Proc. natn. Acad. Sci. USA.* **51**: 569–577.

Gordon, M. S. (1962). Osmotic regulation in the green toad *Bufo viridis*. *J. exp. Biol.* **39**: 261–270.

Hall, F. G. (1922). The vital limits of exsiccation of certain animals. *Biol. Bull. mar. biol. Lab. Woods Hole* **42**: 52–58.

Heatwole, H. & Lim, K. (1961). Relation of substrate moisture to absorption and loss of water by the salamander, *Plethodon cinereus*. *Ecology* **42**: 814–819.

Heatwole, H., Mercado, N. & Ortiz, E. (1965). Comparison of critical thermal maxima of two species of Puerto Rican frogs of the genus *Eleutherodactylus*. *Physiol. Zoöl.* **38**: 1–8.

Heatwole, H., Torres, F., de Austin, S. B. & Heatwole, A. (1969). Studies on anuran water balance. I. Dynamics of evaporative water loss of the coqui *Eleutherodactylus portoricensis*. *Comp. Biochem. Physiol.* **28**: 245–269.

Heller, J. (1930). Uber die Einwirkung von Hypophysenhinterlappenextrakten auf den Wasserhaushalt des Frosches. *Arch. exp. Path. Pharmak.* **157**: 298–322.

Heller, H. (1965). Osmoregulation in Amphibia. *Archs Anat. microsc. Morph. exp.* **54**: 471–490.

Heller, H. & Bentley, P. J. (1965). Phylogenetic distribution of the effects of neurohypophysial hormones on water and sodium metabolism. *Gen. comp. Endocr.* **5**: 96–108.

Heller, H. & Pickering, B. T. (1961). Neurohypophysial hormones in non-mammalian vertebrates. *J. Physiol., Lond.* **155**: 98–114.

Howes, N. H. (1940). The response of the water-regulating mechanisms of developmental stages of the common toad *Bufo bufo bufo* (L) to treatment with extracts of the posterior lobe of the pituitary body. *J. exp. Biol.* **17**: 128–138.

Hutchison, V. H. (1961). Critical thermal maxima in salamanders. *Physiol. Zoöl.* **34**: 92–125.

Imamura, A., Takeda, H. & Sasaki, N. (1965). The accumulation of sodium and calcium in a specific layer of frog skin. *J. cell. comp. Physiol.* **66**: 221–226.

Jameson, D. L. (1966). Rate of weight loss of tree frogs at various temperatures and humidities. *Ecology* **47**: 605–613.

Jørgensen, C. B. (1950). The amphibian water economy, with special regards to the effect of neurohypophyseal extracts. *Acta physiol. scand.* **22**: 1–79.

Kirk, P. L. & Hogben, L. (1946). Studies on temperature regulation II Amphibians and reptiles. *J. exp. Biol.* **22**: 213–220.

Krakauer, T. (1970). Tolerance limits of the toad, *Bufo marinus* in south Florida. *Comp. Biochem. Physiol.* **33**: 15–26.

Lasiewski, R. C. & Bartholomew, G. A. (1969). Condensation as a mechanism for water gain in nocturnal desert poikilotherms. *Copeia* **1969**: 405–407.

Lee, A. K. (1968). Water economy of the burrowing frog *Heleioporus eyrei* (Gray). *Copeia* **1968**: 741–745.

Lee, A. K. & Mercer, E. H. (1967). Cocoon surrounding desert-dwelling frogs. *Science, N.Y.* **157**: 87–88.

Licht, P. & Brown, A. G. (1967). Behavioural thermoregulation and its role in the ecology of the red-bellied newt *Taricha rivularis*. *Ecology* **48**: 598–611.

Lillywhite, H. B. (1970). Behavioral temperature regulation in the bullfrog *Rana catesbeiana*. *Copeia* **1970**: 158–168.

Littleford, R. A., Keller, W. F. & Phillips, N.E. (1947). Studies on the vital limit of water loss in the plethodont salamanders. *Ecology* **28**: 440–447.

Loveridge, J. P. (1970). Observations on nitrogenous excretion and water relations of *Chiromantis xerampelina* (Amphibia, Anura). *Arnoldia.* **5**: 1–6.

MacRobbie, E. A. C. & Ussing, H. H. (1961). Osmotic behaviour of the epithelial cells of frog skin. *Acta physiol. scand.* **53**: 348–365.

Mahoney, J. J. & Hutchison, V. H. (1969). Photoperiod acclimation and 24-hour variations in the critical thermal maxima of a tropical and temperate frog. *Oecologia* **2**: 143–161.

Main, A. R. (1968). Ecology, systematics and evolution of Australian frogs. *Adv. ecol. Res.* **5**: 37–86.

Main, A. R. & Bentley, P. J. (1964). Water relations of Australian burrowing frogs and tree frogs. *Ecology* **45**: 379–382.

Mayhew, W. W. (1965). Adaptations of the amphibian *Scaphiopus couchi* to desert conditions. *Am. Midl. Nat.* **74**: 95–109.

Mayhew, W. W. (1968). Biology of desert amphibians and reptiles. In *Desert biology* **1**: 195–356. Brown, G. W. (ed.). New York and London: Academic Press.

McClanahan, L. (1964). Osmotic tolerance of the muscles of two desert-inhabiting toads, *Bufo cognatus* and *Scaphiopus couchi*. *Comp. Biochem. Physiol.* **12**: 501–508.

McClanahan, L. (1967). Adaptations of the spadefoot toad, *Scaphiopus couchi*, to desert environments. *Comp. Biochem. Physiol.* **20**: 73–99.

McClanahan, L. & Baldwin, R. (1969). Rate of water uptake through the integument of the desert toad, *Bufo punctatus*. *Comp. Biochem. Physiol.* **28**: 381–389.

Mellanby, K. (1941). The body temperature of the frog. *J. exp. Biol.* **18**: 55–61.

Overton, E. (1904). Neununddreissig Thesen uber die Wasserökonomie der Amphibien und die osmotischen Eigenschaften der Amphibien-haut. *Verh. phys.-med. Ges. Würzb.* **36**: 277–295.

Packer, W. C. (1963). Dehydration, hydration and burrowing behaviour in *Heleioporus eyrei* (Gray) (Leptodactylidae). *Ecology* **44**: 643–651.

Ray, C. (1958). Vital limit and rates of desiccation in salamanders. *Ecology* **39**: 75–83.

Reichling, H. (1958). Transpiration und Vorzugstemperaturen mitteleuropaischer Reptilien und Amphibien, *Zool. Jb.* (Physiol.) **67**: 1–64.

Rey, P. (1937). Recherches experimentales sur l'economie de l'eau chez les Batraciens. I + II *Annls Physiol.* **13**: 1081–1144.

Ruibal, R. (1962a). Osmoregulation in amphibians from heterosaline habitats. *Physiol. Zoöl.* **35**: 133–147.

Ruibal, R. (1962b). The adaptive value of bladder water in the toad *Bufo cognatus*. *Physiol. Zoöl.* **35**: 218–223.

Ruibal, R., Tevis, L. & Roig, V. (1969). The terrestrial ecology of the spadefoot toad *Scaphiophus hammondi*. *Copeia* **1969**: 571–584.

Sawyer, W. H. (1951). Effect of posterior pituitary extracts on permeability of frog skin to water. *Am. J. Physiol.* **164**: 44–48.

Sawyer, W. H. (1957). The antidiuretic action of neurohypophysial hormones in amphibia. In *The neurohypophysis*. Heller, H. (ed.). London: Butterworth.

Sawyer, W. H. (1960). Increases water permeability of the bullfrog *Rana catesbeiana* bladder *in vitro* in response to synthetic oxytocin and arginine vasotocin and to neurohypophysial extracts from non-mammalin vertebrates. *Endocrinology* **66**: 112.

Sawyer, W. H. & Schisgall, R. M. (1956). Increased permeability of the frog bladder to water in response to dehydration and neurohypophysial extracts, *Am. J. Physiol.* **187**: 312–314.

Schmid, W. D. (1965a). Some aspects of the water economies of nine species of amphibians. *Ecology* **46**: 261–269.

Schmid, W. D. (1965b). High temperature tolerances of *Bufo hemiophrys* and *Bufo cognatus*. *Ecology* **46**: 559–560.

Schmid, W. D. (1969). Physiological specialization of amphibians to habitats of varying aridity. pp. 135–142 in Physiological Systems in Semi-Arid Environments. C. C. Hoff & M. L. Riedesel (eds). Albuquerque: University of New Mexico Press.

Schmid, W. D. & Barden, R. E. (1965). Water permeability and lipid content of amphibian skin. *Comp. Biochem. Physiol.* **15**: 423–427.

Schmidt-Nielsen, B. & Forster, R. B. (1954). The effect of dehydration and low temperature on renal function in the bullfrog. *J. cell. comp. Physiol.* **44**: 233–246.

Selander, J. A. & West, B. W. (1969). Critical thermal maxima of some Arkansas salamanders in relation to thermal acclimation. *Herpetology* **25**: 122–124.

Shoemaker, V. H. (1964). The effects of dehydration on electrolyte concentration in a toad *Bufo marinus*. *Comp. Biochem. Physiol.* **13**: 261–271.

Shoemaker, V. H. (1965). The stimulus for the water balance response to dehydration in toads. *Comp. Biochem. Physiol.* **15**: 81–88.

Shoemaker, V. H., McClanahan, L. & Ruibal, R. (1969). Seasonal changes in body fluids in a field population of spadefoot toads. *Copeia* **1969**: 585–591.

Spight, T. M. (1967a). The water economy of salamanders. Exchange of water with the soil. *Biol. Bull. mar. biol. Lab. Woods Hole* **132**: 126–132.

Spight, T. M. (1967b). The water economy of salamanders. Water uptake after dehydration. *Comp. Biochem. Physiol.* **20**: 767–771.

Spight, T. M. (1967c). Evaporation from toads and water surfaces. *Nature, Lond.* **212**: 835–836.

Spight, T. M. (1968). The water economy of salamanders: Evaporative water loss. *Physiol. Zoöl.* **41**: 195–203.

Steen, W. B. (1929). On the permeability of the frog's bladder to water. *Anat. Rec.* **43**: 215–220.

Szarski, H. (1964). The structure of respiratory organs in relation to body size in Amphibia. *Evolution* **18**: 118–126.

Taenaka, S. (1963). Electron microscope studies of the temperature effects on the frog skin. *Int. Congr. Zool.* **16**: (**2**): 57.

Thorson, T. B. (1955). The relationship of water economy to terrestrialism in amphibians. *Ecology* **36**: 100–116.

Thorson, T. B. (1956). Adjustments of water loss in response to desiccation in amphibians. *Copeia* **1956**: 230–237.

Thorson, T. B. & Svihla, A. (1943). Correlation of the habitat of amphibians with their ability to survive loss of body water. *Ecology* **24**: 374–381.

Warburg, M. R. (1964). Observations on microclimate in habitats of some desert vipers in the Negev, Arava and Dead Sea region. *Vie Milieu* **15**: 1017–1041.

Warburg, M. R. (1965a). Studies on the water economy of some Australian frogs. *Aust. J. Zool.* **13**: 317–330.

Warburg, M. R. (1965b). The microclimate in the habitats of two isopod species in southern Arizona. *Am. Midl. Nat.* **73**: 363–375.

Warburg, M. R. (1965c). The evolutionary significance of the ecological niche. *Oikos* **16**: 205–213.

Warburg, M. R. (1965d). Studies on the environmental physiology of some Australian lizards from arid and semi-arid habitats. *Aust. J. Zool.* **13**: 563–575.

Warburg, M. R. (1967). On thermal and water balance of three Central Australian frogs. *Comp. Biochem. Physiol.* **20**: 27–43.

Warburg, M. R. (1971a). The water economy of Israel amphibians: The urodeles *Triturus vittatus* (Jenyns) and *Salamandra salamandra* (L). *Comp. Biochem. Physiol.* **40**A: 1055–1063.

Warburg, M. R. (1971b). The water economy of Israel amphibians: The anurans. *Comp. Biochem. Physiol.* **40**A: 911–924.

Zweifel, R. G. (1957). Studies on the critical thermal maxima in salamanders. *Ecology* **38**: 64–69.

Symp. zool. Soc. Lond. (1972) No. 31, 113–131.

SALT AND WATER EXCRETION IN XEROPHILIC BIRDS

ERIK SKADHAUGE

Institute of Medical Physiology A,
University of Copenhagen, Denmark

SYNOPSIS

This paper deals mainly with recent work on two xerophilic, granivorous birds: the domestic fowl (*Gallus domesticus*) and the budgerygah (*Melopsittacus undulatus*). The regulation of the renal and cloacal salt and water excretion has been studied with particular emphasis on the changes induced by dehydration. The glomerular filtration rate and the renal concentrating ability as measured on ureteral urine was studied, and the effects of arginine-vasotocin was investigated by intravenous infusion in the hydrated fowl. The absorptive segment of the lower intestine into which the ureteral urine is passed is the coprodaeum and large intestine. The transmural salt and water transport of this segment was studied by an *in vivo* perfusion technique developed by the author. Finally the interaction of renal function and post-renal modification of urine in the dehydrated bird was evaluated by an analog computer simulation; and the total water balance for a non-drinking budgerygah which can survive on dry seeds alone was calculated.

INTRODUCTION

This survey deals with two aspects of salt and water excretion in xerophilic, granivorous birds. First the output of salt and water in ureteral urine, second the reabsorption which takes place when the urine moves retrograde into the coprodaeum and large intestine. The emphasis is on the changes in glomerular filtration rate (GFR) and the renal concentrating ability brought about by dehydration and the concomitant changes in the transport parameters of the reabsorptive epithelium of the coprodaeum and large intestine. An analysis of the interaction of renal excretion and post-renal modification with respect to salt and water metabolism is finally attempted.

The survey predominantly covers recent work on the domestic fowl (*Gallus domesticus*) and on the budgerygah (*Melopsittacus undulatus*). The former has the advantage of convenient size, the latter is of particular interest since it is able to live without water, fed dry seeds alone (Cade & Dybas, 1962; Greenwald, Stone & Cade, 1967). The general knowledge of bird physiology is probably not yet sufficient to consider ecological or evolutional adaptation of salt and water metabolism in any detail. Neither have attempts to correlate structure and function of the excretory organs revealed special adaptations in desert birds (see later).

Other types of adaptation to life in arid zones related to water metabolism may however exist. The pulmonocutaneous water loss may be low, a salt gland may be present and activated in the dehydrated state, the birds may have a relative low rate of metabolism, the temperature may increase without evaporative cooling, and the tolerance to dehydration (increase in plasma osmolality and decrease in extracellular fluid volume) may be pronounced. The evaporative water loss has consistently been demonstrated to fall when birds are dehydrated (Cade, 1964; Willoughby, 1968, 1969; McNabb, 1969a) and birds (Greenwald *et al.*, 1967; Cade, Tobin & Gold, 1965; Moldenhauer, 1970) like mammals (Schmidt-Nielsen, Schmidt-Nielsen, Jarnum & Houpt, 1957) seem to avoid evaporative cooling by an increase in body temperature, since they have a high upper critical temperature. The evaporative water loss in general appears to be independent of taxonomic group and habitat (Bartholomew & Cade, 1963; Dawson, 1965). Although the salt gland may be functioning in the dehydrated state (R. D. Ohmart, pers. comm.) most xerophilic birds do not possess this organ. Schmidt-Nielsen, Borut, Lee & Crawford, (1963) have proposed that a cloacal salt and water reabsorption of ureteral urine with subsequent excretion of the salt by the salt gland will leave "free" water in the organism to make up for other water losses. Due to the lack of a salt gland this attractive mechanism will not be operating in most xerophilic birds.

RENAL EXCRETION

Glomerular filtration rate

The GFR has been measured in fairly large species such as the domestic fowl, the turkey (*Meleagris pavo*), and the duck (*Anas platyrrhynchos*) (Dantzler, 1966; Holmes, 1965; Korr, 1939; Skadhauge, 1964; Skadhauge & Schmidt-Nielsen, 1967a; Vogel, Stoeckert, Kroger & Dobberstein, 1965). Independent of the size and the habitat of the bird, values of GFR around 2–3 ml/kg have regularly been observed, and this parameter has proven to be relatively stable. In the author's experiments it fell 23% from the hydrated to the dehydrated state in the domestic fowl (Skadhauge & Schmidt-Nielsen, 1967a) and 37% in the budgerygah (Krag & Skadhauge, 1972) (Table I). The fractional water absorption as demonstrated by the inulin urine/plasma (U/P) ratio was always in the dehydrated state observed to be at least 99%

TABLE I

Average values of renal functions in the domestic fowl and the budgerygah

		Urine Osmolality m-osmole/l	Flow μl/kg min	GFR ml/kg min	% of filtrate reabsorbed %	Osmotic U/P ratio
*Gallus domesticus**	Hydration	115	298	2·12	85·8	0·4
	Dehydration	538	18	1·73	99·0	1·6
Melopsittacus undulatus†	Hydration	236	105	4·43	97·6	0·7
	Dehydration	848	28	3·24	99·1	2·3

* From Skadhauge & Schmidt-Nielsen, 1967a.
† From Krag & Skadhauge, 1972.

of the filtered water in the species of birds studied. This is associated with a limited concentrating ability (osmotic U/P ratio 2 – 3). In the mammal a higher urine osmolality would be necessary in order to reabsorb 99% of the filtered water. This is due to the uricotelism of birds as compared with the ureotelism of mammals. This may in itself be viewed as an important adaptation to arid life. As Homer Smith (1956) has pointed out, the excretion of the 320 mg urea formed from 1 g of protein will require 8 ml in blood osmotic solution whereas the same amount as uric acid or urates will be excreted in less than 1·0–0·5 ml. This is because the uric acid and the urates in birds' urine are present in supersaturated colloid suspension with less than 200–300 mg/litre in solution (Porter, 1963; Katz & Schubert, 1970), thus contributing only a few m-osmoles to the urine osmolality.

Concentrating ability

Ureteral urine has been collected only from the species mentioned above, but in several species, particularly small passerines, the liquid droppings have been collected in the salt-loaded state induced by offering saline solutions as the only drinking water. The osmolality thus obtained can safely be assumed to be close to that of ureteral urine due to the high rate of urine flow. This reduces the possible effect of the cloacal sojourn. The possibility that some of the saline solution may pass through the intestinal tract without coming into osmotic equilibrium with blood exists, but is considered unlikely. In the fowl (Dicker & Haslam, 1966; Skadhauge & Schmidt-Nielsen, 1967a), the turkey (Vogel *et al.*, 1965), the duck (Holmes, 1965), and in two carnivorous birds (Calder & Bentley, 1967) the maximal osmotic U/P ratio was around 2·0, in the budgerygah 3·0 (Krag & Skadhauge, 1972), but in the salt-marsh sparrows studied by Bartholomew and co-workers (Poulson & Bartholomew, 1962a,b; Smyth & Bartholomew, 1966) much higher concentrating ability was found: the U/P ratio was 3·2 in *Passerculus sandwishensis brooksi*, 4·5 in *Amphispiza bilineata* and 5·8 in *P.s. beldingi*.

Poulson (1965) has made the very interesting observation in the Savannah sparrows that the osmotic U/P ratio is linearly related to the number of loops of Henle seen on a unit area of the medulla. It may be inferred from Poulson's findings that a steeper concentration gradient is built-up by adding more loops of Henle per unit cross-section area of papillary tissue. If more collecting ducts were added, simply because a larger number of nephrons were added, this would not make the gradient steeper. Therefore it may be suggested that in the birds which concentrate well, a larger fraction of the nephrons have a loop of Henle.

Observations similar to those of Poulson have recently been made by Johnson & Mugaas (1970a,b) and by McNabb (1969b). The interpretation suggested here should be open to further investigation. No special adaptation with respect to structure and function of the medullary cone has been demonstrated in desert birds including the budgerigar (Johnson & Mugaas, 1970a,b). Related to oxygen uptake the GFR of the budgerigar is small (Krag & Skadhauge, 1972), but it should be noted that the kidney weight of the budgerygah is the same as that of the fowl, 0·7 and 0·6% of body weight respectively (Hughes, 1970). They are, however, both low in the range of all birds investigated, which is 0·6–2·0% (Johnson, 1968).

Although the simultaneous occurrence in birds of loops of Henle and an osmotic U/P ratio larger than unity suggest that hypertonicity may develop in the medullary cone presumably due to the presence of a counter-current multiplier system, this is of course not proven until demonstrated. Skadhauge & Schmidt-Nielsen (1967b) dissected the medullary cones in fowls and turkeys after marking of the medullary cones with lissamine green injected intravenously. It was possible to demonstrate a higher osmolality, and a higher NaCl concentration in the cone than in the cortex. Urea contributed less than 0·5% to the medullary cone osmolality.

Action of arginine-vasotocin

The neurohypophysial hormone, arginine-vasotocin (AVT), has been identified in birds both by bio-assay (Munsick, Sawyer & Van Dyke, 1960) and by chemical identification (Acher, 1963). In the hydrated domestic fowl (Fig. 1) this hormone induces an antidiuresis (Skadhauge, 1964; Skadhauge, 1969a; Ames, Steven & Skadhauge, 1971). By mammalian analogy it seems safe to assume that an important action of AVT is to increase the water permeability of the distal tubules and collecting ducts and thereby induce antidiuresis. It is relevant to ask to what extent the changes brought about by dehydration—antidiuresis and fall in GFR—may be attributed to the action of AVT. Since AVT clearly produces antidiuresis, i.e. decreased urine flow associated with increased urine osmolality without large changes in solute excretion (Skadhauge & Schmidt-Nielsen, 1967a) and since AVT in larger but not unphysiologically high doses (Ames *et al.*, 1971) decreases the GFR, it is reasonable to assume that the changes in renal parameters occurring during dehydration are largely due to AVT. Since the experiments with hydrated birds are necessarily associated with an increased extracellular fluid volume and real dehydration is associated with a decreased extracellular fluid volume, which may be a

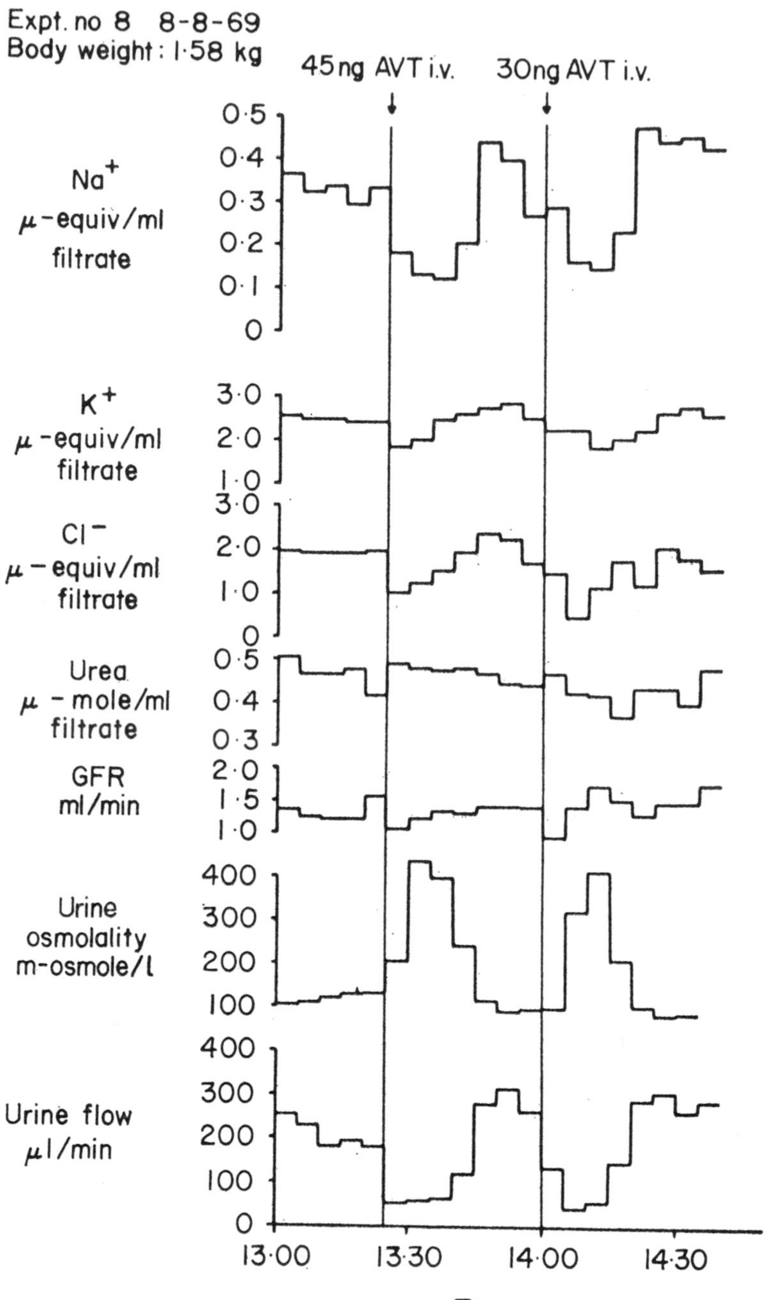

FIG. 1. Effects of intravenous injections of arginine-vasotocin (AVT) into the hydrated domestic fowl. The changes in urinary excretion of Na, K, Cl, and urea, GFR, urine osmolality and flow are recorded. Both GFR and urine flow express excretion from one ureter. A delay of approximately 5 min in rise of urine osmolality is due to the dead space in the collecting funnel sewn over the ureteric orifice. Urine flow and osmolality were recorded by collection from one ureteral funnel, all other parameters were determined on the other ureteral funnel which was rinsed (from Ames *et al.*, 1971).

modifying factor, the emphasis should be placed upon a qualitative similarity between the action of AVT and dehydration rather than on a strict quantitative simulation of the effects of dehydration. In the budgerygah no special adaptation in the neurohypophysial content of antidiuretic material was apparent. This bird was, on a weight basis observed to have the same content as the fowl and the duck (Hirano, 1964).

CLOACAL FUNCTION

Retrograde flow of urine

In recent years several studies have brought attention to the old observation that urine flows back into the coprodaeum and large intestine of birds. Retrograde movement of coloured material instilled in the proctodaeum has been observed as far even as the top of the caeca in the dehydrated fowl (Skadhauge, 1968) and precipitated uric acid has been observed all along the coprodaeum and large intestine also in the budgerygah. Furthermore, the central faeces core reflects the ionic and osmotic composition of the urine as shown in water—or salt-loaded and dehydrated domestic fowls (Skadhauge, 1968). The composition of the central faeces core in the dehydrated domestic fowl is shown in Fig. 2. These observations have been amply confirmed by radiographic investigations (Akester, Anderson, Hill & Osbaldiston, 1967; Nechay, Boyarsky & Catacutan-Labay, 1968; Ohmart, McFarland & Morgan, 1970; Koike & McFarland, 1966).

Since the coprodaeum and large intestine are covered by a single layer epithelium of columnar cells, a reabsorption or secretion of ions may be expected to occur, and a transmural osmotic water flow is likely if the ureteral urine in contact with the epithelium is anisotonic to plasma.

The development of the caecum has been studied in a large number of birds, particularly by Maumus (1902). Since the ureteral urine may flow retrograde into the caecum and fowls with the caeca extirpated have been observed to pass a more watery urine (Röseler, 1929), this organ appears to have a water conserving function in birds. This organ is, however, absent in the budgerygah.

The anatomy of the epithelium of the coprodaeum and large intestine has been studied in a number of birds by Clara (1926). Some birds, particularly the capercailzie (*Tetrao urogallos*), have the reabsorptive area of the epithelium greatly enlarged by the presence of many deep villi which presumably increase the reabsorptive ability, but the

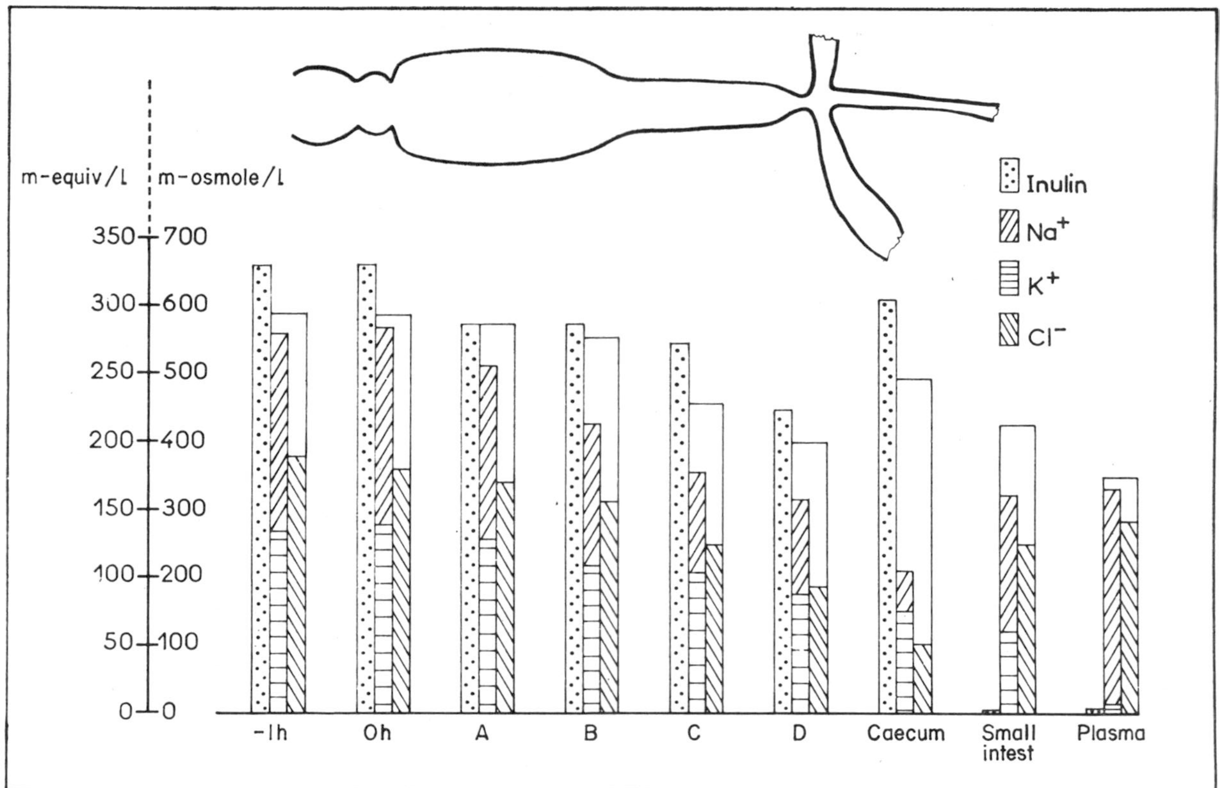

FIG. 2. Composition of the urine-faeces mass in the coprodaeum and large intestine of the dehydrated domestic fowl. The average values of seven roosters are reported. The coprodaeal and large intestinal contents were divided into four fractions (A–D in the figure) and analyses were made on the supernatants after centrifugation. Ureteral urine was collected one hour before (−1 h) and at the termination (0 h) of the experiment. Osmolality of the samples is indicated by the open lines. The inulin concentration remained almost unchanged throughout the coprodaeum and large intestine which

budgerygah has a fairly straight, flat coprodaeal and large intestinal epithelium (E. Skadhauge, unpubl. observ.).

In the following sections of the survey recent investigations into the salt and water flow across the epithelium of the coprodaeum and large intestine of the domestic fowl are considered. This is the only species which has been studied in any detail. A few notes on methods are appropriate. In the older literature there are several estimates of high water reabsorption by the cloaca (Wiener, 1902; Sharpe, 1912; Korr, 1939). But these estimates were based on comparisons between operated birds with the ureters and the cloaca separated, and normal birds. Such comparisons are susceptible to error since the food and water intake in such birds are not normal (Sturkie & Joiner, 1959a,b). Unless careful comparisons on dehydrated birds are made, such studies are not convincing. A more direct approach is to infuse fluids of a composition resembling ureteral urine into the coprodaeum and large intestine where a teflon mass is inserted to simulate the central faeces core (Skadhauge, 1967; Bindslev & Skadhauge, 1971a,b). Such studies can only be carried out on anaesthetized birds, and the normal interaction between urine and faeces is lost. The latter should be no serious objection since the faeces may be viewed simply as an unstirred reservoir of fluid loosely held together by an inert matrix. This may be assumed not to restrict the solute movement, and not to lower the chemical potential of water measurably. Murrish & Schmidt-Nielsen (1970) have in a careful study of lizard urine, determined that only when the water content falls below 45% (w/w) will the matrix potential be measurable. The water content of faeces in dehydrated birds has, however, never been reported to be less than 50% (Cade & Dybas, 1962; Calder, 1964).

SALT ABSORPTION IN THE COPRODAEUM AND LARGE INTESTINE OF THE DOMESTIC FOWL

Sodium absorption

In the author's *in vivo* perfusion studies the Na absorption from NaCl perfusion solutions was observed to be related to the intraluminal Na concentration by saturation kinetics, thus describable by a maximal absorption rate (V_{max}) and a concentration for half maximal flow (K_m). The Na absorption decreased to zero at a zero luminal Na concentration. The absorption was associated with a transmural electric potential difference around 50 mV, lumen negative. Thus the Na absorption is an active, energy-requiring process. Tracer studies revealed a back-flux of isotope of around 40% of the flux in the mucosa to serosa direction. Since the flow in the serosa to mucosa direction was virtually zero when Na was not present in the lumen, this observation is most reasonably explained as an exchange diffusion effect (Levi & Ussing, 1948). The Na absorption was also influenced by the luminal K concentration. The Na absorption was decreased by an intraluminal K concentration higher than 100 m-equiv/1. If the K concentration was lower the Na absorption was associated with a K secretion into the intestinal lumen. The V_{max} for Na was around 280 μ-equiv/kg h and the K_m around 50 m-equiv/1 in dehydrated birds; the V_{max} was unchanged in normally hydrated birds, but the K_m was around 100 m-equiv/1 (Bindslev & Skadhauge, 1971b).

The cloacal Na and K concentrations in the dehydrated domestic fowl are such that the transepithelial K flow is very small, and the Na absorption is operating sufficiently far from the maximal rate for the reduction in the K_m value from the normally hydrated to the dehydrated state to be important for the total Na absorption. This change is responsible for 14% of the 20% increase in fractional water absorption caused by the adaptation of cloacal parameters to the dehydrated state (Skadhauge & Kristensen, 1972). The factor responsible for the change is unknown. Oral Na—loading of the animal suppressed the Na absorption to half the normal value (Skadhauge, 1967), but in a few experiments large doses of AVT did not seem to influence the Na absorption rate. The passive Na mobility and the reflection coefficient of the solutes of plasma—largely NaCl—were zero and unity respectively, both in the normally hydrated and in the dehydrated fowl (Bindslev & Skadhauge, 1971a). Thus NaCl exerts its full osmotic pressure across the cloacal epithelium.

Chloride and potassium flow

Chloride ions were absorbed when NaCl was present in the intestinal lumen, and the absorption rate roughly parallelled that of Na, but at somewhat lower level (Skadhauge, 1967; Bindslev & Skadhauge, 1971b). In some experiments the Cl absorption rate equalled the difference between Na absorption and K secretion (Skadhauge, 1967); in other experiments there was a deficit (Bindslev & Skadhauge, 1971b) which may be accounted for by HCO_3 secretion.

The transepithelial K flow depended upon the luminal K concentration (Skadhauge, 1967), and it seemed to be coupled to the Na flow. If a fairly large Na absorption occurred K was secreted into the lumen, and this secretion was suppressed only by a luminal K concentration of at least 80 m-equiv/1. The K secretion at a luminal K concentration of 40—50 m-equiv/1 was, however, not proportional to the net Na absorption. Independent of the Na absorption, a constant average secretion of 97 m-equiv/kg h was observed (Bindslev & Skadhauge, 1971b). But a complete suppression of Na absorption reversed the K flow which was now absorbed at a rate of 15–50 μ-equiv/kg h. Thus the Na and K flows seemed to be coupled but not in simple stoichiometric proportion.

THE TRANSEPITHELIAL WATER FLOW

The osmotic water flow

The osmotic water flow across the cloacal epithelium of the domestic fowl was measured during *in vivo* perfusion experiments with raffinose as impermeant solute. The water flow was a linear function of the luminal osmolality with a different slope (which expresses the osmotic permeability coefficient) for hypo-osmotic and hyperosmotic perfusion fluids respectively (Bindslev & Skadhauge, 1971a). The osmotic permeability coefficient in the mucosa to serosa direction was significantly larger in dehydrated than in normally hydrated birds. The zero volume flow coincidenced with a zero transepithelial osmolality difference. This indicates that the reflection coefficient is unity (Staverman, 1951; Katchalsky & Curran, 1965).

The solute-linked water flow

The epithelium of the coprodaeum and large intestine of the domestic fowl is able to transport water even against an osmolality difference of 60–80 m-osmole/l (Skadhauge, 1967; Bindslev & Skadhauge, 1971b). This demonstrates that the transmural water flow is influenced by other driving forces than the transmural osmolality difference. Since this water flow is absent when NaCl is not absorbed, both in the present author's experiments as well as on mammalian (Curran, 1960) and fish intestine (Skadhauge & Maetz, 1967; Skadhauge, 1969b) it is a reasonable suggestion that the flow is caused by NaCl flow into a confined region in or between the cells (Curran, 1960). Diamond (1964) has pointed to the lateral intercellular spaces as likely places for this local hypertonicity to develop. At the moment this hypothesis seems the most attractive to account for the apparently non-osmotic water flow against the chemical potential difference for water. In the experiments of Bindslev & Skadhauge (1971b) this water flow was measured as a function of the luminal osmolality. It was described operationally as the difference between the water flow occurring in an experiment with NaCl present in the lumen and an experiment without

NaCl (raffinose perfusion). It was observed to be maximal at plasma osmolality and vanish at luminal osmolalities approximately 200 m-osmole/l higher and lower than plasma osmolality. This does not go against the local hypertonicity hypothesis. More water seemed to be transported as solute-linked water in the dehydrated than in the normally hydrated birds as measured per mole NaCl, but the difference was barely significant. It should be noted that the absorbate at plasma osmolality was hyperosmotic to plasma. This implies that the luminal fluid will be diluted, a phenomenon which was regularly observed in recycling perfusion fluid experiments (Skadhauge, 1967). Since in nature the urine moves retrograde in the narrow space between the cloacal epithelium and the central faeces core the hyperosmotic NaCl resorption will lead to dilution of the fluid; more water will be resorbed than by the solute-linked water flow alone since the general osmotic water flow runs in the same direction. This process is likely to counteract the osmotic water flow into the lumen which presumably occurs in the lower end of the coprodaeum in which the urine moving retrograde is hyperosmotic to plasma. The integrated effect of these flows is explored in an analog computer simulation presented below.

THE EFFECTS OF POST-RENAL MODIFICATION OF URINE IN THE DOMESTIC FOWL

Water and salt loading

Due to the large urine flow in these osmotic situations the cloacal sojourn of ureteral urine will *a priori* be expected to be of minor importance. These conditions are physiological even for xerophilic birds. The ability to excrete an excess water load will be of importance when succulent leaves are ingested, and in some desert regions only salt ponds are occasionally available as sources of drinking water. A calculation of the influence of cloacal sojourn of ureteral urine taking the osmotic composition of the cloacal content in the water- or salt-loaded state into account (Skadhauge, 1968) has demonstrated that only a few per cent of the ureteral water during water-loading and of the ureteral NaCl during salt-loading will be reabsorbed (Skadhauge, 1967).

Dehydration

Retrograde flow in the dehydrated state was simulated by an analog computer model (Skadhauge & Kristensen, 1972). This was fairly realistic since it, with the numerical values of the system parameters as determined by the author, correctly predicted the result of *in vivo* perfusion experiments from a flow rate and composition of the perfusion fluid as the urine in the dehydrated bird. The result of the model simulation was that the fractional water reabsorption in the cloaca was most sensitive to the urine osmolality, moderately sensitive to the urine flow and the Na absorption rate, and virtually unaffected by the osmotic permeability coefficients. The effect of increasing or decreasing these values by 10% from those of the dehydrated fowl is presented in Table II. The total effect of the changes of the cloacal transport parameters from hydration to dehydration made the fractional water

TABLE II

Change in fractional water absorption in the corpodaeum and large intestine of the dehydrated domestic fowl caused by a 10% change of the following parameters

Urine osmolality		16%
Urine flow	approx.	5%
Maximal Na absorption rate		3·7%
Na concentration at half-max Na flow		1·8%
Solute-linked water flow		0·8%
Osmotic permeability coefficients	approx.	0·3%

From Skadhauge & Kristensen, 1972.

reabsorption change from −6 to +14%. Of these 20%, the 14% were due to changing K_m for Na, 5% due to larger solute-linked water flow, and only 1% due to augmented osmotic water permeability coefficients. Thus a minor fraction of ureteral urine is reabsorbed in spite of the urine being 200 m-osmole/l higher than the osmolality of plasma. The water reabsorption, calculated to be 140 μl/g h in the dehydrated bird was, however, limited compared to the salt absorption (117 μ-mole/kg h). Thus the absorbate is strongly hyperosmotic to plasma. The reabsorption in the cloaca will therefore aid in conserving volume by all means but at the expense of a rising plasma osmolality. Since birds seem to tolerate this quite well, the cloacal sojourn of ureteral urine may be of value for the dehydrated bird. The fact that the fractional water absorption is more sensitive to changes in urine osmolality than urine flow leads to a total volume output which is slightly smaller for a lower urine osmolality and a correspondingly higher urine flow, which keeps the ureteral solute output constant. If, however, the slight fall in GFR during dehydration is taken into account the net result is a falling total water loss when the osmolality of ureteral urine increases (Skadhauge & Kristensen, 1972). Thus the sum of events occurring during dehydration seems to be advantageous for water conservation.

THE WATER BALANCE OF THE DEHYDRATED BUDGERYGAH

In the experiments of Krag & Skadhauge, 1972 it was confirmed that budgerygahs may live without drinking water at an ambient relative humidity of 30–40% and at a temperature of 22–24°C. They sustained a weight loss of approximately 10% while increasing the food intake slightly. The water budget of a non-drinking budgerygah was tentatively calculated on the basis of the water intake and water loss (Table III). The water intake came from two sources: the water preformed in food, and the water of oxidation. The latter was calculated on the basis of a measurement of the protein, fat, and carbohydrate content and utilization of the grains eaten by the birds. The water loss was calculated as evaporative and ureteral output. It will appear from the table that this budget seems just to balance. It is reasonable to believe that the estimate of the water loss is minimal. The rate of evaporation was estimated from the six lowest measurements by Cade & Dybas (1962). This is half the value measured by Greenwald *et al.* (1967) on resting, normally hydrated budgerygahs, but Cade (1964) and others (Willoughby, 1968, 1969 and McNabb, 1969a) have observed that dehydration reduces the evaporative water loss to 50%. The ureteral urine flow was based on the six lowest values measured by Krag & Skadhauge (1972). Although this measurement was carried out on anaesthetized birds the concentrating ability seemed to be unaffected since the same maximal urine osmolality, around 1100 m-osmole/l, as in droppings of dehydrated conscious budgerygahs was observed.

The result of the calculation is that the budgerygah may stay in water balance without access to drinking water only if the cloacal sojourn of ureteral urine results in a fractional water absorption just as large as the final faeces water output. Since the cloacal transport parameters of the budgerygah have not been measured the model of Skadhauge & Kristensen (1972) was tentatively applied to the budgerygah assuming the same cloacal transport parameters as in the domestic fowl on a weight basis (Krag & Skadhauge, 1972). The result was that the majority of the urinary solutes would have to be NaCl (or other solutes presumed to be absorbed cloacally) which were reabsorbed in order that one quarter of the urinary water be absorbed. Since the urine contains very little Na, it is likely that the model falls far short of describing the events occurring in the budgerygah correctly. Even if NaCl is delivered to the coprodaeum with the faeces in plasma iso-osmotic solution and quantitatively mixed with ureteral urine an

TABLE III

*Calculation of daily water budget of a non-drinking 30 g budgerygah**

						g/24 h
Food consumption: 16·3% of the body weight						4·9
Water gained:						
Preformed water:						
Water content of food: 10·7%						
10·7% of 4·9 g						0·52
Metabolic water:						
	Protein	Fat	Carbohydrates			
Food composition	14·1%	5·5%	60·5%			
Utilization	75%	80%	100%			
g digested	0·52	0·22	2·97			
g water produced /g food component oxidized	0·50	1·18	0·60			
g water produced	0·26	0·26	1·78		Total	2·30
Total water gain:						2·82
Ml O_2/g food	0·950	2·019	0·828			
Ml O_2 consumed	0·494	0·444	2·459	Total 3·40		
Water lost:						
Evaporation						1·86†
Ureteral urine flow: 21 nl/g min						0·91
Total water loss:						2·77
Water balance:						+0·05

* Data from Krag & Skadhauge (1972).
† Data on evaporation from Cade & Dybas (1962)
Evaporation related to O_2 uptake: 0·55 mg H_2O/ml O_2

almost quantitative NaCl reabsorption can not drag enough water across the cloacal epithelium to let the bird stay in water balance. It is already clear that the combined resorption of Na from faeces and urine must be almost complete, since the grains ingested by the budgerygah contain very little Na. The conclusion of the calculations is that the ability of the budgerygah to withstand dehydration is with our present knowledge not well understood and direct investigation of the cloacal resorption is necessary.

SUMMARY

The GFR is in the domestic fowl and the budgerygah as large as in mammals—around 2–3 ml/kg min, but it is reduced from the hydrated to the moderately dehydrated state, by 23% in the fowl, and by 37% in the budgerygah. At least 99% of filtered water is reabsorbed in the tubules in the dehydrated state in both species. The maximal urine osmolality is around 600 m-osmole/l in the fowl and 1100 m-osmole/l in the budgerygah. The medullary cones of the kidney were found to be hyperosmotic to plasma in the fowl. This suggests a countercurrent multiplier system. Arginine-vasotocin was observed to induce anti-diuresis, involving decrease in urine flow, increase in urine osmolality, and decrease of GFR. This action is similar to the renal response to dehydration which thus may be caused largely by release of this hormone.

The transport parameters of the coprodaeum and large intestine were studied in the domestic fowl. The osmotic permeability coefficient was larger in the mucosa to serosa direction than in the opposite direction. The passive Na mobility of the epithelium was zero, and the reflection coefficient to the solutes of plasma, largely NaCl, was unity. Sodium chloride absorption was dependent upon the luminal Na concentration as describable by saturation kinetics. The V_{max} was around 280 μ-equiv/kg h both in normally hydrated and dehydrated fowls, whereas the K_m concentration was around 50 m-equiv/1 in the dehydrated fowl, 100 m-equiv/1 in the hydrated fowl. A moderate K secretion was observed. Luminal fluids of an osmolality up to 70 m-osmole/l higher than plasma could be absorbed presumably due to solute-linked water flow.

Perfusions of the coprodaeum and large intestine at low flow rate of a fluid similar in composition to ureteral urine and a computer calculation based on the measured cloacal transport parameters, both showed that the hyperosmotic urine formed during dehydration may enter the absorptive segment without leading to a water loss. A minor fraction (14%) may even be absorbed but at the expense of a hyperosmotic NaCl absorption.

In the dehydrated budgerygah the preformed water of the food and the water of oxidation just balanced the evaporative and ureteral urine water loss. Thus the budgerygah can remain in water balance only if cloacal resorption of ureteral urine is equal to the faeces water loss.

Acknowledgements

The collaboration of Drs E. Ames, N. Bindslev, B. Krag and K. Kristensen is gratefully acknowledged. The work was supported by the Danish Medical Research Council and NOVO'S Fond.

References

Acher, R. (1963). The comparative chemistry of neurohypophysial hormones. *Symp. zool. Soc. Lond.* No. 9: 83–91.

Akester, A. R., Anderson, R. S. Hill, K. J. & Osbaldiston, G. W. (1967). A radiographic study of urine flow in the domestic fowl. *Br. Poultry Sci.* **8**: 209–212.

Ames, E., Steven, K. & Skadhauge, E. (1971). Effects of arginine vasotocin on renal excretion of Na^+, K^+, Cl^-, and urea in the hydrated chicken. *Am. J. Physiol.* **221**: 1223–1228.

Bartholomew, G. A. & Cade, T. J. (1963). The water economy of land birds. *Auk* **80**: 504–539.

Bindslev, N. & Skadhauge, E. (1971a). Salt and water permeability of the coprodeum and large intestine in the normal and dehydrated fowl (*Gallus domesticus*). *In vivo* perfusion studies. *J. Physiol., Lond.* **216**: 735–751.

Bindslev, N. & Skadhauge, E. (1971b). Sodium chloride absorption and solute-linked water flow across the epithelium of the coprodeum and large intestine in the normal and dehydrated fowl (*Gallus domesticus*). *In vivo* perfusion studies. *J. Physiol., Lond.* **216**: 753–768.

Cade, T. J. (1964). Water and salt balance in granivorous birds. In *Thirst*: 237–256. Wayner, M. J. (ed.). Oxford: Pergamon Press.

Cade, T. J. & Dybas, J. A. (1962). Water economy of the budgerygah. *Auk* **79**: 345–364.

Cade, T. J., Tobin, C. A. & Gold, A. (1965). Water economy and metabolism of two estrildine finches. *Physiol. Zoöl.* **38**: 9–33.

Calder, W. A. (1964). Gaseous metabolism and water relations of the zebra finch, *Taeniophygia castanotis*. *Physiol. Zoöl.* **37**: 400–413.

Calder, W. A. & Bentley, P. J. (1967). Urine concentrations of two carnivorous birds, the white pelican and the road runner. *Comp. Biochem. Physiol.* **22**: 607–609.

Clara, M. (1926). Beiträge zur Kenntnis des Vogeldarmes. I. Teil. Mikroskopische Anatomie. *Z. mikr.-anat. Forsch.* **4**: 346–416.

Curran, P. F. (1960). Na, Cl, and water transport by rat ileum *in vitro*. *J. gen. Physiol.* **43**: 1137–1148.

Dantzler, W. H. (1966). Renal response of chickens to infusion of hyperosmotic sodium chloride solution. *Am. J. Physiol.* **210**: 640–646.

Dawson, W. R. (1965). Evaporative water losses of some Australian parrots. *Auk* **82**: 106–108.

Dicker, S. E. & Haslam, J. (1966). Water diuresis in the domestic fowl. *J. Physiol., Lond.* **183**: 225–235.

Diamond, J. M. (1964). The mechanism of isotonic water transport. *J. gen. Physiol.* **48**: 15–42.

Greenwald, L., Stone, W. B. & Cade, T. J. (1967). Physiological adjustments of the budgerygah (*Melopsittacus undulatus*) to dehydrating conditions. *Comp. Biochem. Physiol.* **22**: 91–100.

Hirano, T. (1964). Further studies on the neurohypophysial hormones in the avian median eminence. *Endocr. jap.* **11**: 87–95.

Holmes, W. N. (1965). Some aspects of osmoregulation in reptiles and birds. *Arch. Anat. micr. Morph. exp.* **54**: 491–514.

Hughes, M. R. (1970). Relative kidney size in nonpasserine birds with functional salt glands. *Condor* **72**: 164–168.

Johnson, O. W. (1968). Some morphological features of avian kidneys. *Auk* **85**: 216–228.

Johnson, O. W. & Mugaas, J. N. (1970a). Quantitative and organizational features of the avian renal medulla. *Condor* **72**: 288–292.

Johnson, O. W. & Mugaas, J. N. (1970b). Some histological features of avian kidneys. *Am. J. Anat.* **127**: 423–436.

Katchalsky, A. & Curran, P. F. (1965). *Nonequilibrium thermodynamics in biophysics*. Cambridge: Harvard University Press.

Katz, W. A. & Schubert, M. (1970). The interaction of monosodium urate with connective tissue components. *J. Clin. Invest.* **49**: 1783–1789.

Koike, T. I. & McFarland, L. Z. (1966). Urography in the unanesthetized hydropenic chicken. *Am. J. vet. Res.* **27**: 1130–1132.

Korr, I. M., (1939). The osmotic function of the chicken kidney. *J. cell. comp. Physiol.* **13**: 175–194.

Krag, B. & Skadhauge, E. (1972). Renal salt and water excretion in the budgerygah (*Melopsittacus undulatus*). *Comp. Biochem. Physiol.* **41**A: 667–683.

Levi, H. & Ussing, H. H. (1948). The exchange of sodium and chloride ions across the fiber membrane of the isolated frog sartorius. *Acta physiol. scand.* **16**: 232–249.

Maumus, J. (1902). Les cæcums des oiseaux. *Ann. sci. Nat.* (Zool.) **15**: 1–148.

McNabb, F. M. A. (1969a). A comparative study of water balance in three species of quail. I. Water turnover in the absence of temperature stress. *Comp. Biochem. Physiol.* **28**: 1045–1058.

McNabb, F. M. A. (1969b). A comparative study of water balance in three species of quail. II. Utilization of saline drinking solutions. *Comp. Biochem. Physiol.* **28**: 1059–1074.

Moldenhauer, R. R. (1970). The effects of temperature on the metabolic rate and evaporative water loss of the sage sparrow *Amphispiza belli nevadensis*. *Comp. Biochem. Physiol.* **36**: 579–587.

Munsick, R. A., Sawyer, W. H. & Van Dyke, H. B. (1960). Avian neurohypophysial hormones: Pharmacological properties and relative identification. *Endocrinology* **66**: 860–871.

Murrish, D. E. & Schmidt-Nielsen, K. (1970). Water transport in the cloaca of lizards: active or passive? *Science, N.Y.* **170**: 324–326.

Nechay, B. R., Boyarsky, S. & Catacutan-Labay, P. (1968). Rapid migration of urine into the intestine of chickens. *Comp. Biochem. Physiol.* **26**: 369–370.

Ohmart, R. D., McFarland, L. Z. & Morgan, J. P. (1970). Urographic evidence that urine enters the rectum and ceca of the roadrunner (*Geococcyx californianus*) (Aves). *Comp. Biochem. Physiol.* **35**: 487–489.

Porter, P. (1963). Physico-chemical factors involved in urate calculus formation. I. Solubility. *Res. vet. Sci.* **4**: 580–591.

Poulson, T. L. (1965). Countercurrent multipliers in avian kidneys. *Science, N.Y.* **148**: 389–391.

Poulson, T. L. & Bartholomew, G. A. (1962a). Salt balance in the savannah sparrow. *Physiol. Zoöl.* **35**: 109–119.

Poulson, T. L. & Bartholomew, G. A. (1962b). Salt utilization in the house finch. *Condor* **64**: 245–252.

Röseler, M. (1929). Die Bedeutung der Blinddärme des Haushuhnes für die Resorption der Nahring und Verdauring der Rohfaser. *Z. Tiersücht. Zücht-Biol.* **13**: 281–310.

Schmidt-Nielsen, K., Schmidt-Nielsen, B., Jarnum, S. A. & Houpt, T. R. (1957). Body temperature and its relation to water economy. *Am. J. Physiol.* **188**: 103–112.

Schmidt-Nielsen, K., Borut, A., Lee, P. & Crawford, E. (1963). Nasal salt excretion and the possible function of the cloaca in water conservation. *Science, N.Y.* **142**: 1300–1301.

Sharpe, N. C. (1912). On the secretion of urine in birds. *Am. J. Physiol.* **31**: 75–84.

Skadhauge, E. (1964). Effects of unilateral infusion of arginine-vasotocin into the portal circulation of the avian kidney. *Acta endocr., Copenh.* **47**: 321–330.

Skadhauge, E. (1967). *In vivo* perfusion studies of the cloacal water and electrolyte resorption in the fowl (*Gallus domesticus*). *Comp. Biochem. Physiol.* **23**: 483–501.

Skadhauge, E. (1968). The cloacal storage of urine in the rooster. *Comp. Biochem. Physiol.* **24**: 7–18.

Skadhauge, E. (1969a). Activités biologiques des hormones neurohypophysaires chez les oiseaux et les reptiles. In *La Spécificité Zoologique des Hormones Hypophysaires et de leurs Activités*: 63–68, Fontaine, M. (ed.). Paris: Centre National de la Recherche Scientifique.

Skadhauge, E. (1969b). The mechanism of salt and water absorption in the intestine of the eel (*Anguilla anguilla*) adapted to waters of various salinities. *J. Physiol., Lond.* **204**: 135–158.

Skadhauge, E. & Kristensen, K. (1972). An analogue computer simulation of cloacal resorption of salt and water from ureteral urine in birds. *J. theoret. Biol.* **35**.

Skadhauge, E. & Maetz, J. (1967). Étude *in vivo* de l'absorption intestinale d'eau et d'electrolytes chez *Anguilla anguilla* adapté à des milieux de salitités diverses. *C. R. hebd. Séanc. Acad. Sci., Paris* **265**: 347–350.

Skadhauge, E. & Schmidt-Nielsen, B. (1967a). Renal function in domestic fowl. *Am. J. Physiol.* **212**: 793–798.

Skadhauge, E. & Schmidt-Nielsen, B. (1967b). Renal medullary electrolyte and urea gradient in chickens and turkeys. *Am. J. Physiol.* **212**: 1313–1318.

Smith, Homer W. (1956). *From fish to philosopher*. Boston: Little, Brown & Company.

Smyth, M. & Bartholomew, G. A. (1966). The water economy of the black-throated sparrow and the rock wren. *Condor* **68**: 447–458.

Staverman, A. (1951). The theory of measurement of osmotic pressure. *Rev. trav. chim. Pays-Bas* **70**: 344–352.

Sturkie, P. D. & Joiner, W. P. (1959a). Effect of foreign bodies in cloaca and rectum of the chicken on feed consumption. *Am. J. Physiol.* **197**: 1337–1339.

Sturkie, P. D. & Joiner, W. P. (1959b). Effect of cloacal cannulation on feed and water consumption in chickens. *Poultry Sci.* **38**: 30–32.

Vogel, G. I., Stoeckert, I., Kröger, W. & Dobberstein, I. (1965). Harn und Harnbereitung bei terrestrich lebenden Völgeln. Untersuchungen am Truthuhn (*Meleagris pavo* L.). *Zentbl. vet. Med.* **12**: 132–160.

Wiener, H. (1902). Über synthetische Bildung der Harnsäure im Tierkörper. *Beitr. chem. Physiol. Path.* **2**: 42–85.

Willoughby, E. J. (1968). Water economy of the Stark's lark and the grey-backed finch-lark from the Namib desert of South West Africa. *Comp. Biochem. Physiol.* **27**: 723–745.

Willoughby, E. J. (1969). Evaporative water loss of a small xerophilous finch, *Lonchura malabarica*. *Comp. Biochem. Physiol.* **28**: 655–664.

Symp. zool. Soc. Lond. (1972) No. 31, 133–146.

THERMOREGULATION IN AUSTRALIAN DESERT KANGAROOS

TERENCE J. DAWSON

School of Zoology, University of New South Wales, Kensington, New South Wales, Australia

SYNOPSIS

Two species of large kangaroo, the Red kangaroo *Megaleia rufa* (Desmarest) and the Euro *Macropus robustus* (Gould) inhabit the arid interior of Australia. Their thermoregulatory abilities have been investigated to see how the large kangaroos, as marsupials, deal with the problems of hot deserts. The two species also have been examined from a comparative point of view since they appear to approach these problems in fundamentally different ways. The Red kangaroo is an animal of the open plain while the Euro lives around rocky hill country and makes use of small caves as heat refuges.

A study of the heat balance showed that both species had basal metabolic rates considerably below that predicted for eutherians of similar size. The low metabolism, which is characteristic for marsupials, results in a low water requirement for temperature regulation. The body temperatures in the thermoneutral range were approximately 35·5°C. There was some elevation of body temperature at high ambient temperatures but this was not large, 37·7°C at an air temperature of 45°C. The major avenue of evaporative heat loss at these high temperatures was by panting.

The differences between the species are obvious in two areas. The Red kangaroo, which normally is exposed to considerable solar radiation, has fur which is almost twice as reflective as that of the Euro. The fur of the Red kangaroo also has characteristics which prevent the penetration of solar radiation deep into the fur.

The second major difference between the Red kangaroo and the Euro was in the respiratory response to high temperature. Red kangaroos, at all temperatures between 35°C and 45°C, had panting rates much below those of the Euro. This difference may reflect a difference in tidal volumes between the species. A larger panting tidal volume in the Red kangaroo would give greater scope for evaporative water loss before maximum panting rates were reached.

A marked increase in sweating in response to high environmental heat loads was not observed. Sweating was observed to occur in response to an exercise heat load particularly in the Red kangaroo.

INTRODUCTION

The Red kangaroo, *Megaleia rufa* (Desmarest) and the Euro *Macropus robustus* (Gould) are the large kangaroos which inhabit the arid areas of Australia. Apart from being interesting to thermoregulatory physiologists as marsupials that live in the desert, (marsupials until recently being considered as inefficient homeotherms), these two species of kangaroo are of particular interest from a comparative point of view, since they appear to approach the problems of the hot arid environment in fundamentally different ways.

The Red kangaroo is widely distributed over the whole of the interior of Australia, being found on the open plains or in shrub steppe. The Euro is also widely distributed, but generally occurs in association with rocky hill country. In some areas, where the habitat is suitable, they may live in close proximity to each other. When this occurs, however, the two species spend hot summer days resting or "lying up" in entirely different microenvironments. The Red kangaroo is found in the sparse shade of small desert trees in relatively open country, while the Euro can be observed around rocky outcrops in caves and under rock ledges.

Bioclimatological studies by Dawson & Denny (1969) on the microhabitats of the two species of kangaroo have shown that the Euro actually avoids much of the heat load of the desert, particularly the radiation heat load. However, this was not the case with the Red kangaroo. While the small trees under which the Red kangaroos sheltered screened out about 80% of the solar radiation influx, the radiation temperature of this microenvironment still exceeded the animal's body temperature by as much as 30°C when air temperature also exceeded the normal body temperature. It is obvious then that the Red kangaroo is normally faced with a much higher heat load than the Euro. Two questions therefore arise;

1. what are the thermoregulatory responses which the Red kangaroo uses to cope with this high thermal stress; and

2. are there any differences between the two desert kangaroos in thermoregulatory ability?

To help answer these questions studies on the heat balance of these species have been carried out over a wide range of environmental temperatures.

An important aspect of thermoregulation under desert conditions which is often overlooked is the prevention of the flow of heat into the animal from the outside environment. The fur is involved in this role. The usually accepted function of fur is the reduction of the rate of heat loss from the animal when the environment is cold (Scholander *et al.*, 1950a,b,c). In desert environments the fur has the additional functions of (a) reflecting solar radiation and (b) insulating the body of the animal against radiation that is absorbed and converted to heat at or near the surface of the fur. These functional aspects of the thermal properties of kangaroo coats have been examined in collaboration with G. D. Brown (Dawson & Brown, 1970).

MATERIALS AND METHODS

Animals

The Red kangaroos used were animals which had been bred in captivity or hand-reared, the hand-reared young being initially obtained from the far west of New South Wales. The Euros were mostly captured as adults and came from the same area as the young Red kangaroos. The usual weights for mature specimens of these two species are approximately 60 kg ♂, 25 kg ♀ for Red kangaroos and 45 kg ♂, 22 kg ♀ for the Euros. The approximate mean weights of the animals in the current experiments were, Red kangaroos 24·4 kg and Euros 29·3 kg. Both species were fed a diet of lucerne hay and commercial sheep pellets.

Heat balance studies

The heat balance measurements on the two species in summer fur were carried out in a large climate room, the temperature of which could be controlled to ±0·5°C. Temperatures were measured continuously with copper constantan thermocouples and a Honeywell Electronik 15 recording potentiometer. Body temperature was measured as deep colonic temperature, the thermocouples being inserted to a depth of 20 cm.

Oxygen consumption (heat production) and total evaporative water loss were estimated using an open circuit technique, which was essentially similar to the technique used by Dawson, Denny & Hulbert (1969). The animals were fasted for 24–36 h prior to measurement. The kangaroos were placed in a steel mesh cage small enough to prevent them from turning around. This was then positioned inside a large rectangular sheet metal container (152 × 46 × 76 cm) with an air tight lid. The container had large Perspex windows to allow observation of the animal. Inlet and outlet connections were placed at opposite ends of the chamber and the thermocouple leads and the tube attached to the pneumograph were run through a rubber stopper and sealed with rubber cement. Dry air flowed through the chamber at a constant rate, between 70–180 l/min, and was measured with a calibrated gas meter.

Oxygen consumption was measured using a Beckman Model F3M3 paramagnetic oxygen analyser and water loss was continuously monitored using two Hygrodynamics hygrometer indicators, Model 15–3001, and appropriate wide range Hygrosensors. The vapour pressure of the air leaving the chamber was kept below 12 mm Hg at all temperatures. Heat production was calculated assuming a respiratory quotient of 0·8. Brody (1945) gives a conversion factor of 4·8 cal/ml O_2 for this respiratory quotient value. Evaporative water loss was expressed in cal/g h, assuming a conversion factor of 0·58 cal/mg H_2O. Total body insulation (core to environment) was calculated using the equation:

$$\text{Total insulation} = \frac{(T_{\text{body}} - T_{\text{air}}) \times \text{Surface area}}{\text{Heat production} - \text{Evaporation}}$$

Experiments to measure maximum total body insulation were carried out at 3°C.

The respiration rate was measured with a Gilson polygraph Model M5P and Sanborn Model P23BB pressure transducer attached via 2 mm tubing to a small pneumograph taped to the thorax of the kangaroos.

The kangaroos were allowed to come to equilibrium at each air temperature. This was judged to have taken place when the body temperature had changed less than 0·15°C in an hour, when oxygen consumption was also steady. The time for equilibrium to be achieved varied from 3–6 h depending on the ambient temperature.

Fur study

See Dawson & Brown (1970) for detailed methods.

Fur samples

Six summer and six winter skins were obtained from both Red kangaroos and Euros during mid-December and July-August respectively. The skins were collected on the University of New South Wales Arid Zone Research Station, Fowlers Gap, north of Broken Hill in the far west of New South Wales. Estimates of the proportion of the various colour types in the populations of the two species were made by colour coding approximately 300 Red kangaroos and 250 Euros obtained during other studies over a three to four year period. Skins were initially preserved by coating with coarse salt and storing at 4° C. Measurements were made from two regions of each skin, mid-back and hip.

Total reflectance of fur to solar radiation

The reflectance to solar radiation was measured by means of a solarimeter consisting of an evaporative film thermopile (Trickett, 1963) under a clear glass dome. The percentage of solar radiation reflected from fur was estimated by placing the fur sample in sunlight and directing the solarimeter toward it from a fixed point at a fixed distance from the sample. A blackened tube was placed over the dome of the solarimeter to eliminate radiation from beyond the boundary of the sample. A magnesium oxide surface examined in the same manner as the furs was taken to represent 96·3% reflectance.

Spectral reflectance. The spectral reflectance of each type of fur at wave lengths between 0·35 μm and 2·0 μm was measured by means of an integrating reflection spectrometer (Carl Zeiss spectrophotometer PMQII with reflectance attachment RA3) using magnesium oxide as the reflectance standard.

Thermal insulation. The thermal insulation of a sample of the coat of an animal may be calculated from the equation:

$$I = I_c + I_a = \frac{t_s - t_a}{H}$$

where I is the total thermal insulation of the coat (°C cal^{-1} cm^2 h) which is divided into I_c the thermal insulation of the coat and I_a the so-called thermal insulation of the air above the coat, t_s is the skin temperature (°C), t_a is the air temperature (°C), H is the heat flow through the coat (cal cm^{-2} h^{-1}).

To determine the thermal insulation of the coat the quantities t_s, t_a and H must be measured. The heat flow and temperature gradient across the coat sample were measured using the methods described by Hutchinson & Brown (1969) and Dawson & Brown (1970).

RESULTS

Heat balance

Figure 1 shows the effect of air temperature on the basic components of the heat balance of both species, body temperature, heat production, and evaporative water loss, when the kangaroos are in summer fur. The body temperatures of both species are approximately 35·5°C in the thermoneutral range and they rise in response to both cold and heat. At an air temperature of 45°C the mean body temperatures were about 37·7°C, there being no difference between the species.

At air temperatures above the summer critical temperatures (17–18°C) the level of metabolism of Red kangaroos was above that of Euros; the difference was, however, not significant and the overall level for both species was approximately 1·0 cal/g h. This was slightly above the predicted basal level for marsupials (Dawson & Hulbert, 1969, 1970) but since the animals were only kept without food for 24 h prior to measurements this would be expected. A basal metabolism of 1·0 cal/g h is still only 73% of the predicted level for eutherians of comparable size.

The maximum total body insulation (core to environment) at low temperatures for both species in summer and winter is shown in Table I. The total body insulations appear to correlate with the overall values

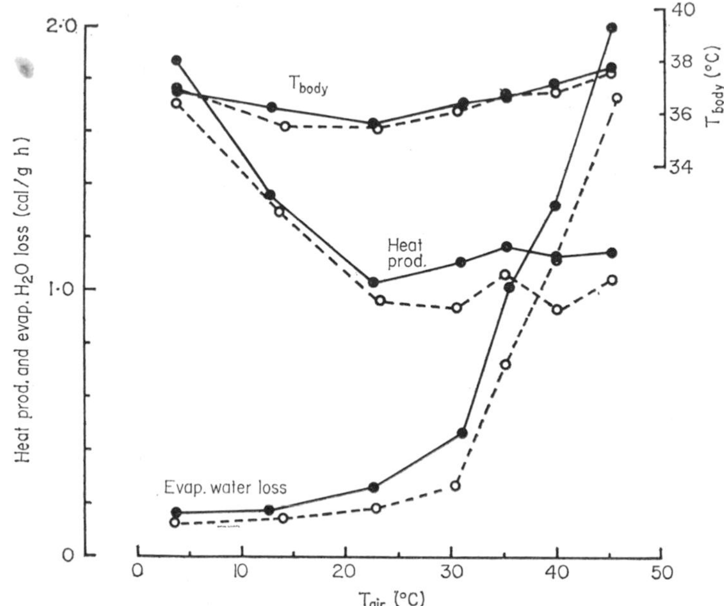

FIG. 1. Heat balance of desert kangaroos in equilibrium with various ambient temperatures. Red kangaroo (*Megaleia rufa*), —●—; Euro (*Macropus robustus*), – –○– –.

for fur insulation. The Red kangaroos have as lightlyl ower, butn on-significant, total insulation in summer and a significantly higher maximum total insulation in winter ($P < 0{\cdot}05$).

The higher evaporative water loss in the euros (Fig. 1) can be only partly explained by the difference in the heat production beween the species. In Fig. 2 is shown the percentage of the metabolic heat production which is lost by the evaporation of water. At air temperatures above 30°C the Red kangaroos tend to loose more water relative to their heat production than do Euros. In view of this tendency it is interesting that at the higher air temperatures there are marked and significant differences in the respiration rates of the two species. The Euros at all temperatures between 35°C and 45°C had much higher respiratory frequencies than the Red kangaroos. At 40°C the respiratory rate per min of the Euros, $N = 7$, was $234 \pm 24{\cdot}8$ (SD) against $162 \pm 22{\cdot}9$ (SD) for Red kangaroos, $N = 8$, and at 45°C the rates were $273 \pm 33{\cdot}4$ (SD) and $238 \pm 9{\cdot}5$ (SD) respectively for Euros, $N = 6$, and Red kangaroos, $N = 7$.

Fur properties

Reflectance

The principal colour types of the two species are listed in Table II together with the percentage occurrence of these types in the wild

TABLE I

Effect of season on fur insulation ($I_c + I_a$) *and maximum body insulation* (*core-environment*) *in desert kangaroos*

	Fur insulation ($I_c + I_a$) °C cal^{-1} cm^2 h				Max. body insulation °C cal^{-1} cm^2 h	
	Summer		Winter			
	Back	Hip	Back	Hip	Summer	Winter
Megaleia rufa (Red kangaroo)	2·5 ± 0·28 (6)	1·4 ± 0·15 (6)	4·2 ± 0·83 (6)	3·2 ± 0·29 (6)	7·9 ± 0·94 (6)	11·4 ± 0·94 (7)
Macropus robustus (Euro)	2·3 ± 0·21 (6)	2·7 ± 0·49 (6)	3·3 ± 0·89 (6)	3·2 ± 0·49 (6)	8·1 ± 1·02 (10)	10·0 ± 1·27 (6)

Values are means ± SD (*N*). Fur insulation values derived from Dawson & Brown (1970).

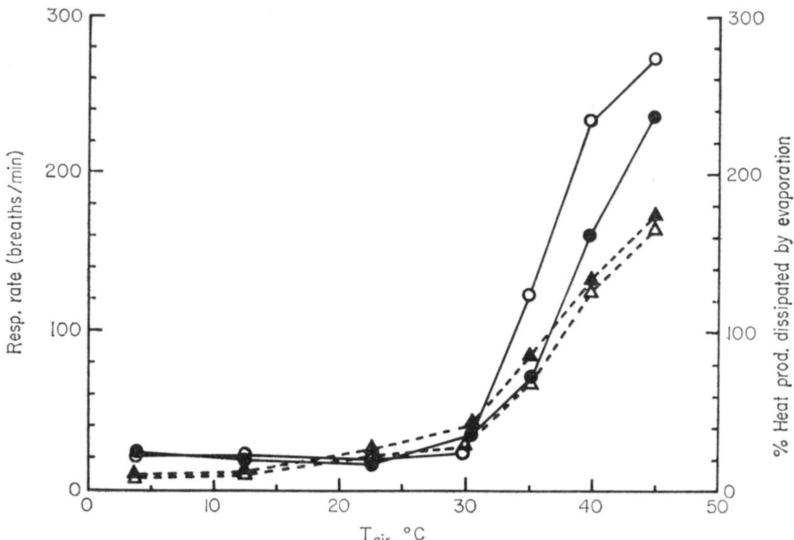

FIG. 2. Respiratory frequencies and percentage of heat production dissipated by evaporation (E/p) of the two species of desert kangaroo. Red kangaroo respiratory frequency —●—; Euro respiratory frequency —○—. Red kangaroo E/p - - ▲ - -; Euro E/p - - △ - -.

populations at Fowler's Gap and the total reflectance to solar radiation of each type.

The Red kangaroo has two distinct colour types, "red" which varies from deep red brown to a sandy brown, and "blue", a grey-blue colour. Table II shows that "red" is the predominant colour for males while "blue" is the usual colour for females. A small number of both sexes have an intermediate type which is variable in colour. The back fur from "red" skins was found to reflect considerably more solar radiation than the fur from "blue" skins from the same site, the "red-blue" type being intermediate. The hip fur from an individual animal was always paler in colour and had a higher reflectance than the back fur, but although the reflectance of "red" hip fur tended to be higher than the "blue" hip fur, differences between colour types were not as clear cut as in the back furs because of considerable overlap. The hip fur with the highest reflectance was almost white.

Categorizing the Euros with respect to colour type was more difficult than for the Red kangaroos, the sandy grey colour type of Euros being just a paler version of the more common dark grey-brown type. This dark grey-brown type had the lowest reflectance of all the coats measured (Table II).

TABLE II

Frequency of occurrence and range of reflectance to solar radiation of the colour types of the fur of the Red kangaroo (Megaleia rufa) *and Euro* (Macropus robustus)

Species	Colour type	Occurrence in wild population (%)		Reflectance to solar radiation (%)	
		Male	Female	Black fur	Hip fur
Megaleia rufa	Red	79·7	12·2	32·4–37·7 (5)	49·1–58·3 (5)
	Red-blue	14·7	19·6	27·4–33·7 (3)	34·6–55·1 (3)
	Blue	5·6	68·2	27·3–28·5 (4)	32·6–54·9 (4)
Macropus robustus	Dark grey brown	82·5	69·0	20·1–24·5 (7)	27·5–38·1 (7)
	Sandy grey	17·5	31·0	27·8–35·2 (5)	34·3–48·7 (5)

Values in parentheses give number of fur samples examined
Reprinted with permission from Dawson & Brown, 1970.

The reason for the differences in the total reflectance is illustrated by the spectral reflectance curves and the curve for the spectral distribution of the energy of solar radiation (Fig. 3).

The curves for the two principal colour types for the Red kangaroos are markedly different. The "blue" is far more reflective than the "red" fur at wavelengths below 0·575 μm, but at wavelengths between 0·575 and 1·30 μm i.e. at the red end of the visible spectrum and in the near infra-red region the "red" fur is much more reflective. The net effect of these differences is that red fur has the higher total reflectance to solar radiation since approximately 53% of the energy of solar radiation occurs between the wavelength of 0·575 and 1·30 μm.

The dark grey-brown Euro fur has a low total reflectance to solar radiation and a typical spectral reflectance curve (Fig. 3) shows that at all wavelengths it is the least reflective of all fur types except below a wavelength of 0·5 μm, where the "red" fur of the kangaroo is slightly less reflective.

Insulation

The total fur insulation (I_c+I_a) of both the summer and winter samples of the back fur of the Red kangaroo tended to be higher than that of the Euro (Table I) but the difference was only marked in the case of the winter sample. The total insulation of the summer samples

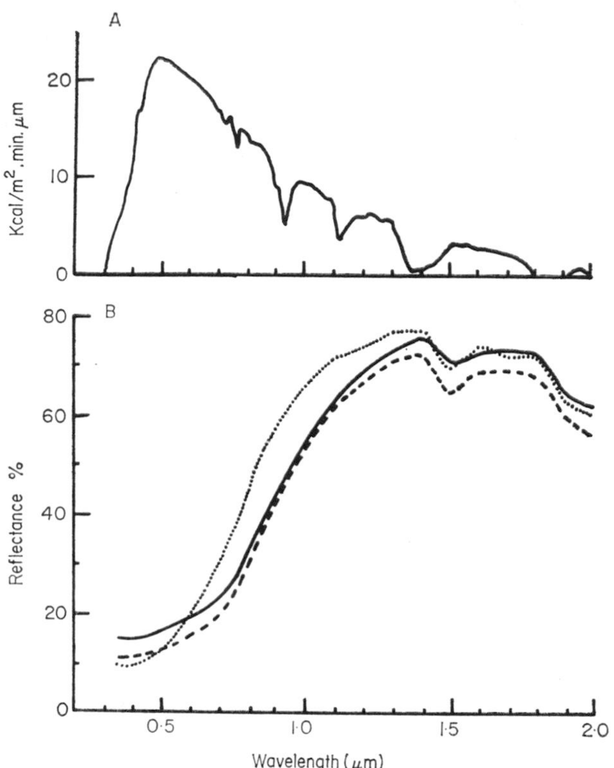

FIG. 3. Comparison of spectral reflectance curves of the furs of desert kangaroos with the spectral distribution of sunlight. A spectral distribution of sunlight with the sun at zenith; H_2O *vp* 20 mm Hg, pO_3 2·8 mm Hg and 300 dust particles/cm^2. B, Typical spectral reflectance curves for the main colour types of Red kangaroos and Euros. Red kangaroos: "red" · · · · · · · ; "blue" ———. Euro: "dark grey brown" – – – – – – –. (Modified from Dawson & Brown, 1970.)

of hip fur of the Red kangaroo is significantly lower than that of the Euro but there were no differences in the total insulation of the winter samples of hip fur of each species.

DISCUSSION

There have been two aspects to this study and these are:

1. how do the large kangaroos, as marsupials, deal with the thermal problems of hot deserts and;

2. are there differences in the thermoregulatory abilities of the Red kangaroo and the Euro in view of the differences in their microhabitat selection?

The low level of metabolism which is characteristic for marsupials in general (Dawson & Hulbert, 1969, 1970) would seem to confer on the desert kangaroos a major advantage with respect to eutherian mammals. At high air temperatures evaporative water loss is required to dissipate the metabolic heat production of the animal and consequently the low heat production of the kangaroos should result in them having a lower water usage. Field studies would tend to confirm this, since in summer both species of kangaroo had much lower rates of tritiated water turnover than did sheep or feral goats when all species were free ranging (T. J. Dawson, M. J. S. Denny & E. M. Russell, unpubl. data).

The comparatively low body temperature of the kangaroos could be considered to be disadvantageous because it would result in a greater gradient for heat flow into the body when the ambient temperature was very high. The body temperatures of both species of kangaroo tended to rise at high air temperatures but whether the kangaroos are capable of allowing the body temperature to fluctuate in the extreme manner that occurs in other desert animals such as the camel (Schmidt-Nielsen, Schmidt-Nielsen, Jarnum & Houpt, 1957), oryx and Grant's gazelle (Taylor, 1970) when they are dehydrated is not known. Examinations of latex injected kangaroo heads have not, however, shown the presence of a *rete mirabile* in the arterial supply to the brain. Such an arrangement allows the dissociation of brain temperatures from the temperature of the bulk of the body (Baker & Hayward, 1968), and this type of carotid *rete* has been reported in the oryx and Grant's gazelle (Taylor, 1970).

The low metabolism of the kangaroos also is not entirely advantageous for thermoregulation in deserts because extremes of temperature are a characteristic of these regions and the question arises as to the mechanisms by which the kangaroos, with their low metabolic rate, maintain their body temperature at low environmental temperatures. The fur insulation of the kangaroo is low, and similar to that of tropical eutherians (Scholander *et al.*, 1950b,c). However, the total body insulation (core to environment) is relatively high compared with that of tropical eutherians and this allows the kangaroos to maintain body temperatures in the cold without large increases in metabolism. Dawson *et al.* (1969) suggested that a high total insulation may be caused by a low peripheral blood flow in marsupials. The variation in total body insulation in both species between summer and winter, however, appears to be largely due to the variation in fur insulation.

In the arid regions where the Euro and Red kangaroo are found, summer temperatures may be very high. The Euro, however, avoids much of this high heat load, particularly that due to intense solar radiation, by spending hot summer days in caves and under rock ledges

(Ealey, 1967; Dawson & Denny, 1969; Russell, 1969). Consequently the reflectance characteristics of its coat may not be important and protective colouration is probably the important influence on coat colour.

The Red kangaroo is usually found in open country in the sparse shade of small desert trees. While these trees reduce solar radiation flux into the "lying up" site of the Red kangaroo by approximately 80%, the effective radiation temperature for a body with zero reflectance still reached 55–65°C (Dawson & Denny, 1969). The summer fur of the Red kangaroo, however, appears to be of a near ideal type to give protection to the animal against high solar radiation. In this role a combination of moderate reflectivity and a high fur density are important, especially in preventing the penetration of solar radiation deep into the fur. The problem of the penetration of solar radiation into the fur of kangaroos is discussed in detail by Dawson & Brown (1970).

The "blue" colour type of the Red kangaroo fur appears to have the same basic characteristics as the "red" type, although it is slightly less reflective. The hip and hind leg fur of the Red kangaroo is short and very pale in summer. It is very highly reflective but penetrance would also be high. However, the insulation of the fur from this region is so low that the protective value against absorbed radiation would also be low. Such fur on the hips and hind legs would facilitate the dissipation of heat, irrespective of whether the heat loss was by radiation, conduction, convection or the evaporation of sweat.

It would appear that there are no gross differences in the thermoregulatory responses of the Red kangaroo and the Euro to high external heat loads. Panting seems to be the principal avenue of evaporative water loss at high air temperatures. In this respect there is an interesting difference between the two species, in that the rate of panting at any given air temperature is much lower in the Red kangaroo than in the Euro. Initially it was considered that this might occur if thermal sweating was an additional heat loss mechanism in the Red kangaroo. Preliminary investigations using ventilated capsules (McLean, 1963) however have failed to demonstrate any marked increase in cutaneous water loss in either the Red kangaroo or the Euro in response to external thermal loads up to 43°C. These studies did indicate that sweating may occur as an auxiliary heat dissipating mechanism in both species in response to severe exercise, but particularly in the Red kangaroos.

The other possibility of an additional avenue of evaporative heat loss is licking. Licking has been traditionally associated with marsupial thermoregulation and until recently it was regarded as a major form of evaporative heat loss (Dawson, 1969). Both the Red kangaroo and the Euro spread water on their fore legs and sometimes on their hind legs during heat stress. It is not actually licking; saliva drips from the mouth during nasal panting and this moisture is wiped on the fore legs. The area covered with saliva is usually small and it is difficult to see how this would result in the large difference in respiratory rate between the two species, since it takes place in both the Red kangaroos and the Euros. It is perhaps more noticeable in the Red kangaroo and this may be the reason for the higher water loss in the Red kangaroos since water spread on the fur is inefficient in its removal of heat from the body (Dawson *et al.*, 1969).

The lower respiratory rates of the Red kangaroos may simply indicate that during panting these animals have a greater tidal volume than do Euros. The Red kangaroos, as we have discussed, are routinely subject to a much higher heat load than is the Euro. There is probably some limit to the increase in respiratory rate imposed by the characteristics of the respiratory system. Another macropodid marsupial, the Tammar wallaby, exhibited second phase breathing after a peak respiratory rate of 440 min was reached in response to severe thermal stress (Dawson & Rose, 1970). If the problems of blood acid-base balance were overcome, a higher tidal volume during panting would mean that a greater amount of heat could be dissipated by the Red kangaroo before its maximum respiratory rate was reached.

References

Baker, M. A. & Hayward, J. N. (1968). The influence of the nasal mucosa and the carotid rete upon hypothalamic temperature in sheep. *J. Physiol., Lond.* **198**: 561–579.

Brody, S. (1945). *Bioenergetics and growth.* New York: Reinhold.

Dawson, T. J. (1969). Temperature regulation and evaporative water loss in the brush-tailed possum *Trichosurus vulpecula. Comp. Biochem. Physiol.* **28**: 401–407.

Dawson, T. J. & Brown, G. D. (1970). A comparison of the insulative and reflective properties of the fur of desert kangaroos. *Comp. Biochem. Physiol.* **37**: 23–38.

Dawson, T. J. & Denny, M. J. S. (1969). A bioclimatological comparison of the summer day microenvironments of two species of arid zone kangaroo. *Ecology* **50**: 328–332.

Dawson, T. J. & Hulbert, A. J. (1969). Standard energy metabolism of marsupials. *Nature, Lond.* **221**: 383.

Dawson, T. J. & Hulbert, A. J. (1970). Standard metabolism, body temperature, and surface area of Australian marsupials. *Am. J. Physiol.* **218**: 1233–1238.

Dawson, T. J. & Rose, R. W. (1970). Influence of the respiratory response to moderate and severe heat on the blood gas values of a macropodid marsupial (*Macropus eugenii*). *Comp. Biochem. Physiol.* **37**: 59–66.

Dawson, T. J., Denny, M. J. S. & Hulbert, A. J. (1969). Thermal balance of the macropodid marsupial *Macropus eugenii* Desmarest. *Comp. Biochem. Physiol.* **31**: 645–653.

Ealey, E. H. M. (1967). Ecology of the euro, *Macropus robustus* (Gould), in North-Western Australia. *C.S.I.R.O. wildl. Res.* **12**: 27–51.

Hutchinson, J. C. D. & Brown, G. D. (1969). Penetrance of cattle coats by radiation. *J. appl. Physiol.* **26**: 454–464.

McLean, J. A. (1963). Measurement of cutaneous moisture vaporization from cattle by ventilated capsules. *J. Physiol.* **167**: 417–426.

Russell, E. M. (1969). Summer and winter observations of the behaviour of the euro *Macropus robustus* (Gould). *Aust. J. Zool.* **17**: 655–664.

Schmidt-Nielsen, K., Schmidt-Nielsen, B., Jarnum, S. A. & Houpt, T. R. (1957). Body temperature of the camel and its relation to water economy. *Am. J. Physiol.* **188**: 103–113.

Scholander, P. F., Hock, R., Walters, V. & Irving, L. (1950a). Adaption to cold in Arctic and tropical mammals and birds in relation to body temperature, insulation and basal metabolic rate. *Biol. Bull. mar. biol. Lab. Woods Hole* **99**: 259–271.

Scholander, P. F., Hock, R., Walters, V., Johnson, F. & Irving, L. (1950b). Heat regulation in some Arctic and tropical mammals and birds. *Biol. Bull. mar. biol. Lab. Woods Hole* **99**: 237–258.

Scholander, P. F., Walters, V., Hock, R. & Irving, L. (1950c). Body insulation of some Arctic and tropical mammals. *Biol. Bull. mar. biol. Lab. Woods Hole* **99**: 225–236.

Taylor, C. R. (1970). Dehydration and heat: effects on temperature regulation of East African ungulates. *Am. J. Physiol.* **219**: 1136–1139.

Trickett, E. S. (1963). An evaporated film thermopile. *J. agric. engng Res.* **8**: 147–155.

Symp. zool. soc. Lond. (1972) No. 31, 147–174.

WATER ECONOMY OF NOCTURNAL DESERT RODENTS

RICHARD E. MACMILLEN

Department of Population and Environmental Biology, University of California, Irvine, California, U.S.A.

SYNOPSIS

In addition to certain preadaptive characteristics including nocturnality, fossoriality, excretion of hyperosmotic urine, and high, sustained body temperatures, nocturnal desert rodents possess combinations of physiological and behavioural strategies which imbue them with measures of water economy necessary for maintenance of positive water balance in an environment where water is at a substantial premium. The physiological strategies include: periodic dormancy; reduced rates of faecal water loss; possession of a respiratory counter-current heat exchange system which may, on cool nights, reduce evaporative water loss to below the level of metabolic water production; and renal concentrating capacities which are consistent with dietary intakes of food and water. The behavioural tactics are difficult to measure and have not been adequately studied; they seem to consist of microhabitat selection and food utilization consistent with physiological limitations. Many laboratory data are available on maximal physiological tolerances and performances with regard to water economy. Studies are currently being conducted in the field to determine on an annual basis states of water balance in Californian nocturnal desert rodents. These studies will reveal the extent to which maximal physiological tolerances and performances are actually employed, and hence, the magnitude of demand the desert places on some of its inhabitants.

INTRODUCTION

Nocturnal desert rodents possess certain basic rodentian characteristics which may be considered preadaptive to a desert existence and which, together with certain other physiological and behavioural adjustments, provide them with appropriate states of water economy and thereby ensure their survival under what are often extremely demanding circumstances. These preadaptive features include those shown below.

Nocturnality

By far the greatest proportion of desert rodents, particularly those which are usually labelled rats and mice, are active on the surface of the desert only at night. By confining activity to the nocturnal periods, these forms can take advantage of the near absence of a greenhouse effect on the desert which promotes maximal heating by day but also maximal cooling at night. Hence, activity is generally restricted, even during the summer, to conditions which are as cool as, if not cooler than, those usually encountered in the laboratory.

Fossoriality

Coupled with nocturnal activity fossoriality is an additional characteristic that virtually all desert rodents share: they spend the inactive times in underground burrows. Such burrows appear to have uniformly moderate temperatures and high humidities (Schmidt-Nielsen & Schmidt-Nielsen, 1950; Kennerly, 1964), which provide an optimal environment for thermoregulation and maintenance of positive water balance for inactive rodents, in summer or winter.

Excretion of hyperosmotic urine

All rodents which have been investigated are capable of producing hyperosmotic urine, to reduce urinary water loss. As we shall see, some desert forms have accentuated this capacity and rely upon it for the maintenance of positive water balance, while others appear to possess no greater powers of urine concentration than rodents which inhabit more domestic situations.

High and constant body temperature

While normothermic, active or resting, nocturnal desert rodents generally have body temperatures (T_B) which range between 36°C and 39°C, and which appear almost invariably to exceed the ambient temperatures (T_A) to which they are exposed. This maintenance of $T_B > T_A$ precludes the necessity for costly evaporative cooling. At times, as will be indicated below, nocturnal desert rodents may abandon normothermia and enter a period of hypothermic dormancy.

While there certainly are morphological attributes of nocturnal rodents which enhance survival, and while there may be other behavioural and physiological characteristics which help a desert existence, the adaptive features indicated above appear to me to be paramount in the lives of desert rodents. These features aptly demonstrate that existence under such extreme conditions depends upon a continual interplay between physiology and behaviour; for the desert environment probably more than any other terrestrial situation on earth, is one where . . . "an individual animal can exhibit its physiological capacities most fully by utilizing its behaviour to place itself in those situations with which it can cope by physiological regulation, or by restricting its period of exposure to intolerable physical conditions, so that its limits of physiological tolerance are not exceeded in spite of its inability to maintain an adequately steady state" (Bartholomew, 1964).

The adaptive strategies for water economy, involving this interplay between physiology and behaviour, are as varied as the nocturnal desert rodents which possess and depend upon them. Generally, however, and in addition to the adaptive characteristics already mentioned above, these strategies may consist of various combinations of the following categories:

1. Temporary escape from the desert environment: circadian or seasonal dormancy.
2. Control of excessive water loss: faecal, pulmocutaneous, and renal.
3. Amelioration of environmental demands by behavioural selection of appropriate environmental components, i.e., microhabitat, food type, consistently with physiological limitations.

The groundwork for the study of the water economy of nocturnal desert rodents was laid in 1935 by the pioneering efforts of Howell & Gersh (1935), with their work on North American desert *Dipodomys* spp. and *Perognathus* spp. Since that time and largely following their examples, the Schmidt-Nielsens, their students and collaborators, and Bartholomew and his students and collaborators, have provided a wealth of information and insight on water regulation of desert rodents from all over the world. These works have been extensively reviewed in the past (see, for example, Chew, 1961; Schmidt-Nielsen, 1964a, b; Hudson, 1964). Therefore, I shall not attempt a further review on the water economy of nocturnal desert rodents. Rather, I shall draw upon examples chiefly from my own work in attempting to assess where we are now, and where, I think, we should go in the future.

THE ADAPTIVE STRATEGIES OF WATER ECONOMY

Circadian and seasonal dormancy

Nocturnal desert rodents, because of their small size and their tendency to restrict activity to finite home ranges, are not highly mobile animals. Hence, if surface conditions become intolerable, migration does not appear to be a practical alternative. If the usual physiological and behavioural capacities are insufficient to cope with the combination of subsurface and surface conditions, certain nocturnal desert rodents resort to periodic bouts of torpor or hypothermia.

The best known examples of periodic torpor among nocturnal desert rodents occur within the North American heteromyid genera *Perognathus* and *Microdipodops* (see Hudson, 1967 for thorough discussion), where apparently all species of these genera undergo circadian periods of shallow torpor during the diurnal period of inactivity and in response to energy restriction; they also occasionally enter torpor spontaneously. Such torpor, with T_B generally no more than 2·0°C above T_A results in considerable energy saving for these small mice which, when normothermic, have inherently high metabolic rates. However, if torpor is employed, even on a circadian basis, under natural circumstances in a cool, moist burrow, it should also result in considerable reduction in respiratory water loss. That is, even though torpid animals expire air saturated with water vapour, respiratory water loss will be minimal if not negligible, due to the inspiration of nearly saturated burrow air at or only slightly below body temperature. Thus, even if circadian torpor in these forms is more directly related to energy conservation, there will be a concomitant although perhaps coincidental conservation of water. It should be noted further, however, that all of the species of *Perognathus* and *Microdipodops* so far studied appear to be independent of exogenous water sources under normal field conditions on the desert, and hence would not appear to be reliant upon torpor as a water-conserving mechanism.

With a single exception, there is no indication from field studies that dormancy in strictly desert species of *Perognathus* and *Microdipodops* is anything other than circadian. This one exception is the little pocket mouse, *Perognathus longimembris*, a very small (8–12 g), common inhabitant of the deserts of North America. Chew & Butterworth (1964), in a field study (1957–1958) of a nocturnal desert rodent population in San Bernardino County, California, noted that *Perognathus longimembris* was one of the most abundant members of the rodent fauna during the months March through July, that they decreased in number during August and September, and were entirely absent from trapping records from October through February. The authors interpreted these data to mean that *P. longimembris* enters a period of seasonal dormancy. In my current (1970–1971) studies near the same area, I have observed a comparable situation with no *P. longimembris* active on the surface from October (when the study commenced) through February. Since their appearance in March through June, they have become one of the most abundant members of the fauna. The time of their disappearance coincides with the very dry period of late summer, but also with the cool, more moist autumn and winter, and with the absence of desert annual vegetation; such conditions at the time of their late summer disappearance could promote maximal water imbalance. Their appearance coincides with the germination and growth of succulent annual vegetation, or conditions promoting optimal states of positive water balance. It is not known whether photoperiod, food availability, moisture availability, or a combination of these factors (or perhaps none) initiates the onset of the period of dormancy. Nor is it known whether, while dormant, the animals employ circadian torpor (as laboratory data would seem to indicate, Chew, Lindberg & Hayden, 1965), or torpor of a longer duration. But certainly such dormancy enables the animal to escape surface conditions and, at the same time, reduce both energy and water expenditures.

In addition to the Heteromyidae, the other rodent family which has met with conspicuous success in the North American deserts is the Cricetidae, including the very successful nocturnal genera *Neotoma*, *Onychomys* and *Peromyscus*. In general, and under usual laboratory conditions, the desert species of these genera are not independent of exogenous water while on a diet of dry seeds. The desert species of *Peromyscus* are of particular interest for recent studies indicate that they are capable of employing torpor (MacMillen, 1965; Morhardt & Hudson, 1966; Morhardt, 1970) at least on a circadian basis.

Through a combination of field and laboratory studies MacMillen (1964, 1965) has demonstrated that semidesert, and presumably desert, races of *Peromyscus eremicus* resort to summer dormancy (aestivation) during the period when water resources are minimal on the surface, and that this dormancy serves chiefly as a water economy measure. Marked individuals in the field were not active on the surface (were untrappable) for two to three month periods between April and August, coinciding with the period of least water availability; when these individuals reappeared, they invariably reappeared in the same locations from which they previously disappeared, suggesting strongly a period of dormancy in their burrows (Fig. 1).

Laboratory studies (MacMillen, 1965) revealed that *P. eremicus* would invariably enter torpor on a circadian basis (torpid by day, active by night) when deprived of food (Fig. 2), but that some individuals during the summer would also enter torpor when placed under conditions of negative water balance with ample food available. In addition torpid animals with $T_B < 16°C$ ultimately perished, indicating that only "shallow" torpor could be meaningful ecologically; winter soil (and burrow) temperatures were invariably below this critical temperature, while summer soil temperatures were invariably above 16°C, suggesting further that torpor in *P. eremicus* is chiefly a summer phenomenon. Measurements of oxygen consumption (Fig. 3) and pulmocutaneous water loss (Fig. 4) in active and torpid animals, indicate that torpor results in considerable savings in both energy and water. Considering that these measurements were made in a dried-air

P.e.	JAN	FEB	MAR	APR	MAY	JUNE	JULY	AUG	SEPT	OCT	NOV	DEC
1♂	X	XX	X					X	X			
5♂	XX	XXX	XXXXX	X X			X	X	XX	X	X	X X
26♀	XX	XXX	XX X	XXX	X			X	X	X	XX	XXX
36♀		XXX	X							X		
55♂			X X	X					X		X	
58♂	X	XX	X X	X			X	XX		XX		
102♀	X	X			XX					XX		XX

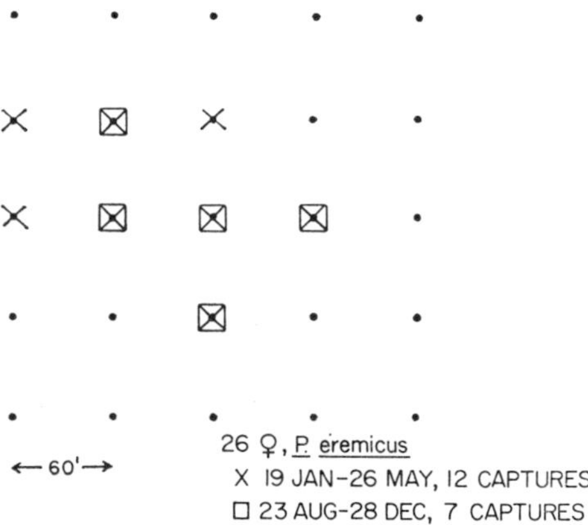

FIG. 1. The incidence of summer dormancy in *P. eremicus* during 1958 (upper), and (lower) the localities of capture of *P. eremicus* No. 26 ♀ before becoming dormant (X), and after emerging from dormancy (⊠). In the upper portion of the figure, each X represents a single capture of an individual; note the near absence of captures in the period May-August, indicating summer dormancy. The lower portion of the figure demonstrates a typical trapping record from one of these *P. eremicus*: a 2–3 month period of disappearance, followed by reappearance at almost the same trapping stations from which the animal had originally disappeared.

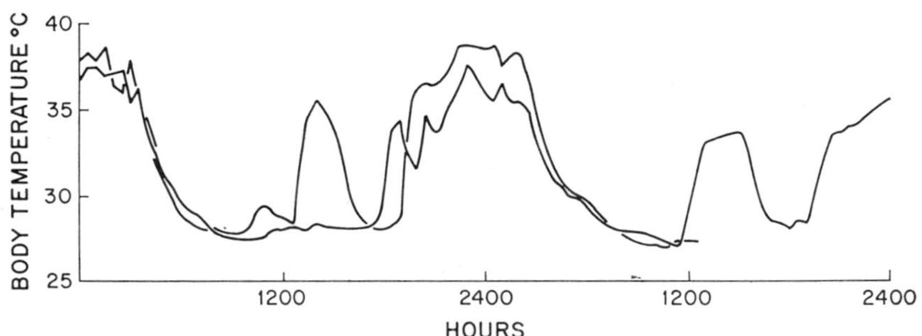

FIG. 2. Circadian torpor as indicated by body temperature in two female *Peromyscus eremicus* after 12 h of deprivation of food and water at $T_A = 25°C$; the two individuals were measured separately under constant conditions of temperature, humidity, and dim illumination. After MacMillen (1965).

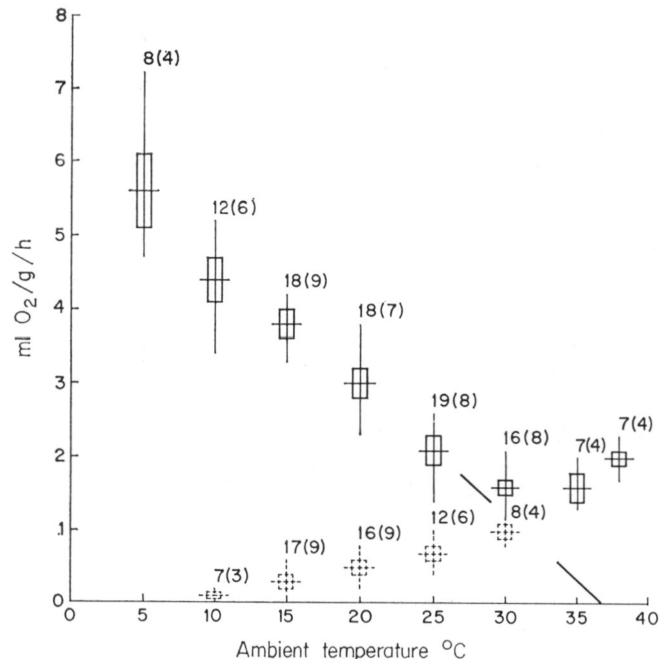

FIG. 3. The relation of oxygen consumption to ambient temperature in active (solid-lined symbols) and torpid (dashed-lined symbols) *Peromyscus eremicus*. The diagonal line is eye-fitted to the mean values and indicates a lower critical temperature of 28°C. The vertical lines represent the ranges. The horizontal lines represent the means ($\bar{x}$). The rectangles enclose the intervals $\bar{x} \pm 2$ SE. The numbers outside the parentheses represent the number of measurements, and the number inside the parentheses represent the number of animals measured. From MacMillen (1965) with permission of the publisher.

stream, and assuming that dormant *P. eremicus* are in cool, moist burrows with stores of seed containing appreciable amounts of moisture, MacMillen (1965) believes that water losses while dormant in the burrows are negligible, even though surface conditions may be intolerable. Again, as in *Perognathus*, laboratory studies indicate that torpor in *P. eremicus* is chiefly circadian, while the field studies indicate the period of dormancy to be two to three months in duration.

Morhardt & Hudson (1966), Hudson (1967) and Morhardt (1970) have more recently surveyed the incidence of torpor in several species of *Peromyscus* and have described starvation-induced circadian torpor in desert and semidesert races of *P. crinitus*, *P. eremicus*, *P. maniculatus*, and the chaparral species *P. boylei* and *P. californicus*. In all of these forms torpor appears to be shallow, generally restricted to $T_B > 16$°C.

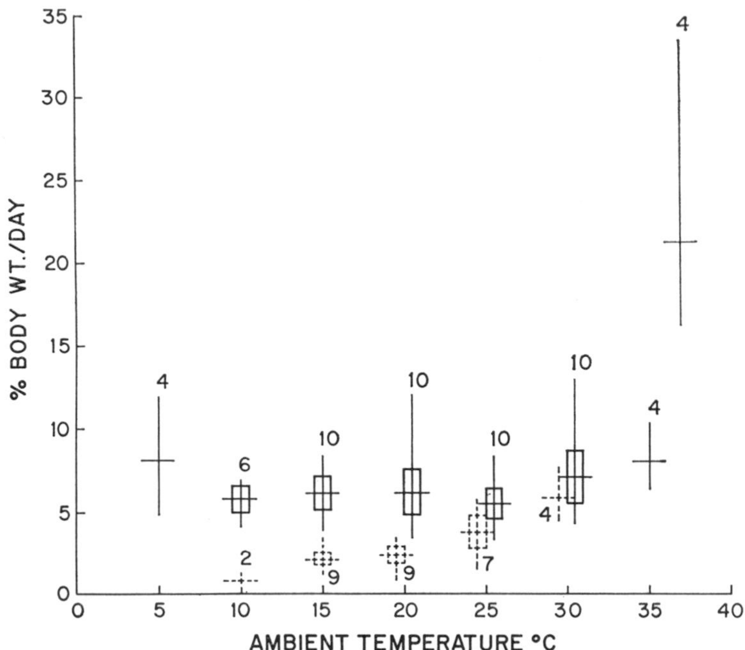

FIG. 4. The relation of pulmocutaneous water loss (expressed as a function of body weight) to ambient temperature in active (solid-lined symbols) and torpid (dashed-lined symbols) *Peromyscus eremicus*. Symbols and numbers as in Fig. 3. From MacMillen (1965) with permission of the publisher.

There are no field data to indicate whether seasonal dormancy is employed by these species (other than for *P. eremicus*), and such data are badly needed. In addition, while apparently all *Peromyscus* will enter torpor when food is deprived or restricted, water restriction or imbalance will also induce torpor in some *P. eremicus*. Detailed studies of the separate and combined roles of water and food intake or restriction in promoting hypothermia and/or normothermia in particularly the desert and semidesert races and species of *Peromyscus* should be very revealing, and should indicate whether aestivation serves primarily as a water-conserving mechanism, as an energy-conserving mechanism, or both. Lastly, the roles of torpor in other nocturnal rodents from the deserts of the world should be intensively examined, to determine whether this is a commonly-employed strategy for desert existence.

Control of excessive water loss

The major avenues of water loss are faecal, pulmocutaneous and urinary.

Faecal water loss

Very few measurements of faecal water content of nocturnal desert rodents are available. Some of these are summarized in Table I and suggest that, when deprived of water the faeces are voided with a water content of about 50% by weight. It is likely that hind gut reabsorption of water in these forms is maximal because Schmidt-Nielsen (1964a) reports the faecal water content of water-deprived white rats (*Rattus norvegicus*) to be 68·5%.

Pulmocutaneous water loss

Many of the comparative data available for rates of pulmocutaneous water loss (expressed as a function of oxygen consumption) of nocturnal desert rodents and at T_A = 28°C or 30°C are summarized in Table I. The data are not strictly comparable, however, since some measurements were made in thermal neutrality while other measurements were made below thermal neutrality, due to inter-specific differences in weight-specific conductance, lower critical temperature, and metabolic rate. For valid inter-specific comparisons, all measurements of pulmocutaneous water loss should be made in thermal neutrality and under basal metabolic conditions. The data for pulmocutaneous water loss (Table I) are variable and suggest that some nocturnal desert rodents have rather high rates of water loss, while others are quite low. However, it is uncertain whether this inter-specific variability is real, or a function of the experimental method (see conflicting data for *Dipodomys merriami* which represent two different geographic races and hence the possibility of different metabolic rates at T_A = 28°C).

Although it has not been documented fully, very likely there is an indirect relationship between pulmocutaneous water loss and body size at thermal neutrality among nocturnal desert rodents, since the level of respiratory water loss in thermal neutrality is indirectly related to metabolic rate and since basal metabolism is indirectly related to body weight. Such a relationship has been fully documented for land birds (Bartholomew & Dawson, 1953). Also, many nocturnal rodents have basal metabolic rates reduced by varying degrees below that predicted by the empirical equation relating basal metabolism to body size. The degree of reduction may well yield some variability of pulmocutaneous water loss expressed as a function of oxygen consumption, even within the same size class of nocturnal desert rodent.

Potential rates of respiratory water loss in rodents appear to be greatly reduced by a counter-current heat exchange system in the

TABLE I

Oxygen consumption, pulmocutaneous water loss, and faecal water content of various nocturnal desert rodents. Faecal water loss was determined in rodents deprived of drinking water, and oxygen consumption and pulmocutaneous water loss were measured at ambient temperatures of 28°C or 30°C. Numbers in parentheses are standard errors of the means

Species	Oxygen consumption (ml/g/h)	Pulmocutaneous water loss (mg H_2O/mlO_2)	Faecal water content (% H_2O)
	Rodents dependent on water		
*Peromyscus eremicus** (North America)	1·56 (±0·27) at 30°C	1·50 at 30°C	
Neotoma lepida† (North America)	0·79 at 30°C	2·04 at 30°C	
	Rodents not dependent on water		
Peromyscus crinitus‡ (North America)	2·88 at 28°C	0·54 at 28°C	
Dipodomys merriami‡§ (North America)	2·24 at 28°C	0·54 (±0·01) at 28°C	45·2
Dipodomys merriami¶ (North America)	1·13 at 28°C	0·80 at 28°C	
Dipodomys spectabilis‡ (North America)	1·40 at 28°C	0·57 (±0·03) at 28°C	
Perognathus spp.‡ (North America)	3·14 at 28°C	0·50 (±0·03) at 28°C	
Acomys caharinus‖ (Israel)	1·01 at 30°C	1·96 at 30°C	
*Notomys alexis***†† (Australia)	2·11 (±0·07) at 28°C	1·05 (±0·11) at 28°C	48·8
*Notomys cervinus***†† (Australia)	2·24 (±0·07) at 28°C	0·76 (±0·08) at 28°C	51·8
*Leggadina hermannsburgensis*** (Australia)	2·86 ± 0·10 at 28°C	1·15 (±0·10) at 28°C	50·4

* MacMillen, 1965; † Lee, 1963; ‡ Schmidt-Nielsen & Schmidt-Nielsen, 1950; § Schmidt-Nielsen, 1964a; ¶ Carpenter, 1966; ‖ Shkolnik & Borut, 1969; ** MacMillen & Lee, 1967; †† MacMillen & Lee, 1970.

respiratory passages, where air is exhaled at a temperature below that at which it is inhaled, resulting in a condensation of water as the air passes out along the respiratory tract, and a recovery of this water by absorption (Jackson & Schmidt-Nielsen, 1964; Schmidt-Nielsen, Hainsworth & Murrish, 1970). The counter-current heat exchange system appears to be characteristic of rodents in general, and the magnitude of water condensation and recovery is indirectly related to ambient temperature (Jackson & Schmidt-Nielsen, 1964; Schmidt-Nielsen *et al.*, 1970; Getz, 1968).

In spite of this reduction in respiratory water loss, it is doubtful that, in thermal neutrality, pulmocutaneous water loss (or evaporative water loss, EWL) in any nocturnal desert rodent is reduced below the level of metabolic water production (MWP). Hence those forms which are referred to as being independent of exogenous water, at least in thermal neutrality, are not truly independent; they rely upon a combination of reduction in EWL through breathing air with some water vapour in it, and augmentation of MWP by eating hygroscopic seeds whose water contents vary with soil or air moisture contents; renal performance then makes up any deficit. Even in the Kangaroo rat, *Dipodomys merriami*, which is extremely economical in terms of EWL, EWL > MWP at $T_A = 25°C$ and at relative humidities below about 12% (Schmidt-Nielsen & Schmidt-Nielsen, 1951).

Because of the magnitude of respiratory water recovery and the effectiveness of the counter-current heat exchange system are indirectly related to ambient temperature (Schmidt-Nielsen *et al.*, 1970), the respiratory component of EWL theoretically should decrease below thermal neutrality. This, in effect happens, and in every nocturnal desert rodent of which I am aware of measurements of the relationship between pulmocutaneous water loss (EWL) and ambient temperature, EWL expressed as a function of oxygen consumption invariably is lower at temperatures below thermal neutrality than at thermal neutrality. Figure 5 demonstrates this phenomenon in the Australian desert hopping mice, *Notomys alexis* and *N. cervinus* (MacMillen & Lee, 1970).

In addition, by definition, metabolic rate increases inversely with T_A at temperatures below thermal neutrality, with the slope of increase (weight-specific conductance) and lower critical temperature inversely related to body weight. Hence nocturnal desert rodents, which almost without exception are small, have high rates of conductance, high lower critical temperatures, and therefore metabolic rates which in-increase maximally with decreases in T_A below thermal neutrality (see for example, Figs 3 and 6, for *Peromyscus eremicus* and *Notomys alexis*, respectively).

Bartholomew (1971) has recently made a similar observation for birds, that below thermal neutrality EWL is essentially independent of T_A while metabolic rate is inversely related. He stated that since metabolic water production (MWP) bears a constant relationship to

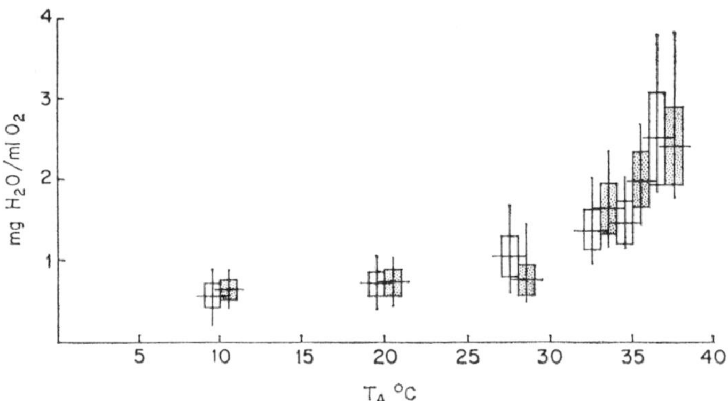

FIG. 5. The relationship between pulmocutaneous water loss (expressed as a function of oxygen consumption) and ambient temperature in ten *Notomys alexis* and *N. cervinus*. Vertical lines represent ranges, horizontal lines represent means ($\bar{x}$), and rectangles enclose the intervals $\bar{x} \pm T_{0 \cdot 95}$ SE. Hollow rectangles indicate *N. alexis* and filled rectangles indicate *N. cervinus*. From MacMillen & Lee (1970) with permission of publisher.

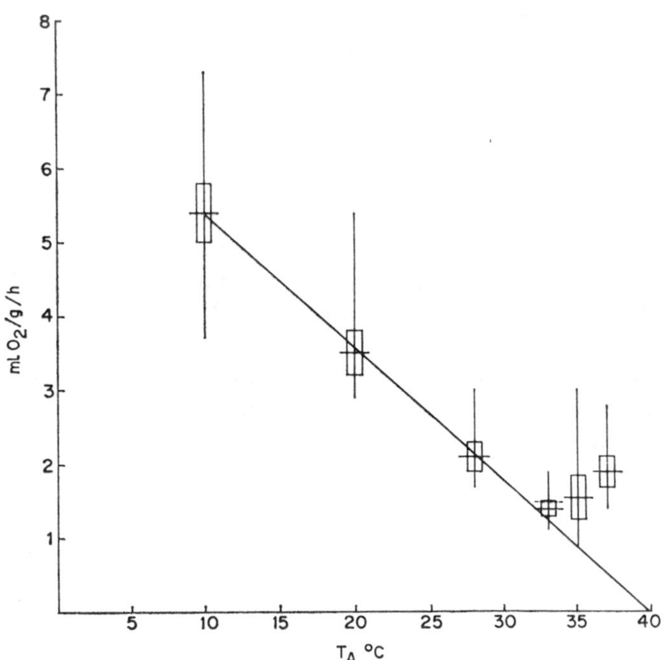

FIG. 6. The relationship between oxygen consumption and ambient temperature in ten *Notomys alexis*. The solid line was fitted to the data below thermal neutrality by the method of least squares. Symbols as in Fig. 5. From MacMillen & Lee (1970) with permission of publisher.

metabolic rate, the difference between MWP and EWL should diminish progressively with decreases in T_A below thermal neutrality. Further, given sufficiently high rates of MWP, low rates of EWL, and cool nights, it is possible for a small desert bird at night to eliminate net water loss due to pulmocutaneous evaporation (Bartholomew, 1971). This has been experimentally verified.

These concepts can be applied to mammals, and are especially meaningful when applied to nocturnal desert rodents. Knowing rates of EWL and oxygen consumption, and assuming that bird seed (the diet on which the desert rodents reported here were maintained) contains approximately the same proportions of nutrients and with the same oxidative requirements for metabolic water production as reported in Schmidt-Nielsen (1964a) for pearled barley, one may calculate the relationship between EWL and MWP. Table II summarizes such data for four species of nocturnal desert rodents, with varying degrees of water independence under laboratory conditions (MacMillen, 1965; MacMillen & Lee, 1967, and unpubl. data). These data indicate that for all of these rodents, even though EWL > MWP in thermal neutrality (*P. eremicus*, 28–35°C; *N. alexis*, 32–34°C; *N. cervinus*, 33°C; *L. hermannsburgensis*, 31–35°C), EWL < MWP from slightly below T_A = 20°C and lower, and at the low relative humidities at which these measurements were made. More data of these kinds are needed from a variety of nocturnal desert rodents before a more definitive statement can be made, but it certainly appears that, within the ranges of nocturnal temperatures and humidities regularly encountered on the surface, far more nocturnal desert rodents than were previously thought are able to compensate entirely for pulmocutaneous water loss by metabolic water production.

Renal water loss

The single physiological means of reducing water loss that appears to be most consistently characteristic of nocturnal desert rodents, is the capacity to concentrate urine while in a water-restricted or water-deprived state. There appears generally to be a direct relationship between the magnitude of concentration and the capacity to withstand water deprivation (by maintaining weight) while on a diet of air-dried seeds. Such a relationship has been demonstrated in some rodent species from virtually every desert and it follows that, among mammals, the most efficient kidneys in terms of water reabsorption and urine concentration belong to nocturnal desert rodents (Table III). Much attention has been paid to these more spectacular rodents, and they are adequately treated in the several review articles mentioned herein,

TABLE II

The relationship between metabolic water production (MWP) and evaporative water loss (EWL) in nocturnal desert rodents at various ambient temperatures and low relative humidities. EWL was measured gravimetrically, and MWP was calculated on the basis that oxidation of mixed bird seed is equivalent to that of pearled barley, and that 1·0 ml O_2 *yields 0·64 mg* H_2O *(after Schmidt-Nielsen, 1964*a*). Bold figures are measurements made in thermal neutrality*

T_A °C	*P. eremicus** rh, %	*P. eremicus** MWP/EWL	*L. hermannsburgensis†* rh, %	*L. hermannsburgensis†* MWP/EWL	*N. alexis‡* rh, %	*N. alexis‡* MWP/EWL	*N. cervinus‡* rh, %	*N. cervinus‡* MWP/EWL
5		1·05						
10		1·26	39·9	1·07	25·8	1·14	30·3	1·00
15		1·08						
20		0·88	14·6	0·97	12·4	0·90	13·9	0·89
25		0·69						
28			9·7	0·56	6·9	0·61	6·0	0·84
30		**0·43**						
33			11·6	**0·34**	5·1	**0·47**	5·5	**0·39**
35		**0·40**	6·7	**0·36**	5·2	0·44	6·9	0·32
37		0·19	9·3	0·31	9·4	0·26	8·0	0·27

* MacMillen, 1965; † R. E. MacMillen, R. V. Baudinette & A. K. Lee, unpubl. data; ‡ MacMillen & Lee, 1970.

Table III

Mean and maximum urine concentrations and urine : blood ratios of nocturnal desert rodents on a diet of dry grain (except O. torridus *on a diet of boiled ground beef and drinking NaCl solutions). Measurements of urine urea and osmotic pressure were not necessarily from the same urine sample. Numbers in parentheses are standard errors of the means.*

Species	Mean value				Maximum value			
	Urine		Urine : blood ratio		Urine		Urine : blood ratio	
	Urea (m-mole/l)	Osmotic concentration (m-osmole/l)	Urea	Osmotic concentration	Urea (m-mole/l)	Osmotic concentration (m-osmole/l)	Urea	Osmotic concentration
Rodents dependent on water								
*Neotoma albigula** (North America)	1230 (±190)	2100** (±170)	36	5·2**	1870	2670**	91	6·7**
Onychomys torridus† (North America)	1710	3180	100·3	9·8	2450	4250	187·0	13·8
Rodents not dependent on water								
Peromyscus crinitus‡ (North America)	1958	3150		9·0	2214	3490		10·4
*Dipodomys merriami** (North America)	2420 (±200)	3780 (±280)	202	9·5**	3840	5540**	352	14·0**
Dipodomys merriami§ (North America)		3990		10·2**		4650		11·8**

TABLE III—*continued*

Mean and maximum urine concentrations and urine : blood ratios of nocturnal desert rodents on a diet of dry grain (except O. torridus *on a diet of boiled ground beef and drinking NaCl solutions). Measurements of urine urea and osmotic pressure were not necessarily from the same urine sample. Numbers in parentheses are standard errors of the means.*

Species	Mean value				Maximum value			
	Urine		Urine : blood ratio		Urine		Urine : blood ratio	
	Urea (m-mole/1)	Osmotic concentration (m-osmole/1)	Urea	Osmotic concentration	Urea (m-mole/1)	Osmotic concentration (m-osmole/1)	Urea	Osmotic concentration
Rodents not dependent on water								
*Dipodomys spectabilis** (North America)	2430 (±120)	3780** (±130)	190	9·5**	2710	4090**	234	10·4**
Gerbillus gerbillus¶ (Egypt)					3410	5500		14·0**
Jaculus jaculus¶ (Africa)					4320	6500		16·0**
Notomys alexis‖ (Australia)	3430 (±340)	6550 (±510)	343 (±31)	17·9 (±1·3)	5430	9370	798	24·6
Notomys cervinus‖ (Australia)	2500 (±150)	3720 (±220)	212 (±32)	9·4 (±1·0)	3140	4920	257	14·2
Leggadina hermannsburgensis (Australia)	2760 (±300)	4710 (±820)	242 (±32)	14·7 (±0·8	3920	8970	381	26·8

* Schmidt-Nielsen, *et al*. 1948; † Schmidt-Nielsen & Haines, 1964; ‡ Abbott, 1971; § Carpenter, 1966; ¶ Schmidt-Nielsen, 1964a; ‖ MacMillen & Lee, 1967.

** Estimates calculated on the assumption that the urine osmotic pressure equals twice electrolyte concentration plus the urea concentration.

so that I will not deal with them in detail. Rather, I shall review briefly typical renal performances among these spectacular rodents, as demonstrated by the Australian hopping mice, *Notomys alexis* and *N. cervinus* (MacMillen & Lee, 1967, 1969).

These murid rodents are widely distributed throughout the more severe desert regions of central Australia. When deprived of water and maintained on an air-dried seed diet, both species lose some weight, followed by complete weight recovery by *N. alexis*, and maintenance of body weight at a reduced level by *N. cervinus*. There was complete survival of a sample of ten *N. alexis*, but two of eight *N. cervinus* perished during the period of water deprivation. Hence, *N. alexis* appeared better able to withstand complete water deprivation than *N. cervinus*, although both species were considered to be independent of water. The renal responses to water deprivation (Fig. 7, Table III) paralleled the weight responses, and the more tolerant form (*N. alexis*) produced significantly more concentrated urine than the less tolerant

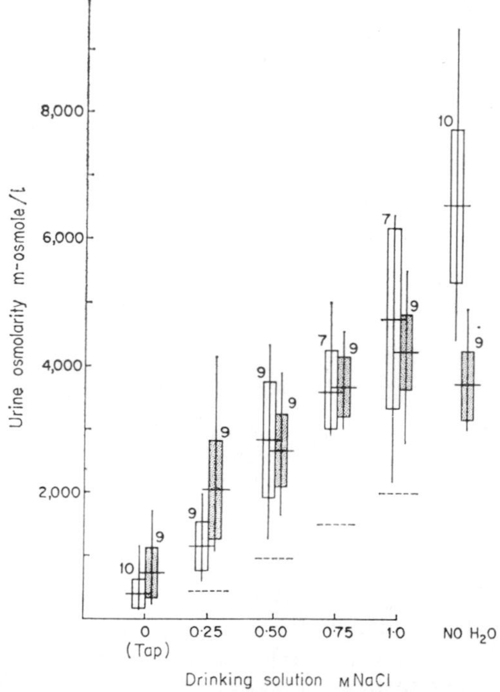

FIG. 7. The relationship between urine osmolarity and the utilization of tap water, various saline drinking solutions, and water deprivation in *Notomys alexis* (hollow rectangles) and *Notomys cervinus* (filled rectangles). Symbols as in Fig. 5. From MacMillen & Lee (1969) with permission of publisher.

form (*N. cervinus*). Rates of pulmocutaneous water loss and the faecal water content appeared to be characteristic of small mammals in general (Table I), thus the major physiological avenue preventing excessive water loss in these forms appeared to be their varying capacities of renal concentration.

Also, as appears typical of these desert rodents, *N. alexis* and *N. cervinus* could drink and apparently process very concentrated NaCl solutions, although *N. alexis* was more reluctant to use the more concentrated solutions (0·75 and 1·0 M NaCl) than was *N. cervinus*. While utilizing these solutions there was a direct relationship between urine concentration and concentration of the drinking solution, and the concentration of the urine exceeded at all times the concentration of the NaCl solution (Fig. 7). Regardless of the kind or amount of drinking solution used, and even when water deprived, the experimental samples of both *N. alexis* and *N. cervinus* maintained weight. In addition blood osmotic properties remained constant (Fig. 8) and

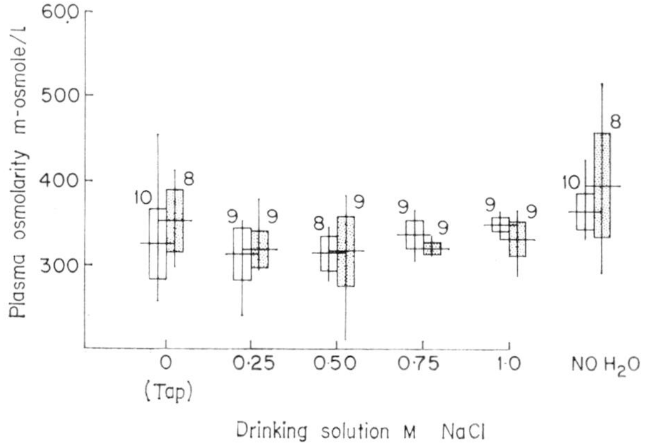

FIG. 8. The relationship between plasma osmolarity and the utilization of tap water, various saline drinking solutions, and water deprivation in *Notomys alexis* (hollow rectangles) and *Notomys cervinus* (filled rectangles). Symbols as in Fig. 5. From MacMillen & Lee (1969) with permission of publisher.

independent of qualitative and quantitative aspects of drinking, indicating maintenance of positive water balance throughout.

Because of the tendency for investigators to concentrate on the unusual forms of life, very little attention has been paid to those desert rodents which have more usual, or typically mammalian, characteristics. These include *Peromyscus crinitus*, *Onychomys torridus*, and *Neotoma albigula*, as indicated in Table III, with only limited capacities of urine concentration. In spite of these limitations, Abbott

(1971) has recently demonstrated water independence in *P. crinitus* under laboratory conditions. It is obvious that *P. crinitus* must rely on other water-conserving mechanisms to augment renal water conservation in order to maintain weight and water balance in a water-deprived state. The demonstration of circadian torpor in *P. crinitus* by Morhardt & Hudson (1966), and of the utility of such torpor as a water-conserving mechanism in the closely related desert form *P. eremicus* (MacMillen, 1965), suggests that *P. crinitus* may well owe its water independence to a combination of moderate renal concentration and a periodic reduction in respiratory water loss through circadian torpor; this would be a fruitful area of investigation.

It is the water-dependent forms among the nocturnal desert rodents which should be of especial interest. Even though their renal functions (Table III) are not unusual, these water-dependent rodents thrive in the desert; therefore they are just as spectacular as the water-independent forms with which they share the same macroenvironment. It is obvious that their water needs are met, in spite of their physiological limitations.

Behavioural amelioration of the desert environment

Behaviour is a very difficult science to quantify, and the natural behaviour of small nocturnal species is almost impossible to measure directly. So that at present, in our attempts to assess the interplay between behaviour and physiology in the adaptive repertoires of nocturnal desert rodents, we have taken the easy way out and have confined our measurements to the more readily quantifiable and interpretable physiological responses. Where, within the same desert macroenvironment there are rodent species whose physiological responses, such as maximal urine concentrating capacity, differ by magnitudes, we have been content to explain that the physiological deficits are made up by behavioural advantages. But what are these advantages? How do they differ inter-specifically? And how are they employed in combination with the physiological capacities to add up to an adaptive repertoire for a desert existence? There are very few, if any, specific answers to these questions, for the entire field of investigation of the behavioural adaptations of nocturnal rodents for a desert existence is virtually untapped.

The behavioural capacities which seemingly would be most significant in coping with a desert existence, in addition to nocturnality and fossoriality, consist of prudent choices of microhabitats and foods. Even within the same desert macroenvironment there is a range of microenvironmental conditions, few of which have been adequately described, from extremely demanding alkaline flats to far less demanding nooks and crannies within rock outcrops. The range of potential foods is equally great, from various seeds to leafy vegetation, to other animals. Since the primary source of water for nocturnal desert rodents is their food, the term as used here is meant to include both the energy source and the water source (whether it be metabolic water, or preformed water). Activity periods, obviously, are also extremely important components of behaviour, for they determine the length of exposure to surface conditions, but fall under the categories of nocturnality and fossoriality.

CURRENT RESEARCH

In an attempt to resolve at least partially the extents to which certain nocturnal desert rodents rely upon urine concentrating capacities on the one hand, and behavioural amelioration on the other, to maintain water balance, I have embarked on a field study of states of water balance of a population of nocturnal desert rodents near the transition between the Mojave and Sonoran Deserts in California. Again, the direct, quantifiable measurements are almost entirely physiological, but also data are being collected on seasonal and circadian surface activity, population structure and fluctuation, and interspecific microhabitat preferences. While these observations will permit some behavioural interpretations, the relative importance of the various behavioural components which contribute to maintenance of water balance will be estimated largely by inference; that is, where measurable physiology leaves off, immeasurable behaviour begins.

In addition, however, the study will reveal on a year around basis states of water balance and, for the several species, the degrees to which renal concentrating capacities actually contribute to water economy, particularly during the critical summer months. The study is aimed at assessing physiological performance in the real world, which should provide a sounder perspective for our laboratory studies.

The study area is two miles south of Joshua Tree, San Bernardino County, California, and consists of a valley 0·8 km wide and 4·8 km long, bounded on each side by parallel granitic ridges. The valley floor is clothed by an admixture of Creosote Bush Shrub (*Larrea divaricata*) and Joshua Tree Woodland (*Yucca brevifolia*), is situated at an elevation of about 970 m and has a mean annual rainfall, recorded at the nearby town of Twenty-Nine Palms, of 105 mm (Bailey, 1966).

The nocturnal desert rodent population consists of the heteromyids *Dipodomys merriami*, *Perognathus fallax*, and *Perognathus longimembris*, and the cricetids *Peromyscus crinitus*, *Neotoma lepida*, and *Onychomys torridus*. Work commenced in October, 1970 and will continue through December, 1971. One hundred permanent trapping stations are employed, which adequately sample each of the obvious microhabitat components. Live trapping is conducted at the dark of the moon each month, the animals are removed from traps twice during the night and urine and blood are collected as soon after capture as is practicable. All animals are marked by toe clipping for identification and, after collection of samples, are released at their points of capture, so that they may be available for future sampling. Urine is collected by placing each animal in a separate cylindrical cage with wire mesh floor, under which is placed a dish with mineral oil. Urine is removed from the mineral oil and placed in small vials, where it is kept frozen until analysed. Blood is removed in heparinized capillary tubes from an orbital sinus, centrifuged, and then the plasma is stored frozen until analysis. Plasma and urine parameters to be measured include osmotic pressure (using a Mechrolab vapour pressure osmometer), urea concentration (Conway microdiffusion technique), and chlorinity (Aminco-Cotlove chloride titrator). In addition, samples of the same species are being maintained in the laboratory under known states of water intake; the same parameters of plasma and urine are measured, and serve as standards of states of water balance, to be compared with field measurements.

Some of the preliminary data are very interesting, and are reported herein. When maintained on an air-dried seed diet in the laboratory and without an additional water source, the response of body weight among the six species falls into two categories: those that maintain or gain body weight without water, and those that lose weight rapidly without water (Fig. 9). The water-independent forms include the heteromyids *Dipodomys merriami*, *Perognathus fallax*, *P. longimembris* and the cricetid *Peromyscus crinitus*. The cricetids *Neotoma lepida* and *Onychomys torridus* lost weight very rapidly and certainly would have perished had not the experiment been terminated. The distribution of these species within the habitat is also interesting. *D. merriami*, *P. longimembris*, and *O. torridus* are the only animals to occur on the valley floor, in seemingly the harshest (with respect to water economy) microhabitat. *P. fallax* occurs generally around the base of the granitic ridges, while *P. crinitus* and *N. lepida* are caught amongst the granitic outcrops, in more sheltered and apparently more mesic microhabitats.

To date, the parameter most extensively analysed from field samples is urine osmotic pressure. Data for the six species over the period November, 1970–June, 1971 are summarized in Figs 10, 11 and 12,

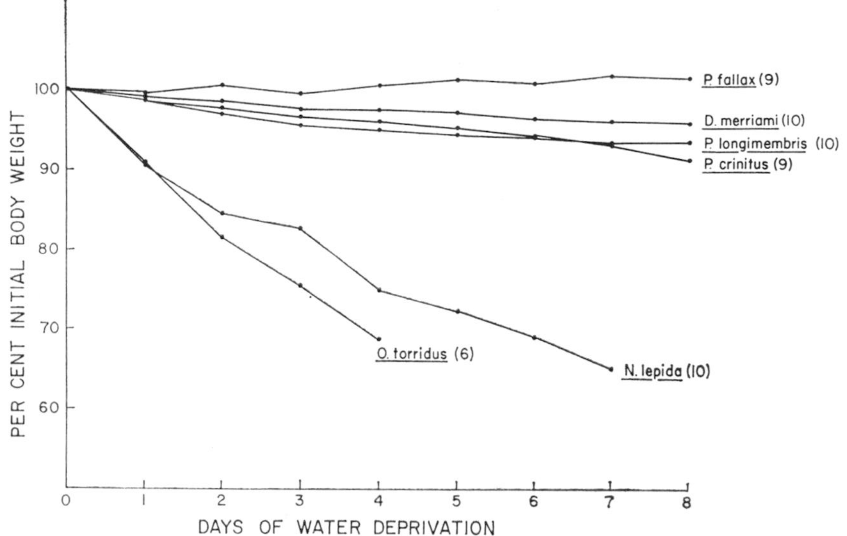

FIG. 9. The response of mean body weight to water deprivation in several sympatric species of California nocturnal desert rodents. The numbers in parentheses indicate sample size. Mean body weights prior to water deprivation were: *Neotoma lepida*, 125·5 g; *Peromyscus crinitus*, 14·5 g; *Onychomys torridus*, 20·2 g; *Dipodomys merriami*, 37·2 g; *Perognathus fallax*, 19·9 g; and *Perognathus longimembris*, 10·1 g.

along with representative urine concentrations for each in the laboratory and in hydrated and dehydrated states.

Data for two of the valley floor residents, *O. torridus* and *D. merriami* are summarized in Fig. 10. *O. torridus*, a carnivorous/insectivorous rodent whose diet is rich in water and protein, has consistently high urine concentrations, probably indicative of high rates of protein intake and urea production. Urine concentrations of *O. torridus* are significantly higher than those of *D. merriami* during the winter and spring months, December through April. Urine concentrations of *O. torridus* deprived of water in the laboratory and kept on a diet of mixed birdseed and sunflower seed approximate field values, but obviously the diets were very different. Laboratory *O. torridus* in a hydrated state and eating birdseed and sunflower seeds had consistently low urine values. Urine concentrations of the water-independent *D. merriami* were very low December through February (coinciding with the period of winter rain), intermediate during March and April (the period of annual plant growth), began to climb in May (the onset of the dry season), and were significantly highest in June (mean concentration, 3858 ± SD 528 m-osmole/l) the first dry, summer month. Since *D. merriami* would not

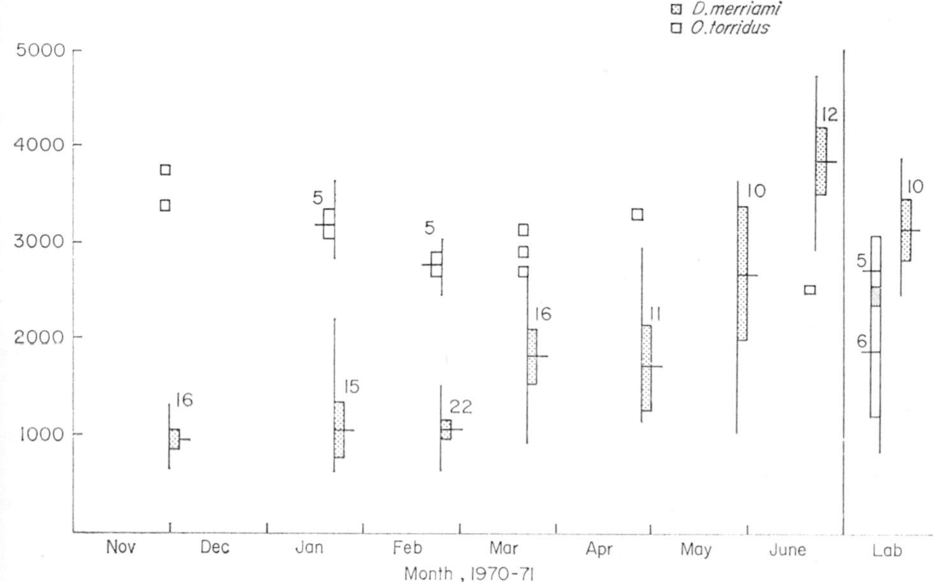

FIG. 10. Field and laboratory urine osmolarities of *Dipodomys merriami* and *Onychomys torridus*. Small squares represent individual measurements where sample sizes were too small for statistical evaluation; vertical lines represent ranges; horizontal lines represent means ($\bar{x}$); rectangles enclose the intervals $\bar{x} \pm T_{0.95}$ SE. Filled rectangles are for heteromyid rodents and hollow rectangles are for cricetid rodents. For lab measurements, areas of overlap between hydrated and dehydrated samples are indicated by cross-hatching.

take water in the laboratory, Fig. 10 indicates only urine concentrations for dehydrated animals; these (mean, 3165 ± SD 417 m-osmole/l) are significantly less concentrated than field urines in June, probably indicating merely that surface conditions in the field were more rigorous than laboratory conditions. Hence, of these two valley floor residents, urine concentrations of *O. torridus* appear to be uniformly high, and with little variation; those of *D. merriami* appear to fluctuate seasonally with very low values during the cooler, moister winter months, and very high values at least during the first hot and dry summer month (June).

In Fig. 11 are summarized the data for the valley floor resident *Perognathus longimembris*, and the inhabitant of granitic outcrops, *Peromyscus crinitus*, both independent of water in the laboratory (Fig. 9). As described above *P. longimembris* was dormant below the surface from at least October through February. They were first trapped in March (the onset of annual plant growth) and have been

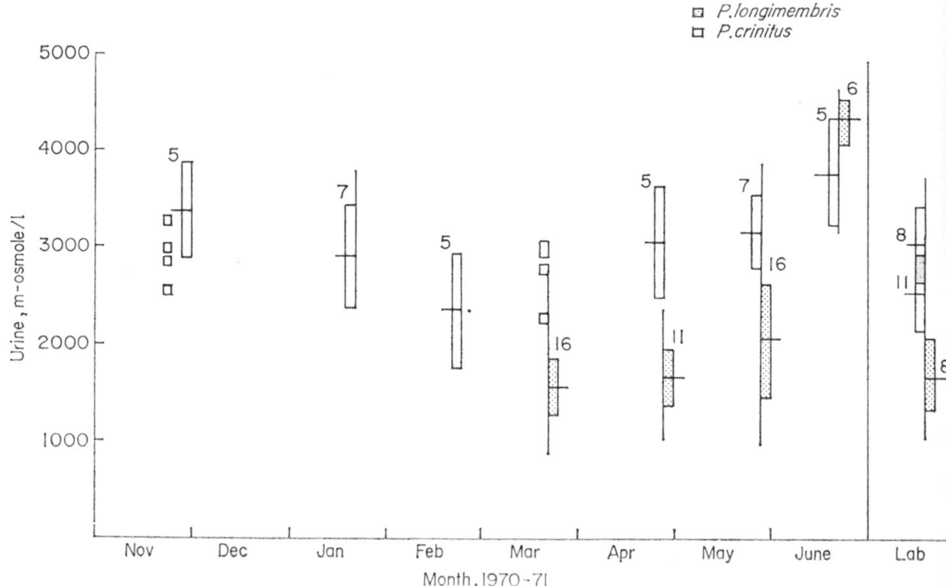

Fig. 11. Field and laboratory urine osmolarities of *Perognathus longimembris* and *Peromyscus crinitus*. Symbols as in Fig. 10.

abundantly represented through June. Their field urine concentrations from March through June (Fig. 11) correspond closely to those of *D. merriami* (Fig. 10), with whom they share the same valley floor microhabitat and presumably subsist on the same foods. The mean field urines of *P. longimembris* in June (4323 ± SD 201 m-osmole/l) are the highest yet recorded in the population, but are not significantly higher than those of *D. merriami*. *P. longimembris,* like *D. merriami*, will not take moisture in the laboratory, and the urine concentrations of animals maintained in the laboratory are unexpectedly low (mean, 1675 ± SD 403 m-osmole/l). The field urine concentrations of *Peromyscus crinitus* are uniformly rather higher than I would have anticipated, and compare rather favourably with those of the insectivorous/carnivorous *O. torridus* (Fig. 10), suggesting that *P. crinitus* may also take in a great deal of animal matter. Highest field urine concentrations in *P. crinitus* were from the June sample (mean, 3783 ± SD 392 m-osmole|l), but this sample was significantly higher than only the February sample. Laboratory urine concentrations of hydrated and dehydrated *P. crinitus* did not differ significantly, and covered a range which corresponded fairly well with the field samples.

The data for the least abundant, rock dwelling species *Perognathus fallax* and *Neotoma lepida* are summarized in Fig. 12. Although the sample sizes are low, the monthly urine concentrations of *P. fallax* appear to follow the same trends as in the other water-independent heteromyids, with low winter values, increased spring values and highest values as summer approaches. Also, as in *Perognathus longimembris*, laboratory urine concentrations of dehydrated *P. fallax* are very low (mean, 1241 ± SD 420 m-osmole/l). The few data available for *Neotoma lepida* indicate that this water-dependent form has uniformly low urine concentrations in the field which range in magnitude between those of fully hydrated and dehydrated animals in the laboratory.

While it is difficult to make a complete assessment of these data until corresponding information is available on plasma osmotic pressure, urine and plasma urea concentrations and chlorinities for the entire annual cycle, the preliminary results indicate that the six species segregate themselves according to microhabitat, and that within these microhabitats the granivorous heteromyids (*D. merriami*, *P. fallax*, and *P. longimembris*) have urine concentrations which vary indirectly with the water contents of the seeds upon which they subsist. The

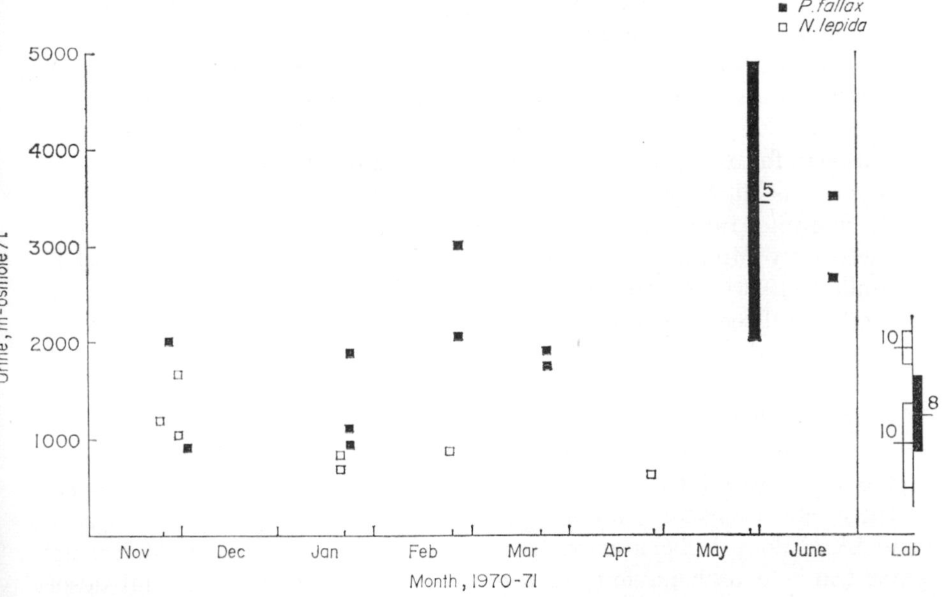

FIG. 12. Field and laboratory urine osmolarities of *Perognathus fallax* and *Neotoma lepida*. Symbols as in Fig. 10.

cricetid *Onychomys torridus*, a very water-dependent form, appears to derive all of the water it needs from its insectivorous/carnivorous diet, resulting in uniformly high urine concentrations. The other highly water dependent form, *Neotoma lepida*, occurs only in the sheltered rocky microhabitat, and its low urine values indicate unusual behavioural capacities for restricting water loss, and the likelihood of meeting water needs by eating vegetation. Lastly, the water-independent cricetid, *Peromyscus crinitus*, with unusually high and uniform urine concentrations, may well subsist on an insectivorous/carnivorous diet, rich both in protein and water.

AREAS OF FUTURE RESEARCH

The wealth of laboratory data we now have available on the water economy of nocturnal desert rodents has been geared primarily toward demonstrations of maximal tolerances and physiological capacities. These data provide us with valid inter-specific, intergeneric, and inter-familial comparisons, but they do not necessarily reflect actual performances in the field. What are needed now are more field-oriented studies and means of assessing states of water balance and rates of water turnover under the conditions actually encountered by the animals in their habitats. The study described above should provide information on states of water balance; we are hoping, in addition, to determine rates of water turnover by measuring the rate of disappearance of tritiated water injected into animals in the field and then released for recapture. Success in recapture of our nocturnal desert rodents is high, making such a study practical. Similar methods of determining rates of water turnover in the field have been used with success by Minnich & Shoemaker (1970) with desert lizards, and by Mullen (1970) who used water labelled with oxygen-18 in *Perognathus formosus*. Precise evaluations of states of water balance, renal performance, and rates of water turnover under natural conditions will enable us then to determine the extent to which the physiological capacities for water economy are employed.

The assessment of physiological capacities in the field emphasizes the role played by behaviour in determining the extents to which these capacities are employed. In water regulation, the reciprocal of physiology is behaviour. Qualitative and quantitative information on the role of behaviour in the water economy of nocturnal desert rodents is sorely needed. Particularly, information on food habits and preferences, and on microhabitat selection and utilization within the desert environment, will enable much more realistic interpretations of physiological performance.

Such primarily field-oriented studies are far more difficult to perform than laboratory studies, but that is where the information is, and the intellectual rewards will be well worth the expenditures.

Acknowledgements

The studies reported herein have been supported in part by National Science Foundation Grants G-18890, GB-5618, and, currently, GB-17833, as well as an advanced research grant under the Fulbright-Hays Act and administered by the Australian-American Educational Foundation.

References

Abbott, K. D. (1971). Water economy of the canyon mouse *Peromyscus crinitus stephensi*. *Comp. Biochem. Physiol.* **38A**: 37–52.

Bailey, H. P. (1966). *The climate of southern California.* Berkeley: University of California Press.

Bartholomew, G. A. (1964). The roles of physiology and behavior in the maintenance of homeostasis in the desert environment. *Symp. Soc. exp. Biol.* **18**: 7–29.

Bartholomew, G. A. (1971). The water economy of seed-eating birds that survive without drinking. *Int. Orn. Congr.* **15.**

Bartholomew, G. A. & Dawson, W. R. (1953). Respiratory water loss in some birds of southwestern United States. *Physiol. Zoöl.* **26**: 162–166.

Carpenter, R. E. (1966). A comparison of thermoregulation and water metabolism in the kangaroo rats *Dipodomys agilis* and *Dipodomys merriami*. *Univ. Calif. Publs Zool.* **78**: 1–36.

Chew, R. M. (1961). Water metabolism of desert-inhabiting vertebrates. *Biol. Rev.* **36**: 1–31.

Chew, R. M. & Butterworth, B. B. (1964). Ecology of rodents in Indian Cove (Mojave Desert), Joshua Tree National Monument, California. *J. Mammal.* **45**: 203–225.

Chew, R. M., Lindberg, R. G. & Hayden, P. (1965). Circadian rhythm of metabolic rate in pocket mice. *J. Mammal.* **46**: 477–494.

Getz, L. L. (1968). Relationship between ambient temperature and respiratory water loss of small mammals. *Comp. Biochem. Physiol.* **24**: 335–342.

Howell, A. B. & Gersh, I. (1935). Conservation of water by the rodent *Dipodomys*. *J. Mammal.* **16**: 1–9.

Hudson, J. W. (1964). Water metabolism in desert mammals. In *Thirst*: 211–235. Wayner, M. H. (ed.) New York: Pergamon Press.

Hudson, J. W. (1967). Variations in the patterns of torpidity of small homeotherms. In *Mammalian hibernation* **3**: 30–46, Fisher, K. C. *et al.*, (eds). New York: American Elsevier.

Jackson, D. C. & Schmidt-Nielsen, K. (1964). Countercurrent heat exchange in the respiratory passages. *Proc. natn. Acad. Sci. U.S.A.* **51**: 1192–1197.

Kennerly, T. E., Jr. (1964). Microenvironmental conditions of the pocket gopher burrow. *Texas J. Sci.* **16**: 395–441.

Lee, A. K. (1963). The adaptations to arid environments in wood rats of the genus *Neotoma*. *Univ. Calif. Publs Zool.* **64**: 57–96.

MacMillen, R. E. (1964). Population ecology, water relations, and social behavior of a southern California semidesert rodent fauna. *Univ. Calif. Publs Zool.* **71**: 1–66.

MacMillen, R. E. (1965). Aestivation in the cactus mouse, *Peromyscus eremicus*. *Comp. Biochem. Physiol.* **16**: 227–248.

MacMillen, R. E. & Lee, A. K. (1967). Australian desert mice: independence of exogenous water. *Science, N.Y.* **158**: 383–385.

MacMillen, R. E. & Lee, A. K. (1969). Water metabolism of Australian hopping mice. *Comp. Biochem. Physiol.* **28**: 493–514.

MacMillen, R. E. & Lee, A. K. (1970). Energy metabolism and pulmocutaneous water loss of Australian hopping mice. *Comp. Biochem. Physiol.* **35**: 355–369.

Minnich, J. E. & Shoemaker, V. H. (1970). Diet, behavior and water turnover in the desert iguana, *Dipsosaurus dorsalis*. *Am. Midl. Nat.* **84**: 496–509.

Morhardt, J. E. (1970). Body temperatures of white-footed mice (*Peromyscus* sp.) during starvation. *Comp. Biochem. Physiol.* **33**: 423–439.

Morhardt, J. E. & Hudson, J. W. (1966). Daily torpor induced in white-footed mice (*Peromyscus* spp.) by starvation. *Nature, Lond.* **212**: 1046–1047.

Mullen, R. K. (1970). Respiratory metabolism and body water turnover rates of *Perognathus formosus* in its natural environment. *Comp. Biochem. Physiol.* **32**: 259–265.

Schmidt-Nielsen, K. (1964a). *Desert animals: physiological problems of heat and water*. London: Oxford University Press.

Schmidt-Nielsen, K. (1964b). Terrestrial animals in dry heat: desert rodents. In *Handbook of physiology—Adaptation to the environment:* 493–507. Dill, D. B. (ed.) Washington D.C.: American Physiological Society.

Schmidt-Nielsen, B. & Schmidt-Nielsen, K. (1950). Evaporative water loss in desert rodents in their natural habitats. *Ecology* **31**: 75–85.

Schmidt-Nielsen, B. & Schmidt-Nielsen, K. (1951). A complete account of the water metabolism in kangaroo rats and an experimental verification. *J. cell. comp. Physiol.* **38**: 165–182.

Schmidt-Nielsen, K. & Haines, H. B. (1964). Water balance in a carnivorous desert rodent, the grasshopper mouse. *Physiol. Zoöl.* **37**: 259–265.

Schmidt-Nielsen, K., Hainsworth, F. R. & Murrish, D. E. (1970). Countercurrent heat exchange in the respiratory passages: effects on water and heat balance. *Resp. Physiol.* **9**: 263–276.

Schmidt-Nielsen, B., Schmidt-Nielsen, K., Brokaw, A. & Schneiderman, H. (1948). Water conservation in desert rodents. *J. cell. comp. Physiol.* **32**: 331–360.

Shkolnik, A. & Borut, A. (1969). Temperature and water relations in two species of spiny mice (*Acomys*). *J. Mammal.* **50**: 245–255.

Symp. zool. Soc. Lond. (1972) No. 31, 175–189.

BLOOD VOLUME REGULATION IN THE SPINY MOUSE: CAPILLARY PERMEABILITY CHANGES DUE TO DEHYDRATION

A. BORUT, M. HOROWITZ and M. CASTEL

Department of Zoology, Hebrew University, Jerusalem, Israel

SYNOPSIS

The spiny mouse, *Acomys cahirinus* Desmarest 1819, maintains its relative blood volume after exposure to acute dehydrating conditions, in contrast to the laboratory rat. The first part of this report deals with changes in permeability of the capillaries due to dehydration, seen as changes in the rate of leakage of marked blood albumin or a non protein tracer from the blood vascular system. Injections of Evans Blue and [^{14}C] dextran (mol. wt 75 000) into the circulation of spiny mice showed an increase in the half life ($t_{\frac{1}{2}}$) of the tracers in the dehydrated animal. In the rat the $t_{\frac{1}{2}}$ of both substances decreased. Blood albumin tagged by *in vivo* injections of [^{14}C] leucine had a $t_{\frac{1}{2}}$ similar to Evans Blue and dextran in both rodents. These findings support the view that a decrease in permeability due to dehydration plays an important part in blood volume regulation by maintaining the level of blood proteins in circulation. The second part of this report looks into the possibility of morphological changes in the fine structure of blood capillaries of spiny mice following the decrease in permeability. Myocardial capillaries were examined by electron microscopy. Horseradish peroxidase was employed as tracer in order to establish the nature of the endothelial cell junction which allows the diffusion of small molecules from the blood stream. The findings substantiate the claim for reduced permeability following dehydration. Most interesting is the presence of tight junctions in the capillaries—similar to those described in brain capillary endothelia. Tight junctions were found both in normal and in dehydrated spiny mice. It is suggested that the changes in permeability may be due to variations in the number of tight junctions.

INTRODUCTION

Acomys cahirinus Desmarest, 1819, the common spiny mouse (subfamily Murinae) inhabits rocky biotopes throughout Arabia, South Persia, the Eastern Mediterranean and spreads into West and East Africa down to Rhodesia (Ellerman & Morrison Scott, 1951). In these areas it penetrates into the most extreme desert regions. Several facts indicate that this mouse is likely to have far reaching adaptations to dehydration.

1. It lives in rocky crevices, does not dig burrows, does not have a padded nest and does not display any form of aestivation (Shkolnik, 1966).

2. The microclimate of its crevices, measured during the summer in a desert biotope (Ein Gedi, on the shores of the Dead Sea) revealed

temperatures around 30°C and relative humidity below 50% (Shkolnik, 1966).

3. Unusually high evaporation from the skin was found in this mouse even at an ambient temperature of 30°C (Shkolnik & Borut, 1969). Its reproductive biology probably also indicates harsh microclimatic conditions—the litter numbers only two to three large and well developed young. All this contrasts with the well known *modus operandi* of other desert rodents minimizing their water loss (Schmidt-Nielsen, 1964).

It is in the ability to preserve a reasonably constant blood plasma volume that we see an important adaptation to withstand dehydration. A disproportionately large amount of water lost from this compartment—as happens in man—will quickly bring about an explosive heat rise due to inability to dissipate the metabolic heat generated (Schmidt-Nielsen, 1964). Such an adaptation was in fact found by exposing spiny mice, kept on a dry diet in the laboratory, to acute dehydration (high ambient temperature and low humidity, henceforth designated as "dehydration" in this paper). As long as the mice remained in good condition their relative blood plasma volume was constant, in contrast to other rodent species serving as comparison: the laboratory rat and the Fat jird, *Meriones crassus* (Horowitz & Borut, 1970).

The mechanisms maintaining the relative distribution of fluid between the vascular and extravascular compartments are still not perfectly understood. But, as pointed out by Starling about 70 years ago, an important role is played by a balance of capillary hydrostatic and colloid osmotic pressures (Wiederhielm, 1968). We know almost nothing about the interplay of hydrostatic pressures in dehydrated animals that conserve their blood volumes. We do, however, know a little about the behaviour of their blood proteins, which are responsible for the colloid osmotic pressure. Schmidt-Nielsen (1964) revealed that in the camel—which conserves its blood volume—Evans Blue, a dye that couples with serum albumin when injected into the blood, remains for an unusually long time in circulation. We found that in the spiny mice the disappearance rate of the same dye from blood is lowered after dehydration (Horowitz & Borut, 1970). These findings support the assumption that the mechanism involved here in conservation is due in some measure to maintenance of proteins in the circulation. Schmidt-Nielsen (1964) also pointed out that the longer life of Evans Blue in the circulation might be due to:

1. Lower metabolism of plasma albumin—or in our case lowered metabolism after dehydration (this includes also the possibility of a more stable binding of the dye).

2. Lower permeability of the vascular bed to proteins.

The first part of this report tries to separate these possible causes by comparing the behaviour of a non-protein tracer, with albumin, in spiny mice and in rats.

Changes in permeability of blood vessels to proteins may be due to two main factors or their interplay.

1. Changes in pressure relations across the vessels, with which we will not deal at present because of lack of sufficient information.

2. Changes in permeability *per se* due to variations in number of functioning capillaries, which alter the effective filtration area (vasoconstriction or vasodilation), or to changes in pore size for protein filtration.

In the second part of this report we shall look into possible morphological evidence on this last point with the help of electron microscopy.

The morphological equivalent of the small pore system, which is responsible for the diffusion of comparatively small water soluble molecules from capillaries with continuous endothelia (muscle, heart, skin, etc.), is the endothelial cell junction. The nature of this junction, which is the narrowed portion of the intercellular endothelial cleft as seen by the electron microscope, has been widely debated. Much has been contributed to resolving this question by the use of tracer molecules (Karnovsky, 1967). In capillaries having a continuous endothelium these cell junctions are now considered to be "gap junctions" with a cleft of up to 40 Å. Horseradish peroxidase, having a mol. wt of 40 000, penetrates and delineates them (Brightman & Reese, 1969). Another system which might transport proteins in the same capillaries (the large pore system) is associated with vesicular transport by pinocytotic vacuoles (Bruns & Palade, 1968). It should be pointed out that the relative importance of the vesicular and intercellular pathway is still unclear. Bearing these contentions in mind we decided to rely in our analysis of spiny mice capillaries only on preparations employing peroxidase as a tracer molecule, and stained with uranyl-acetate *en bloc*. Endocardial capillaries were studied as they have been reported to be consistently open, and because the relevant techniques were perfected on cardiac capillaries in mice (Karnovsky, 1967).

MATERIALS AND METHODS

Animals and treatments

Acomys cahirinus from a stock trapped near the Dead Sea and weighing 30–50 g (males and non-pregnant females) were used. Albino

Rattus norvegicus, Sabar race, were obtained from the Hebrew University Medical School. The specimens used (males) weighed 100–150 g. Both species are routinely reared in the Zoology Department. Dehydration was carried out in a thermostatically controlled room at 37 ± 1°C and relative humidity of 15–20%, proceeding to a body weight loss of around 12% in the spiny mice and 19% in the rats (Horowitz & Borut, 1970). In this series of experiments animals were deprived of food for 6 to 12 h beforehand.

Injection of tracers (dextran and Evans Blue) for permeability measurements

Powdered [^{14}C] dextran (NEN), 2 μCi/100 g body weight with 6% dextran carrier was added to 1% Evans Blue in saline. Both dextrans had a molecular weight similar to plasma albumin, 75 000. Normal (hydrated) and dehydrated animals were anaesthetized with Pentothal, 4·0–4·1 mg/100 g body weight. The tracer solution was then injected into the tail vein (rats) or intracardially (spiny mice). The following volumes were injected: 0·30–0·35 ml into normal rats, 0·20–0·25 ml into dehydrated rats and 0·1 ml into spiny mice. Blood was sampled from the tail hourly during 4 h following the injection. Blood plasma was assayed for Evans Blue photometrically. Plasma (10 μl) was diluted in Bray solution containing 4% Cab–O–Sil (Rapkin, 1963) and assayed for radioactivity in a Packard Tricarb Liquid Scintillation Spectrometer.

Albumin [^{14}C] leucine exchange time

This was calculated from studies on plasma protein turnover in normal and dehydrated spiny mice and rats. These experiments will be reported elsewhere (Horowitz, 1971). Essentially the method entails *in vivo* injections of [^{14}C] leucine into the mice; serial blood sampling; electrophoretic separation of the various plasma proteins and assay of their radioactivity. The albumin exchange between the intra- and extra-vascular compartments was calculated from the appropriate phase of the radioactivity decay curve (Schultze & Heremans 1966).

Electron microscopy of cardiac capillaries

A group of 16 spiny mice, weighing 35–45 g was used in these experiments. Dehydrated and normal mice were anaesthetized with Pentothal and injected intracardially with 3–5 mg horseradish peroxidase (Pentex or Sigma II) in 0·3–0·4 ml isotonic saline. Controls were injected with saline only. At 5, 10, 15 and 30 min after peroxidase injection, both dehydrated and normal animals were sacrificed by decapitation. Myocardium, derived from the lower tip of the heart—well away from the injection site in the middle of the left ventricle—was fixed and treated according to Karnovsky (1967). All tissues were stained with uranyl acetate *en bloc* for 2 h. Thin sections were cut with glass knives on an LKB III Ultrotome, and stained with Reynolds lead citrate prior to examination in an AEI EM6B electron microscope at 60kV or a Philips 300 electron microscope at 60 kV.

RESULTS AND DISCUSSION

Capillary permeability: dextran and Evans Blue injections

Both tracers injected simultaneously show similar behaviour (Figs 1, 2). They are retained longer in the circulation of dehydrated spiny mice and cleared faster in dehydrated rats. The half life ($t_{\frac{1}{2}}$) of Evans Blue in the circulation of spiny mice (Table I) increases by 45·6% and the dextran by 21%. In the rat the $t_{\frac{1}{2}}$ decreases by 44·3% and 33·8% respectively. Both tracers have a similar molecular size. Dextran was used by Mayerson, Wolfram, Shirley & Wasserman (1960) to investigate regional differences in capillary permeability and they found that dextrans of molecular size comparable to albumin are lost at approximately the same rate. Therefore the best explanation seems to be a decrease in capillary permeability of the dehydrated spiny mice, and an increase in the dehydrated rat, which are independent of changes in protein metabolism. The exchange rate of blood albumin [^{14}C] leucine in both species also supports this conclusion (Table I). The decay curve levels off to such an extent in the dehydrated spiny mice that it is impossible to calculate the $t_{\frac{1}{2}}$. However, it decreases to half its value in the dehydrated rat. The values calculated from the exchange experiments are about double those found by Evans Blue injections. Differences in the experimental manipulation and behaviour of the mice might contribute to this. In a previous publication (Horowitz & Borut, 1970) several spiny mice revealed a very long life of Evans Blue in the circulation. This is the reason for the longer $t_{\frac{1}{2}}$ and the large standard deviation which is reported there. Kidney ligation in rats also increased the $t_{\frac{1}{2}}$ of Evans Blue in that instance. Nevertheless, the trend remained essentially the same. Another possibility is the incorporation of [^{14}C] leucine into other sources and its gradual release into newly and continuously synthetized albumin. Changes in albumin metabolism contributed little, if anything, to the above described phenomena. Any increase in synthesis found after dehydration was compensated by increased catabolism (Horowitz, 1971).

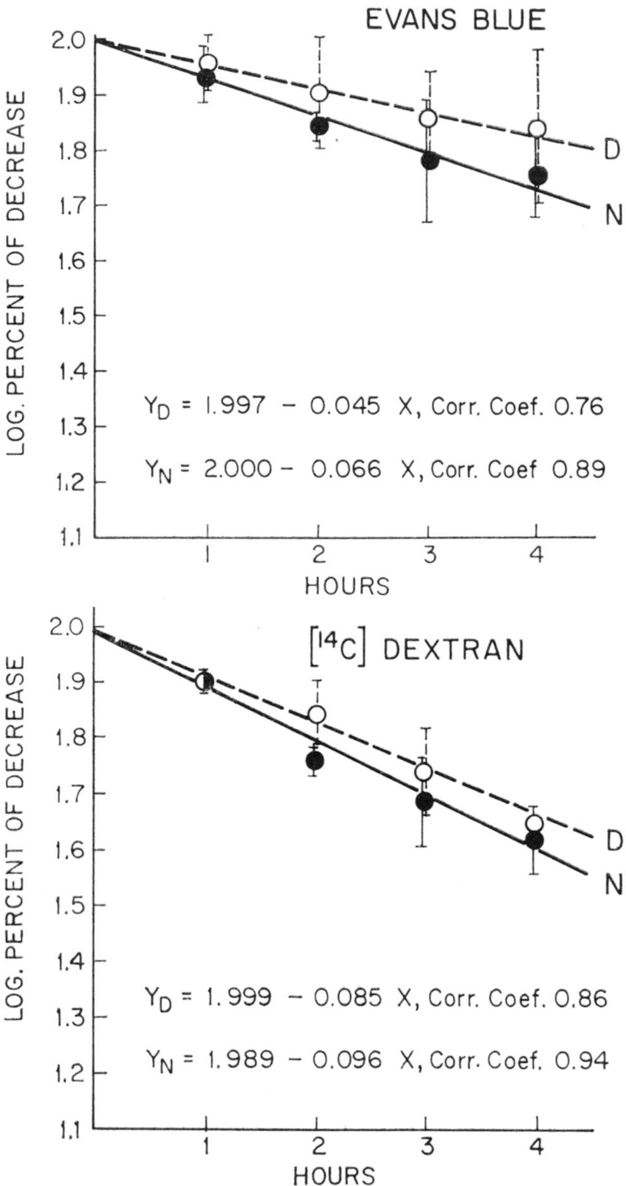

FIG. 1. The decrease in concentrations of [^{14}C] dextran (below) and Evans Blue (above) in plasma of normal (closed circles) and dehydrated (open circles) *A. cahirinus*. Data given as the logarithmic value of the percentage decrease in concentration of the tracers. Vertical line = SD, $n = 6$, dehydrating conditions 37 ± 1°C. 15–20% rh.

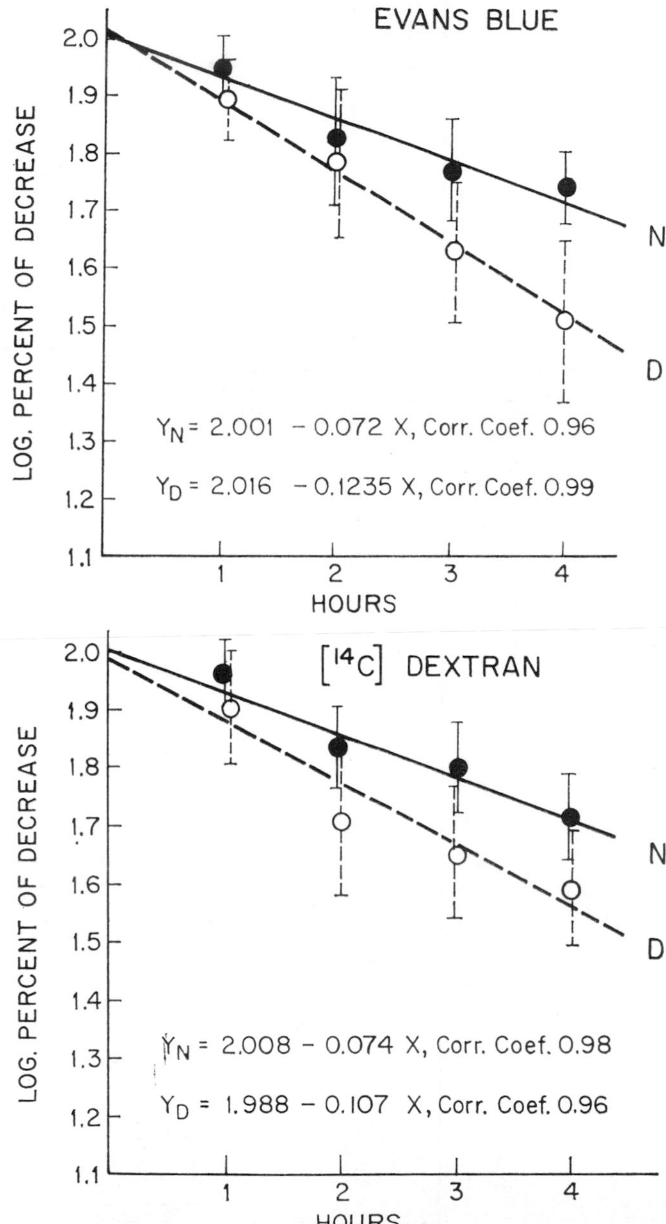

FIG. 2. The decrease in concentrations of [^{14}C] dextran (below) and Evans Blue (above) in plasma of normal (closed circles) and dehydrated (open circles) *R. norvegicus*. Data given as the logarithmic value of the percentage decrease in concentration of the tracers. Vertical line = SD, $n = 6$, dehydrating conditions 37 ± 1°C, 15–20% rh.

TABLE I

Half lives ($t_{\frac{1}{2}}$) *of various tracers in blood of normal and dehydrated* A. cahirinus *and* R. norvegicus. *The data are given in h and min, dehydrating conditions*: 37 ± 1°C, 15–20% *rh*.

	$t_{\frac{1}{2}}$ of Evans Blue*		$t_{\frac{1}{2}}$ of [^{14}C] Dextran*		$t_{\frac{1}{2}}$ of Albumin [^{14}C] leucine†	
	Normal	Dehydrated	Normal	Dehydrated	Normal	Dehydrated
A. cahirinus	4 : 45	6 : 30	3 : 10	3 : 50	8 : 30	∞
R. norvegicus	4 : 15	2 : 25	4 : 15	2 : 45	8	4

* Calculated from regression lines of decrease curve (Figs 1 & 2).

† $t_{\frac{1}{2}}$ of albumin exchanged between plasma and extravascular fluid calculated from decay curve of albumin labelled *in vivo* by injections of [^{14}C] leucine (see methods).

We have considered a nervous control mechanism as a possible means of altering blood vessel permeability. The adrenergic vasoconstrictor centre induces an increase in vascular resistance which decreases capillary permeability. The decrease in permeability with vasoconstriction is due to a decrease in effective pore area consequent to a reduction in the number of functioning capillaries (Renkin & Rosell, 1962a). This does not exclude the alternative possibility of morphological changes in the endothelial intercellular clefts. In contrast to the spiny mice, an increase in rat capillary permeability, which could allow increased leakage of small plasma proteins from the circulatory system was found. Changes in vessel permeability could be the result of increased histamine or serotonin release which could widen the venule endothelial gaps (discussed later). Another possible explanation of increase in capillary permeability may be the decrease of the nervous vasoconstrictor activity, consequently decreasing the blood vessel tonus (Renkin & Rosell, 1962b). In both cases the effective permeable area would increase. The following evidence shows that the idea of changes in capillary pore size rather than changes in available permeable area is more likely:

1. Dextran and Evans Blue half lives differed after dehydration, in the spiny mouse. The percentage change of Evans Blue labelled albumin $t_{\frac{1}{2}}$ was greater than that for dextran, but the observed dextran $t_{\frac{1}{2}}$ was shorter than that of Evans Blue. This indicates that the dextran injected passes more freely than the Evans Blue labelled albumin from the vascular into extravascular pools. This difference can best be explained by changes in pore size, rather than a change in available pore area.

2. The same explanation holds for increased vascular permeability, due to damage by a variety of physical, chemical and thermal agents. It is based on leakage from widening gaps in the endothelia, in this case with a predilection to occur in venules (Cotran, 1967). The same seems to occur in brain capillary endothelia (Brightman, Klatzo, Olsson & Reese, 1970).

Electron microscopy of cardiac capillaries in the spiny mice

Penetration of peroxidase

The behaviour of horseradish peroxidase in the blood system of spiny mice showed a familiar pattern. In capillaries of normal spiny mice, fixed 10 min after injection (Fig. 4), dark, electron-opaque, reaction product, showing the presumed sites of penetration of the enzyme is found extravascularly in high density. In capillaries of dehydrated spiny mice, fixed 10 min after injection, only slight

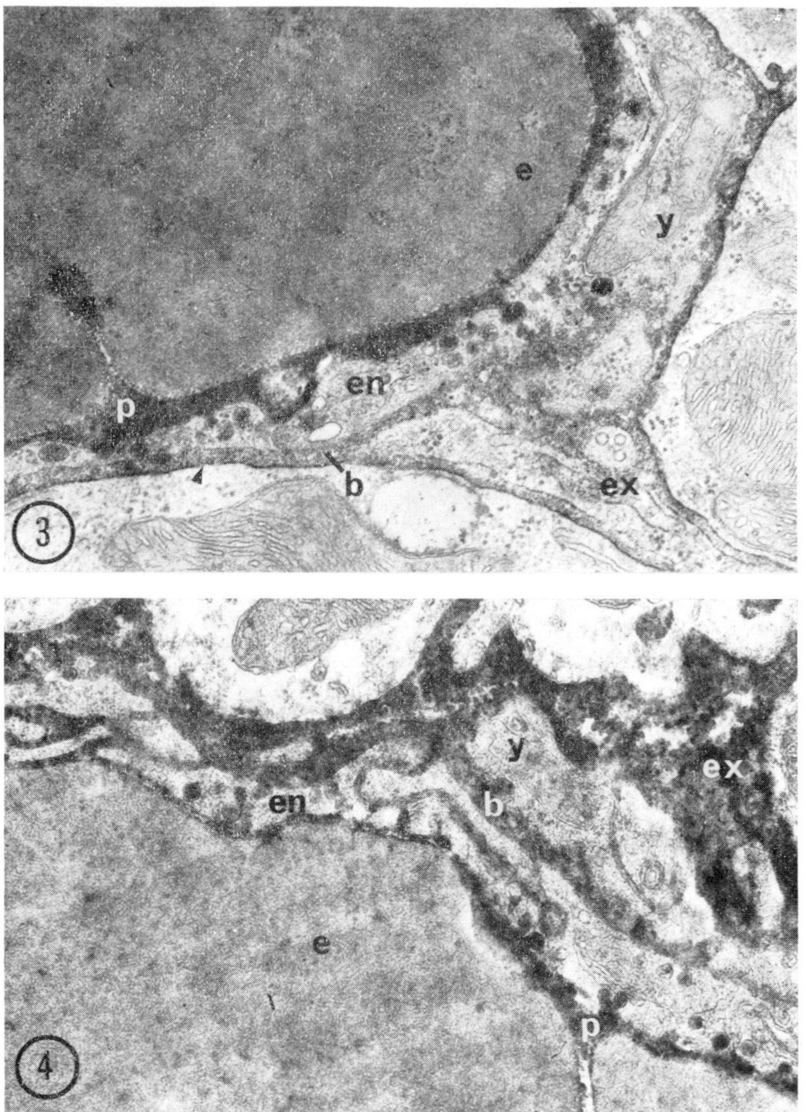

FIG. 3. Cardiac capillary from dehydrated *A. cahirinus* sacrificed 10 min after peroxidase injection. Peroxidase (*p*), the black reaction product, is present in the lumen around the erythrocyte (*e*) and in pinocytotic vesicles of the endothelium (*en*), but the basement lamina (*b*) and the pericapillary extra-cellular space (*ex*) are unstained. Endogenous peroxidase reaction of the sarcolemma (arrow head). Pericyte (*y*) (× 26 700).

FIG. 4. Cardiac capillary from normal *A. cahirinus* sacrificed 10 min after peroxidase injection. Peroxidase (*p*) is present in the lumen around the erythrocyte (*e*), in pinocytotic vesicles of the endothelium (*en*), has reached the basement lamina (*b*), and extensively permeated the pericapillary extra-cellular space (*ex*). Pericyte (*y*) (× 27 000).

extravascular location is noticed—although there are many dense pinocytotic vesicles (Fig. 3). When 30 min elapsed between injection and fixation in normal spiny mice, almost no reaction product could be detected, either intra- or extra-vascularly. Only an occasional electron-dense vacuole indicates that the enzyme had been present, and was probably washed away by the blood stream (Fig. 7). The same phenomenon was found in cardiac capillaries of laboratory mice (Karnovsky, 1967). In dehydrated spiny mice on the other hand, high density of reaction product prevailed, both extra- and intra-vascularly (Figs 5 & 6). In this case a decrease in the glomerular filtration rate may contribute to the longer life of peroxidase in the circulation of the dehydrated spiny mice, but cannot explain the difference after 10 min. It therefore appears that these findings substantiate the claim for reduced permeability.

Intercellular junctions of the myocardial endothelia

Much to our surprise the intercellular junctions look like tight junctions (Fig. 8), such as those described in brain capillaries, choroid plexus epithelium (Brightman & Reese, 1969) and hepatocytes (Goodenough & Revel, 1970), that is, a series of punctate membrane contacts. It is the geometrical arrangement of such contacts, which probably hinders the passage of peroxidase out of the capillary lumen (Orci, Matter & Rouiller, 1971).

Tight junctions were found both in normal and in dehydrated spiny mice. Since there are usually many pinocytotic vesicles filled with the reaction product, in contrast to the situation in the brain (Brightman & Reese, 1969), it is difficult to establish whether there are also gap junctions, because what looks like passage of peroxidase through an intercellular cleft might be due to discharge of pinocytotic vacuoles into the cleft beyond the blocked tight junction (Fig. 8), or vacuolar transport of peroxidase and filling of the gap by backflow from the extracellular space.

The assumption we most favour at present is that during dehydration more junctions close into tight junctions and reduce the permeability of the vascular system to small proteins. Such a system for cellular control over vascular permeability was also suggested by Brightman & Reese (1969) for the mammalian brain. However, the possibility may exist that changes in pinocytotic transport rate of peroxidase are important as well as leakage at other sites. One way to validate the assumption would be to quantitate the tight junctions with lanthanum staining, in which case the stain is added with the fixative and is not influenced by vacuolar transport at all.

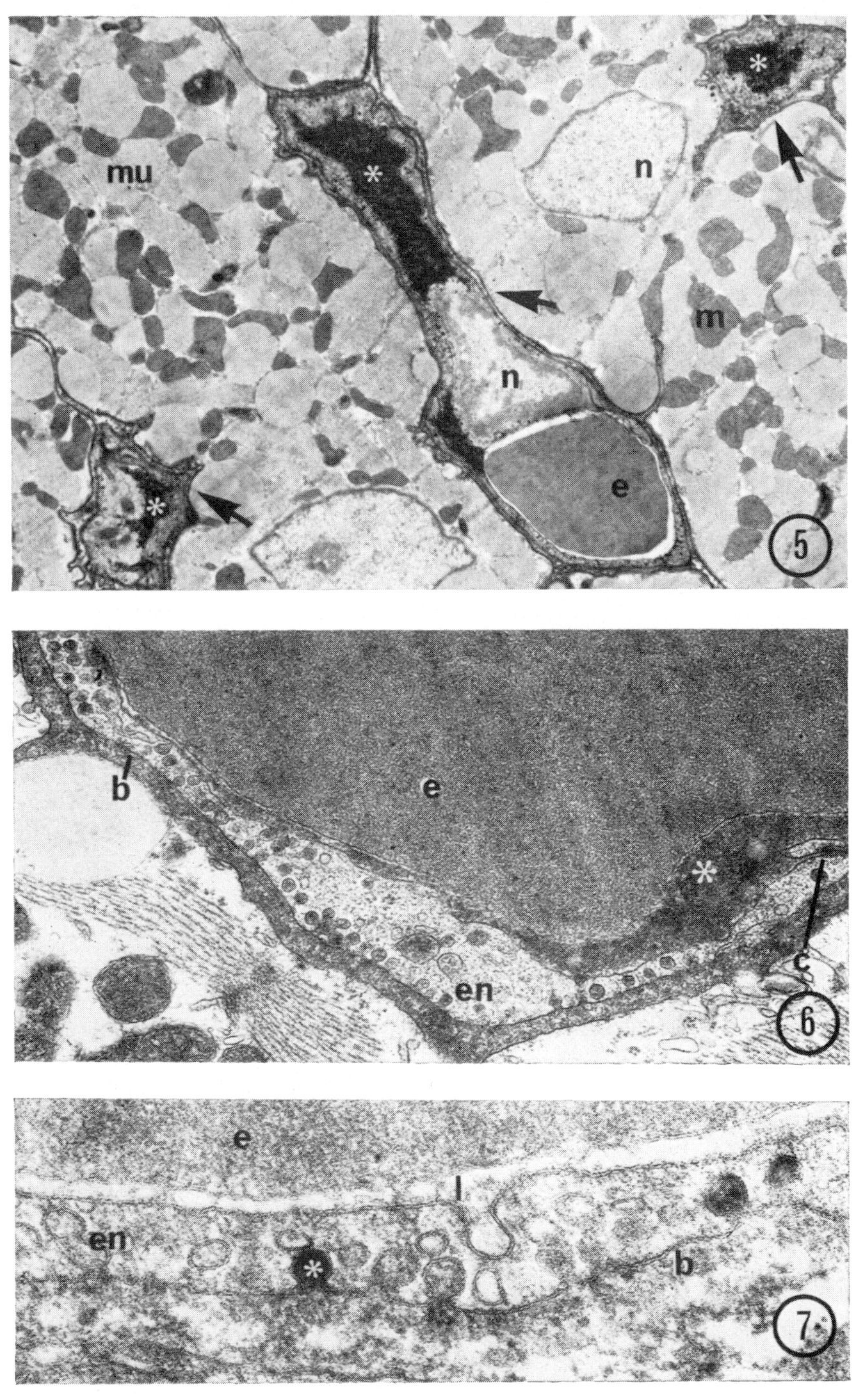
mu
n
m
n
e
5
b
e
en
c
6
e
l
en
b
7

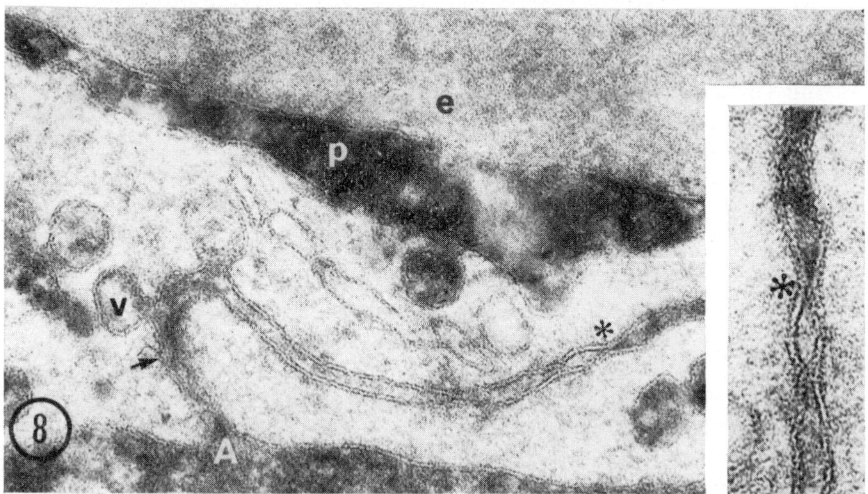

FIG. 8. Intercellular endothelial cleft of cardiac capillary from normal *A. cahirinus* sacrificed 10 min after peroxidase injection. The passage of peroxidase from the lumen through the cleft has been checked at a tight junction (asterisk). The origin of the peroxidase (arrow) in the abluminal (A) end of the cleft is probably from pinocytotic vesicles (*v*). Erythrocyte (*e*) (× 100 000). Inset is higher magnification of the tight junction (asterisk) (× 180 000).

CONCLUSIONS

In the dehydrated spiny mice there is a decrease in permeability of the vascular bed to solutes of a molecular size similar to that of plasma albumin. This might depend at least partially on the unique nature of the junctions found in the myocardial capillary endothelium which is considered representative of capillaries with continuous endothelia. The resulting decrease in permeability contributes to the conservation of colloid osmotic pressure in the blood of the dehydrated spiny mouse (Horowitz, 1971). This assists in conserving the plasma volume by

---

FIG. 5. Low magnification of three cardiac capillaries (arrows) from dehydrated *A. cahirinus* sacrificed 30 min after peroxidase injection, all containing peroxidase (asterisks) within the lumen. Endothelial nuclei (*n*); erythrocyte (*e*); myocardium (*mu*); mitochondrion (*m*) (× 8960).

FIG. 6. Higher magnification of cardiac capillary from dehydrated *A. cahirinus* sacrificed 30 min after peroxidase injection. Peroxidase (asterisk) in lumen around erythrocyte (*e*) and in pinocytotic vesicles of endothelium (*en*); basement lamina (*b*) and pericapillary extracellular space are heavily stained. Intercellular endothelial cleft (*c*) (× 23 000).

FIG. 7. Portion of cardiac capillary from normal *A. cahirinus* sacrificed 30 min after peroxidase injection. Only traces of peroxidase (asterisk) are found in isolated pinocytotic vesicles. No peroxidase in lumen (1). Erythrocyte (*e*); endothelium (*en*); basement lamina (*b*) (× 76 000).

creating a driving force which overcomes the negative hydrostatic pressure of the tissues (Guyton, 1963) and positive hydrostatic pressure of the vessels in the dehydrated animal.

Acknowledgements

We wish to thank Mrs. Y. Shimoni and Mrs. H. Arad for efficient and reliable technical assistance.

References

Brightman, M. W. & Reese, T. S. (1969). Junctions between intimately apposed cell membranes in the vertebrate brain. *J. cell. Biol.* **40**: 648–677.

Brightman, M. W., Klatzo, I., Olsson, Y. & Reese, T. S. (1970). The blood brain barrier to proteins under normal and pathological condition. *J. neurol. Sci.* **10**: 215–239.

Bruns, R. R. & Palade, G. E. (1968). Studies on blood capillaries, II. Transport of ferritin molecules across the wall of muscle epithelium. *J. cell. Biol.* **37**: 277–299.

Cotran, R. S. (1967). The fine structure of the microvasculature in relation to normal and altered permeability. In *Physical basis of circulatory transport*: 249–275. Reeve, E. B. & Guyton, A. C. (eds). Philadelphia: Saunders.

Ellerman, J. R. & Morrison Scott, T. C. S. (1951). *Checklist of Palaearctic and Indian mammals.* London: Brit. Mus. (Nat. Hist.)

Goodenough, D. A. & Revel, J. (1970). A fine structural analysis of intracellular junctions in the mouse liver. *J. cell. Biol.* **45**: 272–290.

Guyton, A. C. (1963). A concept of negative interstitial pressure based on pressures in implanted perforated capsules. *Circulation Res.* **12**: 399–414.

Horowitz, M. (1971). *The physiological adaptations of the blood system of desert animals to dehydration.* Ph.D. Thesis. Jerusalem: Hebrew University.

Horowitz, M. & Borut, A. (1970). Effect of acute dehydration on body fluid compartments in three rodent species, *Rattus norvegicus, Acomys cahirinus* and *Meriones crassus*. *Comp. Biochem. Physiol.* **35**: 283–290.

Karnovsky, M. J. (1967). The ultrastructural basis of capillary permeability studied with peroxidase as a tracer. *J. cell. Biol.* **35**: 213–236.

Manjo, G. (1965). Ultrastructure of the vascular membrane In *Handbook of physiology*—Circulation **3**: 2293–2377, Hamilton, W. F. (ed.). Washington: American Physiological Society.

Mayerson, H. S., Wolfram, C. G., Shirley, H. H. & Wasserman, K. (1960). Regional differences in capillary permeability. *Am. J. Physiol.* **198**: 155–160.

Orci, L., Matter, A. & Rouiller, Ch. (1971). A comparative study of freeze-etch replicas and thin sections of rat liver. *J. ultrastruct. Res.* **35**: 1–19.

Rapkin, E. (1963). Liquid scintillation measurement of radiocativity in heterogenous systems. *Packard Techn. Bull.* **5**: 33–50

Renkin, E. M. & Rosell, S. (1962a). The influence of sympathetic, adrenergic vasoconstrictor nerves on transport of diffusable solutes from blood to tissues in skeletal muscle. *Acta physiol. scand.* **54**: 223–240.

Renkin, E. M. & Rosell, S. (1962b). Effect of different type of vasodilator mechanisms on vascular tonus and on transcapillary exchange of diffusable material in skeletal muscle. *Acta physiol. scand.* **54**: 241–251.

Schmidt-Nielsen, K. (1964). *Desert animals: physiological problems of heat and water.* Oxford: Clarendon Press.

Shkolnik, A. (1966). *Studies in the comparative biology of Israel's two species of spiny mice (genus* Acomys) Ph.D. Thesis Jerusalem: Hebrew University.

Shkolnik, A. & Borut, A. (1969). Temperature and water relations in two species of spiny mice (*Acomys*). *J. Mammal.* **50**: 245–255.

Schultze, H. E. & Heremans, J. F. (1966). *Molecular biology of human proteins* **1**. Amsterdam: Elsevier.

Wiederhielm, C. A. (1968). Dynamics of transcapillary fluid exchange. *J. gen. Physiol.* **52**: 29s–63s.

Symp. zool. Soc. Lond. (1972) No. 31, 191–213.

A COMPARATIVE STUDY OF TEMPERATURE REGULATION IN GROUND SQUIRRELS WITH SPECIAL REFERENCE TO THE DESERT SPECIES

J. W. HUDSON, D. R. DEAVERS and S. R. BRADLEY

Section of Ecology and Systematics, Division of Biological Sciences, Cornell University, Ithaca, New York, U.S.A.

SYNOPSIS

The resting metabolism and pulmocutaneous water loss of *Citellus armatus*, *C. beldingi*, *C. lateralis*, *C. richardsoni*, *C. spilosoma* and *C. townsendi* was measured at night using infra-red and paramagnetic analysis. These ground squirrels are from montane, grassland and desert environments. The basal metabolism of these six species was combined with data from two additional species, *C. mohavensis* and *C. tereticaudus* to establish the mathematical relationship between body weight and metabolism: M (ml O_2/g/h) = $3{\cdot}24\ W^{0{\cdot}66}$ when the mean body temperature is $35{\cdot}7 \pm 0{\cdot}2$ (2 SE) °C. The pulmocutaneous water loss and oxygen consumption of three species was measured during the day at ambient temperatures of 35°C to 41°C. *Citellus armatus*, *C. spilosoma* and *C. townsendi* evaporated 100% of their metabolic heat at ambient temperatures of 39°C to 41°C. The ambient temperature at which the first signs of thermal distress appear in animals exposed to high ambient temperatures varied in conformity with the habitat of the species. The least tolerant was *C. armatus*, a montane species, whereas the most tolerant was *C. tereticaudus*, a ground squirrel which lives in the very hot desert. The thermal conductance exceeded the predicted level by 25–50% for many of the measurements. The high level of conductance and reduced level of basal metabolism are adaptive for coping with a need to dissipate endogenous heat when there is little difference between the body and ambient temperature. It is assumed, however, that these physiological features represent adaptations for hibernation, i.e., rapid cooling and/or warming and have become utilized for desert habitation with slight quantitative shifts in physiological performance. These results confirm the previous observation that *C. tereticaudus* is especially adapted to cope with the severe desert environment.

INTRODUCTION

While there is considerable literature on hibernation in ground squirrels (Baldwin and Johnson, 1941; Bartholomew & Hudson, 1960; Hammel, Dawson, Abrams & Andersen, 1968; Folk, 1960; Lyman & O'Brien, 1960; Strumwasser, 1960; Strumwasser, Gilliam & Smith, 1964; Twente & Twente, 1965) only a few studies (Barnes, 1965; Neumann & Cade, 1965; Popovic, 1959) are concerned with non-hibernating thermoregulatory capacities, and many of those are incomplete, results inconsistent within a single species (Erikson, 1956; Hock, 1960), or fail to consider diurnal differences in metabolism and body temperature (Ogle, 1970) as reported for *Citellus tereticaudus* (Hudson, 1964).

Kayser (1961) described hibernators as characterized by

1. a lower mean central temperature,
2. more marked diurnal temperature rhythms,
3. a marked elevation of metabolism in response to lowering ambient temperature,
4. inadequate physical heat regulation,
5. inadequate physical regulation at ambient temperatures above thermal neutrality, and
6. a basal metabolic rate which decreases during the summer and declines further during the autumn while chemical regulation becomes less intense.

However, some ground squirrels, e.g., *Citellus mexicanus* (Barnes, 1965), *C. tridecemlineatus* (Folk, 1960) and *C. citellus* (Popovic, 1959) have basal metabolic rates (at thermal neutrality) equal to or slightly above the level expected on the basis of body size. In one case (Barnes, 1965), the body temperature at night was unusually high—$37{\cdot}6 \pm 0{\cdot}29$°C ($\pm 2$ SE). Erikson (1956) reported a nocturnal metabolism for two of his *C. undulatus*, weighing 900 and 950 g, between 0·3 and 0·6 ml O_2/g/h—a value he describes as considerably below the "mouse to elephant" curve, although according to the equation of Morrison, Ryser & Dawe (1959), the expected values should be 0·60 and 0·61 ml O_2/g/h, respectively—values similar to Erikson's measurements (1956). The basal metabolism of the desert ground squirrel, *Citellus tereticaudus* is about 60% below the predicted level (Hudson, 1964) and presumably this low level of endogenous heat production is adaptive for coping with high ambient temperatures because there is less heat to be evaporatively dissipated. However, the low basal metabolic rate may be related in some way to its capacity to hibernate and simply be pre-adaptive for desert habitation. It is also possible that this low weight relative metabolism is a consequence of large fat deposits which have the effect of a disproportionate reduction in the total metabolism with the addition of tissue not metabolically active (Hayward, 1965). However, McNab (1968) contends that the low basal rates of metabolism of the desert inhabiting *Peromyscus crinitus* and the naked mole-rat *Heterocephalus glaber* are due not to the accumulation of large amounts of depot fat, but represent adaptations to their environments. Interestingly, neither of these studies has considered the insulative effects of subcutaneous fat and the possible modification of conductance, both with respect to heat gain and heat loss, thus ignoring an important secondary effect of fat deposition with respect to metabolism.

By now there have been many examples which refute the conclusion of Scholander *et al.* (1950) that metabolism is not adaptively modified in homeotherms. In fact, there are even population differences in metabolism as well as other aspects of thermoregulation which adapt homeotherms to different climates (Hudson & Kimzey, 1966). Since ground squirrels live in a variety of habitats, it is reasonable to expect adaptive differences in their non-hibernating thermoregulatory abilities. It has already been demonstrated that the desert ground squirrel, *Citellus* (*Ammospermophilus*) *leucurus*, a non-hibernator is more susceptible to high ambient temperatures than its congener and sympatric species, *Citellus tereticaudus* (Hudson & Wang, 1969). Discernible differences in other species might necessitate comparative studies done within the same laboratory rather than relying on compilation of data from various investigators because of the differences in technique by which various investigators determine basal metabolism, such as whether metabolism is measured during the active or inactive period (Aschoff & Pohl, 1970). A comparative study of ground squirrels which live in desert, montane, and grassland habitats should yield information as to which physiological features are

1. typical of this genus and probably related to hibernation and
2. which features are adaptive to specific environments during the non-hibernating period.

By measuring metabolism with successive levels of fattening, it should also be possible to determine the effect of fat depots on weight relative metabolism, a particularly important consideration with this particular group of mammals.

MATERIALS AND METHODS

Five species of Citellus: *C. spilosoma*, *C. richardsoni*, *C. armatus*, *C. townsendi* and *C. beldingi* were collected during the spring of 1970 near the towns of Albuquerque, New Mexico; Laramie, Wyoming; Provo, Utah; Deseret, Utah and Carson City, Nevada, respectively. Four *C. lateralis* had been obtained the previous summer from Gothic, Colorado. Field weights immediately after capture were determined for *C. spilosoma* and the weight loss of this species which occurred during shipping served to provide an estimated weight level to be maintained in captivity by rationing food. In spite of this procedure, animals fattened somewhat under laboratory conditions, though probably no more than to a level 50% above their field weights.

The data for the eleven *C. tridecemlineatus* is from squirrels purchased from a graduate student at the University of Kansas. Metabolic and body temperature measurements of these animals were made during the fall and winter of 1968. The data for *C. tereticaudus* and

C. mohavensis are from previously published work (Bartholomew & Hudson, 1960; Hudson, 1964; Hudson & Wang, 1969) supplemented by additional metabolic and body temperature measurements from animals (*C. tereticaudus*) purchased from a commercial supplier (Hermosa Reptile Farms) during the period between 1963 to 1965.

The *C. tridecemlineatus* were allowed to gain approximately 25 g between each metabolic determination. The rapidity of weight gain suggests primarily fat deposition. Thus, it is assumed that changes in basal metabolism associated with increased weight are due to the effects of fat. The body weight increased from 139 to 244 g during these experiments.

Animals were kept in $5\frac{1}{2}$ gallon (25 l) aquaria covered with hardware cloth containing wood shavings and cotton batting in windowless rooms on a 12 h photoperiod which extended from 04.00 to 16.00, EST or EDT, depending upon the time of year. Laboratory chow (Agway) and sunflower seeds were given in rations which kept the animals within 50 to 100 g of their capture or receipt weight. Water was supplied *ad libitum*. Animals had been without food for 24 h prior to metabolic measurements, since it had been previously determined that this length of time was required for them to reach their basal metabolic levels, which presumably meant they were then postabsorptive. Animals were weighed, temperatures taken rectally with a Yellow Springs small animal thermister and placed in either a one gallon (4·5 l) paint can (*C. spilosoma*, *C. mohavensis*, *C. tereticaudus* and *C. tridecemlineatus*) or a $2\frac{1}{2}$ gallon (11 l) can, each chamber fitted with ports for the air flow and a copper-constantan or iron-constantan thermocouple to measure chamber temperature. Six of the species (*C. spilosoma*, *C. beldingi*, *C. armatus*, *C. richardsoni*, *C. lateralis* and *C. townsendi*) were supported in the chambers by $\frac{1}{2}$ in. (1·3 cm) mesh hardware cloth so that urine and faeces were collected under mineral oil. The animal chamber was placed in a constant temperature box. Air, measured with a calibrated flow meter (750 ml/min) dried by passing over silica gel before entering the animal chamber, passed through the chamber into a Beckman 315 A infra-red analyser with a CO_2 filter cell. (The instrument had been calibrated by bubbling air through water at a constant and known temperature and collecting the water vapour in drierite trains to determine percent by volume of water in air saturated at known temperatures.) The water vapour in the air leaving the infra-red analyser was absorbed with drierite, and its CO_2 absorbed with ascarite before entering a G-2 oxygen analyser for analysis of its oxygen content. Animals were placed in the measuring system around noon at an ambient temperature of 30°C. By late afternoon or early evening, they reached their resting levels of oxygen consumption and evaporative water loss. The animal was weighed and its body temperature was taken, returned to the chamber and ambient temperature lowered to 20°C. By late evening when the resting level of metabolism and water loss had again been reached, the procedure for removal and return of the animal was repeated and the ambient temperature set for 10°C. The animal was taken out of the chamber the following morning, weighed, body temperature taken and returned to the animal room. In this way it was possible to obtain two daytime and two night-time body temperatures, as well as weight changes throughout the measuring period. The air flow was kept at 750 ml/min in these experiments and it was corrected to STP for calculating metabolic rate. It is important to note that most of the surface area of the animals in the evaporative water loss measurements was exposed to moving air, in contrast to the metabolic experiments in which *Citellus mohavensis*, *C. tereticaudus* and *C. tridecemlineatus* were placed in a chamber which had a layer of shavings in the bottom of the can so that not all of the animal's surface was exposed to moving air. Measurements were made repeatedly between June, 1970 and 1971 for the six species collected in the Spring of 1970. Thus, each of these species has a Summer–Autumn, Winter and Spring measurement.

To measure response to high temperatures over a 2 h period, animals were placed in small wire baskets, placed in a constant temperature box, and viewed through a window to detect any signs of distress as well as count respiratory rate either visually or with a strobotac. Animals were taken out at the end of 1 h for measurement of body temperature. If these were below 42°C, they were returned to the constant temperature box for a second hour. Weight change was used as a crude measure of evaporative water loss since at ambient temperatures of 39°C to 47°C, water loss would be more important than catabolism in its effects on weight change, exclusive of the few instances in which urination and defecation occurred and this data was discarded.

In a second series of experiments, 5–6 individuals of three species representing desert, semi-desert and montane habitats were exposed to temperatures between 35°C and 42°C during the day while metabolism and evaporative water loss were measured. It was necessary to increase flow rate to 1345 ml/min at the very high ambient temperatures to provide the animals with air of sufficient vapour pressure deficit for effective evaporative cooling. The oxygen consumption and evaporative water loss records were planimetered since the animals were frequently restless and a stable reading was difficult to obtain without prolonged exposure to high temperatures which could be fatal.

Table I

Metabolism at thermalneutrality

Species	N	T_A (°C)	T_B* (°C) ($\bar{x} \pm 2$ SE)	Metabolism ($\bar{x} \pm 2$ SE) ml O_2/h	Body weight ($\bar{x} \pm 2$ SE) g
C. armatus	11	29·4 ± 0·3	36·1 ± 0·6	177·0 ± 22·4	298·8 ± 30·1
	9	30·0 ± 0·1	35·6 ± 0·8	136·9 ± 5·2	326·2 ± 33·0
	9	30·2 ± 0·2	35·5 ± 0·7	154·1 ± 15·8	313·5 ± 19·6
C. beldingi	4	29·1 ± 1·2	36·2 ± 0·2	173·5 ± 15·4	253·3 ± 24·0
	3	29·7 ± 0·3	34·9 ± 1·2	122·3 ± 15·6	299·2 ± 13·8
	1	30·3 —	35·4 —	132·8 —	313·2 —
C. lateralis	3	29·9 ± 0·6	36·1 ± 0·6	145·9 ± 31·4	262·7 ± 36·0
	3	30·3 ± 0·6	34·8 ± 0·7	133·5 ± 11·6	290·2 ± 15·2
	3	30·0 ± 0·4	35·8 ± 1·8	113·0 ± 13·2	257·6 ± 43·0
C. mohavensis	7	32·0 ± 0·5	37·0 ± 0·9	111·3 ± 17·9	239·5 ± 44·5
C. richardsoni	10	30·1 ± 0·4	35·3 ± 0·7	128·1 ± 16·4	265·1 ± 13·4
	10	29·7 ± 0·4	35·5 ± 0·4	162·0 ± 24·8	311·9 ± 27·8
	8	30·3 ± 0·3	36·1 ± 0·3	132·0 ± 19·4	252·5 ± 28·0
	9	30·0 ± 0·2	34·9 ± 0·6	103·5 ± 5·4	262·8 ± 10·1
C. spilosoma	9	30·4 ± 0·3	36·3 ± 1·0	81·6 ± 7·6	124·3 ± 13·2
	10	30·1 ± 0·3	37·0 ± 1·0	88·8 ± 14·8	175·8 ± 7·2
	11	29·9 ± 0·2	35·1 ± 1·0	95·5 ± 12·4	173·3 ± 11·8
C. tereticaudus	10	30·0 —	36·3 ± 1·0	93·6 ± 18·2	167·2 ± 12·5
C. townsendi	8	30·8 ± 0·6	36·3 ± 0·5	108·9 ± 19·8	163·8 ± 19·0
	9	29·6 ± 0·4	35·2 ± 0·6	97·5 ± 12·2	233·7 ± 15·2
	8	29·8 ± 0·3	35·3 ± 0·4	119·9 ± 17·4	233·6 ± 18·4
	7	30·0 ± 0·3	35·5 ± 0·6	97·2 ± 17·0	219·0 ± 6·0
C. tridecemlineatus	11(23)†	30·0 —	35·7 ± 0·3	104·5 ± 10·4	182·3 ± 11·7

* Measured at night except for *C. mohavensis*, *C. tereticaudus* and *C. tridecemlineatus*, which include a few daytime measurements.

† Number of measurements.

TABLE II

Ambient temperature, metabolism, and body weight below thermalneutrality

	N	T_A (°C) ($\bar{x}+2$ SE)		Metabolism ($\bar{x} \pm 2$ SE)* (ml O_2/h)		Body weight ($\bar{x} \pm 2$ SE)* (g)	
C. armatus	10	9·6 ± 0·4	19·9 ± 0·4	570·8 ± 50·5	335·0 ± 34·4	271·2 ± 21·8	276·7 ± 22·6
	9	10·1 ± 0·3	19·8 ± 0·6	500·0 ± 47·0	336·0 ± 43·8	313·7 ± 31·8	322·3 ± 31·2
	9	9·7 ± 0·3	19·7 ± 0·3	559·0 ± 33·0	354·6 ± 26·7	308·8 ± 17·8	310·8 ± 16·8
C. beldingi	3	9·5 ± 0·8	20·3 ± 0·6	444·5 ± 88·6	260·4 ± 49·4	244·4 ± 34·0	248·0 ± 33·2
	2	9·7 ± 1·4	20·1 ± 1·2	463·8 ± 156·0	201·8 ± 5·8	277·4 ± 9·2	289·9 ± 5·0
	1	10·4 —	20·0 —	470·9 —	279·6 —	306·6 —	310·4 —
C. lateralis	3	9·9 ± 0·3	20·0 ± 0·4	497·6 ± 74·3	296·0 ± 23·6	255·4 ± 36·4	258·2 ± 36·4
	3	9·6 ± 0·8	20·6 ± 0·5	478·7 ± 28·2	309·4 ± 100·8	283·5 ± 11·0	281·4 ± 13·6
	3	9·8 ± 0·8	19·2 ± 0·3	440·0 ± 59·4	281·0 ± 64·4	251·6 ± 44·8	255·1 ± 44·4
C. richardsoni	10	9·4 ± 0·5	19·8 ± 0·5	577·1 ± 74·0	299·0 ± 20·2	260·0 ± 26·0	256·4 ± 14·6
	10	10·2 ± 0·2	19·8 ± 0·6	646·0 ± 50·8	391·3 ± 45·0	304·4 ± 28·0	307·4 ± 29·6
	8	9·5 ± 0·4	20·3 ± 0·4	464·4 ± 16·6	290·0 ± 23·8	249·8 ± 23·2	247·8 ± 28·4
	9	10·2 ± 0·4	20·4 ± 0·4	489·6 ± 85·6	276·7 ± 26·8	252·3 ± 6·6	261·6 ± 9·2
C. spilosoma	10	10·8 ± 0·3	20·5 ± 0·4	368·3 ± 21·9	202·7 ± 19·4	112·9 ± 8·0	115·1 ± 8·4
	9	10·8 ± 0·3	20·5 ± 0·3	443·7 ± 37·4	244·5 ± 32·6	173·3 ± 8·0	172·0 ± 6·4
	11	10·6 ± 0·3	20·0 ± 0·6	453·3 ± 47·4	290·7 ± 30·4	167·8 ± 11·2	170·7 ± 11·4
C. townsendi	7	10·7 ± 0·8	20·2 ± 0·8	372·8 ± 66·2	216·3 ± 31·2	160·9 ± 20·4	165·1 ± 20·6
	9	9·5 ± 0·8	19·3 ± 0·5	416·0 ± 55·0	273·3 ± 33·8	230·1 ± 14·8	230·0 ± 15·2
	8	9·7 ± 0·4	19·7 ± 0·5	551·4 ± 120·0	302·4 ± 25·6	226·0 ± 18·0	231·8 ± 18·4
	7	9·3 ± 0·6	19·6 ± 0·4	425·9 ± 49·8	277·4 ± 26·8	213·0 ± 20·4	216·8 ± 19·6

* Each of the metabolic and body weight measurements were made at the ambient temperatures given in the first two columns.

RESULTS

The metabolic data are presented in Tables I and II as well as Figs 1, 2, 3, and 4. When the metabolic rate of *C. tridecemlineatus* is plotted as a function of body weight, the points are randomly scattered (Fig. 1). One individual, for example, had a body weight which increased from 139 to 239 g as the metabolic rate successively declined from 0·74 to 0·36, and then increased to 0·65, and then declined to 0·53 ml/g/h, yet the body temperature varied only between 35·0 and 35·9°C. If the metabolic rate of this same species is plotted as a function of body temperature at ambient temperatures of 30°C and 33°C, irrespective of weight (Fig. 2), there is a distinct relationship which can be represented by lines fitted to the points obtained at a T_A of 30°C and 33°C. The standard error of estimate is 0·615 for the 30°C line and 0·676 for the 33°C line. There is almost no correlation between body temperature and metabolic rate at an ambient temperature of 35°C (Fig. 3). The mean metabolic rate of 11 animals measured at a T_A of 30°C at night was 0·62 ± 0·16 (2 SE). Their mean body temperature was 36·1 ± 0·38 (2 SE) and their mean body weight was 184·1 g.

A line fitted by least squares to the metabolic rate of all species measured at 30·0°C (Fig. 4) is remarkably below the level expected for

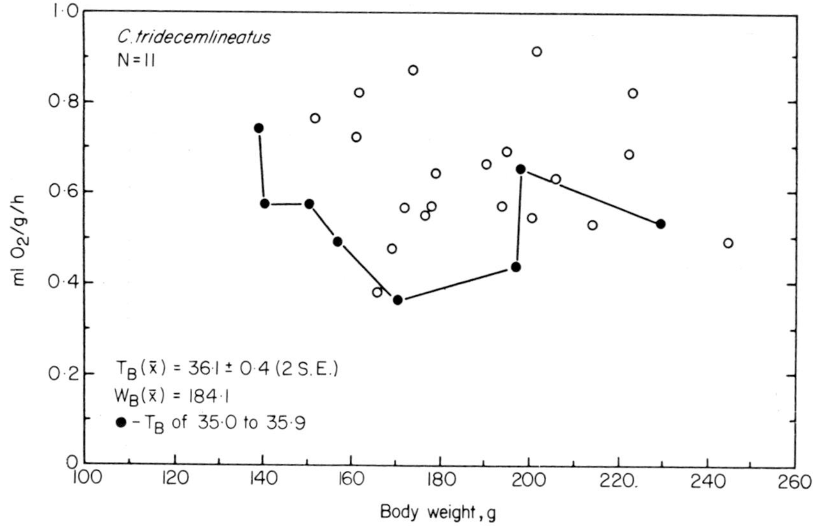

FIG. 1. Relationship between body weight and metabolism of eleven *Citellus tridecemlineatus* allowed to increase their body weight. The closed circles represent points from a single individual whose body temperature varied between 35·0°C and 35·9°C. Measurements include both day and night determinations since these were statistically indistinguishable.

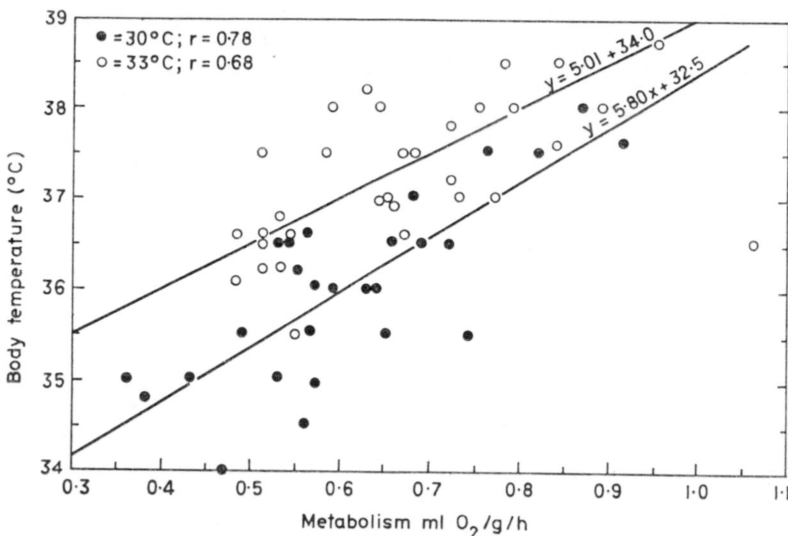

FIG. 2. Relationship between metabolism (metabolic rate) and body temperature of eleven *Citellus tridecemlineatus* measured at ambient temperatures of 30°C (closed circles) and 33°C (open circles) 58 times. Lines have been fitted by least squares to the metabolic values obtained at 30°C and 33°C respectively. The correlation between metabolism and body temperature is 0·78 at 30°C and 0·68 at 33°C. Points are for both day and night determinations since these were statistically identical.

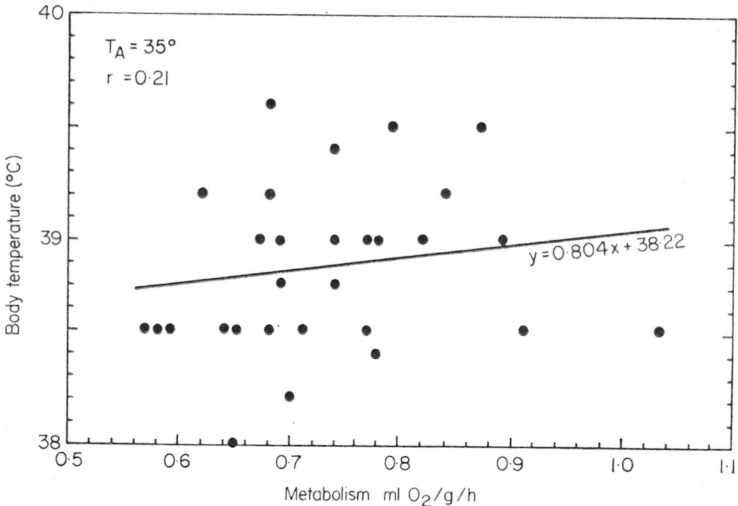

FIG. 3. The relationship between metabolism and body temperature of eleven *Citellus tridecemlineatus* measured at an ambient temperature of 35°C. Points are for both day and night measurements since there were no significant differences. The correlation between metabolism and body temperature is only 0·21.

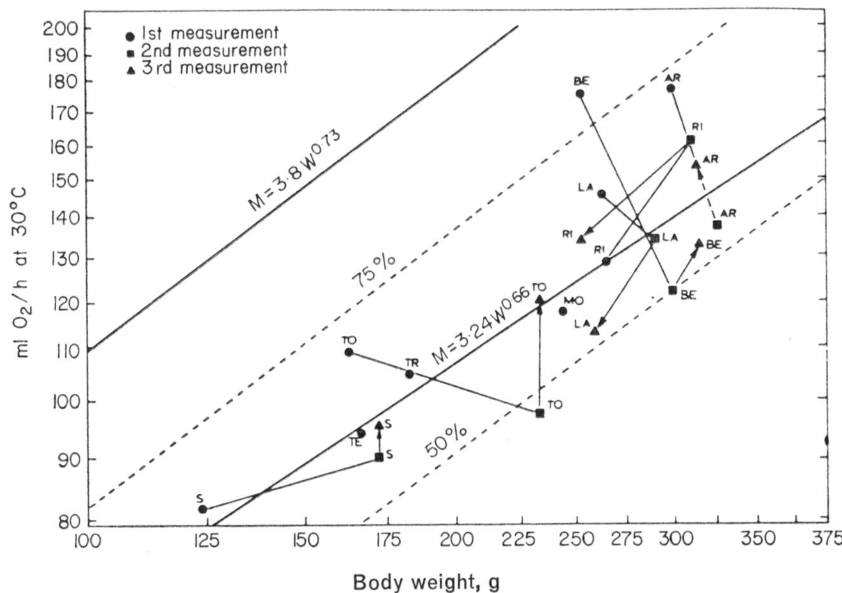

FIG. 4. The relationship between the mean metabolic rate at 30°C and body weight for various species of ground squirrels. The following species, *C. armatus* (AR), *C. beldingi* (B, BE), *C. lateralis* (LA), *C. mohavensis* (MO), *C. richardsoni* (RI), *C. spilosoma* (S, SP), *C. tereticaudus* (TE), *C. tridecemlineatus* (TR). *C. townsendi* (TO), have been included in the line statistically fitted by least squares.

small mammals (Morrison *et al.*, 1959). The equation for our line gives the metabolic rate as $3{\cdot}24\ W^{0.66}$ when the weight is given as g. The mean diurnal body temperature determined from 124 measurements of 43 individuals from six species is $37{\cdot}6 \pm 0{\cdot}2$ (2 SE). The mean nocturnal body temperature of this same group is $35{\cdot}7 \pm 0{\cdot}2$ (2 SE). Thus, there is a marked diel cycle of body temperature with an amplitude of 1·9°C.

The pulmocutaneous water loss, expressed as mg H_2O/ml O_2, is a function of ambient temperature (Fig. 5)—the highest water loss at 30°C and the lowest at 10°C. Except for the *C. spilosoma* at 30°C and the *C. beldingi* at 10°C, all species exhibited one period when the pulmocutaneous loss was markedly reduced (the standard error is so small that it would not be more than a slight bulge in the horizontal line at the top of each rectangle). This lower level coincides roughly with the period of time which would be described under natural conditions as late fall and winter. The two species, *C. spilosoma* and *C. townsendi*, which live under conditions of great aridity have much lower pulmocutaneous water loss at 30°C than some of the other species, three of which live in mountainous habitats, while the fourth lives in regions where there is relatively frequent summer rainfall.

If it is assumed that the consumption of 1 ml oxygen releases 4·8 cal, while the evaporation of 1 mg of water dissipates 0·58 cal, then the evaporative cooling contributes only 6·17% of the heat loss at ambient temperatures between 10°C and 20°C (Table III). Because this evaporative heat loss is so small, it is less confusing, in view of the long history of presenting thermal conductance as heat lost by radiation, convection, conduction as well as evaporation, to present thermal conductance in the traditional manner (Fig. 6). As means of comparison, the Herreid-Kessel (1967) equation for thermal conductance, slightly modified by MacMillen & Nelson (1969) but given in units of oxygen consumption rather than caloric production for mammals, has been given in Fig. 6 for comparative purposes. Except for *C. spilosoma*, there is at least one measurement for each of the six species in which the thermal conductance is at the level expected on the basis of body size alone. The changes in conductance for any species are not correlated with body weight, i.e., conductance may decrease or increase with a decrease in body weight (e.g. *C. townsendi*). The highest levels of conductance, irrespective of body weight, were observed in the species from the relatively arid habitats such as *C. spilosoma*, *C. townsendi* and *C. richardsoni*, while

TABLE III

Percent contribution of evaporative cooling to conductance between 10°C and 20°C

Species	*N*	Percent	Species	*N*	Percent
C. armatus	10	6·03	*C. richardsoni*	10	8·28
	9	4·02		10	5·67
	9	10·09		9	5·81
C. beldingi	3	5·94	*C. spilosoma*	10	6·52
	2	4·57		9	4·31
				11	6·63
C. lateralis	3	5·15	*C. townsendi*	7	5·56
	3	3·80		9	6·40
	3	3·15		8	11·10
				7	4·37

$x = 6{\cdot}17 \pm 0{\cdot}10$ (2SE)

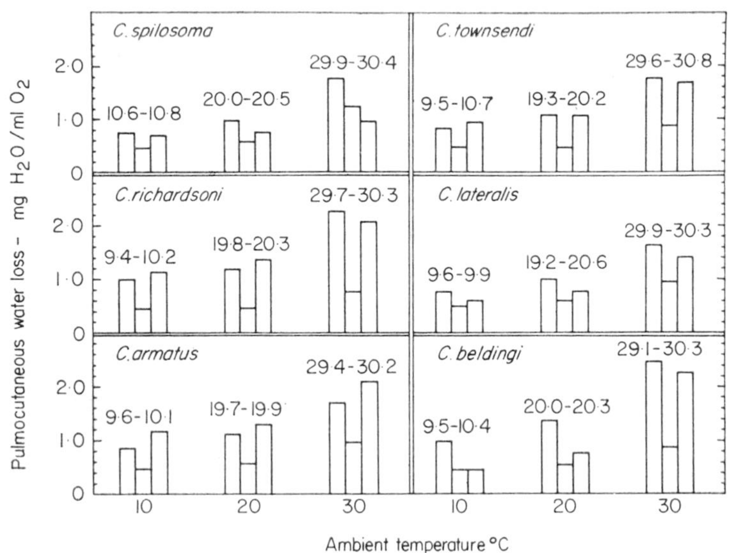

FIG. 5. Pulmocutaneous water loss expressed as mg H_2 O/ml oxygen consumed at three different ambient temperatures (exact ambient temperatures are given above the vertical rectangles) measured three different times between June, 1970 and April, 1971 for the six species of ground squirrels (identified in the upper left corner of the individual graphs).

conductance of high altitude species (*C. armatus*, *C. beldingi* and *C. lateralis*) departed less from the expected levels.

The ability of ground squirrels to tolerate high ambient temperatures varies markedly. The desert dwelling *C. tereticaudus* is much better at withstanding thermal stress than the montane inhabitants, *C. lateralis* and *C. armatus* (Table IV). There is a general correlation between the thermal severity and aridity of the habitat with tolerance to high ambient temperatures. The montane species, *C. lateralis* is unable to cope with temperatures of 39°C; *C. armatus* cannot tolerate 40°C, while *C. leucurus* and *C. spilosoma* from high deserts cannot tolerate ambient temperatures above 41°C and 40°C, respectively. Yet, the ground squirrel which lives in the extremely hot, low deserts, *C. tereticaudus*, can contend with air temperatures up to and including 46°C. When severely stressed by heat, all the species of ground squirrels salivate and rub the saliva over themselves in a behaviourally organized manner.

With increasing ambient temperatures, ground squirrels pant—increasing their breathing rates from values as low as 73/min to rates in excess of 250/min (Table IV).

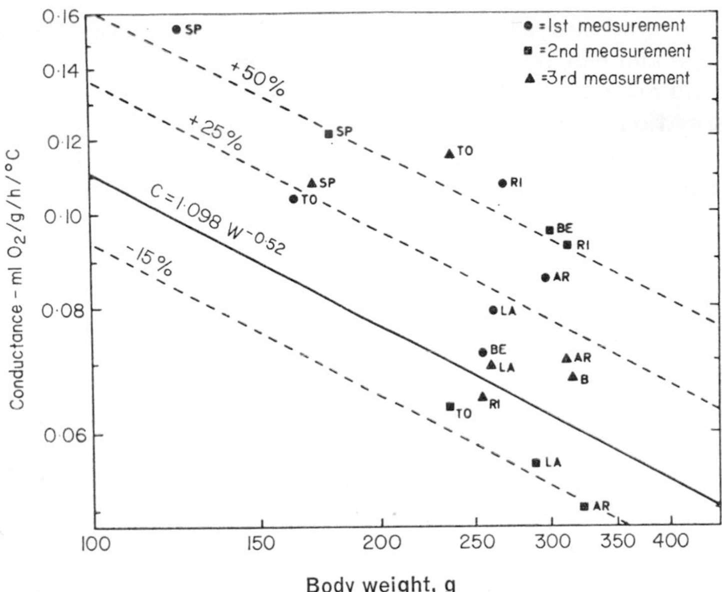

FIG. 6. Thermal conductance, including the evaporative cooling contribution, at ambient temperatures between approximately 10°C and 20°C for the six species of ground squirrels (described and coded in the legend for Fig. 4). The solid line represents the mammalian conductance values compiled by Herreid & Kessel (1967) and reworked by MacMillen & Nelson (1969) to give units of ml O_2/g/h/°C. The dashed lines, beginning with the top, represent conductance values which are 50% above, 25% above and 15% below the level predicted from the Herreid-Kessel equation.

TABLE IV

Respiratory rate and body temperature at highest tolerated ambient temperature

Species	N	Highest T_A (°C) tolerated	Mean breathing rate at 30°C	Mean breathing rate at highest T_A tolerated	T_B (°C)	T_A at which 100% of metabolic heat is evaporated (°C)
C. lateralis	4	<39	—	316	41·4	—
C. armatus	5	39	100	268	41·0	39·0
C. richardsoni	5	39	—	192	41·5	—
C. spilosoma	5	40	142	240	41·0	39·6
C. leucurus	7	41	—	—	41·3	41·0
C. townsendi	5	41	73	230	41·0	40·8
C. tereticaudus	7	46	—	—	41·2	—

The three species selected for measurement of evaporative water loss at high ambient temperatures live in diverse habitats with respect to heat and aridity. The lines fitted by least square to the evaporative heat dissipation (Fig. 7) indicate that 100% of their heat production is evaporated at ambient temperatures of 39·0, 39·6 and 40·8°C, respectively. This corresponds well with the highest ambient temperature at

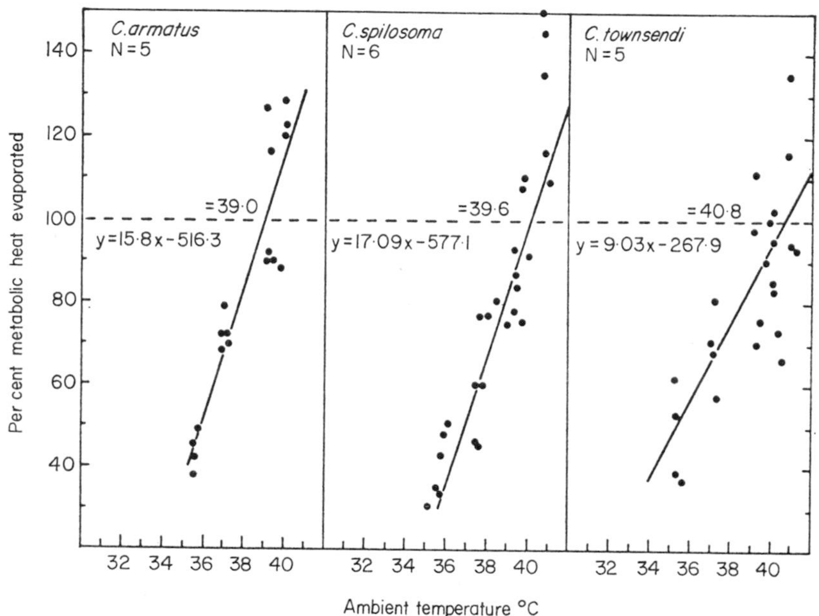

FIG. 7. The relationship between metabolic heat evaporated by pulmocutaneous water loss and ambient temperature of three species of ground squirrels. The equation for the lines, fitted by the least square method, and sample size (N) are given in the figure.

which these same species can keep their body temperatures below 42·0°C for 2 h (Table IV). The overall level is less, and the general variability of evaporatively dissipated heat more, in *C. townsendi* than the other two species. Significantly, *C. townsendi* inhabits a region where summer rainfall is insignificant, whereas *C. spilosoma* inhabits the high desert plateau of Albuquerque which experiences summer rainfall, as does the montane environment of *C. armatus*.

DISCUSSION

The results of this study corroborate McNab's thesis (1968) that fat does not represent a metabolically inert tissue leading to a spurious depression in weight relative metabolism. This does not, however, consider any role subcutaneous fat may have in modifying thermal conductance. Different body tissues vary in both their absolute and their relative contribution to metabolism (Krebs, 1950). To single out one of these tissues and argue that its metabolic contribution is so little in comparison with its total mass that all metabolic values should be determined on a weight basis excluding that tissue (Hayward, 1965), is not only impractical, but it appears to be without substantial experimental support.

The relationship between metabolism and body temperature of *Citellus tridecemlineatus* at thermal neutrality suggests a temperature dependence. However, if one assumed this relationship to be a Q_{10} effect (presuming that body temperature determines metabolism and not the other way around), the Q_{10} value is too high to be real. It is, in fact, more likely that metabolism is determined by something other than body temperature. Thus, it appears that body temperature is probably a dependent variable. This interpretation is supported by the virtually random relationship between metabolism and body temperature when the ambient temperature is 35°C. For example, at 35°C with a body temperature of 38·5°C, the range of metabolic values extends from 0·57 to 1·03 ml O_2/g/h. This variability in metabolic rate is difficult to interpret. To describe it as a "primitive" or "crude" regulation may obscure a phenomenon which contributes in some way to hibernation. Hammel *et al.* (1968) interpret their observations on the golden-mantled ground squirrel, *Citellus lateralis*, to indicate no regulation during hibernation unless a cold stress activates the regulatory system. Perhaps the normothermic thirteen-lined ground squirrels function in a similar manner, with the response to cold or heat not occurring until the body temperature falls or reaches some critical level (set point). Ogle (1970) describes three zones of ambient temperature over which the thirteen-lined ground squirrel varies its level of body temperature and also identifies three significantly different thermal conductance values. If we followed Ogle's description with respect to body temperature, the nocturnal body temperatures of all our species of ground squirrels would be in the zone of hypothermia, although it is measured at a T_A of 30°C, whereas our diurnal body temperatures represent the zone of homeothermia. However, irrespective of definition, there are obvious fluctuations in metabolism which are only partially correlated with variations in body temperature and these may be the result of conductance changes. Kayser (1961, 1965) frequently refers to the physical regulation of hibernators as poor. His observations are doubtlessly correct, but his interpretation might be debated.

Conductance, as typically measured, is a composite of fur thickness, piloerection, subcutaneous fat deposition, vasomotor changes and evaporative cooling. Since the contribution to evaporative cooling in six species of ground squirrels is only $6{\cdot}17 \pm 0{\cdot}1\%$, conductance between 10°C and 20°C is considered primarily a function of physical regulation and insulation. Unfortunately, it is not possible to assess the quantitative contribution of each of these factors, although it is often assumed that physical regulation does not change below the zone of thermal neutrality (Scholander *et al.*, 1950). Dawson & Schmidt-Nielsen (1966) found the lower critical temperature of the Antelope Jack Rabbit to be somewhere between 20°C and 25°C, whereas dry conductance declines markedly until the T_B–T_A difference is about 20°C, or at an ambient temperature somewhere between 15°C and 20°C. Musser & Shoemaker (1965) noted a continuous change in insulation in deer mice as ambient temperature decreased from 33°C to 0°C. However, the conductance of some species, such as *C. richardsoni*, *C. townsendi*, and *C. beldingi* vary from one measurement to the next by as much as 50%. Since body weight changes, assumed to represent changes in fat content, were minimized, it is assumed that there is a variation in physical regulation, i.e., control of peripheral blood flow. This interpretation is consistent with the observations of marked differences in pulmocutaneous water loss from one measurement to the next not accompanied by any consistent lowering or raising of body temperature which profoundly influences pulmonary water loss. A rather high percentage of the pulmocutaneous water loss can occur across the external body surface (Chew, 1965) and it is reasonable to assume the cutaneous water loss could vary with changes in peripheral blood flow. Any reduction in peripheral blood flow also leads to a lower peripheral temperature and therefore a lower mean temperature per unit body mass. Thus, the heat content of animals may vary even though the core body temperature remains constant. In the terminology of Irving (1964), the tissues are heterothermic. Ogle (1970) reported a conductivity of 0·14 cal/h/cm^2/°C from a fresh skin measured with the "hot plate technique", and a conductivity of 0·08 cal/h/cm^2/°C in live thirteen-lined ground squirrels measured with a YSI Kettering radiometer. His data clearly indicate a capacity for reducing conductance. To provide a figure for comparing the values Ogle obtained from direct measurement of conductance with the expected level of conductance, the surface area of a 200 g animal has been computed to convert cal/g/h/°C into cal/cm^2/h/°C. Surface area, calculated from the equation: S (m^2) = 0·091 kg$^{2/3}$ (Lusk, 1928) is 311 cm^2. A 200 g mammal should have a conductance of 0·338 cal/g/h/°C, based on weight. When related to surface area, it should be 0·217 cal/cm^2/h/°C. This predicted level would be even lower if that fraction of heat lost by pulmocutaneous evaporative cooling were to be subtracted. However, it is clear from these figures that the thirteen-lined ground squirrel has a conductance much less than expected, since heat loss measured with the radiometer was 0·08 cal/cm^2/h/°C, or 37% of expected. Thus, in contrast to our squirrels, the thirteen-lined ground squirrels measured by Ogle (1970) are unusually well insulated. This difference cannot be ascribed solely to the inclusion of evaporative cooling in conductance, since we, as well as Dawson & Schmidt-Nielsen (1966), find an evaporative contribution of 10% or less at these ambient temperatures. Until there is better quantitation of comparative insulative capacities of hibernators and non-hibernators, Kayser's conclusion that hibernators lack a well developed capacity for physical regulation should be questioned. Hibernators may not always utilize their maximal capacity for physical regulation. This, of course, begs the question of "why".

Our ground squirrels may have a thermal conductance as much as 50% greater than expected, yet a basal metabolic rate down to 50% below that expected (Figs. 4 and 6). Their basal rates may represent the metabolism of spheres rather than irregularly shaped objects, more typical of mammals (Kleiber, 1961), which results in an exponent of 0·66 rather than 0·73. To maintain a normal body temperature at thermal neutral ambient temperatures while maintaining a reduced metabolic rate implies, *a priori*, an especially effective ability to regulate heat loss by vasomotor control. Since conductance measured at ambient temperatures below thermal neutrality is rather high, it can be assumed that their coat thickness is simply not as dense as expected for animals of their body size. Thus, these squirrels conform to Newton's Law of cooling, as applied to biological systems by Scholander *et al.* (1950), by utilizing an *above average* ability at physical regulation rather than a *below average* ability ascribed to hibernators by Kayser (1961).

These ground squirrels achieve thermal stability in spite of their low basal heat production by virtue of their ability to adjust peripheral heat loss and intensify heat production. This allows them quickly to cool or warm by the appropriate manipulation of heat loss and heat production. Such physiological characteristics are advantageous for hibernators as well as desert dwellers. There do not seem to be significant species differences in metabolic rate and conductance representing specific adaptations to different environments. If there are differences, they're slight and obscured by the variability of metabolism and conductance for any one species.

It may be coincidental that a high degree of regulation of thermal conductance and a low basal metabolism of hibernators are features which can also be advantageous for habitation of hot, dry environments. If so, then hibernators are preadapted for desert habitation. Because the deserts of Western North America are post-pleistocene (Axelrod, 1950), there has been little time for the evolution of dramatic physiological adaptations and probably the physiological differences exhibited by desert mammals are merely slight quantitative shifts, much in the same manner exhibited by house sparrows within the last 100 years (Hudson & Kimzey, 1966; Johnston & Selander, 1964).

The only quantitative shifts in the direction of better adaptation for the desert by diurnal ground squirrels, clearly discernible under laboratory conditions, is the ability to tolerate prolonged exposure to high ambient temperatures. Over a 2 h period, the desert ground squirrels, *C. leucurus*, *C. spilosoma*, *C. townsendi* and *C. tereticaudus* can cope with ambient temperatures of 40°C and above, while the montane species can not tolerate air temperatures above 39°C. Even among the species from desert and semi-desert habitats, tolerance for high air temperatures correlates rather well with the severity of their environment. *C. tereticaudus*, which lives in the severest desert habitats also tolerates ambient temperatures of 46°C for 2 h, while *C. spilosoma* from the high plateau desert of New Mexico can tolerate only 40°C. The other desert species, *C. leucurus* and *C. townsendi* fall between these extremes.

From the three species studied, it appears that the ability to cope with high ambient temperatures is correlated with the extent to which metabolic heat is evaporatively dissipated. Surprisingly, of the three species measured, the one dissipating the most heat by evaporative cooling for a particular temperature, *C. armatus* is the one least able to tolerate high temperatures, whereas *C. townsendi* tolerates the highest temperature yet dissipates the least amount of heat. Some of this is explicable in terms of insulation, i.e., *C. armatus* is better insulated than the other two species and as a result probably loses less of its metabolic heat by radiation, convection and conduction. However, *C. spilosoma* is the least well insulated, yet it has less heat tolerance than *C. townsendi*. Such data on evaporative cooling by *C. tereticaudus* has not been obtained as yet. However, a comparative study of weight change accompanying exposure to high ambient temperatures showed a much smaller loss by *C. tereticaudus* than *C. leucurus* under comparable conditions of exposure to high ambient temperatures (Hudson & Wang, 1969). The heat loss by pulmocutaneous evaporation for *C. leucurus* reaches 100% at an ambient temperature of 41·0°C, a temperature at which *C. tereticaudus* lost 3·1% of its body weight in 2 h whereas *C. leucurus* lost

3·9%. These figures represent very rough approximations, but in conjunction with the other data on evaporative cooling, suggest that *C. tereticaudus* probably also has a low level of pulmocutaneous evaporation. Thus, dependence on water as a means of coping with high ambient temperatures has been minimized commensurate with general moisture availability in the habitat. Differences in ability to cope with high ambient temperatures must depend in part on other mechanisms. There is always the imponderable role of restlessness to be evaluated. Are we observing a behavioural response where species from different habitats are adapted to tolerate only a certain degree of heating before retreating to the cooler environment of their burrows? Have they been forced to remain exposed to conditions they normally avoid and their frantic efforts to escape produces *t* a thermal state inimicable to proper utilization of their physiological capabilities?

The breathing rates of the three species of ground squirrels exposed to high ambient temperatures are 2–3 times greater than thermal neutral rates and can be described as panting, though this term has not been clearly defined or consistently applied (Richards, 1970). From the viewpoint of thermal economy, in order for panting to be adaptive, it should dissipate more heat than it generates without introducing problems of acid-base balance. It is unknown whether these conditions are met by the various species of ground squirrels studied, though some of them can keep their body temperature at 41°C even though ambient temperature exceeds 41°C. It is virtually impossible to determine the metabolic efficiency of rapid breathing in a restless animal which periodically engages in licking itself and spreading saliva over the body. Their restlessness may lead to excessive heat production and prevent them from getting rid of sufficient metabolic heat to prevent fatal hyperthermia. Perhaps under more natural conditions, where they are free to seek relief from heat, they would better integrate their behavioural and thermoregulatory capabilities for survival in hot environments. The ability of ground squirrels to increase breathing rates at high ambient temperatures (i.e., pant) may approach, but is not as great, as that of the jack rabbit, *Lepus alleni* (Schmidt-Nielsen *et al.*, 1965), particularly if our lowest and highest rates (unpubl. obs.) are compared rather than the means as given in Table IV.

A comparison of the thermoregulatory performance of *C. tereticaudus* (Hudson, 1964; Hudson & Wang, 1969) with the species examined in this study clearly reveal the remarkable ability *C. tereticaudus* possesses for coping with extremely high ambient temperatures. Although this physiological capacity may merely represent a quantitative improvement on the general features of this group of ground squirrels, it has enabled *C. tereticaudus* to inhabit one of the most thermally challenging environments in the world, viz., Death Valley, California.

As shown in this study, the ground squirrel widely distributed in the semi-arid Great Basin region, *C. townsendi*, is close to *C. tereticaudus* in its ability to cope with a hot, dry environment. Significantly, chromosomal data, gross morphology, ecology, zoogeography and study of ectoparasites led Nadler (1966) to conclude that *C. townsendi* belongs to a different subgenus than *C. beldingi*, *C. armatus* and *C. richardsoni*, a conclusion which our physiological data supports.

SUMMARY

The resting metabolism and pulmocutaneous water loss of *Citellus armatus*, *C. beldingi*, *C. lateralis*, *C. richardsoni*, *C. spilosoma* and *C. townsendi* was measured at 10°C, 20°C and 30°C during the night using infra-red and paramagnetic analysis. These ground squirrels, all of which can hibernate, live in montane, grassland and desert habitats. The 10°C and 20°C temperatures permitted determination of wet and dry conductance. The metabolism at 30°C of these six species was combined with data from two additional species, *C. mohavensis* and *C. tereticaudus*, either published previously, or unreported, to establish a mathematical relationship between body weight and metabolism for this group. The relationship, M (ml O_2/g/h) $= 3{\cdot}24W^{0.66}$ is applicable only to animals postabsorptive for 24 h and measured at night while maintaining a body temperature of $35{\cdot}7 \pm 0{\cdot}2$ (2 SE)°C. The mean diurnal body temperature is $37{\cdot}6 \pm 0{\cdot}2$ (2 SE)°C. The pulmocutaneous water loss and oxygen consumption of three of the six species, selected to represent montane and desert environments, was measured during the day at ambient temperatures of 35°C to 41°C. *C. armatus*, *C. spilosoma* and *C. townsendi* evaporated 100% of their metabolic heat at ambient temperatures of 39·0°C, 39·6°C and 40°C, respectively, while maintaining body temperatures of 41·0°C. The ambient temperature at which the first signs of thermal distress appeared in animals placed in wire mesh cages and exposed to high ambient temperatures in a constant temperature chamber, varied in conformity with the habitat of the species. The least tolerant was *C. armatus*, a montane species, whereas the most tolerant was *C. tereticaudus*, a ground squirrel which lives in the very hot, low desert including Death Valley, California. The thermal conductance of the six species varied from one measurement to the next. In eight of the determinations, conductance exceeded the predicted level by 25% to 50%. Only 6·17%

of the conductance is due to evaporative heat loss at ambient temperatures between 10°C and 20°C. These ground squirrels are, thus, characterized by an unusually high level of physical regulation and a low level of basal metabolism, features which would be highly adaptive for coping with the need to dissipate endogenous heat when there was little difference between the body and ambient temperature. It is assumed, however, that these physiological features represent adaptations for hibernation, i.e., rapid cooling and/or warming and have become utilized effectively for desert habitation with slight quantitative shifts in physiological performance. These results confirm the previous observation that *C. tereticaudus* is especially adapted to cope with the severe desert environment.

Acknowledgements

Most of the original work reported here was supported by a grant from the National Science Foundation, G.B. 17002, while the support for field work and writing was from the National Institute of Health, GM 15889. The invaluable aid of Mr. Waldo Black, Deseret, Utah, made it is possible to obtain sufficient numbers of the elusive *C. townsendi*. The directions and assistance of Mr. Walter Joyce, Department of Biology, University of New Mexico; Mr. Marvin Maxell, Department of Biology, University of Wyoming and Dr. Clive Jorgensen, Brigham Young University, Provo, Utah, provided us with invaluable information. Mr. Willian G. Parsons, Chief of Enforcement, Nevada Game and Fish Commission, expedited air shipment of freshly captured animals. The unfailing optimism, good judgement and keen observation of Mr. R. A. Hudson contributed much to this study.

References

Aschoff, J. & Pohl, H. (1970). Rhythmic variations in energy metabolism. *Fedn Proc. Fedn Am. Socs exp. Biol.* **29**: 1541–1552.

Axelrod, D. I. (1950). Evolution of desert vegetation in western North America. *Publs Carnegie Instn Wash.* No. 590.

Baldwin, F. M. & Johnson, K. L. (1941). Effects of hibernation on the rate of oxygen consumption in the thirteen-lined ground squirrel. *J. Mammal.* **22**: 180–184.

Barnes, M. (1965). *Seasonal variation of metabolism and thyroid activity in the Mexican ground squirrel, Citellus mexicanus.* Master's Thesis. Rice Univ. Library, Houston, Texas.

Bartholomew, G. A. & Hudson, J. W. (1960). Aestivation in the Mohave ground squirrel, *Citellus mohavensis. Bull. Mus. comp. Zool. Harv.* **124**: 353–372.

Chew, R. M. (1965). Water metabolism of mammals. In *Physiological mammalogy* **2**: 43–178. Mayer, W. V. & van Gelder, R. G. (eds). New York and London: Academic Press.

Dawson, T. & Schmidt-Nielsen, K. (1966). Effect of thermal conductance on water economy in the antelope jack rabbit, *Lepus alleni*. *J. Cell. Physiol.* **67**: 463–472.

Erikson, H. (1956). Observations on the metabolism of arctic ground squirrels (*Citellus parryi*) at different environmental temperatures. *Acta physiol. scan.* **36**: 66–74.

Folk, G. E. (1960). Day-night rhythms and hibernation. *Bull. Mus. comp. Zool. Harv.* **124**: 209–233.

Hammel, H. T., Dawson, T. J., Abrams, R. M. & Andersen, H. T. (1968). Total calorimetric measurements on *Citellus lateralis* in hibernation. *Physiol. Zool.* **41**: 341–357.

Hayward, J. S. (1965). The gross body composition of six geographic races of *Peromyscus*. *Can. J. Zool.* **43**: 297–308.

Herreid, C. F., II & Kessel, B. (1967). Thermal conductance in birds and mammals. *Comp. Biochem. Physiol.* **21**: 405–414.

Hock, R. J. (1960). Seasonal variations in physiologic functions of arctic ground squirrels and black bears. *Bull. Mus. comp. Zool. Harv.* **124**: 155–171.

Hudson, J. W. (1962). The role of water in the biology of the antelope ground squirrel, *Citellus leucurus*. *Univ. Calif. Publs Zool.* **64**: 1–56.

Hudson, J. W. (1964). Temperature regulation in the round-tailed ground squirrel, *Citellus tereticaudus*. *Annales Academiae Scientiarum Fennicae.* (A4) **71**: 219–233.

Hudson, J. W. & Kimzey, S. L. (1966). Temperature regulation and metabolic rhythms in populations of the house sparrow, *Passer domesticus*. *Comp. Biochem. Physiol.* **17**: 203–217.

Hudson, J. W. & Wang, L. C. (1969). Thyroid function in desert ground squirrels. In *Physiological systems in semiarid environments*: 17–33. Hoff, C. C. & Riedesel, M. L. (eds). Albuquerque: University of New Mexico Press.

Irving, L. (1964). Terrestrial animals in the cold: birds and mammals. In *Adaptation to the environment*: 361–377. Dill, D. B. (ed.). Washington, D.C.: American Physiological Society.

Johnston, R. F. & Selander, R. K. (1964). House sparrows: rapid evolution of races in North America. *Science, N.Y.* **144**: 548–550.

Kayser, C. (1961). *The physiology of natural hibernation*. New York: Pergamon Press.

Kayser, C. (1965). Hibernation. In *Physiological mammalogy* **2**: 179–296. Mayer, W. V. & van Gelder, R. G. (eds). New York and London: Academic Press.

Kleiber, M. (1961). *The fire of Life: an introduction to animal energetics*. New York: John Wiley.

Krebs, H. A. (1950). Body size and tissue respiration. *Biochim. biophys. Acta* **4**: 249–269.

Lusk, G. (1928). *Elements of the science of nutrition*, 4th edn. Philadelphia: W. B. Saunders.

Lyman, C. P. & O'Brien, R. C. (1960). Circulatory changes in the thirteen-lined ground squirrel during the hibernating cycle. *Bull. Mus. comp. Zool. Harv.* **124**: 353–372.

MacMillen, R. E. & Nelson, J. E. (1969). Bioenergetics and body size in dasyurid marsupials. *Am. J. Physiol.* **217**: 1246–1251.

McNab, B. (1968). The influence of fat deposits on the basal metabolism in desert homiotherms. *Comp. Biochem. Physiol.* **26**: 337–343.

Morrison, P., Ryser, F. A. & Dawe, A. R. (1959). Studies on the physiology of the masked shrew, *Sorex cinereus*. *Physiol. Zoöl.* **32**: 256–271.

Musser, G. G. & Shoemaker, V. H. (1965). Oxygen consumption and body temperature in the Mexican deer mice, *Peromyscus thomasi* and *P. megalops*. *Occ. Pap. Mus. Zool. Univ. Mich.* No. 643: 1–15.

Nadler, C. F. (1966). Chromosomes and systematics of American ground squirrels of the subgenus *Spermophilus*. *J. Mammal.* **47**: 579–596.

Neumann, R. L. & Cade, T. J. (1965). Torpidity in the Mexican ground squirrel, *Citellus mexicanus parvidens*. *Can. J. Zool.* **43**: 133–140.

Ogle, T. F. (1970). Changes in thermal conductivity of the integument in non-hibernating thirteen-lined ground squirrels (*Spermophilus tridecemlineatus*) in relation to ambient temperature. *Physiol. Zoöl.* **43**: 98–108.

Pengelley, E. T. & Kelly, K. H. (1966). A "circannian" rhythm in hibernating species of the genus *Citellus* with observations on their physiological evolution. *Comp. Biochem. Physiol.* **19**: 603–617.

Popovic, V. (1959). Lethargic hypothermia in hibernators and non-hibernators. *Ann. N.Y. Acad. Sci.* **80**: 320–331.

Richards, S. A. (1970). The biology and comparative physiology of thermal panting. *Biol. Rev.* **45**: 223–264.

Schmidt-Nielsen, K., Dawson, T. J., Hammel, H. T., Hinds, D. & Jackson, D. (1965). The jack rabbit—a study in its desert survival. *Hvalr Skr.* **48**: 125–142.

Scholander, P. F., Hock, R., Walters, V., Johnson, F. & Irving, L. (1950). Heat regulation in some arctic and tropical mammals and birds. *Biol. Bull. mar. biol. Lab. Woods Hole* **99**: 237–258.

Strumwasser, F. (1960). Some physiological principles governing hibernation in *Citellus beecheyi*. *Bull. Mus. comp. Zool. Harv.* **124**: 285–320.

Strumwasser, F., Gilliam, J. J. & Smith, J. L. (1964). Long term studies on individual hibernating animals. *Suomal. Tiedeakat. Toim.* (A4) **71**: 299–414.

Twente, J. W. & Twente, J. A. (1965). Effects of core temperature upon duration of hibernation of *Citellus lateralis*. *J. appl. Physiol.* **20**: 411–416.

Symp. zool. Soc. Lond. (1972) No. 31, 215–227.

THE DESERT GAZELLE: A PARADOX RESOLVED

C. RICHARD TAYLOR

Museum of Comparative Zoology, Harvard University, Cambridge, Massachusetts, U.S.A.

SYNOPSIS

Grant's and Thompson's gazelle are small East African antelopes. They are similar both in size and markings and often run in the same herds. The range of the Grant's gazelle, however, extends into the hot, arid regions of East Africa while that of the Thomson's gazelle does not. It is surprising, therefore, that the Grant's gazelle requires about $\frac{1}{3}$ more water per kg body weight than the Thomson's gazelle in a simulated desert environment (12 h/day at 22°C alternating with 12 h/day at 40°C).

This paper tries to resolve this apparent paradox by investigating the response of the two gazelles to short, but very intense, heat loads. Most of the water loss in a simulated desert is through evaporation and helps keep the animal cool. Intense solar radiation occurs together with high air temperatures in the arid regions of Africa. During a short period at mid-day, Grant's gazelle might frequently encounter a more severe heat load than the air temperature of 40°C provided in the simulated desert.

At high air temperatures both gazelles dissipate heat primarily by panting. When dehydrated neither gazelle began to pant until air temperature exceeded 40°C and steady state rectal temperature was higher than air temperature. This effect was greater in the desert-dwelling Grant's gazelle than in the Thomson's gazelle. For example, when air temperature was 45°C body temperature of the Grant's gazelle was as high as 46·5°C while that of the Thomson's gazelle did not exceed 42·3°C.

The higher body temperature and lower evaporation of the Grant's gazelle at air temperatures exceeding 40°C help to resolve the apparent paradox between water requirements and habitat of the gazelles.

INTRODUCTION

East Africa holds a peculiar fascination for a biologist because of its tremendous diversity both of habitats and of plant and animal species. Within a day's drive of Nairobi one can reach: the snow on Mount Kilimanjaro; a tropical rain forest; expansive plains; the shore of one of the many lakes of the Rift Valley System; a tropical coast replete with palms, white sand beaches and buxom native girls; the agriculturally productive highlands; or the southern edge of the hot, arid Saharan desert.

Vast herds of ungulates still inhabit the East African plains. Ungulates are abundant not only in numbers of individuals but also in numbers of species. Allen (1939) has listed 66 species of wild ungulates

K

FIG. 1. A mixed herd of Thomson's and Grant's gazelles. The white stripe above the tail of the desert-dwelling Grant's gazelle is the most reliable way to distinguish it from the non-desert Thomson's gazelle.

inhabiting East Africa with 47 in Kenya. Two-thirds of the land mass of Kenya is arid or semi-arid (as distinguished by having less than 250 mm of rainfall per year). As one travels further north the rainfall may be less than 25 mm per year. Air temperatures are high (the daily maximum may exceed 40°C for several months during the year). Prolonged droughts are common and a particular area may be without rain for several years. During droughts cattle are moved out of these arid northern regions to better pastures. Many die from thirst and starvation in the process. There are several species of antelope, however, which continue to inhabit these inhospitable areas even during prolonged droughts. It has been consistently reported by explorers, local inhabitants, game wardens and naturalists that these animals can survive without drinking (Taylor, 1968a). Oryx and gazelles are particularly interesting since they do not seek shade during the middle of the day.

About 8 years ago I set out for Africa to try to find out if antelope could indeed survive in deserts without drinking; and if they could, to determine the physiological mechanism by which they accomplished this remarkable feat. Among the ungulates which I studied were two small East African antelopes: the Grant's gazelle (*Gazella granti*) and the Thomson's gazelle (*Gazella thomsonii*). Adults weigh between 10 and 50 kg. It is difficult for the novice to distinguish between them, for in many areas both species run together in the same herds, and they are similar both in size and markings (Fig. 1). There is one important difference between these two species: Grant's gazelle are found in the hot, arid sub-Saharan regions of East Africa while Thomson's gazelle are not. *A priori*, then, one would expect that the Grant's gazelle would be more frugal in their handling of water than the Thomson's gazelle.

Five years ago I contributed to another symposium of the Zoological Society of London on the Comparative Nutrition of Wild Animals. My paper was concerned with the water requirements of a number of East African ungulates (Taylor, 1968a). Much to my chagrin I had found that under simulated desert conditions, the desert-dwelling Grant's gazelle required more water than the non-desert Thomson's gazelle. I expressed hope that this paradox might be resolved by further study. In this paper I would like to discuss:

1. the experiments where I determined the water requirements of these two animals under simulated desert conditions;
2. some experiments under conditions which approximate the intense solar radiation of the arid regions of Africa; and finally
3. to propose an explanation which would resolve the apparent paradoxical picture of the two gazelles' water requirements.

WATER REQUIREMENTS IN A SIMULATED DESERT

Before discussing the water requirements of a gazelle, it is worthwhile to consider the question of how water enters and leaves a gazelle. A gazelle may acquire water by drinking; through preformed water in the food that it eats; and by formation of water as it oxidizes its food. Water leaves the gazelle through evaporation (taking place both from the respiratory tract and from the skin); with the urine; and with the faeces. When considered for any prolonged period of time, a gazelle must be in water balance, i.e., the water that comes in must equal the water that leaves.

It was possible to quantify each of these avenues of water intake and loss by housing an animal in a metabolism cage in the laboratory. The amount of water an animal drank was easily measured. The amount of water in its food was determined by measuring the water content of the food and multiplying this by the amount of food which the animal ate. The composition of the food and faecal samples was determined. Then it was possible to calculate oxidation water. Approximately 0·5 g of oxidation water was produced from each gram of hay which a gazelle digested.

The water loss from a gazelle was also measured in the metabolism cage. Urine was collected beneath a layer of oil and its volume measured. Faeces were collected; their moisture content was determined; and the amount of water lost through the faeces was calculated by multiplying the amount of water contained in a gram of dry faeces by the number of grams of dry faeces which the animal produced. I was thus able to measure directly all of the avenues of water intake and two of the three avenues of water loss. Since water intake must equal water loss, I could calculate the evaporative water loss by subtracting faecal loss plus urinary loss from total water intake.

The next problem was simulation of the hot desert environment in the laboratory. Heat and aridity are two of the critical parameters which need to be included in a simulated desert. One possibility would be to provide a constant high temperature and restrict water intake. A constant high temperature allows heat exchange between the animal and the environment to be measured easily. It is very different, however, from the periodic high temperature of a desert. A cycling temperature has an important advantage over a constant high temperature for studying water conserving mechanisms. Some strategies which an animal might use to reduce its water requirements in the desert, such as a temporary hyperthermia at mid-day or a temporary hypothermia in the morning and slow warming during the day, depend on a cycling temperature.

Figure 2 shows the simulated desert environment used. Air temperature was raised quickly from 22°C to 40°C in the morning (between 08.00 and 08.30); remained constant at 40°C for 11·5 h and returned to

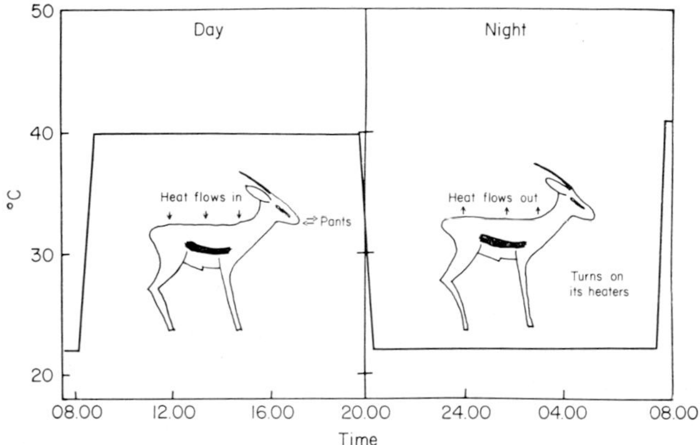

FIG. 2. A desert environment was simulated in the laboratory by a periodic heat load. Each morning between 08.00 and 08.30 air temperature increased from 22°C to 40°C. It remained at 40°C for 11·5 h. Between 20.00 and 20.30 it returned to 22°C and remained at 22°C until 08.00 the next morning. A periodic heat load has advantages over a constant high air temperature for investigations of mechanisms a gazelle might use to conserve water in a hot desert (see text).

22°C in 30 min (between 20.00 and 20.30 h). A temperature of 40°C is higher than the gazelle's body temperature and heat would flow into the animal from the environment. A gazelle might normally encounter air temperatures of about 40°C for a few hours each day, but not for 12 h. I thought that the extra hours at 40°C would compensate for the extra heat an animal might gain from solar radiation (which was not included in our simulated laboratory desert). The 11·5 h at 22°C would enable an animal to dissipate stored heat without evaporation and provide a period for recovery from a temporary hyperthermia.

Using this simulated desert, I found that evaporation accounted for most of the water loss from both the Grant's and the Thomson's gazelle, at least when they have drinking water freely available: 82% of the total water lost for the Thomson's gazelle and 83% for the Grant's gazelle (Fig. 3) (Taylor, 1970a). What function does this evaporation serve and can evaporation be reduced when water supply is restricted? Some evaporation occurs each time an animal exhales air. Air is saturated with water vapour at body temperature when it arrives at the lungs and unless it can be cooled before it leaves the animal, each litre of exhaled air will contain about 45 mg of water.

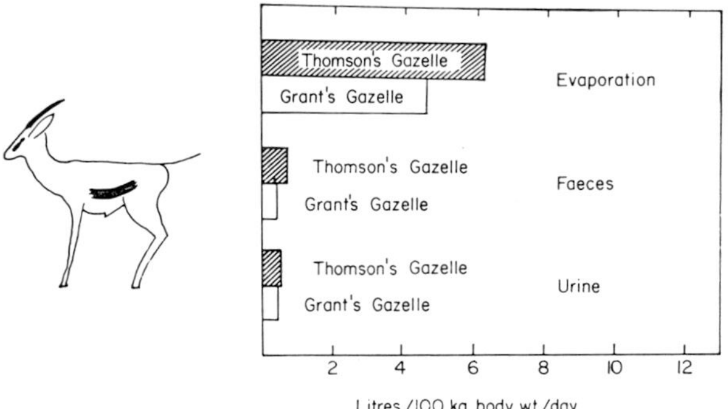

FIG. 3. When animals could drink at will, evaporation accounted for about 80% of the water lost by both Thomson's and Grant's gazelles in a simulated desert (12 h/day at 40°C alternating with 12 h/day at 22°C). Water lost with faeces and urine was relatively unimportant. Any major reduction in water loss when the water supply is limited must involve a reduction in evaporation.

Most of the gazelles' evaporation is used for keeping cool. Figure 4 illustrates the high rate of evaporation which occurs during the simulated desert day. As air temperature increased from 22°C to 40°C, the average respiratory rate of both Thomson's and Grant's gazelle increased from about 15 to about 200 per min. The gazelles could no longer lose their metabolic heat without evaporation, and both animals increased evaporation by panting. The gazelles possess functional sweat glands. The level of cutaneous water loss, however, is not increased significantly at high ambient temperatures (Robertshaw & Taylor, 1969). Although the frequency with which individual glands release sweat onto the skin increases in the heat, the rate of cutaneous water loss over an interval of time longer than several minutes does not increase. This is explained by a lower rate of water loss between periods of glandular activity.

This is the situation where the gazelles have water freely available to them. What happens when their water intake is restricted? To check this I gradually cut down the amount of water which I gave to an animal until it was just able to maintain its weight at 85% of the initial level. If I gave it any more water it gained weight and if I gave it any less water it lost weight. I then maintained this 85% weight for a period of two weeks and measured the animal's water balance (Taylor, 1968a).

Figure 5 shows that evaporation was reduced in both the Thomson's and Grant's gazelle when water intake was restricted. Unexpectedly the Thomson's gazelle showed a greater decrease than the Grant's

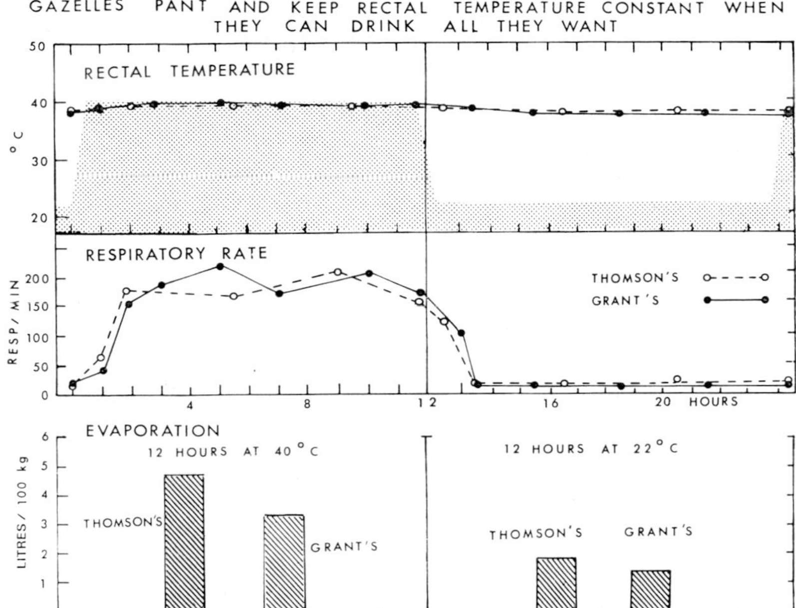

FIG. 4. Rectal temperature (top) and respiratory rate (middle) of a Thomson's (dashed line) and Grant's gazelle (solid line) at intervals during 24 h in a simulated desert. The top of the stippled area represents air temperature. Evaporation (bottom) during the 24 h period was divided into the amount taking place during the 12 h at 40°C and the amount taking place during the 12 h at 22°C. The data were selected from a day which was representative of other days when gazelles had water freely available. Both gazelles panted and maintained their rectal temperatures below air temperature when air temperature was 40°C.

gazelle (63% versus 31%) and evaporation was less by an amount equal to 1% of body weight per day (Taylor, 1970a). During the 12 h at 40°C, neither species panted. Instead, both animals apparently abandoned evaporative cooling. Their body temperatures climbed above air temperature to a point where they were in thermal balance with their environment without panting (41·6°C in the Thomson's and 41·0°C in the Grant's gazelle). During the simulated desert night (22°C) body temperature fell again to the normal level (37·8°C in the Thomson's and 38·1°C in the Grant's gazelle). So we find that when water is in short supply, both the Thomson's and the Grant's gazelle have adopted a strategy of an elevated body temperature during the hot part of the day, thereby conserving water which they normally would use to keep cool. We are left, however, with the paradoxical situation of the Grant's gazelle, a desert-dwelling species, requiring more water for evaporation

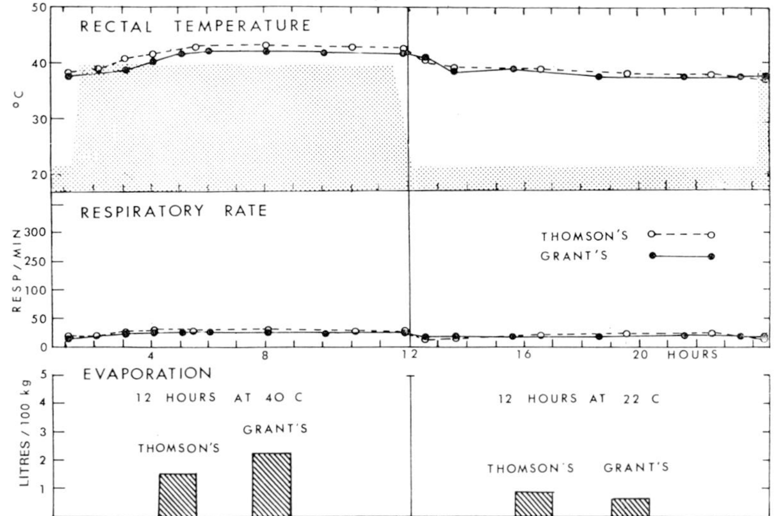

Fig. 5. Rectal temperature, respiratory rate, and evaporation in Thomson's and Grant's gazelles under simulated desert conditions. This figure is similar to Fig. 4 except that the gazelles were dehydrated and their water intake was restricted (see text). Neither gazelle panted during the 12 h at 40°C; rectal temperature exceeded air temperature; and evaporation was drastically reduced. The data were selected from a day which was representative of other days.

than the Thomson's gazelle, a non-desert-dwelling species. This seems unreasonable.

From these results one wonders if there is something missing in the experimental design. It seems likely that while a heat load of 12 h per day at 40°C probably equals any heat load an animal might encounter in a hot desert environment, for a short period each day the heat load might be much more intense. Perhaps the paradox between the water requirements of these two species of antelopes might be resolved if we could look at what was happening during the short period of the day when solar radiation is intense.

EFFECTS OF AN INTENSE HEAT LOAD AND RESTRICTED WATER INTAKE ON TEMPERATURE REGULATION OF GAZELLES

It is difficult to simulate the sun in a laboratory. It is not difficult to give a more intense heat load by increasing air temperature. Body temperature of the dehydrated gazelles exceeded air temperature at 40°C. A body temperature of 41°C or 42°C seems possible, but what happens when air temperature reaches a higher level, say 45°C? To investigate this, I measured respiratory rate, cutaneous water loss, and body temperature while animals were in a steady state at air temperatures between 20°C and 50°C (Taylor, 1970b). I defined a steady state as being achieved when body temperature varied less than ±0·1°C and respiratory rate less than ±5 resp/min during an hour. Measurements were made both on fully hydrated animals and on animals which had lost 15% of their weight while kept at 40°C without access to water.

Figure 6 shows the results of these experiments. Both gazelles dissipated excess heat primarily by panting. Sweating contributed little to heat dissipation. The onset of panting in hydrated gazelles occurred at air temperatures between 26°C and 30°C in both species. The average rate of panting over a period of 10 min (gazelles pant at a constant frequency between 200–300 resp/min and modulate evaporation by panting or not panting) increased at higher air temperatures, and body temperature was about 40°C when air temperature was 50°C.

Dehydrated gazelles did not pant until air temperature exceeded 40°C and their steady state rectal temperatures were higher than 40°C. This is similar to what we observed in the simulated desert experiments. If instead of 40°C for the simulated desert day I had picked 45°C, our results probably would have been entirely different. The Grant's gazelle would probably have required nearly the same amount of water while the Thomson's would have required much more. This is because at air temperatures above 42°C the Thomson's gazelle increased evaporative cooling by panting and maintained a body temperature well below that of the air. It had a body temperature of about 42·5°C when air temperature was 45°C. The desert-dwelling Grant's gazelle, on the other hand, had a body temperature of about 46°C, still in excess of the air temperature. Thus during the brief, very hot period of the desert day, the Grant's gazelle could avoid evaporative cooling, while the Thomson's gazelle could not.

INDEPENDENT REGULATION OF BRAIN AND BODY TEMPERATURES

Body temperatures above 45°C raise a new question of how animals survive such high body temperatures. I observed a Grant's gazelle which had a rectal temperature of 46·5°C for as long as 6 h with no observable ill effects. Such high rectal temperatures would be lethal in most mammals. In the gazelles, however, a high body temperature does not necessarily mean a high brain temperature. The arterial blood

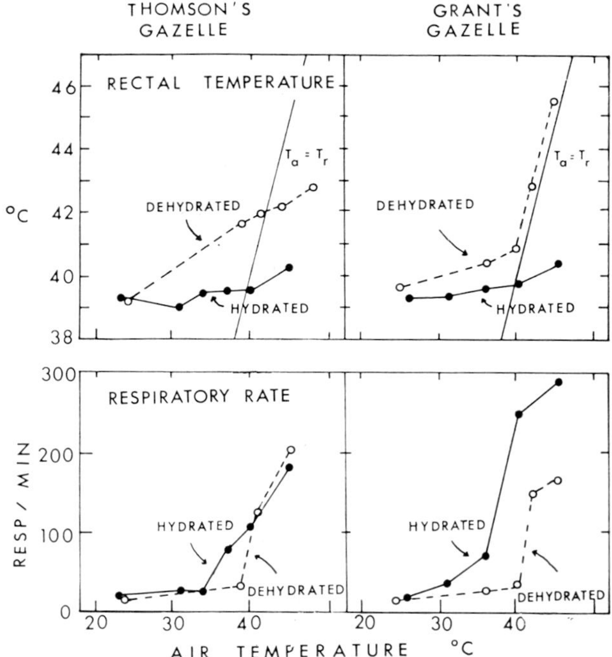

FIG. 6. Steady-state rectal temperature of hydrated (solid lines) and dehydrated (dashed lines) gazelles at air temperatures between 20 and 50°C. Each point represents the mean of from 9 to 30 measurements on three or four individuals. Thin diagonal lines indicate equal air and rectal temperatures. The desert-dwelling Grant's gazelle had a rectal temperature which exceeded an air temperature of 45°C when dehydrated (Taylor, 1970b).

supplying the brain may be selectively cooled. In ungulates there is no internal carotid artery and most of the arterial blood supplies the brain through the external carotid artery. At the base of the brain this artery breaks into a carotid *rete mirable* consisting of hundreds of small parallel arteries and then reforms to supply the brain. This *rete* lies in a venous pool, the cavernous sinus (Daniel, Dawes & Prichard, 1953). Venous blood, cooled by evaporation from the walls of the nasal passages as the animal breathes, drains through the cavernous sinus (Baker & Hayward, 1968). This cool blood then comes in close contact with the warm arterial blood on the way to the brain and an exchange of heat occurs, cooling the arterial blood supplying the brain and warming the venous blood draining the nasal mucosa as shown in Fig. 7. Selective cooling of the brain has been observed in the goat (Taylor, 1966), and

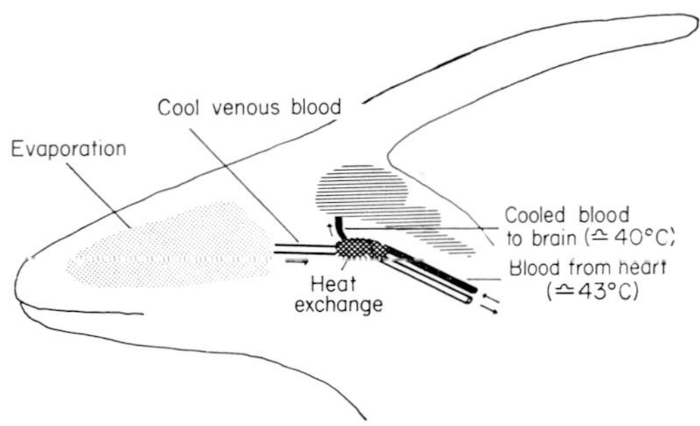

FIG. 7. A schematic representation of the proposed counter-current cooling of the gazelle's brain (see text).

Baker & Hayward (1968) have rather elegantly demonstrated an exchange of heat in the carotid *rete* of sheep. A counter-current cooling of the brain may be an important factor in the antelope's tolerance of extremely high body temperatures. There is also considerable evidence that hydrated antelopes normally use this mechanism while they are running (Taylor & Lyman, 1971).

CAN DESERT ANTELOPE SURVIVE WITHOUT DRINKING?

Now that the paradox between the Thomson's and Grant's gazelle seems to be resolved, let us return to the validity of reports that desert antelopes can survive without drinking. Specifically, I will try to answer the question of how the Grant's gazelle survives without drinking in a hot desert. The assumption is made that the water required in the simulated desert environment approximates the situation in a real desert. We have seen that even utilizing the strategies of very high body temperatures to avoid evaporative cooling, the Grant's gazelle still requires water equal to about 4% of its body weight each day. The stories of explorers and of the local inhabitants thus seem unreasonable. Where would the gazelles acquire 1–2 l of water each day? The possibilities would be:

1. preformed water in the food, and
2. oxidation water.

In an attempt to resolve the matter, I spent some time following Grant's gazelle in the hot arid Northern Frontier District of Kenya (NFD) toward the end of a severe drought. The animals were eating the most abundant plant, *Disperma* sp. The leaves of this plant were so dry and brittle that they disintegrated into a fine powder on touch. They contained less than 1% water. Using this 1% water content together with a calculation of oxidation water available from this plant, the animals would require drinking water amounting to about 3% of their body weight per day. Over the period of two weeks that I observed the animals, they did not drink nor did they appear emaciated. All of our collections of plants to determine their moisture content had been made during the middle of the day, when the animals were rather inactive. Relative humidity increases as the temperature falls at night. The dew point was seldom reached in this particular area, but relative humidity on the average reached 85%. It seemed entirely possible that these plants could pick up water from the relatively humid night air as Buxton (1923) had suggested. To check this I collected some plants and kept them at different humidities in the laboratory (Taylor, 1968b). I found leaves dried to 1% water content picked up water rapidly at 17°C and 85% relative humidity (conditions which approximate those found during the night in the arid NFD). After 4 h the *Disperma* leaves contained about 30% water, and after 8 h about 40% water. A fairly simple calculation shows how much water would be available to a gazelle if it fed on the *Disperma* at night instead of during the day (Table I). If the average moisture content were 20%, then the Grant's gazelle would have about 2·3 l/100 kg body weight/day available; 3·10 l if it contained 30% water and 4·12 l if it contained 40% water. In a simulated desert the gazelle required 3·86 l/kg body weight each day. Thus by eating predominately at night, the Grant's

TABLE I

Comparison of water requirements and water available to Grant's gazelle feeding on Disperma

Minimum water requirements (l/100 kg body wt/day)		Preformed and metabolic water available from eating *Disperma* sp. containing:		
22°C	22°–40°C	20% water	30% water	40% water
2·08	3·86	2·30	3·10	4·12

Daily minimum requirement determined at constant moderate temperature (22°C) and at 12 h heat load (40°C) alternating with 12 h moderate temperature (22°C). Calculations of water intake based on twice fasting metabolic rate (7·1 l of O_2/kg/day), 50% digestibility of feed, 4·8 kcal/l of O_2 and 0·54 g of metabolic water/g of digested dry matter (Taylor 1968b).

gazelle could be independent of surface water. This seems a likely explanation for its independence of free water.

Acknowledgements

The work discussed here was carried out at the East African Veterinary Research Organization, Muguga, Kenya. I am most grateful for the facilities and support provided by this organization. Support for the research was also provided by NIH grant 11, 816– 01, 02, 03, 04 and the paper was written during a period of support by NSF grant GB 27539. The author thanks Messrs P. Kamoyo, S. Thuku, E. Ngugi, J. Njoroge and J. Njenga for able technical assistance and for care of experimental animals.

References

Allen, G. M. (1939). A checklist of African Mammals. *Bull. Mus. comp. Zool. Harv.* **83**: 1–703.

Baker, M. A. & Hayward, J. N. (1968). The influence of the nasal mucosa and the carotid *rete* upon hypothalamic temperature in the sheep. *J. Physiol., Lond.* **198**: 561–579.

Buxton, P. A. (1923). *Animal life in deserts, a study of the fauna in relation to the environment.* London: Arnold.

Daniel, P. M., Dawes, D. K. & Prichard, M. M. L. (1953). Studies of the carotid *rete* and its associated arteries. *Phil. Trans. R. Soc.* (B.) **237**: 173–215.

Robertshaw, D. & Taylor, C. R. (1969). A comparison of sweat gland activity in eight species of East African bovids. *J. Physiol., Lond.* **203**: 135–143.

Taylor, C. R. (1966). The vascularity and possible thermoregulatory function of the horns in goats. *Physiol. Zool.* **39**: 127–139.

Taylor, C. R. (1968a). The minimum water requirements of some East African bovids. *Symp. zool. Soc. Lond.* No. 21: 195–206.

Taylor, C. R. (1968b). Hygroscopic food: a source of water for desert antelopes? *Nature, Lond.* **219**: 181–182.

Taylor, C. R. (1970a). Strategies of temperature regulation: effect on evaporation in East African ungulates. *Am. J. Physiol.* **219**: 1131–1135.

Taylor, C. R. (1970b). Dehydration and heat: effects on temperature regulation of East African ungulates. *Am. J. Physiol.* **219**: 1136–1139.

Taylor, C. R. & Lyman, C. P. (1971). Heat storage in running antelopes: independence of brain and body temperatures. *Am. J. Physiol.* **222**: 114-117.

Symp. zool. Soc. Lond. (1972) No. 31, 229–242.

WATER ECONOMY OF THE BEDUIN GOAT

A. SHKOLNIK, A. BORUT* and J. CHOSHNIAK

Department of Zoology, University of Tel-Aviv, Israel

SYNOPSIS

A breed of black dwarf goats is raised by the Beduin inhabiting the extreme desert along the Gulf of Eilat in the eastern Sinai. The body weight of these Sinai goats ranges from 11–22 kg. They thrive where few other domestic animals are found. The water economy in five of these goats was studied in a hot room at a temperature of 30°C, 30% relative humidity, with and without drinking water. Two black goats representing the breed commonly known as the "mountain goat" were studied under the same experimental conditions for the purposes of comparison. The mountain goats are common all over Israel and thrive in the deserts of its eastern and southern regions.

After two weeks of water deprivation, on a diet of dry hay and barley only, the Sinai goats lost about 30% of their body weight, but did not lose appetite. At the end of the first week under the same conditions, the mountain goats lost about 25% of body weight and consumed no more food. Both breeds maintained body water content during the water deprivation period within levels normal to ruminants, and their drinking capacity, at the termination of the water deprivation period, was very high: 23–26% of the body weight in mountain goats, and 30–40% in Sinai goats. When normally watered the water content in all body compartments was high in both breeds. The total water content amounted to 75–78% of body weight and the blood plasma to 6–8%. The Sinai goats, however, were more efficient in preserving water. The following features found in the Sinai goat may contribute to its efficient water economy: low metabolic rate, 30% lower than the value predicted according to body weight; smaller evaporative water loss during water deprivation (541 mg H_2O/kg/h compared with 710 mg in the mountain goat); dry faeces with only 40% water content and urine output per kg less than half that found in the mountain goat. The daily caloric value of the food consumed per day by a Sinai goat was a third of the intake per day by a mountain goat and the daily amount of water consumed by a Sinai goat was one fourth to one sixth the amount needed by a mountain goat although there is only a factor of two difference between the weights of the breeds.

INTRODUCTION

Black goats are conspicuous in the landscape of Israel and its adjacent deserts. Archaeological sources indicate that their original domestication took place in this part of the world, where their wild ancestors still survive (Harris, 1961; Zeuner, 1963). Skeletons of domesticated goats are frequently found in excavations of Stone Age cultures dating from the 8th millenium BC and more recently.

The dominant breed of goats in this area, *Capra hircus mambrica* L. 1758, has a shiny, black, hairy coat, long hanging ears and, usually,

* Address: Department of Zoology, Hebrew University, Jerusalem, Israel.

blue eyes (Bodenheimer, 1935). Body weight ranges from 25 to over 40 kg. Arab villagers raise them in the northern part of Israel, where the animals are called "Maaz Jabali"—meaning "mountain goats". There they browse mainly on the Mediterranean bush and pasture, generally on steep and rough terrain. In the arid Negev, however, they constitute the main livestock of the Beduin. With these nomads, mountain goats thrive even in hot and dry deserts.

Goats are also found in eastern Sinai, the harshest of all deserts in the area (Atlas of Israel, 1970), but the mountain breed previously described is not found there. The Sinai goats, although also coloured black, differ from the mountain goats in many morphological features. They are dwarfish animals—averaging 16 kg in weight. They are brown-eyed and have stiff, erect and highly vascularized ears.

About thirty years ago this breed was described from Hejaz, to the east of the Gulf of Eilat (Epstein, 1963). The approximate distribution of the Sinai goat along both sides of the Gulf of Eilat is shown in Fig. 1. Few deserts in the world can match the barren terrain where these domesticated ruminants thrive (McGinnies, Goldman & Taylor, 1968). Rain in the area is rare and sporadic. The annual average amounts to less than 25 mm. It is a land of practically eternal summer. For seven to eight months of the year, the daily maximum temperature may be well above 40°C, and relative humidity drops below 10%. Cloudy skies are rare even in wintertime, and radiation is intense all year round. Water sources are few and several days' walking distance apart from each other. The vegetation is extremely meagre. Scattered thorny *Acacia* trees and low desert scrub are relatively abundant only in wadi beds (Atlas of Israel, 1970).

Camels, donkeys and a few dogs and sheep are the only animals that accompany the small herds of goats owned by the sparse Beduin population. Horses, the pride of the Beduin in the desert, are absent here.

Ruminants of the size of these Sinai goats lack the advantages of large mammals. On the other hand, they are too large to be able to evade the full impact of the desert climate in the manner of small mammals—by withdrawing during the day to protective shelters (Schmidt-Nielsen, 1964). This handicap first drew our attention to these creatures.

Our curiosity was aroused further when we realized that even during the hottest part of the summer these goats, exposed all day to the harsh climate, were sometimes watered only once every fourth day. This information focussed our interest on their ability to withstand dehydration, and on their drinking capacity.

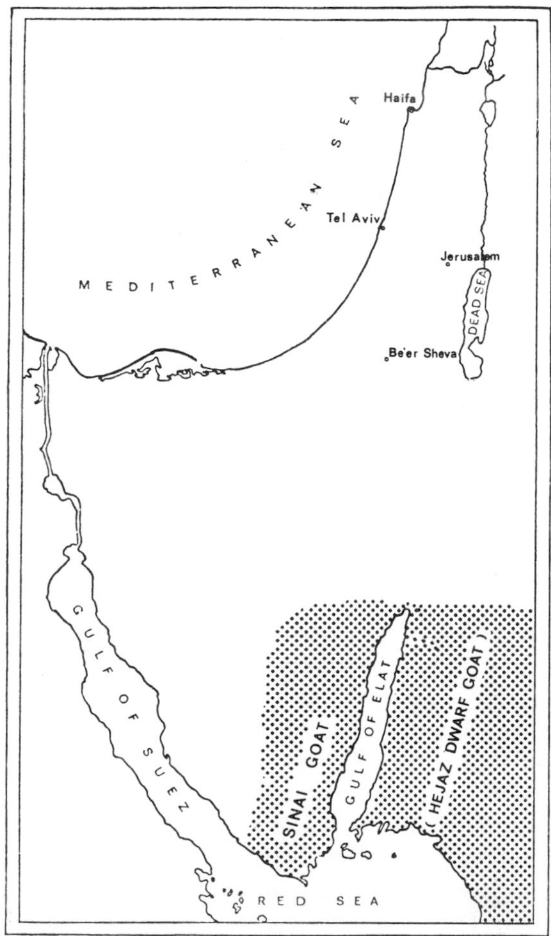

FIG. 1. The approximate distribution of the Sinai goat along both sides of the Gulf of Eilat. The distribution of this breed in Saudi Arabia (Hejaz) is given according to Epstein (1943).

MATERIALS AND METHODS

Five Sinai goats were studied in our laboratory under controlled conditions. Their standard diet was barley and wheat hay. Water was offered once a day, and even this was sometimes refused. Two mountain goats were also studied for purposes of comparison. The mountain goats would have lost weight on the diet given to the Sinai goats and we had to replace the wheat hay by alfalfa hay and often water twice a day. Food analysis was kindly carried out in the Quality Control Laboratory of "Milobar" Central Feed Mill Co. Ltd., Haifa. Analyses included the percentage of digestible cellulose established in actual feeding experiments on ruminants.

An environmental room ("Hot pack" model 682–17) enabled us to regulate temperature and humidity. For some measurements, a metabolic cage was built into this chamber and connected to an open air-flow system.

After being weighed and connected to iron-constantan thermocouples and EKG electrodes, the goats readily entered this cage. Two hours were allotted to equilibration prior to the measurements which lasted 60 to 90 min. The goats yielded simultaneously recorded data on oxygen consumption (Beckman Paramagnetic O_2 Analyser), ambient, deep core and skin temperatures (Leeds and Northrup Speedomax), as well as heart and respiration rates (Beckman Dynograph). Evaporative water loss was measured by collecting and weighing the water in the air leaving the metabolic cage. An air flow of 0·5 l/min was diverted from the entire flow of 25 l/min into specially-devised glass collecting tubes immersed in a freezing bath (−70°C). Each tube served during a collecting period of 20 min and after being replaced, sealed and its outside dried, was weighed on a Mettler analytical balance (accuracy of 0·1 mg). Control measurements were carried out to test the system, and $98 \pm 3{\cdot}2\%$ of the water lost from an open container in the cage was recovered.

The experiments were all carried out under standard conditions of 30°C and 30% rh (unless otherwise stated). Two weeks were allowed for acclimation to these conditions, during which the animals were fed and watered normally, maintaining a relatively constant body weight. For the study of water-deprived goats the water supply was then cut off. The regular food, kept in the climate room for equilibration, was offered as usual. The water content of this food dropped, however, during this procedure to 1–2% of its weight.

Measurements of total body water (HTO space), extracellular space (inulin space) and blood plasma volume (Evans Blue space) were assayed by injecting the markers simultaneously into the jugular vein. (0·1 mCi of HTO (N.EN. Co.), inulin (BDH) 50 mg/kg and Evans Blue (Warner-Chilcott) 0·5 mg/kg). Blood was withdrawn from the jugular vein 6–8 times during 5–6 h after the injection. Plasma for HTO determination was diluted in Bray solution with 4% Cab-o-Sil and read in a Packard Tricarb Scintillation counter (Rapkin, 1963). Inulin in the plasma was determined by a modification of Heyrovsky's (1956) method. Evans Blue in plasma was colorimetrically determined. The decrease in the concentration of all the markers during the sampling period was followed and then extrapolated to zero time.

RESULTS AND DISCUSSION

The rate of loss in body weight in Sinai and mountain goats is shown in Fig. 2. The difference between the two breeds lay not only in the rate of their weight loss. More striking was the capacity of Sinai goats to continue eating even at a loss of 30% of body weight. Water depletion, however, greatly affected the appetite of the mountain goats, and after a week no more food was consumed. Soon afterwards, at a loss of 25% of the initial body weight, the experiment had to be terminated in order not to jeopardize the life of the animal.

At the termination of all experiments, the goats were given free access to water (Fig. 3). In the Sinai goats the volume of water consumed—even when it amounted to 40% of their body weight—was imbibed within 90–150 sec. No more water was drunk when offered later during the same day and the volume consumed during the

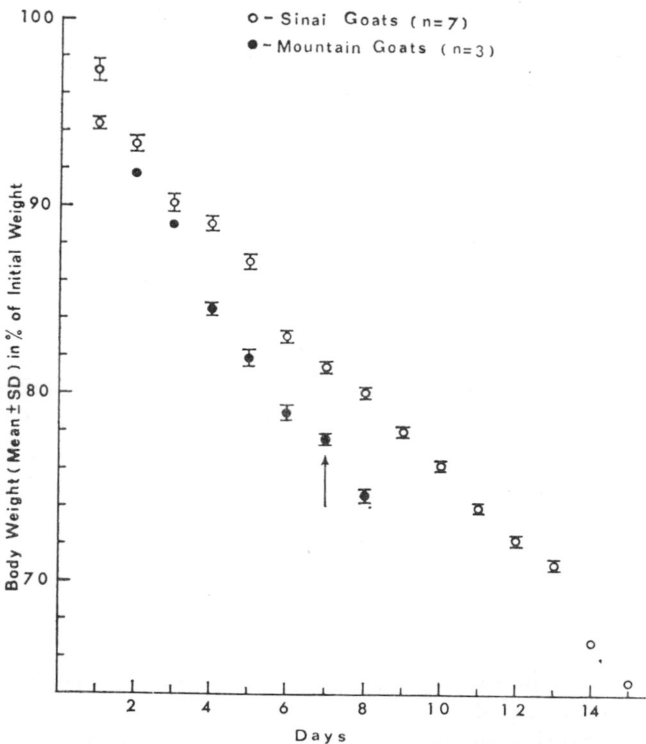

FIG. 2. Loss of body weight by Sinai and mountain goats when deprived of drinking water at 30°C and 30% relative humidity. The arrow points to the time where no more food (dry hay and barley) was consumed.

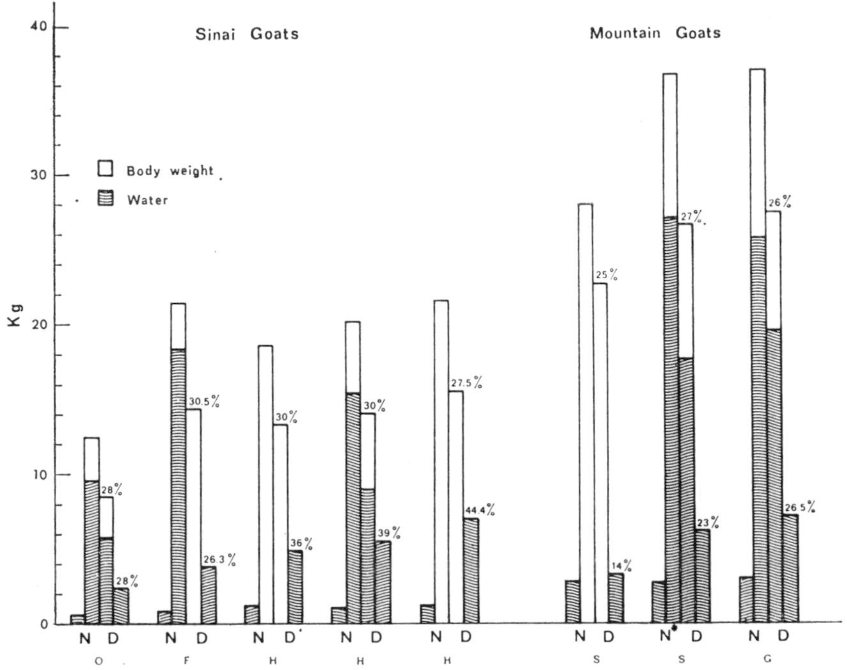

FIG. 3. Normal mean daily water consumption (first bar from left); body weight and total body water in a normally watered goat (second bar); body weight—in kg and percentage of initial weight—and total body water at the termination of water deprivation experiment* (third bar); water consumption at the termination of water deprivation experiment* in kg and percentage of body weight at that time. O, F, H, S, G—individual goats; N—normally watered; D—after water deprivation.

following days did not exceed the normal. In the mountain goats, drinking took much longer and for a few days the volume of water consumed was higher than normal. It may be of interest to note that in the few experiments we have made, the loss of body weight in the dehydrated Sinai goats exactly equalled the drop in their water content.

Water depletion did not significantly affect the body temperature of the Sinai goat as measured at 30°C and 40°C (Fig. 4). The body temperature level was well regulated within the range typical for ruminants.

The metabolism of goats was first studied in normally-watered animals at temperatures ranging from 10°C to 40°C (Fig. 5). The oxygen consumption per kg body weight of the breeds in relation to ambient temperature, is different. Most striking is the lower minimal

* See Fig. 2.

metabolic rate found in the Sinai goats in spite of their smaller body size.

Table I emphasizes this difference, which may be of adaptational significance in a hot environment: a low metabolism generates less heat, and thereby saves the water otherwise needed for its dissipation. It reduces the ventilation of the lungs and the amount of food needed, which is important in an area where food is so scarce.

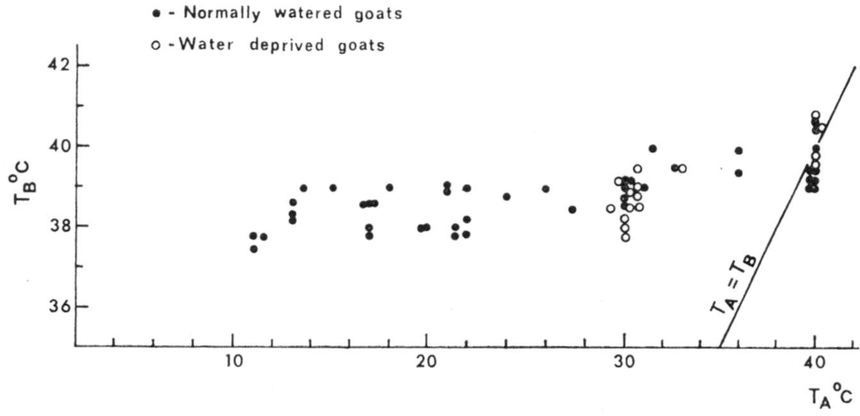

FIG. 4. Body temperature in Sinai goats at different ambient temperatures.

TABLE I

Minimal metabolism of Sinai and Mountain goats

Goat	Body weight in kg	Minimal metabolic rate ml O_2/kg/h ($\bar{M} \pm SD$)*	Deviation in % from the expected†
		Sinai goats	
O	12·300	207 ± 17	−37
T	12·800	212 ± 30	−28
F	22·000	192 ± 42	−33
H	18·000	237 ± 32	−20
$\bar{M}$		224	−30
		Mountain goats	
S	28·900	275 ± 40	+ 4
G	36·200	280 ± 42	+10

* Each figure is the mean of 4–5 experiments.
† From Kleiber's (1961) equation: kcal/day = 70 $kg^{3/4}$, assuming 4·8 kcal/lO_2.

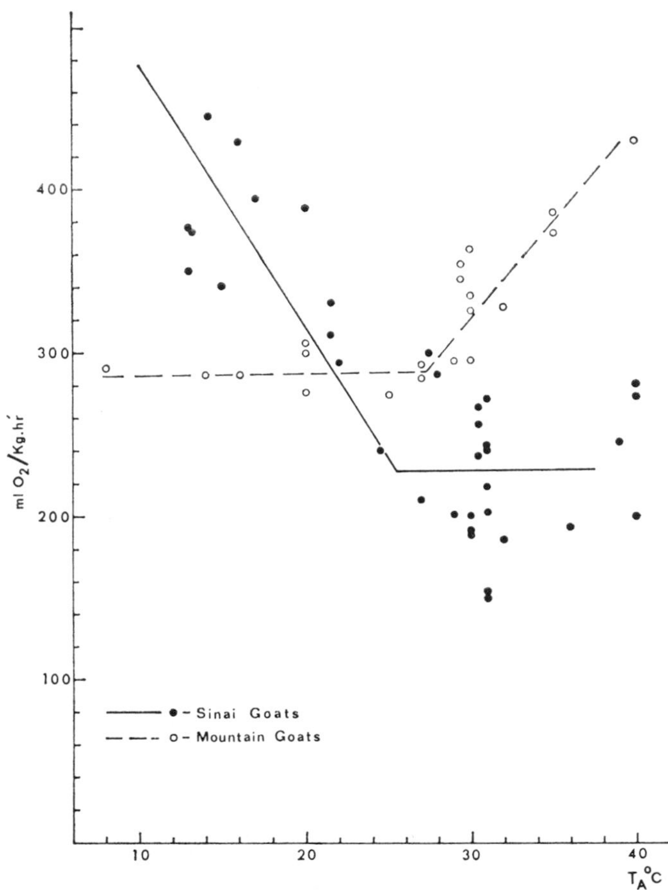

FIG. 5. Oxygen consumption of Sinai goats and mountain goats in relation to ambient temperature.

Water depletion did not change the rate of oxygen consumption in the Sinai goats, but it reduced it by 30% in the mountain goats (Table II). Evaporative water loss, on the other hand, in dehydrated goats, was reduced to 50% of its normal value in both breeds. Along with this drop, respiratory rates in the water-deprived goats were also markedly reduced. This change in respiration may contribute to reduction in the evaporative loss even though oxygen consumption is equal in the normal and dehydrated Sinai goats.

Evaporation loss is generally the largest single factor in the water balance, and its value in the Sinai goats—which is low even when

TABLE II

Metabolism, evaporative water loss and respiratory rates in Sinai and mountain goats at 30°C and 30 % rh

Goat	Normal body weight kg	Minimal metabolism O_2 ml/kg/h		Evaporative loss H_2O mg/kg/h		Respiration rate Resp/min	
		N	D	N	D	N	D
				Sinai goats			
O	12·300	207	208	950	583	19	6·7
T	12·800	212	215	1086	516	—	8
F	22·000	192	186	963	497	38	7·1
H	18·000	237	226	1310	591	23	6·2
$\bar{M} \pm SD$		$212 \pm 18·7$	208 ± 16	1077 ± 25	547 ± 47	27 ± 10	$7 \pm 0·76$
				Mountain goats			
S	36·000	337	236	1440	692	162	16
G	36·200	295	235	1065	728	77·5	12
$\bar{M} \pm SD$		316 ± 30	$235·5 \pm 0·7$	$1252·5 \pm 5$	710 ± 25	$119·75 \pm 59$	$14 \pm 2·8$

N—Normally watered goats; D—Water deprived goats (each figure represents five different experiments).

compared to other desert ruminants—is of importance especially for a small animal (Schmidt-Nielsen, 1964).

The amount of food consumed by the normally-watered animals and its caloric value is given in Table III. Table IV presents its composition. Even when calculated on body weight, more food was consumed by the mountain goats than by the Sinai breed. One Sinai goat consumed one-third or even one-fifth of the amount needed to maintain a mountain goat under the same experimental conditions. The significance of this advantage in a desert needs no further emphasis.

TABLE III

Food requirements at 30°C and 30% rh

Goat	Bw/kg	Food consumed g/kg day*		Caloric value of food kcal/kg day
		Sinai goats		
O	12·3	Barley	18	94·98
		Hay	10	
F	21·5	Barley	17	100·35
		Hay	13	
H	19·0	Barley	17	100·35
		Hay	13	
		Mountain goats		
G	36·9	Barley	18·1	161·9
		Alfalfa	12·3	
S	36·0	Barley	17·6	165·1
		Alfalfa	13·0	

* Calculated as average from more than 5 days.

TABLE IV

Food analysis—g/100 g

	Preformed water	Protein	Fat	Cellulose	Carbohydrates (other than cellulose)	Ash
Barley	12·8	10·4	2·2	4·8	67·7	2·1
Alfalfa hay	8·3	18·6	—	22·0	41·1	10·0
Wheat hay	7·0	3·9	1·3	38·5	44·7	4·6

The faeces of both species were very dry. In the water-deprived Sinai goats, faecal water amounted to only 40% of its fresh weight—the same was found only in the dehydrated camel (Schmidt-Nielsen, 1964). Water in the faecal pellets of the mountain goats never dropped below 50%. When normally watered, 50% water in the faeces of Sinai goats and 60% in the others were frequently found and these values were used for the calculations presented later on.

Urine was collected under oil in the metabolic cage or in plastic bags when the goats stayed in the climatic room. A water balance for the two breeds was worked out on the basis of the measurements made (Table V). There was only a small loss of water by the Sinai goats so that a goat of this small size can thrive on one-seventh the daily volume of water a mountain goat drinks under identical conditions.

A study of the water distribution in the different body compartments of normally watered and water-deprived goats has only just begun. In a few animals it has, however, been measured (Fig. 6). Large volumes were found for both total body water (HTO space) and plasma volume in the normally watered goats. Such high volumes, although striking, have already been reported for normally watered goats (Hix, Underbjerg & Hughes, 1959).

It is difficult to interpret the inulin space measured as long as the rate of inulin penetration into the gastrointestinal tract of our animals is not accurately known. No less striking than the high water content in all body compartments of normally-watered goats, is their ability to maintain the space of these compartments within the limits normal for ruminants and mammals in general (Hix *et al.*, 1959; Macfarlane, 1964; Macfarlane, 1968).

It is interesting to point out that concentration of plasma and its constituents does not deviate much, if at all, from normal values during dehydration in both breeds (results in preparation).

On one occasion we measured the water content of the gastro-intestinal tract in a goat. In about 7 kg of the material taken from the entire tract (six from the stomach and one from the intestine), about 6·5 l were water, which amounted to over 28% of the animal's weight. Previous to this measurement the goat—a mountain goat from an arid part of the Negev—was fed for two weeks on barley and hay and normally watered. The volume of gastro-intestinal tracts as reported in the literature amounts to 14–18% of body weight (Macfarlane, 1964).

In summary, both breeds of black goats thriving in hot and dry deserts withstand prolonged water deprivation at 30°C. The Sinai goat continues to eat even at a loss of over 30% of its body weight in two

TABLE V

Water economy of Sinai and mountain goats at 30°C and 30 % rh

Goat	Body weight kg	Food consumed*		Water intake with food g/kg/day: Preformed and oxidative water		Total	Water output g/kg/day: Minimal evaporative loss†	Urine	Loss in faeces‡	Total	Drinking ml/kg/day
Sinai goats											
O	12·3	Barley	18	3·0	12·0	15·0	22·8	12·4	7·8	43	41·8
		Wheat hay	10								
F	21·5	Barley	17	3·1	12·7	15·8	21·2	13·3	7·8	42·3	39·5
		Wheat hay	13								
H	19·0	Barley	17	3·1	12·7	15·8	26·1	25·6	7·8	59·5	55·7
		Wheat	13								
Mountain goats											
G	36·2	Barley	25·8	5·4	19·0	24·4	25·5	33·9	14·3	73·7	95·6
		Alfalfa	23·7								
S	36·0	Barley	25·1	5·3	19·2	24·5	34·6	33·9	14·3	82·8	106·5
		Alfalfa	25·4								

* Calculated as average from more than 5 days.

† Measured in resting animals. The apparent difference between total loss and total intake would probably be balanced by additional evaporative loss under exercise.

‡ Calculated as average for each group.

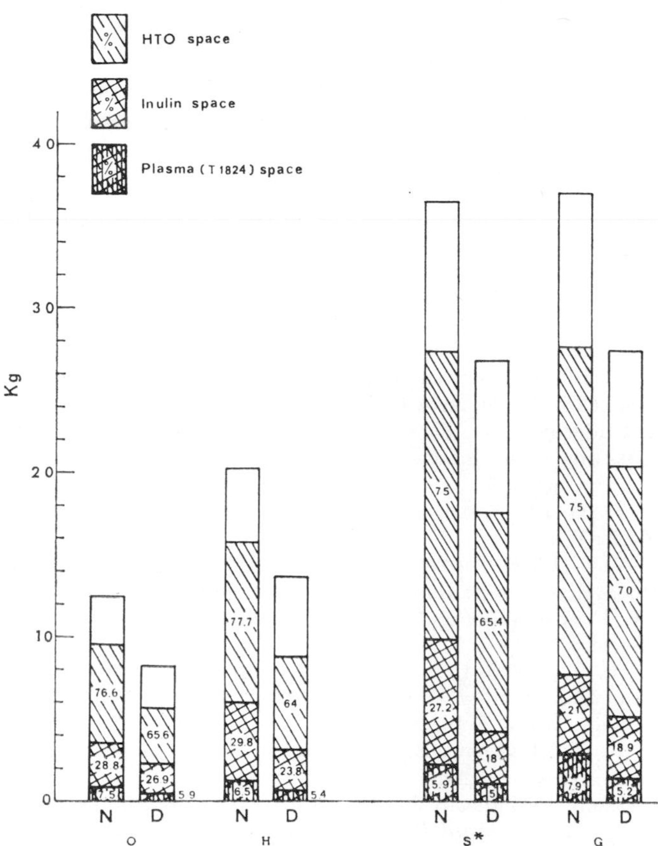

FIG. 6. Volume of the different body fluid compartments in normally watered and water-deprived goats. O, H, S*, G—individual goats; N—normally watered; D—after water deprivation.

weeks. Both breeds have a high drinking capacity and when normally watered maintain the water content of the compartments at a high level. The Sinai goat is efficient in conserving water due to a low metabolic rate and economical water expenditure through all physiological avenues studied. The low water and food requirements found in the Sinai goat are of advantage in the desert in which it lives.

These conclusions were drawn from studying only a few animals, and only in the experimental conditions mentioned above. In addition to increasing the number of animals studied, other experiments are planned. These include studies at ambient temperatures ranging from 22–40°C as well as under natural conditions, including exposure of the black goats to direct solar radiation.

Acknowledgement

This research was kindly supported by a grant from the Israeli National Council for Research and Development.

References

Atlas of Israel (1970). *Jerusalem: Survey of Israel.* Amsterdam: Elsevier.

Bodenheimer, F. S. (1935). *Animal life in Palestine.* Jerusalem.

Epstein, H. (1943). The Hejaz dwarf goat. *J. Hered.* **37**: 345–352.

Harris, D. R. (1961). The distribution and ancestry of the domestic goat. *Proc. Linn. Soc. Lond.* **173**: 79–91.

Heyrovsky, A. (1956). A new method for the determination of inulin in plasma and urine. *Clin. Chem. Acta* **1**: 470–474.

Hix, E. L., Underbjerg, G. K. L. & Hughes, J. S. (1959). The body fluids of ruminants and their simultaneous determination. *Am. J. vet. Res.* **20**: 184–191.

Kleiber, M. (1961). *The Fire of Life: an introduction to animal energetics.* p. 212. New York: Wiley.

Macfarlane, W. V. (1964). Terrestrial animals in dry heat: Ungulates. In *Handbook of physiology, section 4: Adaptation to the environment* 509–539. Dill, D. B., Adolf, E. F. A. & Wilberg, C. C. (eds). Washington D.C.: American Physiological Society.

Macfarlane, W. V. (1968). Comparative function of ruminants in hot environment. In *Adaptation of domestic animals:* 264–276. Hafez, E. S. E. (ed.). Philadelphia: Lea & Febiger.

McGinnies, W. G., Goldman, B. J. & Taylor, P. (1968) *Deserts of the World.* Tucson: University of Arizona Press.

Rapkin, E. (1963). Liquid scintillation measurement of radio-activity in heterogeneous systems. *Packard Tech. Bull.* **5**: 33–50.

Schmidt-Nielsen, K. (1964). *Desert animals.* Oxford: Oxford University Press.

Zeuner, F. E. (1963). *A history of domesticated animals.* London: Hutchinson.

Symp. zool. Soc. Lond. (1972) No. 31, 243–259.

RENAL SALT AND WATER EXCRETION IN THE CAMEL (*CAMELUS DROMEDARIUS*)

G. M. O. MALOIY

Animal Physiology Division,
East African Veterinary Research Organization
*Muguga, Kabete, Kenya**

SYNOPSIS

Previous studies on the water balance of the one-humped camel have shown that it can resist severe dehydration in part because the kidney can excrete an osmotically highly concentrated urine (2800 m-osmole/kg). Since there is little other quantitative information about the renal function in the camel, a study was undertaken to examine glomerular filtration rate (GFR) and renal salt and water excretion in the camel under a variety of controlled experimental conditions. Changes in urine flow and concentration and inulin clearance (C_{IN}) during dehydration and salt loading were measured. Slow dehydration at 0·8%/day weight loss, involving a gradual reduction in daily water intake until body weight decreased by 20–22%, caused a 57% decrease in urine flow and a 30% reduction in GFR. Salt loading increased GFR and urine flow by about 52% and 103% respectively.

In dehydrated and in salt-loaded camels, respectively 99·8% and 99·2% of the water filtered at the glomerulus was reabsorbed. The observed changes in urine flow appeared to be brought about by alteration in GFR and renal tubular water reabsorption.

Urine and plasma osmolality increased during salt loading and dehydration as did the osmolal U/P ratio and the concentrations of both urinary and plasma electrolytes and urea. The most concentrated urine excreted by the camel was 3200 m-osmole/kg with urea contributing 900–1400 m-mole/1.

The overall water expenditure of the camel was investigated in normally hydrated and dehydrated animals exposed to two ambient temperatures in a climatic chamber. The donkey in the same environment was found to consume and excrete more water and urine respectively than the camel.

The response of the camel to drinking NaCl solutions of various concentrations as its only source of drinking water was also investigated and it was concluded that the one-humped camel could drink 3·5–5·5% NaCl solutions which were even more concentrated than sea water.

INTRODUCTION

Previous studies on the water balance (Schmidt-Nielsen, Schmidt-Nielsen, Houpt & Jarnum, 1956), urea excretion (Schmidt-Nielsen, Schmidt-Nielsen, Houpt & Jarnum, 1957a), temperature regulation (Schmidt-Nielsen, Schmidt-Nielsen, Jarnum & Houpt, 1957b), metabolism (Schmidt-Nielsen *et al.*, 1967) water turnover (Macfarlane, Morris & Howard, 1963; Macfarlane & Howard, 1970) and renal function (Siebert & Macfarlane, 1971) of the one-humped camel

* Present address: Department of Animal Physiology, University of Nairobi, P.O. Box 30197, Nairobi, Kenya.

have shown that its ability to withstand severe dehydration is partly due to

1. the excretion of concentrated urine,
2. its tolerance to dehydration (30% of initial body weight),
3. a low overall water expenditure,
4. the reduction of faecal as well as evaporative water loss.

More recently Macfarlane & Siebert (1967) have examined kidney function in hydrated and dehydrated camels exposed to the sun (1000 kcal/m^2 h) in the central Australian desert (air temperatures 35–42°C).

The present study was undertaken to examine further

1. the water economy,
2. the rate of urine flow and the ability of the kidney to excrete a concentrated urine,
3. the mechanism by which the camel's kidney regulates salt and water balance and
4. to estimate glomerular filtration rate and tubular reabsorption of salt and water under a variety of controlled experimental conditions.

The ability of the camel to drink NaCl solutions of increasing concentrations as its only source of drinking water was also investigated. The Somali donkey, another domestic animal which is herded by nomadic pastoralists in hot semi-arid regions and occupies a similar habitat to that of the camel, was used for a comparison. A brief account of part of this work has been published (Maloiy, 1971).

MATERIALS AND METHODS

Animals

Three young adult one-humped camels (*Camelus dromedarius*) (two females and one male) weighing between 190 and 460 kg were used. The donkeys (two females and two males) weighed between 130 and 180 kg. All the animals which were bought originally from nomadic pastoralists dwelling in the hot semi-arid northern part of Kenya, had previously been used for other physiological studies.

PROCEDURE

Water balance experiments

The overall water balance was estimated in experimental animals housed in metabolism cages as described by Taylor, Spinage & Lyman (1969) and Maloiy (1970). An animal was assumed to be in water balance when water gain equalled water loss.

The water balance of the animals was estimated daily for 20–30 days in a moderately cool environment (22°C) and in a simulated desert environment (changes between 22°C and 40°C at 12 h intervals). The relative humidity never exceeded 40%. Measurements were made at each air temperature both in hydrated and dehydrated animals.

The food and water consumption, the volume of the urine voided and the total weight of the faeces excreted were measured daily. A fresh sample of food and freshly voided faecal samples were each weighed and dried to constant weight at 105°C in a forced air oven and the total daily water intake and faecal water loss were calculated. Metabolic water formed as a result of tissue respiration was estimated daily by analysing the composition of the hay, calculating the amount of water produced per gram of food utilized by the animals, and multiplying this figure by the intake of apparently digested dry matter (determined by the difference between food dry matter intake and faecal dry matter excreted, divided by dry matter intake). Evaporative water loss was calculated by subtracting the amount of water lost in faeces and urine from the total water intake (water drunk + free water in food + metabolic water).

Urine was collected in buckets underneath the metabolic cages. Toluene was used as a preservative and the buckets were covered with a polyethylene sheet to prevent evaporation. Occasionally, small samples of urine were collected by either catheterizing the bladder of female animals or by attaching polyethlene bags to male animals. Blood taken from the jugular vein was centrifuged immediately. The plasma and urine samples were immediately frozen at −20°C and later analysed for osmolality and electrolytes.

Dehydration and water deprivation

Macfarlane & Siebert (1967) dehydrated camels in the central Australian desert (maximum air temperatures 35–42°C) by exposing them to the sun (1000 $kcal/m^2 \cdot h$) and depriving them of water. Under these conditions the camels lost weight at 1·8–2·5% each day. In the present study the animals were dehydrated in the climatic chambers by gradually restricting water intake until they had lost 20–22% of their initial body weight. In the absence of solar radiation, the Kenya camels lost weight at about 0·8–1·8%/day. One camel in our 22°C environmental room was deprived of drinking water for 45 days but was offered dry hay (water content 12%) *ad libitum.*

Diet

The animals were offered chopped poor quality hay (*Cynodon dactylon*) *ad libitum*. The composition of the hay on a dry matter percentage basis contained 6–7% crude protein; 0·02% Na; 1·36% K; and 10–12% water. The tap water offered to the animals contained 31·3 mg Na/l and 8·12 mg K/l.

Salt-loading experiments

Salt tolerance and urinary Cl excretion were examined in both camels and donkeys. The animals were offered NaCl solutions of increasing concentrations (0·25–5·50% NaCl) as their only source of drinking water. Each concentration of NaCl solution was given to each animal for a period of 7 days. Plasma and urinary concentrations of electrolytes, osmolality, fluid intake and urine volume were measured, and observations made on food intake and body weight changes. During these experiments the animals were kept at an ambient temperature of 22°C. At this air temperature, cutaneous evaporation of water is minimal.

Inulin clearance (GF)R

Glomerular filtration rate was estimated in each of the two female camels; once when they were normally hydrated, once when dehydrated and once when salt loaded. The right and left jugular veins were catheterized with polyethylene tubing (Portex Co. PE 160 or 190). One catheter was used subsequently for taking blood samples and the other for the infusion of solutions. Urine was collected by gravity flow through a self-retaining urethral catheter (French Gauge 18) with a 5 ml inflatable balloon.

The inulin solution consisted of either 10% or 5% pyrogen free inulin (Thomas Kerfoot & Co. Ltd., Vale of Barsley, Lancashire, England) dissolved in sterile 0·9% (w/v) NaCl solution. A priming dose of this solution was injected intravenously over 4–7 min and followed by a continuous infusion for 120–240 min.

To allow equilibration, the first clearance period was not begun until 50–60 min after the start of the continuous infusion of inulin. Glomerular filtration rate was measured in 8 successive clearance periods of 10–30 min, the duration depending on the state of hydration of the animals. Blood samples were taken at the mid-point of each period for determination of plasma inulin concentration. During the last minute of each clearance period the bladder was washed twice with 10–20 ml of sterile distilled water at 37°C. The bladder was, however, not washed when the animals were dehydrated. During periods of salt loading, while on a diet of dry hay, the animals were first acclimatized to the salt load by withdrawing drinking water and 2·75% NaCl was offered as water for seven days prior to estimating the GFR.

Chemical analysis

The concentration of inulin in plasma and urine samples was measured by the alcoholic resorcinol method of Schreiner (1950). Sodium and potassium in urine and plasma samples were estimated by flame photometry. The osmolality (m-osmole/kg) of plasma and urine was determined with an Advanced Instrument wide-range laboratory Osmometer (model 68-3W). Chloride was estimated by the method of Schales & Schales (1941) and urea in the urine by the microdiffusion method of Conway (1962). The pH of the urine was determined with a Pye pH meter (model 79).

RESULTS

Water balance

It will be seen from Fig. 1a,b that the water loss of camels fed on dry hay was low both in a moderately cool environment (22°C) and in a simulated desert environment (22–40°C) compared with that of the donkey. When the animals had free access to water, the estimated total intake of water from all sources averaged 2·06 l/100 kg body wt/day and 3·84 l/100 kg body wt/day for the camel in the 22°C and 22–40°C environment respectively. Comparable figures for the donkey were 7·45 and 8·82 l/100 kg body wt/day for the same environmental conditions.

Faecal water loss

Table I shows changes in the dryness of the faeces and the food intake of three camels both when water was freely available and when the animals were dehydrated in either the 22 or 22–40°C environment. Following dehydration both the camels and donkeys (see Maloiy, 1970) excreted drier faeces and reduced their food intake. The camel, however, excreted drier faeces than the donkey under all these experimental conditions.

Evaporative water loss

At 22°C, with water either freely available to the camel or restricted, about 50% of the total water loss was through evaporation. Dehydration of the camel in either the 22°C or 22–40°C environment reduced

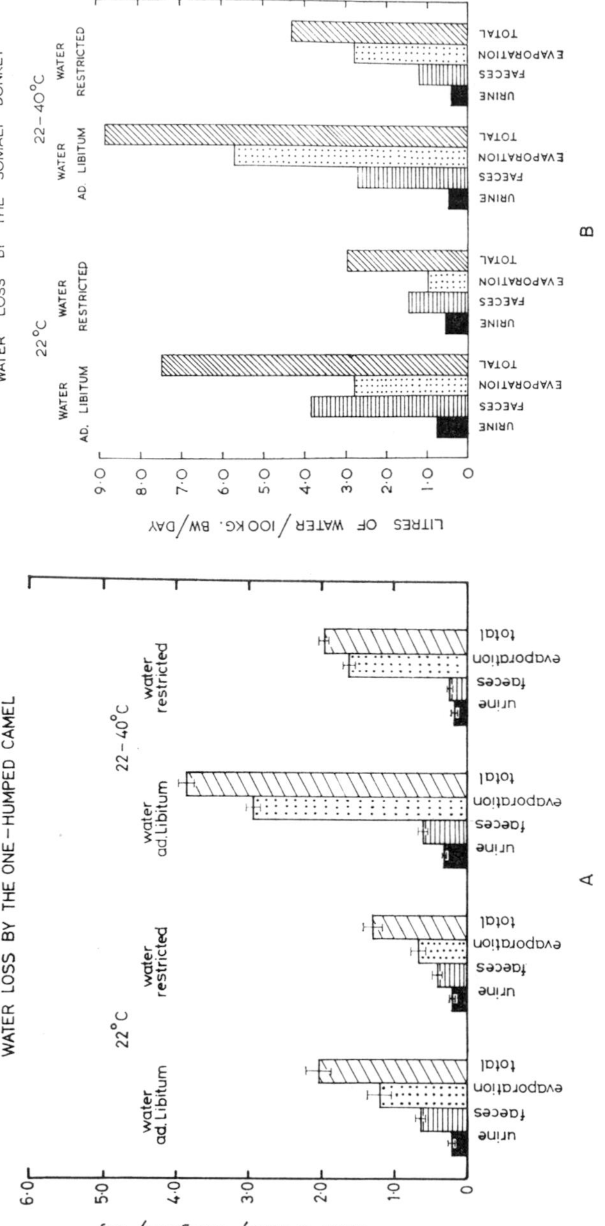

FIG. 1. Amounts of water loss in faeces, urine, and evaporation when (A) the camel and (B) the Somali donkey were watered *ad libitum* and when water was restricted to near minimal levels at ambient temperatures of 22°C and 22–40°C (data for the donkey are from Maloiy, 1970).

TABLE I

Changes in dryness of faeces and food intake of three camels when normally hydrated and when water intake was restricted

Ambient temperature	Water intake *Ad libitum*	Restricted	% Change
	Faecal water content %		
22	57 ± 0·37	46 ± 0·44	−19
22–40	53 ± 0·58	44 ± 0·49	−16
	Food intake kg/day		
22	2·9 ± 0·12	1·7 ± 0·99	−41
22–40	2·8 ± 0·10	1·9 ± 0·07	−32

Mean values ± SE.

evaporative water loss by 50% or more (Fig. 1a,b), whereas a periodic heat load (22–40°C) increased the amounts of water lost by evaporation by the donkey and the camel at least when water was available freely to the animals. When exposed to high air temperatures (T_a 40°C) the camel dissipated excess heat by sweating (cutaneous evaporation). At such high ambient temperature the camel allows its temperature to increase by as much as 5–6°C thereby conserving water through heat storage.

Urinary water loss

On dry *Cynodon* hay, camels excreted alkaline urine (pH 8·2–8·6). Table II shows the urine volume and concentrations in hydrated and dehydrated camels. Less than a third of the total water loss of the camel was used to form urine (Fig. 1a). Restriction of water intake in either the 22°C or 22–40°C environment reduced the daily urine output, but increased the concentration of the urine. Maximal urinary osmolar concentrations of the camel and other East African mammals are compared in Fig. 2. Urea accounted for a substantial fraction of the osmotic concentration (Table II). Further rates of urine flow of hydrated, dehydrated and salt-loaded camels are given in Table III.

Effect of complete water deprivation in the camel

Figure 3 shows the daily changes in body weight, food intake, urine volume, plasma and urine osmolality in one camel deprived of

TABLE II

Urine volume and concentrations of its constituents in the one-humped camel subjected to heat and dehydration in the climatic chamber

Ambient and experimental conditions	Water intake l/day	Urine volume ml/day	Sodium m-equiv/l	Potassium m-equiv/l	Chloride m-equiv/l	Urea m-mole/l	Osmolality m-osmole/kg H_2O
22°C Water *ad lib.*	2·93 ± 0·45	702·0 ± 43·4	2·3 ± 0·48	778·0 ± 30·7	250·0 ± 20·8	538·0 ± 88·6	2094·0 ± 79·6
22°C Minimum water	1·86 ± 0·11	442·0 ± 29·9	9·0 ± 1·0	987·0 ± 66·3	278·0 ± 32·6	608·0 ± 107·5	2581·0 ± 99·4
22–40°C Water *ad lib.*	8·38 ± 0·58	857·0 ± 80·5	2·2 ± 0·27	423·0 ± 76·8	130·0 ± 28·3	618·0 ± 108·9	1473·0 ± 212·1
22–40°C Minimum water	2·83 ± 0·21	205·0 ± 7·4	6·0 ± 0·75	630·0 ± 28·6	153·0 ± 22·6	954·0 ± 66·8	2230·0 ± 68·5

n = three camels; values are means ± SE; 18 samples were taken from each animal when water was available freely and 10 samples when the animals were dehydrated.

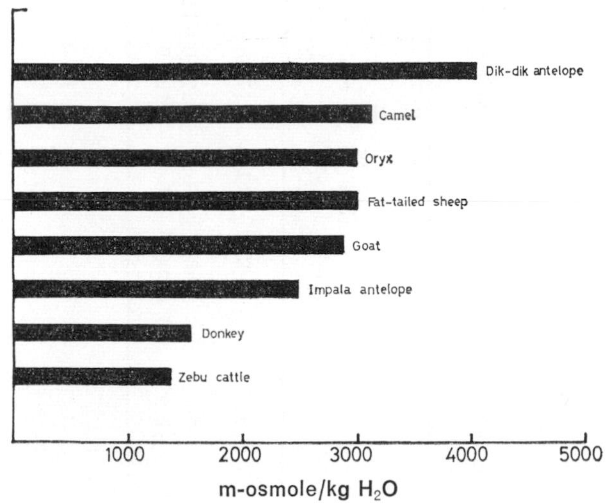

FIG. 2. The maximal urinary osmolar concent rations of severalEast African mammals. Urinary osmolalities were measured after the animals had been severely dehydrated. (Data for oryx and Zebu cattle were kindly supplied by C. R. Taylor.)

drinking water in the 22°C climatic chamber over 45 days. Dry hay (12% water) was available *ad libitum*. During this period, there was a gradual decline in body weight from (460 to 360 kg, a loss of 22% body wt), food intake and urine volume. Urine osmolality rose to about 3000 m-osmole/kg during the first week then declined to about 2300 m-osmole/kg then rose slightly to 2500 m-osmole/kg. Plasma osmolality rose to about 460 m-osmole/kg. On the 46th day when this animal was to be rehydrated, it had lost 22% of its body weight yet it then drank in 10 min an amount of water equivalent to 60% of its initial body weight.

Plasma composition

Plasma Na, K, Cl and osmolality increased during dehydration (Table IV). In severely dehydrated camels, plasma osmolality increased to about 460 m-osmole/kg.

Renal tubular function and glomerular filtration rate (GFR)

Table III gives the GFR (measured as inulin clearance) of camels subjected to different states of osmotic stress. Gradual dehydration involving a 20–22% loss of body weight caused a 30% decrease in

Table III

Inulin clearance, the urinary osmotic and ionic composition of urine of the one-humped camel during states of osmotic stress

Experimental conditions	Sodium m-equiv/l	Potassium m-equiv/l	Chloride m-equiv/l	Urine flow ml/min	Osmolality m-osmole/kg H_2O	GFR Inulin clearance ml/min
Normal hydration	2·0 ± 0·64	650·0 ± 45·0	209·0 ± 8·4	0·56 ± 0·07	1463·0 ± 121·9	179·0 ± 9·1
Salt loading (2·75% NaCl)	203·0 ± 32·2	130·0 ± 21·3	639·0 ± 49·2	1·14 ± 0·02	2049·0 ± 38·2	272·0 ± 11·4
Dehydration	8·9 ± 0·71	846·0 ± 33·2	281·0 ± 11·3	0·24 ± 0·02	2230·0 ± 50·8	124·0 ± 5·2

Mean values ± SE of 8 clearance periods for each of the two female camels.

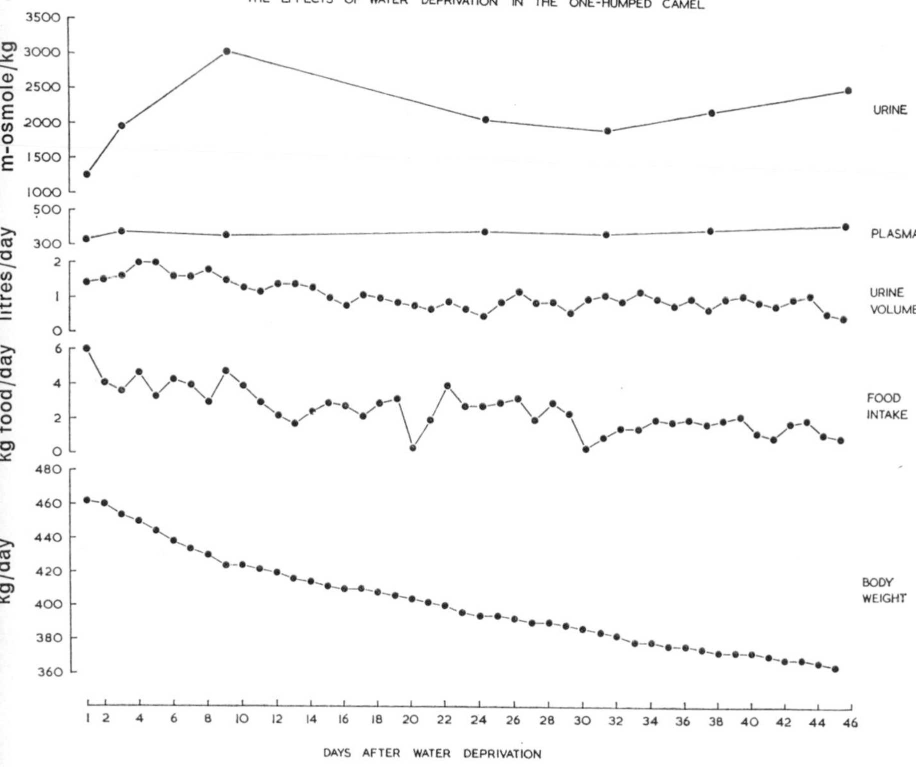

FIG. 3. Day-to-day changes in body weight, food intake, urine volume, plasma and urine osmolality of one camel deprived of drinking water in the 22°C environmental room, for 45 days but with access to dry chopped hay (12% water) *ad libitum*.

GFR ($P < 0{\cdot}01$) whereas salt loading (2·75% NaCl) caused a 57% increase in GFR ($P < 0{\cdot}01$). The data on GFR and urine flow rates (Tables III, IV) permit calculation of the percentage of renal tubular water absorption as well as osmolal and free water clearance under the different experimental conditions. In the dehydrated animals, the percentage of filtered water reabsorbed from the glomerular filtrate was 99·8%. After administration of saline (2·75% NaCl), the proportion of water reabsorbed fell to 99·2%.

The observed change in rate of urine flow (Tables II, III) is the net result of both alteration in GFR and changes in renal tubular water reabsorption. Dehydration and salt loading resulted in the elevation of osmolal U/P ratio from 5 to 8.

Table IV

Plasma ionic and osmotic composition of the one-humped camel subjected to heat and dehydration

Temperature and experimental conditions	Sodium m-equiv/l	Potassium m-equiv/l	Chloride m-equiv/l	Osmolality m-osmole/kg H_2O
22°C Water *ad lib.*	154·0 ± 1·6	4·6 ± 0·21	116·0 ± 1·2	341·0 ± 2·8
22°C Minimum water	165·0 ± 1·7	8·8 ± 0·99	122·0 ± 1·2	359·0 ± 1·7
22–40°C Water *ad lib.*	153·0 ± 1·4	3·1 ± 0·12	112·4 ± 1·7	333·0 ± 2·1
22–40°C Minimum water	161·0 ± 1·3	5·6 ± 0·24	119·0 ± 1·3	352·0 ± 1·5

Figures are means ± SE; 12 samples were taken from each animal when water was available freely and eight samples when the animals were dehydrated; $n =$ three camels.

Salt tolerance

Can camels drink sea water? Although we did not give the camels sea water to drink, we nevertheless offered them NaCl solutions of equivalent or higher concentrations than that of sea water. On drinking NaCl solutions of graded concentrations (0·25–5·50%), both the camel and the donkey increased the volume of their fluid intake. The camel's fluid intake increased two to fourfold, from a mean of 2·93 ± 0·45 l of tap water to about 5–12 l NaCl solution per day. Similarly, urine volume increased from 0·70 ± 0·41 l/day when tap water was drunk, to 3–9 l/day when drinking salt solutions. Food intake also increased under these conditions from 2·8 kg to 3–7 kg food daily.

Urine Cl concentrations fluctuated between 280 and 1000 m-equiv/l. Under these conditions, no marked changes were observed in plasma Cl concentrations (136–150 m-equiv/l). Urinary osmolality increased from 1000–1560 m-osmole/kg to well over 3000 m-osmole/kg. No great changes occurred in plasma osmolality (340–360 m-osmole/kg). The camel maintained its body weight even when drinking 4·0% NaCl solution.

The donkey, unlike the camel could only tolerate NaCl solutions at concentrations of 0·75–1·00%. When drinking NaCl solutions with a concentration above 1·00% the animal lost weight and reduced both fluid and food intake as well as urine volume (Fig. 4). The urinary Cl concentration reached a high level at about 680 m-equiv/l. and the osmolality was between 1500 and 1600 m-osmole/kg. However, as in the camel, only small changes were observed in plasma Cl concentrations and osmolality.

DISCUSSION

Although the one-humped camel and the Somali donkey both are herded in the same habitat by pastoral nomads, the camel can better adapt to adverse conditions. Although the two species adapt qualitatively similarly to water deprivation and high environmental temperatures, the camel possesses more fully developed physiological and behavioural mechanisms for coping with heat and aridity than does the donkey (Maloiy, 1970). The camel, even in a cool environment turns over less water than the donkey; this supports the conclusions of Schmidt-Nielsen *et al.* (1956) and Macfarlane & Howard (1970). At high ambient temperatures, the camel adapts to water deprivation by reducing faecal, urinary and evaporative water losses. The mechanism or site of the reduction in evaporative water loss at low environmental temperatures has not been studied.

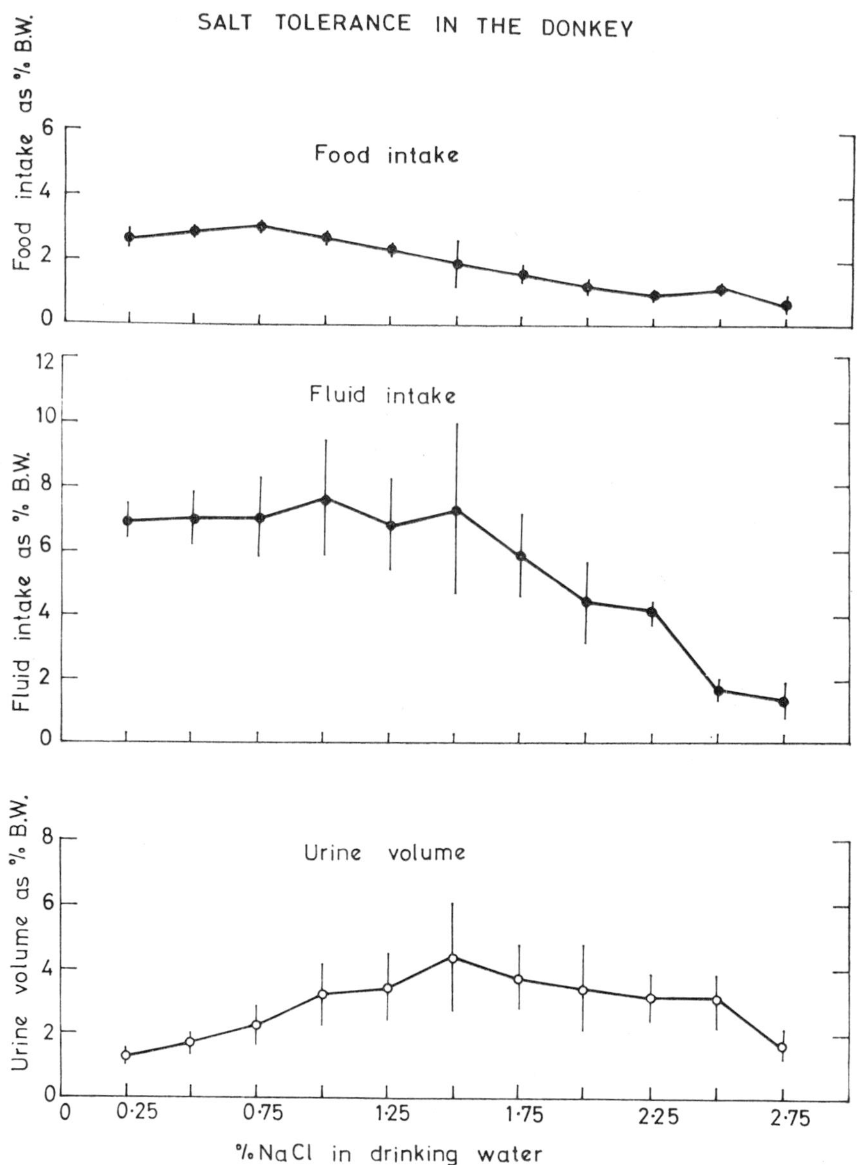

FIG. 4. Effects of *ad libitum* drinking of various NaCl solutions on mean fluid intake, urine volume and food intake in the donkey. Mean figures ± SE for three donkeys.

What role does the kidney play in regulating water balance in the camel? During dehydration, the kidney reduces urinary water loss both by decreasing GFR and by increasing tubular reabsorption of water. Macfarlane *et al.*, (1967) found that the infusion of vasopressin into camels increased GFR. Thus under these conditions, vasopressin may well have been responsible for the increased excretion of a highly concentrated urine by acting on the collecting ducts making them more permeable to water. The possible involvement of adreno-cortical hormones in this response (Chester-Jones, 1957) should not be overlooked.

Water absorption from the alimentary canal can be increased during dehydration and this occurs to a greater extent in the camel than in the donkey (Maloiy, unpubl. obs.). Intestinal absorption of salts and water is known to be affected by such hormones as aldosterone and angiotensin (Crocker & Munday, 1970; Edmonds & Marriott, 1970). Possibly angiotensin may be involved in the camel in the effects on the intestine, but might also be mediating the observed decrease in renal plasma flow. The decrease in renal plasma flow (and therefore GFR) could be mediated by this substance. Macfarlane & Siebert (1967) found that the reduction in GFR was accompanied by a decrease in renal plasma flow. Moreover, in many mammals, angiotensin helps stimulate thirst (Fitzsimons & Simons, 1969). Both the camel and the donkey drink large quantities of water in a short time after prolonged dehydration which might indicate high angiotensin levels. Thus, until the endocrine state of the dehydrated camel is known, it seems justifiable to suggest tentatively that vasopressin and angiotensin may well promote water retention.

Do camels thrive when drinking sea water? In camels offered NaCl solutions they tolerated 850 m-mole NaCl. Kangaroo rats tolerated the same concentrations of NaCl solutions (Schmidt-Nielsen & Schmidt-Nielsen, 1948, 1950). The experiments in which hypertonic saline was given confirm that the camel can excrete a more concentrated urine than the donkey which suggests a basic difference between the kidneys of the two species. The increased GFR induced by salt-loading was also observed in camels by Schmidt-Nielsen *et al.* (1957) but since it also occurs in the rat (Chester-Jones, 1957) this response does not reflect a specific adaptation to the desert environment. Again it would seem that hormonal mechanisms are involved.

It has long been suspected that the camel can drink saline as concentrated as sea water (Schmidt-Nielsen, 1964) but whether it could drink actual sea water which contains magnesium sulphate and other salts, remains to be confirmed. The camels used in these experiments, like the Kangaroo rat (Schmidt-Nielsen & Schmidt-Nielsen, 1948, 1950) suffered no ill effects from drinking NaCl solutions which were even more concentrated than sea water (3·5–5·5% NaCl) and could excrete urine with a Cl concentration above 1000 m-equiv/l and osmolality of 3200 m-osmole/kg which justifies Schimidt-Nielsen's (1964) contention. The donkey, however, was unable to exist on these high NaCl solutions. This difference between the two species in salt tolerance could be explained by the inability of the donkeys' kidneys to excrete a highly concentrated urine (1500 m-osmole/kg as opposed to 3000 m-osmole/kg for the camel).

These experiments together with those of Schmidt-Nielsen; Macfarlane and their co-workers have shown how the camel and the donkey can withstand heat and survive in hot arid regions. The gross mechanisms involved in water conservation have now been described but the actual regulatory and cellular mechanisms involved in the responses to dehydration or salt-water drinking at high environmental temperatures now require investigation.

Acknowledgements

I would like to thank Messrs P. Kamoyo, S. Thuku, P. Njomo, J. Njoroge and J. Njenga for able and reliable technical assistance and for the care of experimental animals. I am also grateful to the Wellcome Trust for a travelling grant which enabled me to participate in the Symposium.

References

Chester-Jones, I. (1957). Comparative aspects of adreno-corticol neurohypophysial relationships. In *The neurohypophysis*: 253–275. Heller, H. (ed.). London: Butterworths.

Conway, E. J. (1962). *Microdiffusion and volumetric error*, 5th Ed. London: Lockwood.

Crocker, A. D. & Munday, K. A. (1970). The effect of the renin-angiotensin system on mucosal water and sodium transfer in everted sacs of rat jejunum. *J. Physiol., Lond.* **206**: 323–333.

Edmonds, C. J. & Marriott, J. (1970). Sodium transport and short-circuit current in rat colon *in vivo* and effect of aldosterone. *J. Physiol., Lond.* **210**: 1021–1039.

Fitzsimons, J. T. & Simons, B. J. (1969). The effect on drinking in the rat of intravenous infusion of angiotensin given alone or in combination with other stimuli or thirst. *J. Physiol., Lond.* **203**: 45–57.

Macfarlane, W. V. & Howard, B. (1970). Water in the physiological ecology of ruminants. In *Physiology of digestion and metabolism in the ruminant*: 362–374. Phillipson, A. T. (ed.). Newcastle upon Tyne: Oriel Press.

Macfarlane, W. V. & Siebert, B. D. (1967). Hydration and dehydration of desert camels. *Aust. J. exp. Biol. med. Sci.* **45**: 29.

Macfarlane, W. V., Morris, R. J. H. & Howard, B. (1962). Water metabolism of merino sheep and camels. *Aust. J. Sci.* **25**: 112.

Macfarlane, W. V., Morris, R. J. H. & Howard, B. (1963). Turnover and distribution of water in desert camels, sheep, cattle and kangaroos. *Nature, Lond.* **197**: 270–271.

Macfarlane, W. V., Kinne, R., Walmsley, C. M., Siebert, B. D. & Peter, D. (1967). Vasopresins and the increase of water and electrolyte excretion by sheep, cattle and camels. *Nature, Lond.* **214**: 979–981.

Maloiy, G. M. O. (1970). Water economy of the Somali donkey. *Am. J. Physiol.* **219**: 1522–1527.

Maloiy, G. M. O. (1971). Renal salt and water excretion in the one-humped camel. *Int. Cong. Physiol. Sci.*, **25**: 365.

Schales, O. & Schales, S. S. (1941). A simple and accurate method for the determination of chloride in biological fluids. *J. biol. Chem.* **140**: 879–884.

Schmidt-Nielsen, B. & Schmidt-Nielsen, K. (1950). Do kangaroo rats thrive when drinking sea water? *Am. J. Physiol.* **160**: 291–294.

Schmidt-Nielsen, B., Schmidt-Nielsen, K., Houpt, T. R. & Jarnum, S. A. (1956). Water balance of the camel. *Am. J. Physiol.* **185**: 185–194.

Schmidt-Nielsen, B., Schmidt-Nielsen, K., Houpt, T. R. & Jarnum, S. A. (1957). Urea excretion in the camel. *Am. J. Physiol.* **188**: 477–484.

Schmidt-Nielsen, K. (1964). *Desert animals: Physiological problems of heat and water.* Oxford: Oxford University Press.

Schmidt-Nielsen, K. & Schmidt-Nielsen, B. (1948). Salt excretion in desert mammals. *Am. J. Physiol.* **154**: 163–166.

Schmidt-Nielsen, K., Schmidt-Nielsen, B., Jarnum, S. A. & Houpt, T. R. (1957b). Body temperature of the camel and its relation to water economy. *Am. J Physiol.* **188**: 103–112.

Schmidt-Nielsen, K., Crawford, E. C., Jr., Newsome, A. E., Rawson, K. S. & Hammel, H. T. (1967). Metabolic rate of camels: effect of body temperature and dehydration. *Am. J. Physiol.* **212**: 341–346.

Schreiner, G. E. (1950). Determination of inulin by means of resorcinol *Proc. Soc. exp. Biol. Med.* **74**: 117–120.

Siebert, B. D. & Macfarlane, W. V. (1971). Water turnover and renal function of dromedaries in the desert. *Physiol. Zool.* **44**: 225–240.

Taylor, C. R., Spinage, C. A. & Lyman, C. P. (1969). Water relations of the waterbuck, an East African antelope. *Am. J. Physiol.* **217**: 630–634.

Symp. zool. Soc. Lond. (1972) No. 31, 261–296.

COMPARATIVE WATER AND ENERGY ECONOMY OF WILD AND DOMESTIC MAMMALS

W. V. MACFARLANE and BETH HOWARD

Department of Animal Physiology,
Waite Agricultural Research Institute,
University of Adelaide, South Australia

SYNOPSIS

Over 99% by number of the molecules present in a rumina nt are water. Measurement of tritiated water turnover provides ecophysiological information on the water metabolism of breeds, species or genera, compared in the field while exposed to the same environment. The powerful effects of solar radiation on water demand in the desert are integrated with those of air temperature and food supply by this approach. Water turnover is influenced by age, environmental temperature, food supply, density, lactation and behaviour. Yet the intrinsic rate at which each species uses water brings about the same rank order of water turnover among those species in different environments.

This rank order for water turnover is closely correlated with the metabolic rate or oxygen turnover, which is high in some desert animals with high water turnover (eland, cattle, reindeer, *Sminthopsis*) and low in others (camel, goat, oryx, musk ox, *Dasycercus*) which economize water. Other correlated variables are the rates of pulmocutaneous evaporation, and movement of water from gut to blood, which are rapid in animals with high rates of oxygen and water metabolism, low in the others. Low rates of movement of water and energy through animals allow them longer survival in, and better adaptation to the desert. Sensitivity to vasopressin is high in desert mammals with low water turnover and low in those with high water demands.

The recent distribution of mammals in arid areas shows anomalies of ecophysiology which could be explained if the functional evolution of some mammals took place in non-arid regions, followed by migration into the desert without modification of their functions. Others, evolved in the desert, remain there when high-rate animals perish.

INTRODUCTION

More than 200 megayears have passed since some amphibia crawled from the water to remain on dry land. Yet water is still the matrix in which the living processes of mammals take place. In dry air and under the heat of the sun, structural and functional water economies developed. The squamous surface became less permeable, the colon reabsorbed water more effectively and renal concentration was acquired. Yet the number of molecules of water relative to the number of other molecules in the body remained much as in aquatic vertebrates. Water is by far the most numerous molecule in a mammal (Table I) comprising about 99·2% of all molecules present in ruminants. Fats and electrolytes are the next most numerous molecules, but they make up only 0·8% of the total number (Macfarlane & Howard, 1970).

TABLE I

Molar composition of a 100 kg tropical ruminant

	% Body weight	Content mole	Content mole %	Turnover mole/24h
Water	70·0	3889·0	99·207	300·0
Fat	12·0	15·0	0·382	1·0
CHO protein	14·0	0·1	0·002	2·0
Ca	3·5	10·0	0·255	0·002
Na, K	0·5	6·0	0·153	1·0
	100·0	3920·1	100·00	304·0

Oxygen and carbon compounds from which energy is released are carried through tissues in a stream of water which transports them from lung or gut through cells and out to the renal filter or evaporative cooler. The turnover of water by an animal appears in this way to be linked with the turnover of energy. A 50 kg sheep in dry conditions is likely to move 150 moles of water (2·7 l) per day through its active tissues. The water comes from food water, oxidation of hydrogen or water ingested as such. On this stream about 20 moles of oxygen are carried each day. There is, overall, a close relationship in any genus or species between the amount of water and of oxygen used. Lifson & McClintock (1966) employed $D_2{}^{18}O$ to measure water and oxygen consumptions at the same time, and they found some relation between the two in the rat.

It could be expected in the desert that different types of mammal would show some uniformity in rate of water handling. This expectation has been investigated among animals undisturbed in their outdoor environments.

CONTENT AND TURNOVER OF WATER IN FIELD MAMMALS

In an ecological niche energy flows from the sun through plants to herbivores and from them through carnivores towards entropic distribution after death. This flow of energy is carried by water through plants and animals.

Large quantities of water are needed for effective plant growth, so that the water cost of 1 kg of dry grass is 150–250 l of water. Water for animal maintenance includes that needed for the plants that are eaten, and that required to sustain herbivores during periods of drought as well as of sufficiency. McMillan (1965) estimates that 1000 metric tons of water are required by sheep for each kg of wool formed; and for steak 110 tons/kg, or 400 tons/kg dry protein. There is rarely 1% efficiency of energy use for wool production and the efficiency in water use is even less.

A satisfactory measurement of the content and movement of water through the animal phase of an ecosystem in the field is obtainable by using tritiated water (TOH). This approach brings minimal disturbance to the normal feeding and behaviour patterns. If animals of different breeds or species are maintained in the same environment over the same period of time, the physical impact of sun, wind, air temperature and humidity is similar for all, so that only animal variables are significant. For ruminants with the same grazing habits, food-water intake and metabolic water are also held constant. Even if they are not, the reaction of the animal to potential food supply is not distorted in the field situation as it is in the laboratory conditions, where often artificial feed components are offered, and sun is excluded. Desert insolation doubles the heat load of sheep (Macfarlane, 1964, 1968) and alters feeding behaviour: but these effects are integrated with and included in the TOH dilution measurement.

METHODS

A group of animals is weighed, identified individually and injected with TOH (5–10 μCi/kg) intramuscularly at a known time. The labelled water is allowed to equilibrate. In the case of man, carnivores or milk-drinking young ruminants, equilibration throughout extracellular and intracellular spaces is complete in less than 2 h. In adult ruminants, however, the rate of equilibration is slowed because mixing of TOH from the blood through the saliva to the large volume of fluid in the reticulorumen takes considerably longer. In sheep or goats, equilibration requires 5–6 h, cattle 7–8 h, camels 8–12 h (Macfarlane, 1968) and the process is slowed by dehydration which reduces the rate of salivation (Stepankina & Tashenov, 1958). Correction can be made for the loss of concentrated TOH in fluids by kidney or gut during equilibration, but unless the animals have a very high excretion rate, this is less than 1% of the dose. An intramuscular route of administration lessens the height of the peak in plasma concentration that occurs after intravenous injection, and thus renal loss of marker is reduced.

After time for equilibration has elapsed (without the introduction of new water as food or fluid) the concentration of ^{3}H relative to ^{2}H is measured by scintillation counting of a sample of body fluid (saliva, blood, urine). A convenient approach is to inject the marker in the evening, leave animals overnight away from food and water then to take blood samples in the morning. Animals are released to their normal field activities. The dilution of marker by drinking or from food or metabolic water integrates intake to the time of the next sample. This may be between 4 and 10 days according to the turnover rate. If the water content of the animal changes during this period there will be an apparent change in the dilution of the TOH. This can be adjusted by taking a blood sample after 7–10 days then injecting another known amount of TOH to get a further total body water estimation.

The amount of exchange of tritium with protium is small and has been estimated at between 0·5% and 2% (Morris, Howard & Macfarlane, 1962). In sheep deprived of food a 4–5% decrement of TOH concentration took place during 7 days without water. Metabolic water was produced from the food in the rumen, which would account for more than 3% of the dilution. The accuracy of the method appears to be greater than the usual measurements on confined animals, where the amount of food water, metabolic water and drinking water may be estimated but it is not easy to compensate for spillage and evaporation. Agreement to 2% was obtained in the turnover of TOH by identical twins grazing together in the field, but when measurements were made on water intake by similar cattle in stalls wide discrepancies appeared (Macfarlane & Howard, 1966) between TOH determinations of their water turnover and bucket-measured quantities.

WATER DISTRIBUTION

Total body water

The dilution of a known quantity of marker distributed throughout body fluids measures the total body water content. Cell water, extracellular fluid and transcellular water such as that in the gut, is estimated. Cell water is almost fixed at 72% of the fat-free weight although under the stress of heat or dehydration some cell water changes occur.

Cell water content

This is regulated by electrolyte pumps in cell membranes moving K into the cell. This appears largely to be the activity of Na^+, K^+ATPases which result in a balanced removal of Na from and secretion of K into cells. This maintains cell turgor and flow of water and energy. Control of cell electrolytes is probably intrinsic to cells, with regulation partly by thyroxin action, partly by aldosterone and cortisol. Water is also the convecting medium for gases, anabolites and katabolites, in the circulating blood, then from interstitial fluid to cells. The estimated volume of body water is a momentary stasis in a dynamic flow-through process.

Transcellular water

Transcellular water of the alimentary tract is drawn upon by the animal during water deprivation, and ruminants have a larger proportion (up to 18% of body weight) available from this source than non-ruminant animals. Alimentary water is the product of intake drives determined in the hypothalamic and forebrain area, and is derived from food water, ingested water and secretions. The gut, as part of the external world, receives saliva, gastric, pancreatic and intestinal fluids to aid the movement and digestion of food. The volume of water egested is controlled by the amount of Na reabsorbed by the colon, with aldosterone affecting the rate of uptake.

The extracellular component

This component of body fluids is regulated by absorption from the intestine, by volume sensors in the hepatic portal system and the atrium of the heart, as well as by concentration sensors in the juxtaglomerular cells of the kidney working through angiotensin on the glomerular layer of the adrenal cortex. This complex is concerned with the volume of Na retained, which in turn retains water in extracellular fluid. Extracellular and gut fluids are labile and respond considerably to the environment. Extracellular fluid volume rises when animals are without adequate food (Macfarlane, Morris, Howard & Budtz-Olsen, 1959) or when an increased metabolic rate induced by shearing sheep in winter, with limited food intake, produces starvation (Morris *et al.*, 1962). During summer, body water, particularly the extracellular volume, increases relative to body weight as Na is retained. Removal in summer of the insulation provided Merinos by a fleece increased extracellular fluids 17% and doubled water turnover (Macfarlane, Howard & Morris, 1966b).

INTER-SPECIFIC WATER METABOLISM

Ecologically, total body water provides useful indications of the energy and water reserves of an animal. If there is more fat there is less water per unit of weight; if there is excess body water, starvation or disease is likely.

The metabolic rate of mammals varies with size as mass$^{0.75}$ (Kleiber, 1947). Water turnover, however, is not quite parallel with the flow of energy since water is used also for convection and for evaporative cooling. To allow comparison of water use between animals of different size, an exponential relation to body mass is needed. Adolph (1949) found that most water parameters were related to the $^{0.8}$ to $^{0.85}$ power of the mass. Richmond, Langham & Trujillo (1962) used weight $^{0.8}$. We found that the empirical regression of body weight on water turnover is described by weight $^{0.82}$. Since, however, body weight varies with fat and bone content, turnover is usefully related to the body water pool expressed as $1^{0.82}$. Since, also, the interaction of molecules is by number rather than mass it is useful to measure water, oxygen or carbon metabolism in molar terms. In subsequent tables the water content is expressed as a fraction of the body weight, and the turnover as l/day, ml/kg/day or mole/$l^{0.82}$/day, each of which gives information on a different aspect of water economy.

TABLE II

Identical twins and wool growth selection in the genetics of water turnover

Breed or species		Body weight kg	Body solids % body wt	Water turnover/24h ml/kg	ml/kg$^{0.82}$	Environment
Bos taurus	*A*	235	26	136	364	Kenya
twins	*B*	257	32	131	359	highlands
Bos taurus	*A*	520	37	90	276	lush
twins	*B*	515	40	88	270	pastures
Bos indicus	*A*	420	30	87	261	
twins	*B*	430	33	87	261	
Merino sheep						28°S
selected	wet	40·3	38·3	128	250 ± 36	summer rain
(12)	dry	46·2	43·7	98	197 ± 16*	hot, dry
Merino sheep						
unselected	wet	41·4	36·1	133	259 ± 20	summer rain
(12)	dry	44·9	42·9	88	174 ± 15*	hot, dry

Identical twin cattle on the same pasture showed identity of water handling among twin pairs, but large differences between breeds or species.
Merino sheep in the summer wet season used more water than during the hot dry part of summer, at Cunnamulla (lat. 28°S). In the wet season water was freely available from lush pasture. Sheep, selected genetically to produce 13% more wool than control sheep, turned over more water during the dry summer than those producing less wool (statistically significant* $P = 0{\cdot}01$). The high producing sheep also had 16% higher rates of metabolism than unselected sheep. Mean ± SD.

GENETIC COMPONENT OF WATER METABOLISM

The identity of water turnover amongst identical twins grazing together and the differences between twin pairs on the same pasture gave indications of a strong genetic control of water turnover (Table II). This was reinforced by studies on sheep selected for wool growth in the arid areas of Australia. Those with the greatest wool growth had the greatest water turnover (Macfarlane, Dolling & Howard, 1966a; Macfarlane & Howard, 1966, 1970) and higher metabolic rates (Graham, 1968). There appear not only to be inter-family and inter-specific differences in the rates of water turnover, but also differences between groups in a breed or line of animals. These relations have been pursued in the field over several continents and orders of mammal.

WATER METABOLISM IN ARID AREAS

Two-thirds of Australia are dry and one third is desert: while one-fifth of the earth's surface is arid. The original marsupials of Australia have been, in part, displaced by Merino sheep (from Spain and North Africa, through Germany, Britain and France), by cattle, mainly from Britain and more recently from India, camels from Pakistan, and donkeys from the mediterranean area. The water consumption of some of these genera—cattle, sheep, kangaroos and camels—has been compared in the field near Alice Springs in the central desert area (lat. 24°S) during summer (Fig. 1). Kangaroos (*Megaleia rufa*) remained in shade during the heat of the day but the sheep, Shorthorn cattle and dromedaries were exposed to solar radiation (1000 kcal/m^2/h) as well as to air temperatures reaching a daily maximum of 38–42°C. There was dry summer grass and saltbush to eat with some supplement of lucerne hay. The environment was the same for all animals and they remained at large during the period of measurement except for the shaded kangaroos (Table III). The animals with the smallest proportion of body water and the greatest fat reserves were camels and sheep, then kangaroos while cattle had most water in the body (Macfarlane, Morris & Howard, 1963). The proportion of body water turned over daily and integrated over 2 weeks, was lowest amongst the camels. Kangaroos had lower water turnovers than sheep but since the sheep were in the sun, and kangaroos in the shade during the day, the sheep needed more evaporative cooling than kangaroos. There was thus a hierarchy of water turnover among differing types of animals in the same environment. Body water content tended to be high when turnover was high. This rule, that the more water passes through mammals the more remains in them, seems to

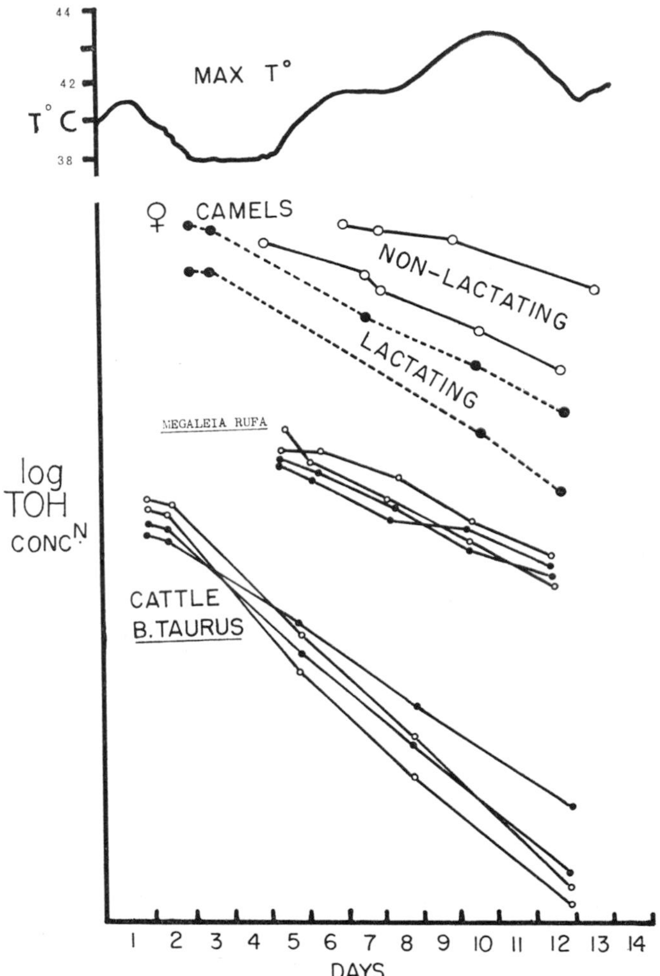

FIG. 1. Dilution curves of tritiated water in mammals near Alice Springs during summer. The water turnover was highest in cattle (Shorthorn) lower in kangaroos (*M. rufa*) and least in camels though lactation by two camels increased the rate of water use.

apply whether water turnover is altered by seasonal heat, lactation or by food supply.

EFFECT OF BREED, SPECIES, GENUS ON WATER TURNOVER RATES

The evolutionary history of a group of animals forming a genetic unit has presumably determined the water functions of that gene pool.

Table III

Summer comparison of water metabolism of grazing animals

		Total body water ml/kg	Water turnover/24 h litres					
			litres	% body water	ml/kg	ratio	ml/$l^{0.82}$	ratio
PERIOD A								
Camel	(3)	623	27·5	9·0	62	1	250	1·3
Kangaroo (*M. rufa*)	(4)	769	2·08	11·5	88	1·4	191	1·0
Cattle (Shorthorn)	(3)	755	28·9	19·6	148	2·4	486	2·5
PERIOD B								
Camel	(3)	715	38·1	12·0	82	1	355	1·0
Sheep (Romney)	(5)	554	5·2	18·7	104	1·3	430	1·2
Cattle (Shorthorn)	(3)	826	53·4	19·1	162	2·0	540	1·5

These animals shared the same desert environment near Alice Springs 24°S lat. During Period A temperatures were lower than during B, when maximum air temperatures were 41–43°C.

In a shared environment the different types of animal have characteristic water turnover rates and thus maintain a rank order. When the environmental temperature or food supply is changed the rank order of a group is closely held at a characteristic rate of water turnover.

Merino and Leicester sheep grazing arid summer chenopods, or grass pastures near Deniliquin maintained the same order of difference on each type of food—the Leicesters turned over 58–78% more water than Merinos (Table IV). Macfarlane, Howard & Siebert (1967) reported this using TOH in the field and Wilson (1969) found the same response using penned sheep. On winter pasture with lush growth of grass a similar difference was found between the breeds.

TABLE IV

Water content and turnover of Merino and Border Leicester sheep grazing saltbush (Atriplex) *or* Danthonia *during summer*

		Body weight kg	Total body water ml/kg	Water turnover/24 h litres	ml/kg	$ml/kg^{0.82}$
Danthonia grass						
Merino	(6)	52	720	5·85	111	227 ± 53
Leicester	(6)	40	772	6·91	173	337 ± 40
$\Delta \frac{L}{M}$ %			7·8	19·5	58	49 $P < 0{\cdot}001$
Saltbush						
Merino	(6)	48	745	9·44	196	395 ± 117
Leicester	(6)	39	774	13·75	350	677 ± 126
$\Delta \frac{L}{M}$ %			4·0	45	78	74 $P < 0{\cdot}001$

The Leicesters took more water daily on *Danthonia* than Merinos, and when the sheep required more water to excrete salts (Na, K) from *Atriplex*, Leicesters took in even more water. Wilson (1969) showed that increased water intake was, in pens, paralleled by greater food consumption. Leicesters also had greater body water contents than Merinos, on each pasture. Mean ± SD. Differences between the breeds were statistically significant.

Identical twin pairs of cattle were measured for water consumption on the grazing areas in the uplands of Kenya (Macfarlane & Howard, 1966) where Boran twins used 261 $ml/kg^{0.82}$ each day in the same context as *B. taurus* twins turning over 362 $ml/kg^{0.82}$ (Table II). So within a species or between species there are genetic groupings with different rates of water metabolism.

TABLE V

Groups of mammals compared for water metabolism between the equator and the Arctic

	Breed or species		Body solids % wt	Body weight kg	Water turnover/24 h ml/kg	Water turnover/24 h $ml/kg^{0.82}$	Environment
A	Cattle (Boran)	(6)	28	417	76	224 ± 14	Arid
	Eland	(5)	20	247	78	213 ± 43	equatorial
	Wildebeest	(1)	27	175	53	137	grassland
	Kongoni	(2)	15	88	52	116	winter
	Oryx	(1)	30	136	29	70	lat. 1°S
B	Cattle (Boran)	(4)	23	197	135	347 ± 12	Equatorial
	Sheep (Ogaden)	(12)	32	31	107	197 ± 29	desert
	Goats (Somali)	(4)	31	40	96	185 ± 32	NFD Kenya
	Camel (Somali)	(4)	30	520	61	188 ± 37	lat. 3°N
C	Buffalo	(3)	21	354	212	535 ± 33	Summer
	Shorthorn	(4)	26	322	168	461 ± 48	wet season
	Santa Gertrudis	(2)	37	523	141	373 ± 60	pasture
	Banteng	(4)	23	372	132	348 ± 22	tropical
	Zebu	(3)	38	532	121	350 ± 36	lat. 12°S
D	Reindeer	(6)	23	100	128	293 ± 65	Winter
	Moose	(1)	23	186	111	284	Central Alaska
	Goats	(3)	33	70	52	112 ± 10	Taiga
	Musk oxen	(2)	34	324	35	99	lat. 65°N

Mean ± SD

This is further illustrated (Table V*C*) in a study of bovids in the tropics (lat. 12°S) during the summer rains (Siebert & Macfarlane, 1969). The buffalo (*Bos bubulus bubulis*) grazing tropical grasses maintained its swamp functions and used more water than any other bovid. Shorthorn (*B. taurus*) cattle also had higher water turnover rates, followed by the zebu cross (*Santa Gertrudis*) then the banteng (*Bibos banteng*) with zebu (*B. indicus*) cattle using least water. The *B. indicus* types used less water than *B. taurus* or the buffalo. The water content followed the reciprocal order, so that buffalo had least and zebu most tissue, including fat. There was greater water content in the high-turnover animals.

SEASON AND TEMPERATURE

Camels and cattle measured together during summer in the central desert, and again in winter, showed parallel changes in total body water and water turnover (Table VI*A*). Winter is dry and sunny with little evaporative cooling, so that extracellular volume is reduced. In summer increased thermal loading raised total body water as an increase in water turnover took place (Siebert & Macfarlane, 1971). Cattle contained more water and used at least twice as much as camels in the same environment.

In the hottest region of Australia (lat. 21°S near the west coast) sheep have minimal shelter from the sun on the spinifex plains. Water turnover was measured on the same sheep during a period of cool weather, then during high levels of summer radiation and heat (Table VI). Four-month-old Merinos used less water per $kg^{0.82}$ than older sheep, but turnover rose 41% between the maximum temperatures of 29°C and 40°C. Ewes put through less water than rams per metabolic kilogram in the cooler period and increased water turnover 28% in the heat. The turnover by rams rose only 19% at 40°C above that at 29°C. The rams found some meagre shelter from the sun: but all sheep showed the effects of heat by increasing evaporative cooling.

Young Merino ewes bred in the tropics were compared during summer and winter. They had higher body water content (Table VIII) during summer than winter and turned over three times more water in the hot season. When half of the group was exposed to a temperate climate with succulent grass during winter, they took three times more water in winter (from food rather than drinking) than in summer. With this high turnover, however, went greater water retention so that body water was higher during the wet winter than in summer, in contrast with summer increments in body water in the tropics, where there is summer rain and a demand for evaporative cooling.

TABLE VI

A. Water content and turnover of cattle and camels during summer and winter near Alice Springs

	WINTER Body water	WINTER Turnover	SUMMER Body water	SUMMER Turnover
	ml/kg	ml/kg$^{0.82}$/24 h	ml/kg	ml/kg$^{0.82}$/24 h
B. taurus				
Shorthorn (3)	764	325	842	482
C. dromedarius				
Camel (3)	626	110	715	238

B. Effects of heat and radiation on the water turnover of Merino sheep in the arid tropics at Abydos, lat. 21°S, during summer

	Weaned lambs (18) 13 kg		Ewes (28) 35 kg		Rams (10) 55 kg	
	l/24 h	ml/kg$^{0.82}$/24 h	l/24 h	ml/kg$^{0.82}$/24 h	l/24 h	ml/kg$^{0.82}$/24 h
Max T° 29	1·19	143·9	3·09	170·5	4·85	180·2
Max T° 40	1·68	201·7	3·90	217·9	5·78	214·6
Rise %	41	40	26	28	19	19

The turnover rates are integrals over six days in the cooler conditions and five days during hot weather without cloud.

Water turnover falls rapidly in the first year of life, then more slowly with age in a given environment (Table XII).

LACTATION

Lactating and non-lactating camels (Table VII*A*) together in the desert during summer differed by 27 ml/kg/day (44%) in water turnover rate because of the water used in milk production. Lactation not only is energetically expensive to a mammal but is also a costly function in terms of water use. Camel lactation lasts up to 18 months and is associated with increased body water content as the fat reserve of the hump is depleted.

Amongst Merino ewes on lat. 21° the water turnover during pregnancy is virtually the same at a given air temperature and food supply as that of non-pregnant ewes. When lactation begins, however, water turnover increases (Table VII*B*). These measurements made during summer integrated the cost of both evaporative cooling and feeding the young. Ewes produced about 1·2 l of milk daily to feed the lambs. Their own water turnover was accordingly increased by the amount of metabolic water produced in forming milk and the water requirement for milk. This increased the ewes' water turnover by 44% for lactation relative to non-lactating and non-pregnant ewes.

The water turnover of young animals while suckling is a close measure of the milk intake (Macfarlane, Howard & Siebert, 1969) correlating ($r = 0{\cdot}98$) with bottle-fed quantities. TOH may be used to estimate body solids gain per litre of milk, also, in the field.

FOOD SUPPLY

Clark & Quin (1949) emphasized the close relationship between water and food intake. Among Merino sheep near Pretoria, reduction of food intake lessened water consumption: and a reduction in available water was associated with less food consumption. This linkage of functions arises in part from the interaction of neighbouring neurones of the ventro-medial hypothalamus where food and water intake is regulated on afferent information and blood composition (Anand, 1961). There are other inputs in the regulation, such as rumen fill and the osmotic pressure of the duodenal contents which also feed back to the brain stem to form a regulatory loop.

The turnover of water by ruminants is closely related to the succulence or dehydration of pasture plants. In the tropical summer there may be low rates of water intake when dry vegetation is eaten but

TABLE VII

Water lost of lactation.
A. Female camels near Alice Springs during summer. Effect of lactation on water turnover

Camels		TBW ml/kg	Water turnover/24 h litres	ml/kg	$ml/l^{0.82}$
Lactating	(2)	725	42·8	88·5	364
Non-lactating	(2)	695	27·5	61·5	253
Lact.-Non-lact. Δ%		4·5	54	44	44

Lactating camels were less fat, and used 44% more water per metabolic unit than the non-lactating camels in the same environment.

*B. Water metabolism of Merino ewes lactating during summer, lat. 21°*S

Sheep		TBW ml/kg	Water turnover/24 h litres	ml/kg	% increase
Lactating 1 month	(22)	763	4·6	121	+44%
Non-lactating (lamb died)	(9)	722	3·9	91	+9%
Not pregnant	(4)	681	3·5	84	0

The average daily milk yield to lambs from lactating ewes was 1·2 l/24 h, measured separately by TOH dilution in the lamb.

summer rain rapidly increases water turnover when lush vegetation grows (Table VIII). This is eaten in greater quantity than dry pasture, so that animals may become fat and at the same time have two or three times more water and dry organic matter passing through them daily because of the high water content (80–90%) of freshly grown plants. This is illustrated by Merino sheep (lat. 28°S) in the semi-arid *Astrebla* regions. Prior to rains, water turnover was 93 ml/kg/24 h on dry pasture and after the rains this rose to 130 ml/kg/24 h, when sheep ate succulent new growth though air temperatures were lower (Table II). Sheep do not need to drink when pasture carries 60–70% water (Macfarlane *et al.*, 1966a). Similar summer-winter differences of water turnover are shown in Table VIII where in a mediterranean climate

TABLE VIII

Seasonality of water content and turnover of Merino ewes in the tropics (lat. 21°S) and in temperate zone (lat. 35°S)

20 ewes at Julia Creek	21°S	*Summer* (Hot)	*Winter* (Dry)
Body water ml/kg		762	690
l/24 h		6·0	2·4
ml/kg/24 h		190	62
20 ewes at Adelaide	35°S	(Dry)	(Wet)
Body water ml/kg		640	737
l/24 h		2·9	8·5
ml/kg/24 h		69	250

Half of the flock of 40 ewes (15 months old initially) remained in the tropics, the other half was transferred to Adelaide.
On lat. 21°S the summer is hot and wet, the winter dry, so water is used in summer by sheep for cooling.
On lat. 35°S the summer is warm, and dry, but most pasture grows with winter rains, when large amounts of water are ingested with food.

the winter use of water was more than three times greater than in summer.

Water turnover influences food intake in at least two ways. When there is little food there is reduced drinking of water. But when food is lush and freshly grown there is much greater food intake than in the dry season (by two or three times). With each kg of dry matter the animal takes 4 kg water, so that turnover is increased. Total metabolism is also increased. Sheep can pass 30 l of water daily through the kidneys, so the water content of food is not likely to limit intake once the water is released from the ingesta.

STOCKING RATE

When a pasture is heavily stocked, the amount of food consumable daily is reduced and with this the water intake falls. In compensation, however, animals seem to replace fat by increments of body water. On lat. 35° during the summer heat, sheep held at 2·5/ha used more water than those at 17/ha. Water turnover was inversely proportional to the stocking density. Similarly in Israel where Merino and Awassi sheep were compared on the same pasture, an increase in density resulted in a decrease in water turnover and an increase in body water content

(Table IX). Water measurement allowed a comparison of food intakes and mobilization of fat with reduced food supply.

TABLE IX

Merino and Awassi sheep grazing together in the Negev

Pasture stocking rate		Merino Body solids %	Merino $ml/kg^{0.82}/24$ h turnover	Awassi Body solids %	Awassi $ml/kg^{0.82}/24$ h turnover
Wheat-legume	1:4	24·9	218	23·2	272
	1:1·5	12·2	186	22·6	209
	1:1	10·0	176	13·0	202
Native pasture	1:4	26·4	218	24·8	229

Sheep on pastures in southern Israel during summer, held at different stocking rates ranging from one sheep on four dunums, to one sheep per dunum (10 dunums = 1 hectare). The fatness of the sheep declined with increased density of stocking, and the water turnover fell as food became less easily available. But Merinos turned over less water at each stocking rate than the fat-rump Awassi sheep.

TRANSLOCATION OF RUMINANTS

Use of arid pasture requires nomadism, either of the traditional type, or by moving animals in trucks during drought. This type of migration is increasingly employed.

Measurements were made on Merino sheep living in the tropics as well as on Merinos from lat. 35° transferred to Abydos (lat. 21°S) in the hottest part of arid Australia where for six months of the year mean maximum temperatures are over 35°C. At Abydos the water turnover of sheep exposed to high summer temperatures was proportional to the amount of wool grown. Newly imported animals from temperate regions grew the most wool but used most water. Poorly adapted sheep grew little wool and used little water. Local Merinos derived from sheep imported more than 20 years earlier grew little wool (2 kg or less) and used the least amount of water (Table X). Similarly these long-term survivors of the tropics had low fertility and produced few lambs. It appeared that the surviving Merinos in the dry tropics were those with little competence in keratin formation or reproduction. The reduced metabolic drains arising from low productivity would be likely to increase survival in drought.

TABLE X

Wool growth and water metabolism of Merino ewes in Western Australia in tropics lat. 21°S during summer

		Total body water ml/kg	Water turnover/24 h ml/kg	ml/$kg^{0.82}$	Wool growth g/kg/year
Local sheep (tropically adapted)	(9)	704	103	201	52
Recently imported (unproductive)	(10)	788	119	219	74
Recently imported (more productive)	(10)	806	125	233	102

The local sheep had been naturally selected in this very hot dry tropical region for 20 years. Recently imported animals were in their second year on spinifex (*Triodea*) country. These sheep were separated into two groups on prior performance: unproductive ewes had grown less than 2 kg wool and reared no lamb; the more productive had grown more than 2 kg wool/year and reared a lamb in the previous winter. (Sheep in the sun with maximum air $T°$ 38–43°C.)
The sheep most highly adapted for survival had low water turnover rates and more body solids. The more productive newcomers had higher water consumptions and less body solids.

On lat. 21° at Julia Creek, the total body water of Merinos was 762 ml/kg amongst the local sheep in summer but incoming Merino sheep from lat. 35°S within a few months, achieved the same high water content, compared with their temperate zone water content, 640 ml/kg (Table VIII, Fig. 2). Tropical sheep on *Astrebla* pasture grew less wool each year than the temperate zone sheep, but these within a year adjusted to a lower wool output. The water turnover of the translocated sheep came to be similar to, although a little higher than local tropical sheep (Fig. 2). A converse situation on lat. 35° (winter rainfall area) led to transferred tropical sheep having a lower water turnover rate than the local Merinos (presumably from lower rates of feeding on the same pasture and 35% lower milk output to their lambs). In addition, translocated sheep failed to synthesize more wool when large amounts of green pasture grew in winter. The local sheep grew most of their wool in this period and produced more milk for lambs. It was not until the second year that translocated sheep adjusted water use, wool growth and endocrine functions to the new, cool and plentiful environment.

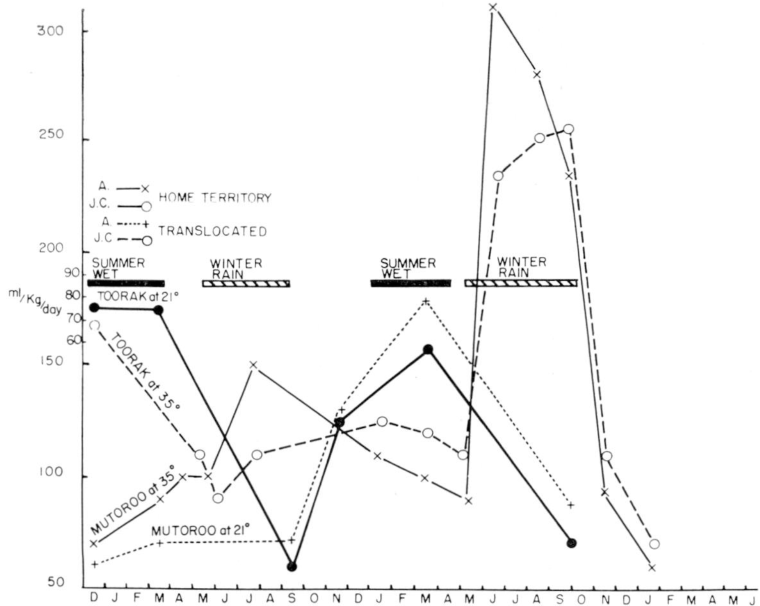

FIG. 2. Patterns of water use by Merino ewes translocated between pastures in 21°S and 35°S latitudes. There is summer rainfall on lat. 21°S and winter rainfall on lat. 35°S, so that succulent foodstuff occurs with heat in the north, and during the cool season in the South. The Toorak strain of Merino belongs to the arid tropics, while the Mutooroo strain comes from saltbush country on lat. 34°S. When Toorak sheep were transferred south they did not eat the plentiful winter pasture or reach the water turnover of the local sheep. Nor were the water turnovers as great as Mutooroo sheep in the second year. Mutooroo sheep in the tropics used more water than the locally bred sheep.

SALTBUSH

Niches for halophytes occur in the arid zones of the Middle East, Africa and Australia. The intake of *Kochia* or *Atriplex* by ruminants is usually small since these plants are not preferred foods. When, however, grasses and succulents have disappeared in the dry season, saltbush is used as a source of food (Wilson, 1966, 1969). In summer, with daily temperatures of 35–38°C Merino and Leicester sheep were exposed in the field to *Atriplex nummularia* or to *Danthonia* as sources of food (Table IV). Water was freely available. The eating of saltbush almost doubled the water turnover relative to low-salt pasture. Leicester sheep in the same environment as Merinos consistently used over 60% more water (per $kg^{0.82}$) on grass than Merinos (Macfarlane *et al.*, 1967), and the difference was increased by eating saltbush, to 74%.

Thus, the intrinsic rate of water use which runs in parallel with metabolic rate was maintained regardless of the amount of electrolyte passing. Electrolytes were washed out by fresh drinking water. Salty drinking water will thus limit the amount of saltbush that could be taken. Sheep tolerate about 1·3% NaCl in drinking water (220 m-mole/l) and cattle about 1·0% (170 m-mole/l) but if salt is taken while fresh water is available large quantities can be excreted as thirst increases. Sheep, for instance, take about 4 mole of Na and K salts daily when eating saltbush and wash it through with 10–18 l of water (Macfarlane *et al.*, 1967). This does not require an osmolality of urine above 2500 m-osmole/l for removal of salts.

REGIONAL HIERARCHIES OF WATER TURNOVER

Equatorial arid zone of Africa

The unusual equatorial desert areas of Somalia and northern Kenya sustain a nomadic pastoral way of life. In this economy camels provide the transport. Boran cattle are traded, while fat-tailed Ogaden sheep and goats provide milk or meat to the Somali herdsmen (Fig. 4B1). In the arid *Acacia* scrub 4–6°N of the equator, temperatures are high but food and water supplies are poor. Through the courtesy of Hadji Issa and Mr. John Golds, field studies were made on the water turnover of this animal complex in the scrub near Wajir (Table V*B*). All the animals sweated as the daily temperatures reached 35°C or more under the equatorial sun. In this environment goats and camels used the least amount of water, sheep somewhat more, and *Bos indicus* used twice as much water as camels. Thus, these different species of animals and similar genera in Australia fell into the same genetic rank order of water requirement (Table III). Cattle were the most demanding on water, sheep intermediate and camel were least water dependent. All these tropical animals had high total body water contents of 75–80% of body weight.

Taylor (1968) found that the intake of water by *Bos indicus* cattle studied indoors was low relative to eland. The food intakes he reports seem low and this may have depressed water intake in the stalls. Similar low intakes were found in stalled cattle eating dry *Cyanodon* hay (Macfarlane & Howard, 1966). Freely grazing animals probably eat more, select more succulent food and behave more normally than penned animals.

The eastern slopes of Kenya are hot and moderately arid. Two comparisons of ruminants were made on these regions. In the first at

Katumani, three breeds of sheep grazing *Cyanodon* grass showed a rank order sequence in which Karakuls consumed most water and had the highest body temperatures—presumably because the curly black coat became more heated in the sun than that of other breeds. Merinos on the same pasture used less water, and Dorpers (a cross between Dorset and the so-called black-head Persian or Ogaden sheep) used the least. The Dorper was also the fattest animal in this complex (Table XI*C*).

TABLE XI

Comparison of breeds of sheep in different environments

			Body solids %	Water turnover/24 h ml/kg	ml/kg$^{0.82}$	Environment
A	Merino sheep	(6)	28	89	160	Dry grassland
	Dorset × Merino	(6)	32	70	130	autumn
B	Awassi	(2)	19	121	236	Kenya
	Ogaden	(2)	14	109	178	highlands
	Merino	(2)	24	104	193	cool
	Masai	(1)	33	77	135	
C	*Katumani*					
	Karakul	(4)	24	111	205 ± 41	Eastern slope
	Merino	(6)	29	94	180 ± 34	of Kenya
	Dorper	(6)	31	88	170 ± 43	hot, moist
D	*Naivasha*					
	Awassi	(7)	31	112	229 ± 38	Rift Valley
	Merino	(10)	26	128	239 ± 26	dry and hot

The rank order of water turnover of different breeds of sheep is maintained in various environments. The Merino in these diverse contexts is a marker of the relative status of other breeds.

In this way it is possible to rank breeds of animals for relative water turnover (Table XI). Currently the rank order ascertained by these methods would put Leicester and Karakul sheep at the highest rating, then Romney, Dorset, Merino, Merino cross, Ogaden and Masai sheep. The Dorper would be lowest in the list although it is probable that such sheep as the Meidob and Kababish of the Sudan would have lower requirements still. These have not yet been tested.

Antelopes

Since bovids differ considerably in water turnover between species and since there was a wide range of turnover between camels, sheep, goats and cattle in the same environment, it seemed likely that similar hierarchies might occur amongst antelopes. On the Athi River plains of Kenya, the environment is hot and dry. With the kind collaboration of Mr. David Hopcraft and Dr. G. Maloiy measurements were made on Boran cattle (*B. indicus*) synchronously with eland, kongoni and wildebeest living together on the same pasture (Table V*A*). The Boran and eland (*Taurotragus oryx*) had the least body water and thus were the fattest animals (Fig. 4A2). They were the animals with the largest water turnovers and the two genera were almost identical in the same environment. Eland, the largest of the antelopes, are like cattle in many of their functions. The wildebeest (*Connochaetes taurinus*) used about half the water taken by eland, while kongoni (*Alcelaphus buselaphes*) turned over a little less—at about the rate of sheep in these circumstances. Since antelope accumulate very little fat on their normal range, comparison between cattle, even Boran, and kongoni is best made on the basis of water content (ml/$l^{0.82}$). The kongoni contained 15·7% solids compared with 28·7% in Boran cattle running with them. Daily water turnover was 127 ml/$l^{0.82}$ for kongoni and 259 ml/$l^{0.82}$ for eland, relative to 295 ml/$l^{0.82}$ in the cattle. The turnover of the water pool was thus less than in the Boran.

In the rather cooler environment of Muguga, west of Nairobi, measurements on oryx (*Oryx gazella*) indicated that this animal has an even lower water turnover than camels and less than Thomson's gazelle. The daily turnover rate of five *Gazella dorcas* in Professor Mendelssohn's vivarium, University of Tel Aviv, averaged 84 ml/kg (135 ml/$kg^{0.82}$). These animals are in the same functional group as the Kenya gazelles. There is thus a hierarchy (with a threefold range) in water turnover rates amongst the antelope living on the equator (Table V*A*).

Alaskan ruminants

Another type of desert beside the hot deserts of the subtropics, is the cold deserts in the arid arctic. Precipitation in central Alaska is irregular, but rarely is above 250 mm a year. The air in winter is intensely dry and most water is in the solid state. Near Fairbanks, with air temperatures of 0° to −30°C at the end of winter, water turnover studies were made on ruminants living outdoors (Table V*D*). The daily water turnover of reindeer (*Rangifer tarandus*, 365 ml/$l^{0.82}$) and moose (*Alces alces*, 353 ml/$l^{0.82}$) were highest—nearly twice the amount turned over by sheep in the same environment (202 ml/$l^{0 \cdot 82}$). Goats required rather less and musk oxen (*Ovibos moschatus*) were found to turn over water at rates (142 ml/$l^{0 \cdot 82}$) comparable with those of camels, about one third the rate of reindeer (Fig. 4A1). Thus in the cold desert, a hierarchy of water turnover also occurs, in which the reindeer may be compared with cattle or eland, while the musk ox is in the class of the camel and oryx, with very low turnover rates.

FUNCTIONAL CORRELATES

Water turnover can be measured with some precision in the field amongst animals moving and feeding freely. This helps understanding of the ecological competence and selection pressures on a mammal. It is part of an energy flow system in which the easiest variable to measure is that of water flow. This is not, however, an isolated function. It is part of the complex carrying oxygen and its carbon or nitrogen katabolites. Sodium and K distributions determine the water content of extracellular and intracellular fluids and are also linked with water through the action of electrolyte pumps. Field measurement of total energy or of chemical fluxes is difficult. When animals are constrained or incarcerated differences in function, behaviour and particularly in water requirements are induced. In the open, radiant energy can double the flux of heat through desert mammals: yet the effect of sun is difficult to imitate in the laboratory. Similarly, the choice of foods and the social conditioning of the penned animals are often restrictive, relative to free range life. So field measurements of water content and turnover have useful ecological and physiological implications.

Metabolic rate

Although it is not easy to measure metabolic rate in the field, some indication of the energy turnover can be obtained from faecal collection. For growing sheep, TOH turnover correlated well ($r = 0 \cdot 93$) with faecal dry matter output (Fig. 3) which in turn correlates with food intake. Similarly, Siebert (1971) working with tropical cattle obtained a correlation of $r = 0 \cdot 84$ between measured feed intake and water turnover. Water intake varies of course with the type of food, and rises with high nitrogen or K levels that demand water for excretion.

Age, water and energy metabolism

There is an increase of body tissue and fat as water content declines with age. Similarly water turnover decreases rapidly in the first six months of life (Table XII) then more slowly. A parallel decrement of energy turnover takes place with age. This appears to be part of the water-energy linkage in which the two rates of turnover vary together.

When the standard metabolism of different species or genera is compared with the water turnover rates (compensated exponentially for size) a good correlation is found between water and energy use. The

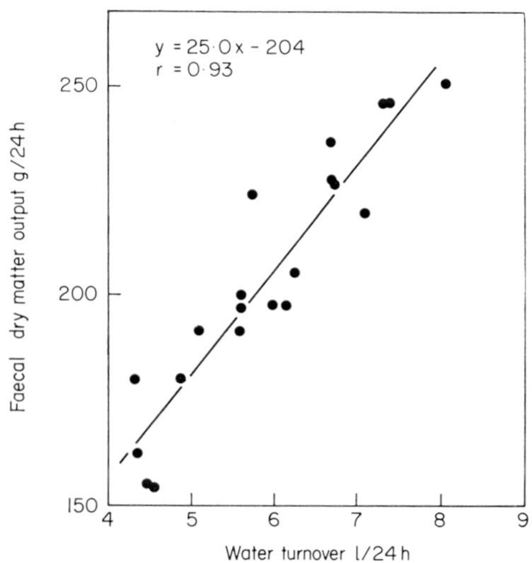

Fig. 3. The faecal dry matter output of young Merino sheep was measured synchronously with the TOH turnover. There is a correlation (r = 0·93) between the two, indicating a relationship between food energy intake and water use.

Table XII

Relationship between water and energy metabolism with increasing age in Merino lambs during summer lat. 35°S

Age	Body water ml/kg	Water turnover/24 h ml/kg	Water turnover/24 h $ml/1^{0.82}$	Energy metabolism $kcal/kg^{0.73}/24$ h*
Birth	807	229	366	204
4 weeks	736	152	288	180
6 months	725	122	299	97
1·5 years	635	77	221	88
2·5 years	617	56	170	90
3·5 years	540	48	168	90

There is a parallel decrement between water turnover and oxygen consumption in lambs as they increase in age. Measurements of water metabolism were made with the sheep on dry pasture during summer. Body water also decreases with age.

* Ritzman & Benedict (1931), sheep starved 18–32 h.

water turnover of Merino sheep in the arid sub-tropics during summer was greater in animals selected for high rates of wool growth than in unselected controls (Macfarlane, Dolling & Howard, 1966a). The metabolic rates of the selected sheep at rest were 16% higher (Graham, 1968) than those of the control group. On the same pasture, therefore, increased water turnover was associated with higher rates of wool production and of energy consumption.

Energy metabolism was measured by Schmidt-Nielsen *et al.* (1967) in dromedaries while water turnover was also determined (Macfarlane *et al.*, 1963) on the same animals. As the camels became dehydrated, their energy consumption was reduced. The rate of energy turnover by resting, hydrated camels when related to the Brody-Kleiber metabolic kg (mass $^{0 \cdot 75}$) is about 50 kcal/kg$^{0 \cdot 75}$/day which is well below the average mammalian value of 70 kcal. Through each metabolic mass, sheep and goats pass about 60 kcal/day, *Bos indicus* uses 80–90 and *Bos taurus* cattle 90–110 kcal/day (Blaxter, 1962). In Kenya, determinations by Rogerson (1968) of standard metabolism of the eland indicated that it was well over a 100 kcal/kg$^{0 \cdot 75}$/day but the kongoni ran at a lower rate, nearer to that of sheep. McEwan (1970) has determined the metabolic rate of caribou (*Rangifer*). He finds rates at or above the cattle group (102 kcal/kg$^{0 \cdot 75}$/day). In general, therefore, the hierarchy of water turnovers is paralleled by a similar rank order of energy turnover amongst these ruminants.

A similar relationship appears in small desert marsupials and rodents. Among fat-tailed dasyurids of the Australian desert there are animals through which energy and water run parallel at high or low rates of turnover. *Dasycercus cristicauda* is a fossorial marsupial which eats insects and lives in the same desert environment of *Sminthopsis crassicaudata* which is a more surface-living animal, but also insectivorous (Fig. 4B2). Both animals in resting conditions put through about 5 mole of water to 1 mole of oxygen (Kennedy & Macfarlane, 1971). But *Sminthopsis* metabolizes both water and oxygen three times faster than *Dasycercus*. *Dasyuroides* is similar to *Dasycercus* in this respect, while *Antechinus* resembles *Sminthopsis*. Amongst the small rodents a similar pattern emerges but the metabolic rate is higher than that of marsupials (MacMillen & Nelson, 1969). The water turnover is correspondingly higher (Table XIII). The kangaroo has a water turnover a little lower than that of sheep and its metabolic rate is also lower (Dawson & Hulbert, 1970). The wombat has a lower water consumption than the camel per kg$^{0 \cdot 82}$ and an extremely low metabolic rate (Wells, pers. comm.). Over a wide range of orders, families and genera, therefore, there is a close parallel between energy and water metabolism (Fig. 4).

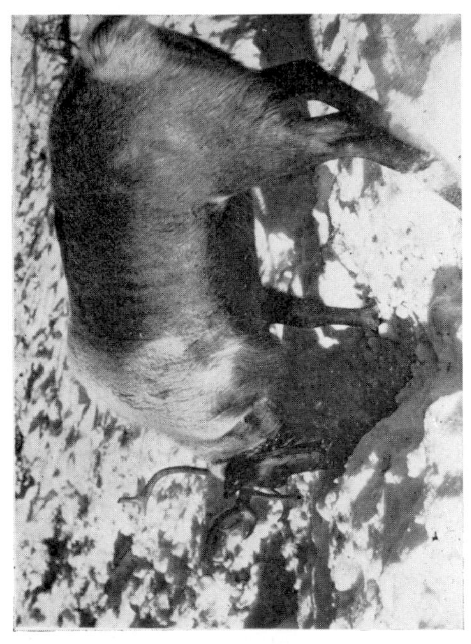

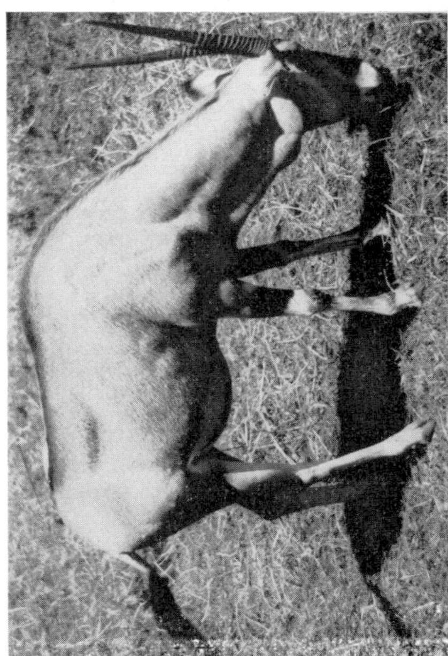

1

A

2

B

1

2

Birds

Since this relationship between water and energy holds for mammals it seemed possible that these functions might be found among birds. Information is available (Dawson & Bartholomew, 1968) on water intake; while the energy consumption of a number of bird genera has been collated by Lasiewski & Dawson (1967). Passerine birds with body weights up to 1 kg have energy consumption rates higher than those of cattle (average metabolic rate of passerines = 129 $kg^{0 \cdot 72}$). For non-passerines there is a greater range of body weight but the metabolic rate = 78 $kg^{0 \cdot 72}$, which is within the statistical range for eutherian mammals (Kleiber, 1947). The average water consumption of passerines is also greater (by about 40%) than that of non-passerine birds of the same weight. Yet the average ratio (5·8 : 1) of moles of water to the moles of oxygen passing through the birds daily is the same for the passerine and non-passerine groups. It appears that the passerines (finches, sparrows, grosbeaks) differentiated early in evolution as high-rate animals. Yet zebra finches and some sparrows survive in deserts when they have access to water resources. Non-passerines like doves, parrots or budgerigars have lower energy and water turnovers and seem better adapted to the deserts where a number of them live. Succulent plants have also, relative to xerophytes, higher rates of both respiration and transpiration of water.

Permeability of skin and gut

Associated with metabolic rate is the rate at which insensible water loss or transpiration occurs in mammals. Large mammals show greater permeability of skin when metabolic rates are high and this occurs also in small mammals (Table XIII). The permeability of skin and respiratory surfaces in dasyurids is closely proportional to metabolic rate and water turnover, those of *Sminthopsis* reaching nearly three times the rate of *Dasycercus*.

FIG. 4A. Mammals with low water turnover rates (camel, musk ox, oryx and *Dasycercus*) are on the left, paired with high turnover rate mammals using water two or three times faster (cattle, eland, reindeer, and *Sminthopsis*) on the right. Metabolic rate is known to be lower than average in camel and *Dasycercus*, and higher than average in cattle, eland, reindeer and *Sminthopsis*. The members of each pair share the same environmental niche. 1. Reindeer (high) digging for lichens, and musk ox (low) in Alaska. 2. Boran (*B. indicus*) cow and eland (both with high energy and water turnover) compared with oryx (low) in the arid equatorial region of Kenya. Note the faecal stipes of the eland.

B. 1. Boran cattle (high water turnover) and dromedaries (low) in the *Acacia* scrub of the desert Northern Frontier District of Kenya. 2. *Sminthopsis crassicaudata* (high) and on the left *Dasycercus cristicauda* (low), dasyurid marsupials of the central Australian desert. They are both nocturnal insectivores.

The permeability of the gut to water has similar characteristics in ruminants. Uptake of water from the cattle rumen, for instance, is rapid so that when tritiated water is put into the rumen it moves halfway to a steady level in the blood within 0·5 h while TOH from sheep rumen requires 1–2 h and in camels 3–4 h to reach the same relative distribution to plasma. Thus the rate of water movement from gut to blood is proportional to the rates of water turnover and oxygen turnover, which appear to be correlated functions.

Renal and colonic reabsorption of water

When animals are without water, particularly in summer, the colon reduces water output while the kidney concentrates urine. Dry cattle lower the water content of faeces to 60%, sheep to 50% and camels to 45% (Macfarlane, 1964). On the renal side, cattle concentrate urine to 2·6 osmole/l, camels to 3·1, and sheep to 3·8 osmole/l. The concentrating power is not entirely a matter of vasopressin sensitivity. Although cattle are about 100 times less sensitive to vasopressin than camels, sheep are 3–5 times less sensitive than camels (Siebert & Macfarlane, 1971). Kongoni have about the same sensitivity as sheep. In the Arctic, however, there is an anomalous response since neither reindeer nor musk ox is at all sensitive to vasopressin, either at the level of reducing urine flow, or in terms of increasing the secretion of K (which is a characteristic of ruminant renal responses to vasopressin, Macfarlane *et al.*, 1969). Cattle, sheep and camels all increase K output 3–10 times when vasopressin is administered but reindeer and musk oxen increase K excretion only 20–30% with large doses of 1–2 units of vasopressin.

Rates of dehydration

Desert survival of mammals is acutely determined by the availability of water and more chronically by food supply. The rate at which water is lost from the body is a major determinant of survival time. Cattle during summer in the desert, receiving 1000 kcal/m^2/h of solar radiation with air at 40°C lost water at an average rate of 7–8% per day, sheep lost 4–6% per day and camels 1–2%/day. The rate of loss of water is a function of the evaporative cooling as well as of the amount of water expended in urine and faeces. Cattle are slow to turn off urinary and faecal loss: sheep do so rather more rapidly than cattle, but camels reduce filtration within 24 h of restricted fluid intake and they save water both by lower filtration and by increased reabsorption (Siebert & Macfarlane, 1971). Survival time without water at daily temperatures of around 40–42°C is 3–4 days for *Bos taurus* cattle, 6–8 days for Merino

TABLE XIII

Water turnover and oxygen consumption of desert Dasyurids and rodents at 25°C

		Average weight g	% body water	Water turnover/24 h		Oxygen consumption/24 h		Molar ratio water/O_2
				ml/kg	mole/$l^{0.82}$	l/kg	mole/$kg^{0.75}$	
DASYURIDS								
Sminthopsis crassicaudata	(8)	19	68	460	17·2	111·0	1·91	5·1
Dasycercus cristicauda	(35)	87	20	134	6·7	36·0	0·87	5·5
Dasyuroides byrnei	(5)	130	20	120	6·2	29·8	0·81	5·0
RODENTS								
Notomys alexis	(11)	35	25	190	9·3	66·0	1·26	4·6
Notomys cervinus	(10)	41	21	149	7·4	65·0	1·30	3·6
Pseudomys australis	(6)	50	22	139	6·3	62·6	1·32	3·4

sheep and 15–20 days or more for dromedaries. Amongst small dasyurids a similar pattern emerges. *Sminthopsis* will die without water in 3–5 days because of its very high rate of water turnover, while *Dasycercus*, if insect food is available lives on indefinitely without water (Schmidt-Nielsen & Newsome, 1962).

Rehydration

Most desert animals replace water rapidly after dehydration. This is true of both birds and mammals and it is interesting that some desert birds learn to drink with suction rather than by the normal tongue and head movements (Dawson & Bartholomew, 1968). Cattle, sheep, camels or donkeys can all take large amounts of fluid rapidly when they have been deprived of water (Schmidt-Nielsen, 1964). In our experience 20–25% dehydrated camels in the desert will drink about 60% of weight loss as water in the first stage intake of 80–100 l. Sheep take 65% (Macfarlane *et al.*, 1961; Macfarlane, 1964) and cattle about 75% of the weight lost during dehydration in the initial drink, with complete rehydration in one or two days. These observations differ somewhat from earlier reports of drinking times, but 4–10 animals in each group have been studied in the summer desert and repletion did not occur on the first drink.

After taking on a load of water equal to about one fifth of the body weight after dehydration, cattle, sheep and camels respond in different fashions. Cattle begin to excrete some of the load within 4 h and Merino sheep within 12 h, but camels have a very slow rate of uptake of water and there may be no diuresis for a day, after the second or third drink has been taken. After drinking 84 l a camel that lost 20% of body weight during summer dehydration, reduced renal water, Na and K output for 20 h while osmotic adjustment of the water took place (Macfarlane, 1968). The plasma Na, raised to 180–205 m-equiv/l by dehydration, is reduced and urea stored in the extracellular fluid (up to 600 mg/100 ml), is moved into the rumen. Salivary flow is speeded up and the salts added to the newly-taken fresh water bring it to near isotonic levels before being absorbed. After this re-use of the electrolytes and urea retained in extracellular fluid, urinary water and salts are again excreted.

The success of camels in coping with long periods of deprivation of water (for instance, Giles' journey of 17 days in summer across the Victoria Desert of southern Australia in 1875 with camels receiving one drink on the 13th day only, of 8 l) arises from retaining a high plasma and extracellular volume (Macfarlane *et al.*, 1963). Part of this fluid conservation appears to be due to thick capillary walls with low permeability, partly to the conservation of albumin in the plasma so that oncotic pressure is maintained, and partly to drawing on cell and gut fluids to sustain the circulating plasma volume. Other animals, like cattle, lose plasma and pass into circulatory failure about the fourth day. Sheep, although losing extracellular volume, have a peculiarly resiliant circulation which can be maintained even with low (45% of normal) plasma and extracellular volumes (Macfarlane *et al.*, 1961) for 5–8 days without water in summer temperatures around 40°C.

MECHANISMS

The relationship between water and energy turnover is probably based on hypothalamic neuronal activities controlling food and water intakes and outputs (Anand, 1961). But in addition, the rate of metabolism is in part intrinsic to cells and in part modulated by thyroid activity. The action of thyroxin in increasing oxygen consumption is largely determined by its control of the $Na^+ - K^+$ activated ATPase in cells, according to Ismail-Beigi & Edelman (1970). If the Na–K pump system of the cell wall runs at a high rate, water and energy turnover through cells would be increased. This would apply to muscles and brain as well as to gut and kidney. It seems probable that the different rates of water use found in desert animals derive from different rates of centrally determined action (though thyroxin) although measurements in this area are few.

There remains the anomaly of a range of mammals with different rates of function living in the desert. It seems likely that water and energy functions have rates of evolution which are similar to those for bodily structures. It is usually calculated (Simpson, 1953) that evolutionary processes require three to eight million years to produce a new genus. If the generic differences in function which are found between cattle, sheep and camels require the same order of time for evolution, the current physiology of these animals is likely to be of Pliocene origin. Yet between the Pliocene and the present, many changes of climate have occurred which presumably would encourage migration (Martin, 1970). Recently, migration has been forced upon animals, as in the case of cattle, camel and sheep imported to central Australia. These were moved by men over the last 170 years. It appears that cattle originated in swamp lands such as those of Indochina, if the guar and banteng are near the root stock of bovid radiation (Zeuner, 1953). Indian cattle developed in drier country and have lower rates of metabolism and water turnover than *Bos taurus* which developed largely in temperate regions through the auroch. Sheep on the other hand seem to have originated in Asia Minor in a dry and mountainous habitat like that of goats. Goats and sheep have similar metabolic rates and water turnovers, though goats run at slightly lower rates than sheep. Camels developed in the dry western plains of America but they walked out in Pleistocene times to Asia and finally to Africa. If these be the roots and origins of the camel then it was functionally evolved for deserts, and although exposed to other climates it has retained its original physiology. The sheep is intermediate in these functions, and tropical swamp animals of cattle-type are migrants to desert areas where they remain highly dependent on water. If the water supply fails, the food supply later fails also and the animals either die or migrate. They can, however, reinvade. A similar pattern shows with *Sminthopsis* and *Dasycercus*. *Dasycercus* has a centre of distribution in the desert (Kennedy & Macfarlane, 1971), while *Sminthopsis* is mainly found in moist coastal regions but migrates to and occupies niches in the same central dry area as *Dasycercus*. If drought persists, *Sminthopsis* would die out within a few days without water, whereas *Dasycercus* could live on continuously without water provided insect food was available.

Presumably, similar events in the evolutionary history of eland, kongoni and oryx have occurred. The possibility would be that the oryx originated in the desert and eland in wetter country. But both come to occupy the same niches in many parts of central Africa. It would be a reasonable extrapolation to expect that the musk ox originated in arid arctic environments and died out during warmer pluvials while reindeer and moose presumably came from the wetter less cold zone and migrated into the arctic, where they have not yet changed their physiology. The high water and energy turnover rates of the reindeer and the great dissipation of heat through growing antlers (which maintain 35°C in an ambient of -30°C) are not efficient, thermodynamically, for the arctic. This concept assumes that, for a dry environment, there is some long-term advantage in a low metabolic rate with a low water turnover and a water-conserving kidney and colon. Certainly in any extended exposure to desert conditions, the camel, oryx, *Dasycercus* or musk ox would survive while cattle, eland, reindeer or *Sminthopsis* would be eliminated.

Acknowledgements

We appreciate the help with supply or handling of animals given in Australia by Drs. C. Letts, B. Hart, B. D. Siebert, C. Watts and Mr. R. Inns; in Africa by Drs. W. Payne, G. Maloiy and Mr. D. Hopcraft; in Israel Drs. E. Eyal and M. Morag and Mr. R. Benjamin and in Alaska by Drs. P. R. Morrison, J. Luick, J. Teal and their colleagues. Grants from the Australian Research Grants Committee, the Australian Wool Board, the Reserve Bank of Australia and the Australian Meat Board have contributed to the investigations and we are grateful for their assistance.

References

Adolph, E. F. (1949). Quantitative relations in the physiological constituents of mammals. *Science, N.Y.* **109**: 579–587.

Anand, B. K. (1961). Nervous regulation of food intake. *Physiol. Rev.* **41**: 677–708.

Blaxter, K. L. (1962). *The energy metabolism of ruminants.* London: Hutchinson.

Clark, R. & Quin, J. I. (1949). Studies on the water requirement of farm animals in South Africa. I. The effects of intermittent watering of Merino sheep. *Onderstepoort J. vet. Sci.* **22**: 335–343.

Dawson, W. R. & Bartholomew, G. A. (1968). Temperature regulation and water economy of desert birds. In *Desert Biology* **1**: 357–393. Brown, G. W. (ed.). New York & London: Academic Press.

Dawson, T. J. & Hulbert, A. J. (1970). Standard metabolism, body temperature and surface area of Australian marsupials. *Am. J. Physiol.* **218**: 1233–1238.

Graham, N. McC. (1968). The metabolic rate of Merino rams bred for high or low wool production. *Aust. J. agric. Res.* **19**: 821–824.

Ismail-Beigi, F. & Edelman, I. S. (1970). Mechanism of calorigenic action of thyroid hormone: role of sodium transport. *Fedn Proc. Fdn Am. Socs exp. Biol.* **29**: 582 Abs. No. 1881.

Kennedy, P. M. & Macfarlane, W. V. (1971). Oxygen consumption and water turnover of fat-tailed marsupial *Dasycercus cristicauda* and *Sminthopsis crassicaudata*. *Comp. Biochem. Physiol.* **40**A: 723–732.

Kleiber, M. (1947). Body size and metabolic rate. *Physiol. Rev.* **27**: 511–541.

Lasiewski, R. C. & Dawson, W. R. (1967). A re-examination of the relation between standard metabolic rate and body weight in birds. *Condor* **69**: 13–23.

Lifson, N. & McClintock, R. (1966). Theory of use of the turnover rates of body water for measuring energy and material balances. *J. theoret. Biol.* **12**: 46–74.

Macfarlane, W. V. (1964). Terrestrial animals in dry heat: ungulates. In *Handbook of physiology-environment,* **4**: 509–531. Dill, D. B. (ed.). Washington, D.C.: American Physiological Society.

Macfarlane, W. V. (1965). Water metabolism of desert ruminants. In *Studies in physiology*: 191–199. Curtis, D. R. and McIntyre, A. K. (eds). Berlin: Springer Verlag.

Macfarlane, W. V. (1968). Comparative studies in the adaptation of ruminants to hot environments. In *The adaptation of domestic animals*: 164–182. Hafez, E. S. E. (ed.) Philadelphia: Lea and Febiger.

Macfarlane, W. V. & Howard, B. (1966). Water content and turnover of identical twin *Bos indicus* and *B. taurus* in Kenya. *J. agric. Sci. Camb.* **66**: 297–302.

Macfarlane, W. V. & Howard, B. (1970). The ecophysiology of water. In *The physiology of digestion and nutrition in ruminants.* Phillipson, A. T. (ed.). Newcastle: Oriel Press.

Macfarlane, W. V., Morris, R. J. H. & Howard, B. (1963). Turnover and distribution of water in desert camels, sheep, cattle and kangaroos. *Nature, Lond.* **197**: 270–271.

Macfarlane, W. V., Dolling, C. S. H. & Howard, B. (1966a). Distribution and turnover of water in Merino sheep selected for high wool production. *Aust. J. agric. Res.* **17**: 491–502.

Macfarlane, W. V., Howard, B. & Morris, R. J. H. (1966b). Water metabolism of Merino sheep shorn during summer. *Aust. J. agric. Res.* **17**: 219–225.

Macfarlane, W. V., Howard, B. & Siebert, B. D. (1967). Water metabolism of Merino and Border Leicester sheep grazing saltbush. *Aust. J. agric. Res.* **18**: 947–958.

Macfarlane, W. V., Howard, B. & Siebert, B. D. (1969). Tritiated water used to measure intake of milk and tissue growth of ruminants in the field. *Nature, Lond.* **221**: 578.

Macfarlane, W. V., Morris, R. J. H., Howard, B. & Budtz-Olsen, O. E. (1959). Extracellular fluid distribution in tropical Merino sheep. *Aust. J. agric. Res.* **10**: 269–286.

Macfarlane, W. V., Morris, R. J. H., Howard, B., McDonald, J. & Budtz-Olsen, O. E. (1961). Water and electrolyte changes in tropical Merino sheep exposed to dehydration during summer. *Aust. J. agric. Res.* **12**: 889–912.

Macfarlane, W. V., Kinne, R., Walmsley, C. M., Siebert, B. D. & Peter, D. (1967). Vasopressins and the increase of water and electrolyte excretion by sheep, cattle and camels. *Nature, Lond.* **214**: 979–981.

MacMillen, R. E. & Nelson, J. E. (1969). Bioenergetics and body size in dasyurid marsupials. *Am. J. Physiol.* **217**: 1246–1251.

Martin, P. S. (1970). Pleistocene niches for alien animals. *Bioscience* **20**: 218–221.

McEwan, E. H. (1970). Energy metabolism of the barren ground caribou (*Rangifer tarandus*). *Can. J. Zool.* **48**: 391–392.

McMillan, J. R. A. (1965). Water, agricultural production and world population. *Aust. J. Sci.* **28**: 135–147.

Morris, R. J. H., Howard, B. & Macfarlane, W. V. (1962). Interaction of nutrition and temperature with water metabolism of Merino wethers shorn in winter. *Aust. J. agric. Res.* **13**: 320–334.

Richmond, C. R., Langham, W. H. & Trujillo, T. T. (1962). Comparative metabolism of tritiated water by mammals. *J. cell. comp. Physiol.* **59**: 45–53.

Ritzman, E. G. & Benedict, F. G. (1931). The heat production of sheep under varying conditions. *Tech. Bull. New Hamps. agric. Exp. Stn* No. 45.

Rogerson, A. (1968). Energy utilization by the eland and wildebeest. *Symp. zool. Soc. Lond.* No. 21: 153–162.

Schmidt-Nielsen, K. (1964). *Desert animals*. Oxford: Oxford University Press.

Schmidt-Nielsen, K. & Newsome, A. E. (1962). Water balance in the mulgara (*Dasycercus cristicauda*) a carnivorous desert marsupial. *Aust. J. biol. Sci.* **15**: 683–689.

Schmidt-Nielsen, K., Crawford, E. C., Newsome, A. E., Rawson, K. S. & Hammel, H. T. (1967). Metabolic rate of camels: effect of body temperature and dehydration. *Am. J. Physiol.* **212**: 341–346.

Siebert, B. D. (1971). Growth and water metabolism of cows and progeny on fertilized and unfertilized tropical pastures. *Aust. J. agric. Res.* **22**: 415–428.

Siebert, B. D. & Macfarlane, W. V. (1969). Body water content and water turnover of tropical *Bos taurus*, *Bos indicus*, *Bibos banteng* and *Bos bubalus bubalis*. *Aust. J. agric. Res.* **20**: 613–622.

Siebert, B. D. & Macfarlane, W. V. (1971). Water turnover and renal function of dromedaries in the desert. *Physiol. Zoöl.* **44**: 225–240.

Simpson, G. G. (1953). *The major features of evolution.* New York: Columbia University Press.

Stepankina, M. K. & Tashenov, K. T. (1958). Water metabolism in the camel. *Sechenov physiol. J. USSR* **44**: 942–947.

Taylor, C. R. (1968). The minimum water requirements of some East African bovids. *Symp. zool. Soc. Lond.* No. 21: 195–206.

Wilson, A. D. (1966). The intake and excretion of sodium by sheep fed on species of *Atriplex* (saltbush) and *Kochia* (bluebush). *Aust. J. agric. Res.* **17**: 155–163.

Wilson, A. D. (1969). Water economy and food intake of sheep when watered intermittently. *Aust. J. agric. Res.* **21**: 273–281.

Zeuner, F. E. (1963). *A history of domesticated animals.* London: Hutchinson.

Symp. zool. Soc. Lond. (1972) No. 31, 297–314.

THE ROLE OF ADVECTIVE FOG IN THE WATER ECONOMY OF CERTAIN NAMIB DESERT ANIMALS

GIDEON N. LOUW

Zoological Institute, University of Stellenbosch, Stellenbosch, South Africa

SYNOPSIS

The Namib desert is a long narrow coastal desert on the southwestern coast of Africa. The presence of the cold Benguella current on the western margin of the desert has a profound effect upon the climate of the Namib and is responsible for the frequent occurrence of advective sea fog over the desert. The frequency of fog and the accumulation of wind-blown plant detritus in those areas of the desert which are almost devoid of vegetation, provides sufficient water and energy to support a surprisingly varied endemic fauna. Certain of these animals, such as the tenebrionid beetle *Lepidochora argentogrisea* and the psammophilous lizard *Aporosaura anchietae*, have evolved a physiological dependence upon fog water and are capable of a considerable degree of water storage. Other animals within the ecosystem such as the ostrich and Namib gerbil, are physiologically well adapted to desert life but are not able to store water or exist indefinitely on dry food. These animals, are, however, indirectly dependent on fog water by feeding on succulent plants which are sustained by the regular condensation of fog.

INTRODUCTION

The Namib is a desert on the southwestern coast of Africa. In length it is over 16 000 km and it extends southwards from Mossamedes in Angola to below the mouth of the Orange River (lat. 15 to 30°S). In contrast with this great length the Namib is comparatively narrow, seldom extending for more than 130 km into the interior of the continent. The eastern border of the desert is demarcated by the foothills of the Western Escarpment which rises to an undulating plateau at 1200–1800 m above sea level. The Atlantic Ocean forms the western margin of the desert and the northern and southern halves of the Namib can be roughly divided on geomorphological criteria at the Kuiseb River. The northern half consists of flat gravel plains occasionally interrupted by *Inselberge*, while in the southern portion the plain is overlain by a massive dune system which extends southwards from the Kuiseb without interruption for over 320 km. These physiographic features are illustrated in Fig. 1. They exert a profound effect on the climate of the desert and consequently on the ecology and physiology of the endemic fauna and therefore warrant further brief description.

The cold Benguella current which sweeps up the western coast of southern Africa is indirectly responsible for the extreme aridity of the

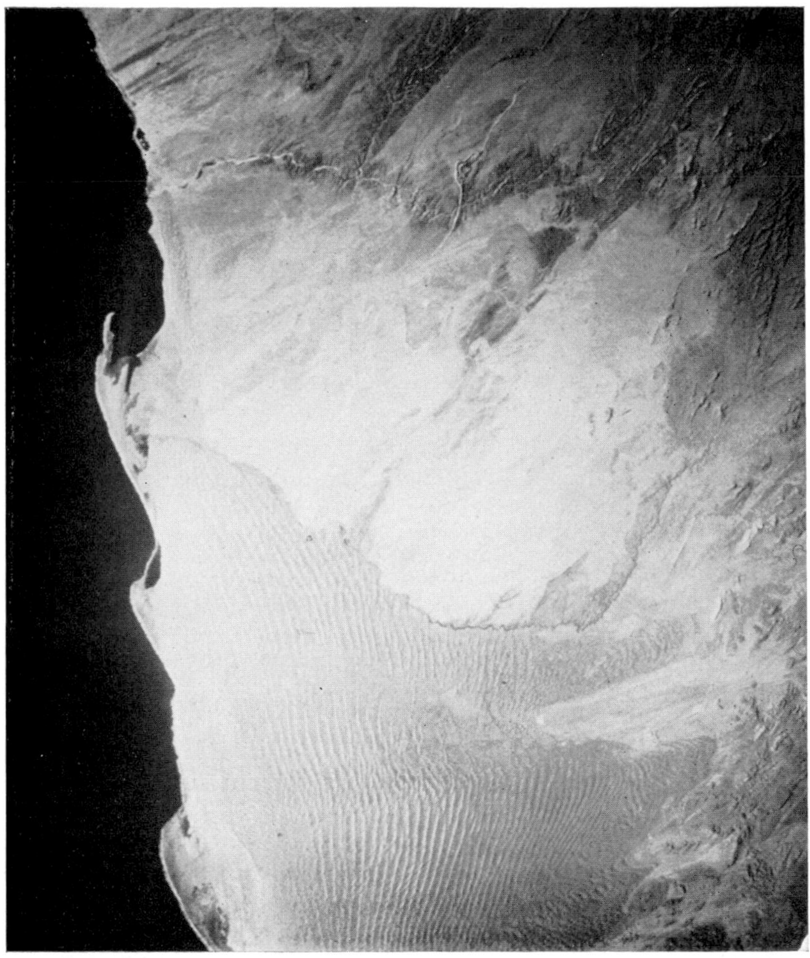

FIG. 1. A view of the central Namib Desert taken from outer space. The massive parallel dunes which end abruptly along the Kuiseb River bed are clearly visible, as are the foothills of the escarpment on the right (Courtesy, United States Information Service).

Namib. In this respect it is important to note that in the western half of the desert, the area in which the present investigations were conducted, the rainfall is so low and variable that it can be considered negligible for the purposes of this discussion. As a result vegetation in the western half of the desert is extremely sparse and limited to a few specialized species such as *Zygophyllum*. In contrast the eastern half of the desert receives some rain (25–50 mm per annum), although very sporadically. These sporadic thunderstorms result in a dramatic growth of the grass cover, predominately *Stipagrostis* species, on the gravel plains and between the parallel dunes on the so-called dune streets. The escarpment on the eastern border of the desert receives sufficient rainfall to support a mixed plant cover of shrubs and perennial grasses.

An additional and equally important effect of the proximity of the cold Benguella current is the regular occurrence of advective sea fog and the cool, moist southwesterly sea breeze. Fog occurs most frequently on the coast but has also been recorded infrequently as far as 130 km from the coast. The frequency of fog at Gobabeb, some 56 km east of the coast, has been summarized in Fig. 2. These data were originally compiled by Schulze (1969) over a five year period and show

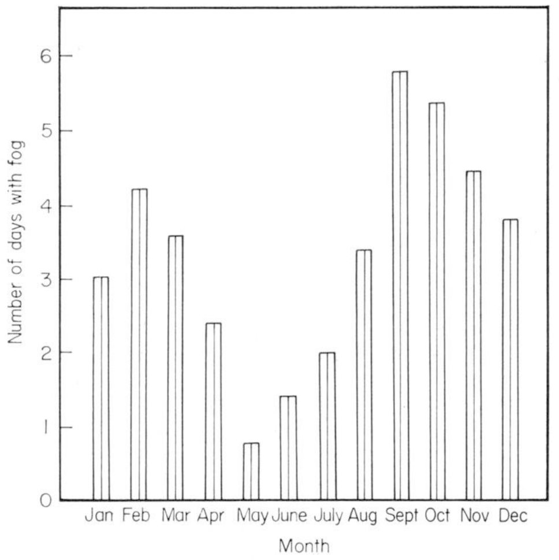

FIG. 2. Mean number of days per month on which fog occurs at Gobabeb, some 56 km East of the Atlantic coast. (Compiled from data in Schulze, 1969.)

that fog can be expected at least once per month throughout the year. The fog frequently, although not always, condenses on the surface and on wind-blown plant detritus in the form of fine droplets of water. We have collected fog water in glass containers and from the surface of plants and wind-blown detritus. The osmolality of these samples ranged from 14–38 m-osmole/l which is surprisingly low and emphasizes the suitability of fog as a source of water for the endemic Namib fauna.

The prevailing winds of the Namib are the cool, southwesterly sea breeze and the desiccating, easterly *berg* wind. These winds are responsible for sculpting the large parallel sand dunes of the southern Namib. As a result of wind action the sand on the windward side of the dunes becomes compacted while the leeward side consists of soft wind-blown sand which is an ideal medium in which burrowing animals can escape from extremely high or extremely low surface temperatures. For example, while studying the temperature profile of a dune we found that the temperature of the sand 7·5 cm below the surface was 38°C at 14.00 h compared with 60°C on the surface. Conversely, at 18.00 h the temperature on the surface had dropped to 20°C while at a depth of 7·5 cm below the surface the temperature was 33°C.

In addition to the sculpting effect of the prevailing winds they have other extremely important influences. The southwesterly sea wind, which usually begins to blow in the early afternoon in response to the intense insolation of the fore-noon, cools the surface of the sand rapidly and raises the relative humidity of the air. In this way more favourable conditions are created for diurnal animals. The easterly *berg* wind, on the other hand, orginates over the escarpment on the eastern border of the desert and, because of the sudden drop in altitude between the escarpment and the desert plain, the temperature of the air mass increases rapidly giving rise to a very strong, hot and desiccating wind. The strength of this wind is such that dry grass stems and seeds are lifted into the air and blown into the vegetationless dune system where they accumulate in the form of cushions of detritus. This detritus has a gross energy value of approximately 3800 cal/g and represents a very important source of energy for the dune fauna.

In summary, then, the Namib Desert is a true desert of extreme aridity which experiences very high temperatures at times. These hostile conditions are, however, tempered by a cool moist sea wind and the fairly frequent occurrence of advective fog. In addition, some of the areas without vegetation receive a secondary supply of food energy in the form of wind-blown plant detritus. As a result the apparently lifeless, barren dunes and gravel plains support a surprising variety of animal life. The first authorative description of this fauna was written by Koch (1961). Until recently, however, no attempts have been made to correlate the physiology of any of these species with the unusual, if not unique, habitat provided by the Namib. This paper, then, is a brief summary of physiological studies carried out over the past three years on several key species inhabiting the Namib. Special attention has been given to water economy and thermoregulation in an attempt to elucidate the physiology of adaptation of these species to the desert environment.

METHODS

The methods employed were all of a standard nature and require little elaboration. Field observations of thermoregulatory and feeding behaviour were supplemented by laboratory observations in a temperature controlled chamber and in artificially constructed enclosures in the open air. Blood, urine and haemolymph samples were collected from freshly killed animals in the field and from animals kept in the laboratory. These were analysed by standard methods using flame photometry for determining electrolyte concentrations and an osmometer (Advanced Instruments) for determining the osmolality of large samples and the method of Gross (1954) for small samples. Temperatures were recorded with a variety of instruments including fast registering cloacal thermometers, a YSI telethermometer and radiotelemetry.

The studies were conducted mostly at the Namib Desert Research Station, Gobabeb, South West Africa.

RESULTS AND DISCUSSION

The selection of suitable species to illustrate physiological adaptation to the Namib environment is difficult because of the large variety of interesting examples. For instance, the organisms inhabiting the bare gravel plains in the western half of the desert exhibit interesting adaptations and occupy unusual microhabitats. On first inspection, however, this habitat appears to be a lifeless plain covered with scattered quartz stones. Closer examination of these stones, nevertheless, reveals that the regular occurrence of advective fog and the presence of wind-blown detritus have created suitable conditions for animal life beneath the stones. The sea fog condenses frequently upon the stones and provides water for lichens which grow on the upper surface. If the condensation of fog water is sufficiently heavy, the water will reach the lower surface of the stone, thus creating a moist environment which is sufficiently cool for the growth of green algae. In addition, wind-blown grass frequently collects on the eastern side of the stones and in this way an ideal microhabitat and niche is created for arthropod life (Fig. 3).

In spite of the interesting adaptations encountered on the gravel plains the vegetationless dunes represent the most unusual habitat and it is from this ecosystem that five samples will be taken to illustrate physiological dovetailing with the previously described habitat.

The tenebrionid beetle Lepidochora argentogrisea

The wind-blown grass or detritus which collects on the leeward side of the vegetationless dunes represents the most important primary source of energy to the psammophilous fauna inhabiting the soft wind-blown sand on the leeward side or slip-face of the dune. One of the most important direct utilizers of this energy is the tenebrionid beetle

Lepidochora argentogrisea. For this reason we have examined thermoregulation, digestion, metabolism and water economy in this species (Louw & Hamilton, 1971).

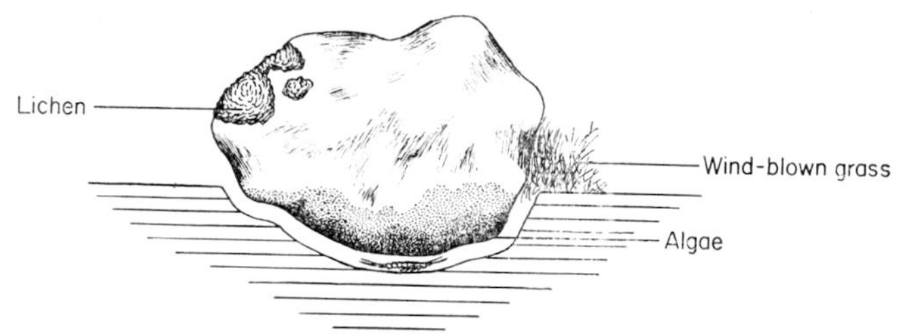

FIG. 3. Diagrammatic representation of the effect of fog on stones covering the vegetationless gravel plains. Lichens grow on the upper surface of the stone while condensed fog water reaching the lower surface creates a suitable microhabitat for algae and arthropods, the latter feed upon wind-blown grass collecting on the windward side.

These beetles are morphologically very well adapted to their ultrapsammophilous existence (Fig. 4) and as they are largely nocturnal in habit they escape from the extremely high surface temperatures, experienced on the slip-face during the day, by burrowing beneath the sand. Their strict nocturnal activity pattern can be changed by a facultative response to surface wind. Whenever strong winds occur the surface of the sand is cooled and the beetles emerge in large numbers to feed upon the detritus brought in by the wind. Nevertheless, this species appears to have a wide temperature tolerance since active individuals have been observed on the surface of the sand when the surface temperature was as low as 6°C. They seldom emerge, however, at surface temperatures approaching 40°C and for the most part are exposed only to cool night temperatures. In this way excessive water loss experienced during high temperature conditions is avoided.

The ability of *L. argentogrisea* to digest the wind-blown detritus was examined and it was found that they were able to obtain sufficient nutrients from the detritus to satisfy their calorific requirements, which were determined in a separate metabolism experiment. The digestible cellulose and other nutrients obtained from digestion can, after absorption, naturally serve as an important source of metabolic water. This fact, coupled with the ability of *L. argentogrisea* to withstand desiccation at 0% rh, as efficiently as the familiar *Tenebrio molitor*, would lead one to believe that they are independent of free water. This was not found to be the case since the animals slowly lose weight on air dry food.

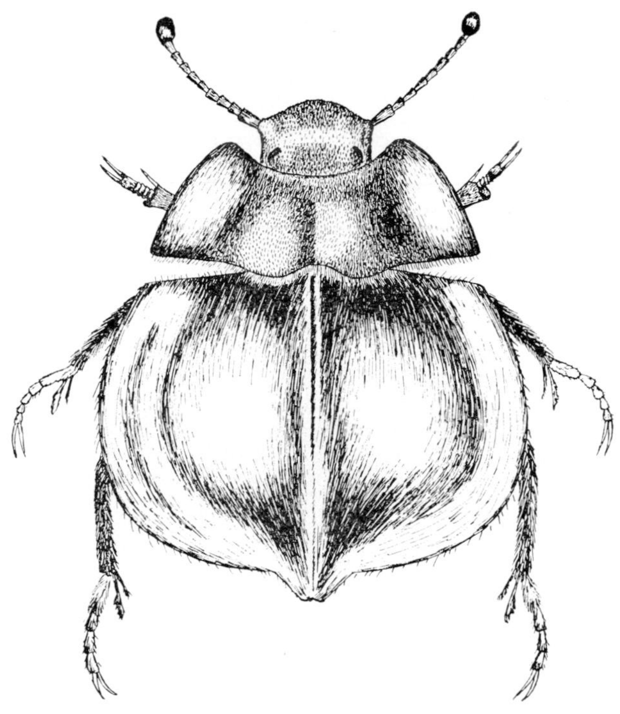

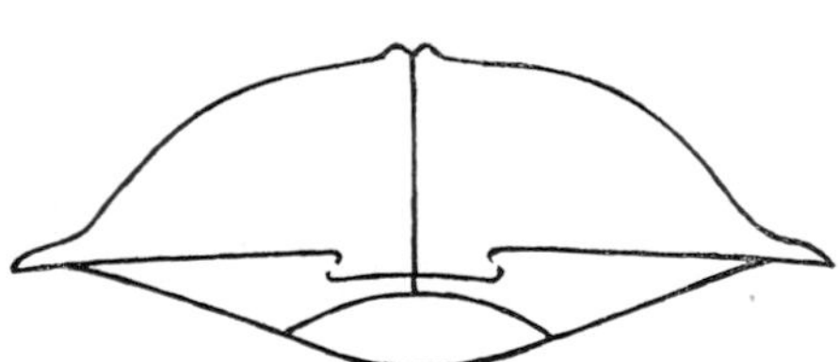

FIG. 4. Dorsal view of the psammophilous tenebrionid *Lepidochora argentogrisea*. The body outline (below) shows the projecting epipleura, beneath which droplets of fog water collect. (Adapted from original by Koch, 1962.)

These beetles thus require a source of free water and the most obvious choice would be fog water. It was not surprising, therefore, to find beetles above the surface of the sand during a heavy condensing fog. The fog had condensed on the dorsal surface of the elytra in the form of fine drops. Moreover, in the afternoon of the same day, several hours after

TABLE I

The effect of hydration upon the osmolality of the haemolymph of L. argentogrisea*

Group	*N*	Osmolality of the haemolymph (m-osmole/l) Mean	SD	% difference
Hydrated beetles	12	339	±20·3	
Dehydrated beetles	12	427	±15·9	+26%

* From Louw & Hamilton (1971).

the fog had cleared, water drops were still found on the ventral surface of beetles which had been removed from beneath the sand. These drops were found to be clinging to the ventral surface of the epipleura. Subsequent laboratory studies showed that water drops, sprayed on to the dorsal surface of the elytra, are not directly absorbed through the cuticle. Nevertheless, these drops do not evaporate as quickly as similar sized drops placed on an inert ceramic surface, which may mean that the water drops coming into contact with the cuticle are surrounded by a lipid layer.

Laboratory studies did, however, show that water sprayed on dehydrated beetles entered the digestive tract and subsequently caused a marked reduction in the osmolality of the haemolymph (Table I). In this way water is stored in the soft tissues of the insect until the next fog occurs.

The sand-diving lizard Aporosaura anchietae

These lizards inhabit the soft wind-blown sand of the dune slip-face. Unlike the *Lepidochora* beetles they are diurnal animals but, nevertheless, escape extremely high and low surface temperatures by adopting a bimodal activity rhythm which coincides with surface sand temperatures between 30–40°C. Because of the prevalence of these animals on the dune slip-face we have examined their feeding habits, thermoregulation and water economy in some detail (Louw & Holm, 1971).

In their feeding habits *Aporosaura* are opportunistic. For example, on the dunes immediately adjacent to the Atlantic Ocean they feed almost exclusively on kelp flies. The flies have a high moisture content which is sustained by the precipitation of fog water upon their wings.

On the other hand, *Aporosaura* which inhabit the inland dunes feed mostly on dry grass seed which is an important constituent of the wind-blown detritus which collects on the vegetationless dunes. The latter group therefore, although they will capture the occasional arthropod when the opportunity arises, are, as a result of the nature of their diet, exposed to a greater risk of dehydration.

This risk of dehydration is further aggravated by their preferred temperature range of 30–40°C. Temperatures within this range are experienced for a relatively short period on the dune slip-face but the animals make maximum use of this short period by employing a characteristic thigmothermic behaviour pattern. When surface temperatures approach 30°C on the slip-face the lizards emerge from beneath the sand and press the ventral surface of their bodies against the substrate. In order to achieve maximum contact with the substrate all four limbs and the tail are raised off the surface of the sand and the body temperature of the animal rises swiftly. The lizards then begin to forage on the slip-face but, as the temperature of the surface approaches 40°C, they move the body as far as possible away from the surface of the substrate by straightening the limbs. They will occasionally interrupt this stilt-like walk to raise diagonally opposite limbs while using the base of the tail for support (Fig. 5). This thermoregulatory dance allows the lizards to remain above the surface for as long as possible but when the surface temperature exceeds 40°C they dive beneath the surface to reach a cooler environment.

The exposure of the lizards, although only briefly, to the strong insolation on the slip-face at temperatures between 30–40°C must result in a considerable loss of moisture. Moreover, the nature of their diet, which contains a large percentage of dry grass seed, aggravates the situation further and they are therefore compelled to utilize a source of free water. The most obvious source is again fog water and, although we have never observed the animals drinking fog water, we have strong circumstantial evidence that they do. For example, when the animals are killed and dissected shortly after the occurence of a heavy condensing fog, the stomach is enormously distended and filled with water. Subsequently this water is transferred to the caecum which expands to accommodate it and even after eight weeks there is a significant amount of fluid still present in the caecum. Moreover, in captivity the animals drink readily when water is sprayed in the form of fine drops on the glass side of the terrarium. In doing so they consume about 10% of their body weight in water and exhibit twisting and writhing movements of the body during the last phases of drinking. These movements presumably facilitate the consumption of an abnormally large volume of

FIG. 5. The psammophilous lizard *Aporosaura anchietae* engaged in thermoregulation on the dune slip-face. (See text for explanation.)

fluid. In Table II the effect of dehydration upon the plasma osmolality of *Aporosaura* is illustrated. These data show that, similar to *Lepidochora*, the plasma osmolality of *Aporosaura* appears to be fairly labile and is influenced by the degree of dehydration. It would appear, then, as if *Aporosaura* is capable of a considerable degree of water storage and that its physiology in this respect is well adapted to dependence upon the peculiar Namib weather pattern of regular advective sea fog. It is also important to note in this respect that the known distribution of *Aporosaura* is limited to the fog belt of the Namib.

TABLE II

The effect of dehydration upon the plasma osmolality of the lizard Aporosaura anchietae*

Group	*N*	Plasma osmolality (m-osmole/l) Mean	Range
Freshly captured after recent fog	8	312	275–320
Dehydrated in captivity for three weeks	5	420	410–435

* Adapted from Louw & Holm (1971)

The side-winding viper Bitis peringueyi

This viper with its characteristic side-winding mode of locomotion is fairly common in the dune ecosystem of the Namib. They have been observed to be active on the surface of the sand both during the day and at night. It is, however, not yet known whether they are diurnal or nocturnal. In any event, the ease with which they are able to submerge themselves beneath the sand allows them to escape the dehydrating effect of extremely high temperatures. Moreover, they have been seen to feed upon *Aporosaura* lizards which would ensure a high moisture content of their diet. It is not surprising therefore that these animals have been successfully kept for over four months in captivity without access to water. Nevertheless, acting on an original observation of K. Schaer in 1969 I was interested in determining whether these animals made use of fog water. In order to determine this, two individuals were placed in an enclosure which prevented fog condensing either on the snakes or near them. They were regularly fed on small live lizards.

After two months the snakes were sprayed with water in the form of a fine mist which settled on the dorsal surface of the animals. As soon as a snake became aware of the water droplets it became excited and immediately flattened its body against the substrate in order to increase the surface area exposed to the spray. At the same time the snakes coiled up and the head moved back and forth over the dorsal surface of the body as the animal licked off the water droplets. This behaviour was interrupted every few minutes to raise the head some 10 cm above the ground to assist the flow of water into the digestive tract by gravity (Fig. 6). This well defined behaviour pattern would appear to indicate that *Bitis peringueyi* makes regular use of condensing fog water under natural conditions. It is also of significance in this respect that the distribution of *B. peringueyi*, like *Aporosaura* is confined to the Namib fog belt.

The ostrich Struthio camelus

The ostrich, unlike the species described previously, cannot escape to a favourable microclimate to avoid excessively high temperatures. Moreover it has the added disadvantage of maintaining a fairly constant body temperature (Crawford & Schmidt-Nielsen, 1967). Nevertheless, it successfully inhabits some of the most arid regions of the Namib and for this reason we have examined thermoregulation and renal function in these birds (Louw, Belonje & Coetzee, 1969).

Although the ostrich maintains a fairly constant body temperature of 38–40°C it makes maximum use of convective and radiant cooling in order to reduce water loss to a minimum. This is achieved by erecting the feathers over the body and moving the wings away from the body to expose the thorax and thighs which are not covered by feathers. In this way the convective cooling action of the slightest breeze is utilized and the temperature of the air space between the feathers and the skin is reduced sufficiently to allow loss of body heat. Only as a last resort, when there is no wind will the ostrich employ evaporative cooling by raising its respiration rate suddenly from approximately 4 to 40/min. Conversely, at low ambient temperatures the feathers are folded closely against the skin and the temperature of the air space between the feathers and the skin rises rapidly to form an insulative layer (Fig. 7).

The ostrich also has efficient renal function. When deprived of water and fed only on air dry food (9% water) the urine volume decreased dramatically and the osmolality rose sharply to reach a maximum of 800 m-osmole/l. The concentration of potassium in the urine rose to a value of 139 m-equiv/l while the concentration of sodium fell from 76 to 30 m-equiv/l indicating efficient aldosterone control. Concurrently

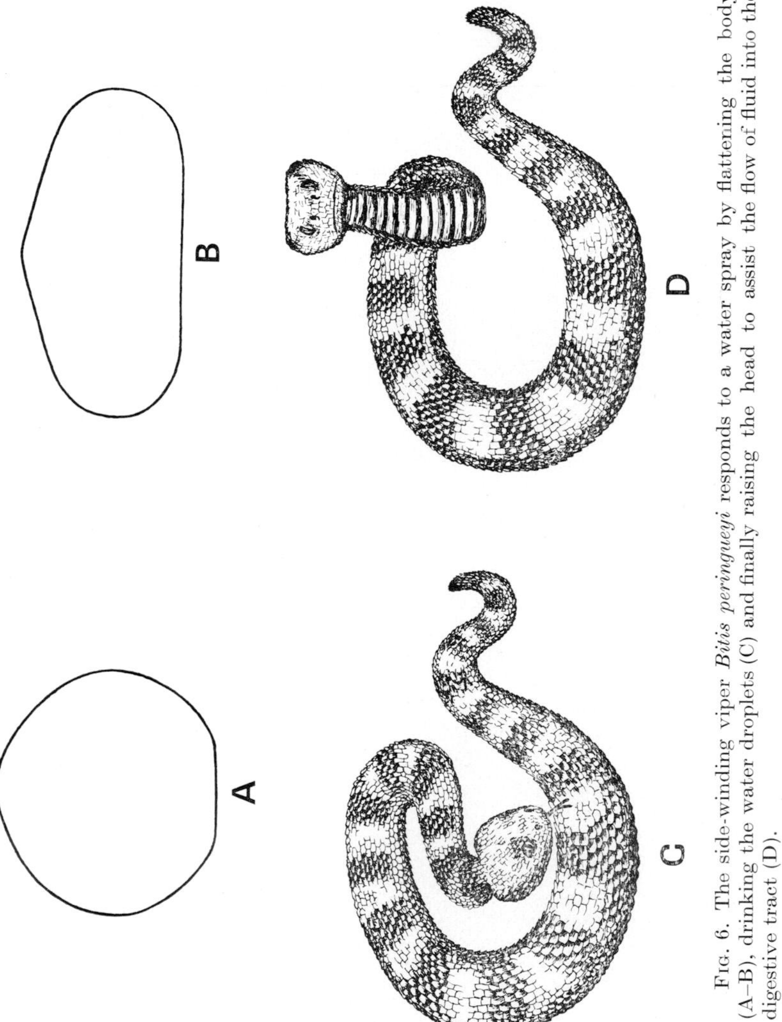

Fig. 6. The side-winding viper *Bitis peringueyi* responds to a water spray by flattening the body (A–B), drinking the water droplets (C) and finally raising the head to assist the flow of fluid into the digestive tract (D).

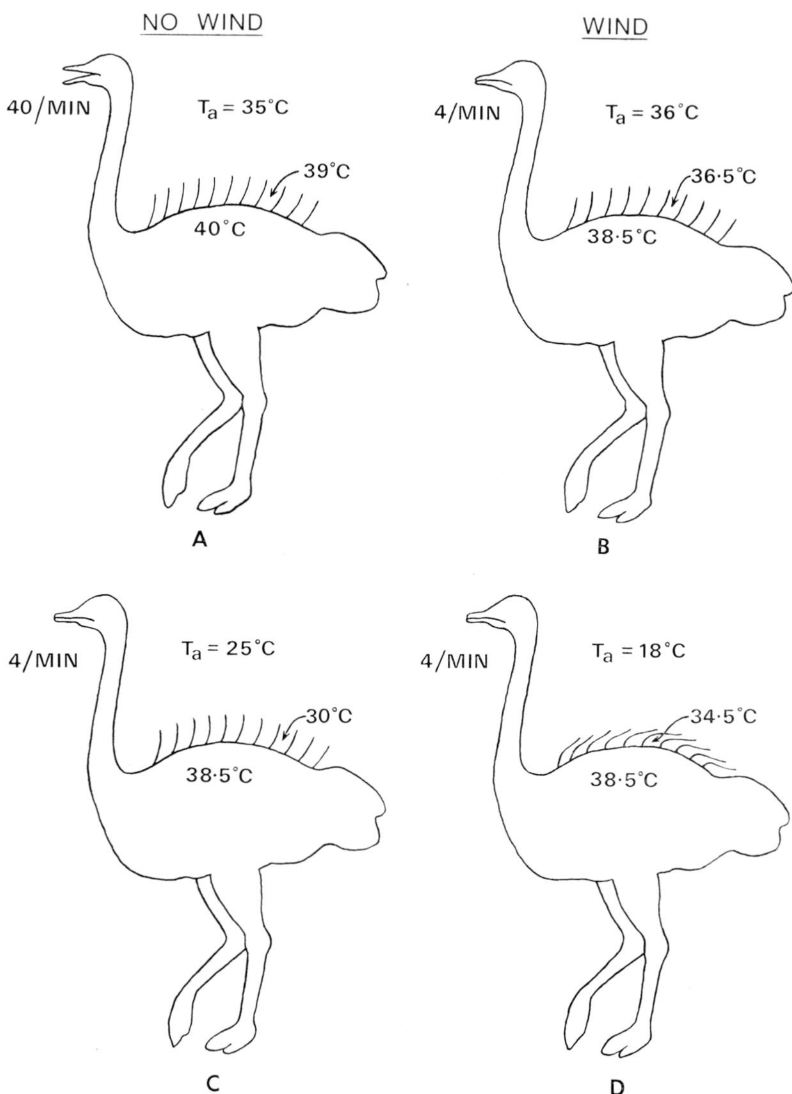

FIG. 7. Thermoregulation in the ostrich involves thermal panting and feather erection under conditions of no wind and high ambient temperature (A). In windy conditions feather erection alone is frequently sufficient to allow body cooling (B, C) while at low ambient temperatures at night the feathers are flattened to provide an insulating layer of air (D).

the undissolved uric acid content increased by approximately 1500% and its excretion was facilitated by copious mucus secretion from the epithelial lining of the ureter. Finally, during the dehydration period osmolality of the plasma remained remarkably constant.

With the above physiological background in view, it is therefore not surprising that the ostrich cannot exist indefinitely on dry food. After eight days they refuse to feed and lose weight steadily. Moreover, if they are forcibly hydrated by administering 11 l of water to them (10% of body wt), the excess water is rapidly excreted and the plasma osmolality is not significantly affected as it is in the species discussed previously. Very little, if any, water is therefore stored yet the animals survive in areas without surface water. The answer to the question of their means of survival is to be found in the high moisture content of certain plants, the frequent occurrence of condensing fog and the comparatively high relative humidity of the air at night in the Namib. For example, we have recently examined the effect of the relative humidity of the air on the moisture content of a dry perennial desert grass *Stipagrostis uniplumus* which is favoured by ostriches (M. K. Jensen & G. N. Louw, unpubl. obs.). The results are illustrated in Fig. 8 and show how closely the moisture content of the grass follows the humidity of the air. It is also clear that when grazing in the early hours of the morning the ostriches are feeding on grass with a moisture percentage of almost 27%. At 13.00 h the moisture percentage had dropped to below 10% but at the same time a succulent species of *Bohenia* which had been heavily grazed contained 68% moisture. Naturally after a heavy condensing fog the moisture intake during grazing would also be very high for several hours. Finally, when faced with extreme water deprivation the ability of the ostrich to move rapidly over long distances would allow it to visit isolated water holes.

It would appear then that, although the ostrich cannot use fog water as efficiently as the species described previously, it nevertheless is of direct importance and probably of secondary importance in sustaining succulent plants upon which the ostrich feeds.

The Namib gerbil Gerbillus paeba

The Namib gerbil is one of the very few mammals to be found in the dune ecosystem. It is strictly nocturnal and during the day remains hidden in fairly deep burrows which it frequently constructs in the fairly compact sand which surrounds the root system of the leafless but thorny narras plant *Acanthosicyos horrida*. The entrance to the burrow is always closed during the day and these animals are never exposed to the dehydrating effects of high temperatures. They are herbivorous and never drink water. A study of their water economy was therefore undertaken.

It was found that when these animals are fed exclusively on a commercial mixture of bird seed, high in carbohydrate and low in protein and kept at an ambient temperature of 24°C and a relative

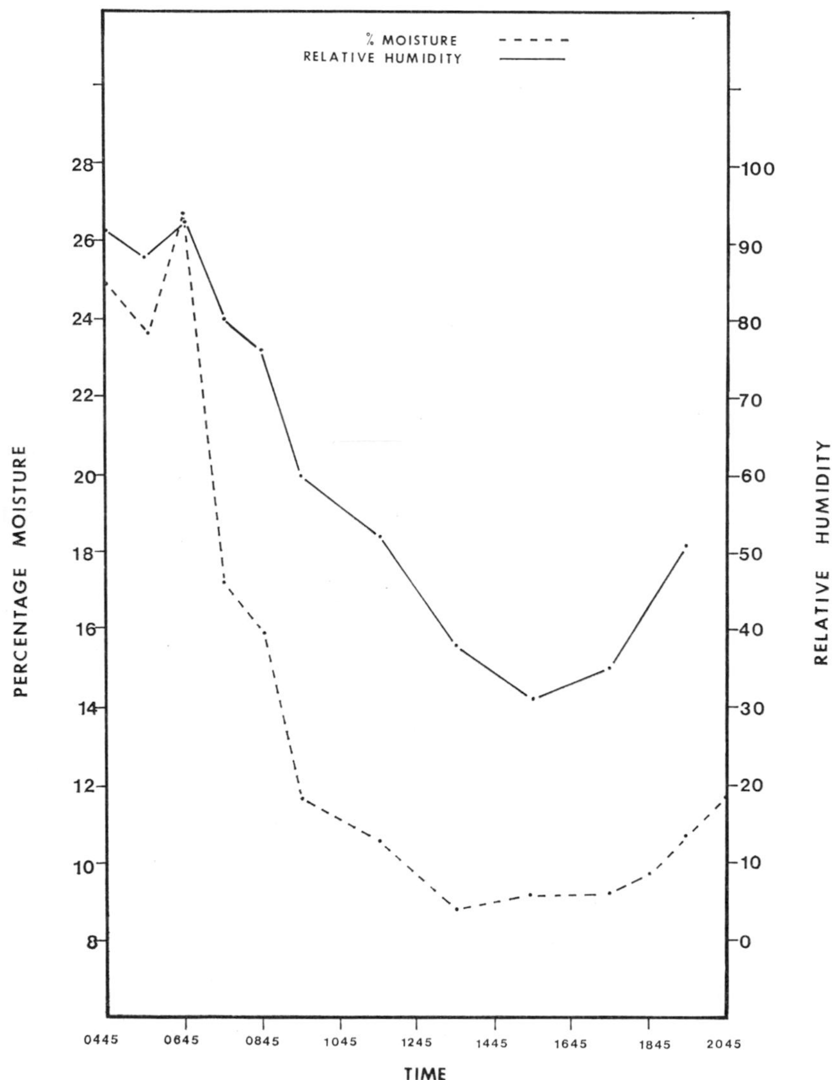

FIG. 8. The effect of the relative humidity of the air at various times of the day upon the moisture content of a perennial desert grass *Stipagrostis uniplumus*.

humidity of 50–55% that they lost weight rapidly. On the fifth day the mean percentage loss in weight of five animals was 22% and the experiment had to be terminated. The provision of fresh lettuce leaves at this stage swiftly restored the animals to their original body weight. In a similar experiment, also on five animals, but conducted at 19°C and 70–75% relative humidity the animals lost weight at a slower rate, taking seven days to lose 22% of their body weight. Nevertheless, the animals could not survive on the seed and the experiment again had to be terminated.

These results were confirmed by a third experiment in which five animals were again fed the same diet and kept overnight in metabolism cages which allowed for the collection of urine under mineral oil. Temperatures were kept constant at 19°C and relative humidity at 70–75%. When the animals received fresh lettuce leaves in their diet the mean osmolality of the urine was 2860 m-osmole/l (range 2246–3490 m-osmole/l) and the maximum mean osmolality achieved during dehydration was 4035 m-osmole/l (range 3767–4475 m-osmole/l). The Namib gerbil therefore has efficient renal function but not sufficiently spectacular to allow it to survive on dry grass seed. Moreover, unlike *Aporosaura* and *Lepidochora* it is not able to store water and cannot therefore rely on the periodic condensation of fog water. These animals must therefore obtain some source of succulent feed within their habitat and this supposition was confirmed by the presence of succulent plant material (*Trianthema hereroensis*) among the food stored in their burrows. It would appear, then, as if these gerbils, like the ostrich, are not directly dependent on fog water but indirectly on the few succulent plants sustained by the fog.

Acknowledgements

The South African Council for Scientific and Industrial Research are thanked for their generous financial support. Thanks are also due to Dr. M. K. Jensen, Director of the Namib Desert Research Station, for her help and enthusiastic encouragement. The technical assistance of Alex Dürr and Robin Gibbs is gratefully acknowledged.

References

Crawford, E. C. & Schmidt-Nielsen, K. (1967). Temperature regulation and evaporative cooling in the ostrich. *Am. J. Physiol.* **212**: 347–353.

Gross, W. J. (1954). Osmotic responses in the sipunculid *Dendrostomum zostericolum*. *J. exp. Biol.* **31**: 402–423.

Koch, C. (1961). Some aspects of abundant life in the vegetationless sand of the Namib Desert dunes. *Jl. S.W.A. Scient. Soc.* **15**: 8–34.

Koch, C. (1962). The tenebrionidae of Southern Africa XXXII. New psammophilous species from the Namib Desert. *Ann. Trans. Mus.* **24**: 107–159.

Louw, G. N. & Hamilton, W. J. (1971). Physiological and behavioural ecology of the ultrapsammophilous tenebrionid, *Lepidochora argentogrisea*. *Madoqua*, Ser. II, **1**: 87–95.

Louw, G. N. & Holm, E. (1971). Physiological, morphological and behavioural adaptations of the ultrapsammophilous, Namib Desert lizard *Aporosaura anchietae* (Bocage). *Madoqua*, Ser. II, **1**: 67–85.

Louw, G. N., Belonje, P. C. & Coetzee, H. J. (1969). Renal function, respiration, heart rate and thermoregulation in the ostrich (*Struthio camelus*). *Scient. Pap. Namib Desert Res. Stn* No. 42: 43–54.

Schulze, B. R. (1969). The climate of Gobabeb. *Scient. Pap. Namib Desert Res. Stn* No. 38: 5–12.

Symp. zool. Soc. Lond. (1972) No. 31, 315–326.

ENERGY EXCHANGES WITH THE ENVIRONMENT OF TWO EAST AFRICAN ANTELOPES, THE ELAND AND THE HARTEBEEST

VIRGINIA A. FINCH

Department of Animal Physiology, University of Nairobi, Nairobi, Kenya

SYNOPSIS

The energy exchange between animals and their thermal environment was assessed by estimating each flux of radiant energy absorbed and each mode of heat dissipated in the field under conditions of intense solar radiation. Two representative species were chosen, the eland which uses sweating primarily and the hartebeest which uses panting primarily as a means of evaporative cooling. Absorptivity to short-wave radiation is 0·58 for the fur of the hartebeest and 0·78 for the fur of the eland, while absorptivity to long-wave radiation is considered to be 1·0. The largest single component of the heat load at mid-day is thermal radiation from the ground. The total long-wave radiation from the ground and atmosphere contributes more than one-half to the effective radiative heat load. The heat absorbed at the fur surface is approximately nine times that of the metabolic heat. Of the heat absorbed, two-thirds by the eland and three-quarters by the hartebeest is liberated from the fur surface as long-wave radiation. Convectional heat loss is small in both species. At the peak period of radiation, evaporative heat loss accounts for 20% in the hartebeest and 31% in the eland of the total dissipation of the effective radiative heat load.

INTRODUCTION

The exchange of energy between an animal and its thermal environment has interested scientists for many years. However, difficulties in determining reliable measurements of the effects of solar radiation on organisms have limited research in the past in this area of environmental physiology. There have been, nevertheless, a few instances of field experiments which describe some of the relationships of solar radiation to thermal exchanges of animals (Riemerschmid & Elder, 1945; Kelly, Bond, & Heitman, 1954; Macfarlane, Morris & Howard, 1956; Priestley, 1957). More recently there has been increasing information available concerning the application of engineering and physical principles of heat transfer to biological systems (Birkebak, 1966; Gates, 1968; Porter & Gates, 1969). This has increased the feasibility of experimental field research, particularly in the area of energy exchange. Accordingly this study is an attempt to determine quantitatively thermal exchanges with the environment of two species of East African antelope, the eland (*Taurotragus oryx*) and the hartebeest (*Alcelaphus buselaphus cokii*) under conditions of intense solar radiation. These two species were chosen because the eland uses sweating primarily and the hartebeest panting primarily as a means of evaporative cooling. The measurements are based on the physics of heat transfer and the physical and physiological responses of animals to radiation. It forms part of an investigation into the effects of solar radiation on temperature regulation and heat balance in several species of East African herbivores.

THE RADIATIVE ENVIRONMENT

The radiative environment of the locality presently under investigation is described in Fig. 1 in terms of the individual fluxes of energy irradiating the upward and downward facing surfaces of a flat horizontal plate. Energy coming from the upper hemisphere which irradiates the upward facing surface of the plate consists of direct solar radiation (short-wave), diffuse radiation (short-wave) and thermal radiation (long-wave) from the atmosphere. Energy coming from the lower hemisphere which irradiates the downward facing plate consists of thermal radiation (long-wave) emitted from the surface of the ground and direct and diffuse radiation reflected from the ground. The total radiative heat load on the horizontal surface is equal to the sum of the downward and upward streams of radiant energy and represents the total potential heat load on an animal. The effective radiative heat load is that portion of the potential radiation actually absorbed by the animal.

ESTIMATION OF THE EFFECTIVE RADIATIVE HEAT LOAD

The total quantity of radiant energy absorbed by the fur covering of an animal is the sum of the amount absorbed by the different areas of its body on which the radiation falls. For the purpose of calculating mean absorptivity, the body of the animal is regarded as a cylinder, a model which is considered to be a reasonable approximation of the animal's shape (Clapperton, Joyce & Blaxter, 1965). The direct sunlight, diffuse light, and atmospheric radiation coming from the upper hemisphere irradiate approximately the top half of the animal's body, while reflected sunlight and thermal radiation coming from the lower hemisphere irradiate approximately the lower half of the animal's body. Therefore, a total of one-half of the potential environmental radiation impinges on the animal at any one time. The spectral absorptivity to short-wave radiation of each animal's coat will determine further the effective radiative heat load. For the purpose of this estimation,

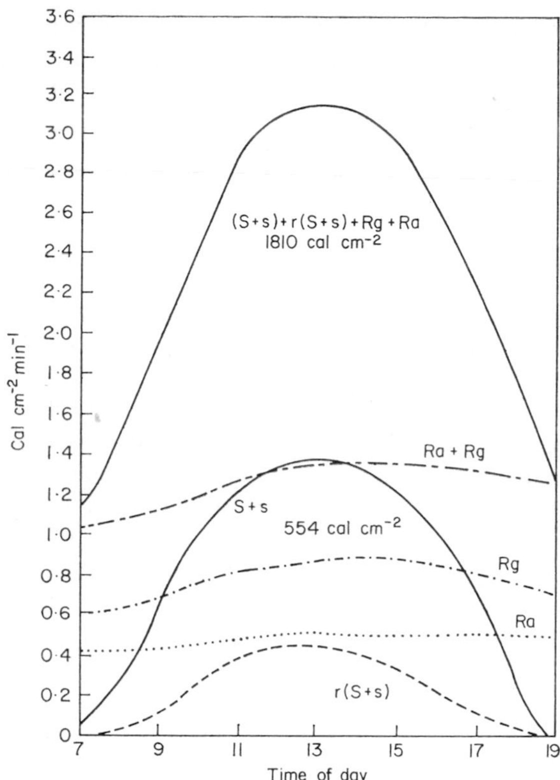

FIG. 1. The daily variations of the potential radiant heat load near Nairobi, Kenya, on February 9, 1971, on a flat horizontal surface receiving a downward stream of direct solar radiation, S, diffuse radiation, s, and atmospheric thermal radiation, Ra; and receiving the upward stream of reflected direct and diffuse radiation, $r(S+s)$, and thermal radiation from the ground, Rg. The total radiant energy, H, the total short-wave radiations, $S+s$, and the total long-wave thermal radiation, $Ra+Rg$, are summed separately.

absorptivities to sunlight, diffuse light, and reflected light are assumed to be the same. The absorptivity to infra-red radiation is considered to be between 0·95 and 1·0.

All absorbed heat does not necessarily penetrate to the skin of the animal. Some of it is lost directly to the environment through the emission of long-wave radiation and through convectional heat loss. Any heat which penetrates to the skin surface and is absorbed into the body will be lost through evaporative cooling. The rate of absorption of environmental heat together with the rate of heat production by metabolism must equal the rate at which heat is eliminated from the body in order for an animal to maintain a constant body temperature.

It is the purpose of this paper to evaluate and compare measurements and calculations of each flux of radiant energy absorbed and each mode of heat dissipated by the two species under investigation, the eland and the hartebeest.

METHODS

The two eland, obtained from a local farmer, were approximately one and one-half years of age when captured. The two hartebeest were purchased from a trapper at an approximate age of eight months. After a training period of several months, the animals submitted calmly to experimental procedures. During the experiments reported in this paper, the eland weighed between 365 and 400 kg and the hartebeest between 95 and 100 kg. The animals were maintained at an experimental site close to Nairobi in semi-arid bush country at an altitude of 1450 m. Measurements were made between 09.00 and 15.00 h on cloudless days. During this time the animals stood quietly in a crush made of steel piping, the horizontal axis of which was oriented at right angles to the incoming radiation. The animals were starved 16 h prior to and during the experiments, but had constant access to water.

A solarimeter (Yellot Sol-A-Meter, Mark I-G, spectral response 0·3 to 1·5 μm) was used to measure short-wave radiation. This instrument was mounted 100 cm above the ground to receive incoming short-wave radiation from the sun, and then rotated 180° downward to receive short-wave radiation reflected from the ground. A shield placed over the sensing cell allowed diffuse light to be recorded. The percent of reflectance of short-wave radiation from the coat was measured on a spectrophotometer from fur samples of each species. Values of spectral absorption were then calculated by subtracting the reflectance values from unity. As the amount of sunshine received by any one area of fur varies according to the angle between that area and the solar beam, calculations as described by Porter & Gates (1969) were used to estimate the average direct radiation from the sun.

An infra-red field radiometer (Model PRT-10, Barnes Engineering Co., spectral sensitivity 6·9 to 20 μm) was used to measure long-wave radiation from the ground and the fur surface. Mean ground temperature was determined from measurements taken every 3 m along a line perpendicular to and bisecting the longitudinal axis of the animal's body. Fur surface temperature was averaged from six readings around the circumference of the animal's body. The quantity of reradiated heat emitted from both the ground and fur surfaces was calculated from the absolute temperatures of each taken to the fourth power, emissivity of the surfaces (considered to be one in both cases), and the Stefan Boltzmann constant for radiation.

Shade temperature and relative humidity, from which atmospheric thermal radiation was estimated according to Brunt's empirical formula (1939), were recorded from a dry and wet bulb thermometer housed in a Stevenson's screen near the crush. To measure average wind speed a three-cup anemometer with recorder was placed near to the side of the animal at a height level with its flank. Convectional heat loss was estimated from the ratio of the wind velocity to the diameter of the animal's body, and the temperature gradient between the fur surface and air according to the formula derived by Gates (1962).

Metabolic rate and respiratory heat loss were measured separately from the other physiological and environmental parameters. Expired air was collected in Douglas bags connected by flexible tubing to gas masks. Respiratory rate, counted visually by watching flank movement, was not significantly altered in the eland by wearing the masks; however, in the hartebeest, rates over 60/min were lowered by 15% to 20%. Respiratory heat loss was calculated, therefore, from the data on minute volume assuming that the expired air was saturated at body temperature. Body temperature was obtained with a clinical thermometer inserted in the rectum a depth of 10 cm. To determine oxygen tension, gas samples were analysed on an oxygen electrode (Cambridge blood gas analyser, Model 48C, Electronic Instrument Ltd.). Sweating rates were measured with non-ventilated sweat capsules using calcium sulphate (Drierite) as the desiccant. These were applied to four areas of the skin previously determined in earlier mapping trials to give a reasonable estimate of the average sweating rates over the trunk of the animal.

RESULTS

The amount of heat absorbed from each component of the effective radiative heat load at midday is given in Table I. At this hour, direct and diffuse light impinge on the animals at an average rate of 1·37 cal/cm^2.min, while light is reflected from the ground at 0·34 cal/cm^2.min. The absorptivity coefficient to short-wave radiation is 0·78 for the fur of the eland and 0·58 for the fur of the hartebeest, whereas absorptivity to long-wave radiation is 1·0. The largest single component of the heat load at this hour of the day is thermal radiation from the ground. For the eland the total long-wave radiation from the ground and atmosphere contributes slightly over one-half to the effective radiative heat load

TABLE I

The quantity of heat absorbed from each component of radiation which comprises the effective radiative heat load (e.g. the total absorbed heat) for an eland and a hartebeest at solar elevation 90°. Values are in cal/cm².min

Species	Short-wave radiation: Direct	Short-wave radiation: Diffuse	Short-wave radiation: Direct and diffuse reflected from the ground	Long-wave radiation: Atmosphere	Long-wave radiation: Ground surface	Effective radiative heat load
Eland	0·317	0·047	0·191	0·245	0·429	1·229
Hartebeest	0·230	0·035	0·127	0·244	0·424	1·060

whereas for the hartebeest the long-wave radiative heat load is almost twice that of the short-wave.

Metabolic rate remained relatively constant over the period of measurement for the two animals described above at a mean value of 0·113 cal/cm^2.min for the hartebeest and a mean value of 0·131 cal/cm^2.min for the eland. The heat absorbed at the fur surface is approximately nine times as great as the fasting metabolic heat load.

Heat loss through reradiation of absorbed heat during one day's measurement is given in Table II. Measurements were taken hourly and recorded according to solar elevation. Fur surface temperature is given as the mean value of six readings around the circumference of the animal's body. There is, however, considerable variation between temperatures of different areas. For instance, at a solar elevation of 90° fur surface temperature on the dorsal side of the eland was 44°C and on the ventral side 36°C, while in the hartebeest, fur surface temperature dorsally was 53°C and ventrally 39°C. At midday, the hartebeest, with a hotter fur surface, loses 7% more heat by reradiation than the eland. Of the heat absorbed, approximately two-thirds by the eland and three-quarters by the hartebeest is liberated as long-wave radiation. Determination of convectional heat loss (Table III), based on the gradient between the fur surface and air temperature, wind speed, and body diameter, shows that the hartebeest loses almost twice as much heat through convection as the eland.

Evaporative heat loss from the hartebeest amounts to 45% of that lost from the eland (Table IV). Calculations given in Table IV further show that 78% of the total evaporative heat loss from the eland is cutaneous while 62% in the hartebeest is respiratory. The rate of

TABLE II

Mean fur surface temperature and long-wave radiative heat loss from the fur surface during one day's measurement for an eland and a hartebeest

	Eland		Hartebeest	
Solar elevation	Fur surface temperature, °C	Heat loss cal/cm².min	Fur surface temperature, °C	Heat loss cal/cm².min
40°	35·7	0·742	37·6	0·760
52°	37·6	0·760	41·0	0·792
65°	38°6	0·769	43·6	0·816
78°	39·0	0·774	44·2	0·822
90°	39·5	0·778	46·0	0·839
78°	39·0	0·774	44·8	0·828
65°	38·5	0·768	43·4	0·814

TABLE III

Difference between fur surface and air temperature, wind speed, and convectional heat loss during one day's measurement for an eland and a hartebeest

	Eland			Hartebeest		
Solar elevation	Fur surface to air temp. difference, °C	Wind speed mph	Heat loss cal/cm².min	Fur surface to air temp. difference,°C	Wind speed mph	Heat loss cal/cm².min
40°	13·0	6·4	0·036	16·6	1·8	0·038
52°	11·6	11·2	0·039	16·5	11·6	0·069
65°	9·9	10·4	0·038	16·6	8·8	0·063
78°	9·0	9·3	0·029	15·5	9·6	0·061
90°	8·5	12·0	0·030	15·0	8·8	0·057
78°	8·0	12·0	0·028	14·8	8·8	0·054
65°	6·5	10·6	0·022	11·9	8·4	0·045

cutaneous and respiratory heat losses in the eland and respiratory heat loss in the hartebeest vary in proportion to the intensity of the solar heat load, while cutaneous heat loss in the hartebeest increases only slightly. Rates of evaporative heat loss appear to bear no relation to changes in air temperature, which is assumed to be within the thermoneutral zone of both species. During the period of measurement body temperature increased in the eland 0·5°C and in the hartebeest 0·6°C.

TABLE IV

Evaporative heat losses, shade temperature, and direct and diffuse radiation during one day's measurement for an eland and a hartebeest

		Eland			Hartebeest		
Solar elevation	Shade temp. °C	Direct and diffuse radiation cal/cm².min	Respiratory heat loss cal/cm².min	Cutaneous heat loss cal/cm².min	Direct and diffuse radiation cal/cm².min	Respiratory heat loss cal/cm².min	Cutaneous heat loss cal/cm².min
40°	22	0·800	0·069	0·166	0·750	0·050	0·048
52°	26	1·080	0·079	0·230	1·070	0·058	0·060
65°	29	1·250	0·098	0·027	1·250	0·100	0·071
78°	30	1·340	0·104	0·354	1·350	0·140	0·077
90°	31	1·380	0·104	0·390	1·360	0·145	0·080
78°	31	1·340	0·091	0·370	1·300	0·142	0·068
65°	32	1·260	0·085	0·350	1·230	0·120	0·069

DISCUSSION

Radiant energy must be absorbed before it becomes available for producing heat. In studies of heat tolerance of cattle the importance of reflectance of solar energy from the animal's fur coat has been recognized for a long time (Rhoad, 1940; Brody, 1945). Stewart (1953) and more recently Hutchinson & Brown (1969), in detailed quantitative studies of the physics of absorption and reflectance of cattle hair, have demonstrated the influence of coat colour on the absorption of solar energy and given definite values for spectral reflectivity of various colours of cattle coats. Coat structure as well as colour of the eland and hartebeest are significant contributing factors in the environmental adaptability of these species. In structure the coat of the hartebeest is uniformly dense throughout (effective thickness 8 mm), whereas the coat of the eland (effective thickness 1 to 2 mm) is thin and sparsely distributed over its body. In colour the fur of both species is a light reddish-brown, a colour more or less common to many antelopes and gazelles in East Africa. However, the tip of each hair of the hartebeest is white. Therefore, the shade of coat colour of this species is somewhat lighter in appearance than the eland. This difference in shade results in a reflectance of sunlight of 22% in the eland and 42% in the hartebeest. These values of reflectance as determined by the spectrophotometer are for an angle of incidence of the sun of 0°. A greater reflectance takes place, with a consequent decrease in absorption, as the angle of incidence approaches 90°. However, the values reported in Table I were calculated at midday when the incoming sky radiation impinges on the animals at angles of incidence close to 0° with respect to the upper part of the body. This means that for the hartebeest slightly over one-half of the incident short-wave radiation is actually available for absorption and thus able to contribute to the heat load. In the eland as much as three-quarters of the incident sunlight is absorbed. Objects normally gain heat from their environment in direct proportion to their surface area. Although the surface area of the hartebeest is one-half that of the eland, the higher proportion of reflected short-wave radiation from its fur results in the short-wave solar heat load on this species being 30% less than on the eland.

Assessment of the heat load from solar radiation is usually discussed as if absorption of radiation occurred only at the surface of the fur coat. Hutchinson & Brown (1969), however, have shown that radiation is absorbed over a range of levels within the coat extending from the surface to deeper layers inside the coat. The findings of these workers have demonstrated that radiation penetrates more deeply in loose coats than in flat, dense coats. Thus, the difference in coat structure for the eland and hartebeest would undoubtedly be important in evaluating the heat load on each species. Penetrance of radiation would be small through the thick coat of the hartebeest, and therefore the protective value of the fur of this species in terms of thermal insulation would be high. In contrast, penetrance of radiation through the shallow coat of the eland would be high, and in areas of the body where the hair is sparse, absorption would be directly by the skin. The coat of this species, then, would have little protective value against the sun as the thermal insulation of shallow coats is low (Bennett, 1964).

Absorptivity of long-wave radiation which the animal receives from the ground and atmosphere is considered to be nearly 1·0. The surface of the ground radiates nearly as a black body. In this study the ground on which the animals stand is bare, hard packed soil, the surface temperature of which may reach 60°C. However, mean soil surface temperature, which includes readings within the animal's shadow, is generally between 45°C and 50°C. Thermal radiation from the atmosphere is calculated from air temperature, which is typically 29°C to 31°C at midday, and relative humidity, which is generally 20% to 25%. Together, the two components of thermal radiation from the ground and atmosphere appear to be the major contributing factor in the effective radiative heat load. However, both the eland and hartebeest are emitting long-wave radiation in quantities which are larger than those being absorbed (Table II). Therefore, the net flow of thermal radiation is back to the environment rather than into the body of the animal. Because of a higher fur surface temperature, the hartebeest reradiates a larger proportion of its absorbed heat than the eland.

The primary compensation for the heat load is by the physical process of reradiation. Convectional heat loss, as determined in this study, is only of secondary importance. The effective radiative heat load is, in fact, three to four times that which an animal would be able to compensate for through the mechanisms of evaporative heat loss alone. At the peak period of radiation, evaporative heat loss accounts for 20% in the hartebeest and 31% in the eland of the total dissipation of the effective heat load (Table IV). The eland loses several times more heat through sweating than through panting, whereas in the hartebeest the major mode of evaporative heat loss is through the respiratory tract. Heat dissipation through panting is nearly twice that through sweating. Although the hartebeest possesses functional sweat glands, cutaneous evaporation increases only slightly under conditions of solar radiation. Similar relationships of cutaneous to respiratory water loss have been reported for the eland by Taylor & Lyman (1967) and for the hartebeest by Maloiy & Hopcraft (1971) in the environment of the climatic chamber. Robertshaw & Taylor (1969), in experiments investigating this interesting difference in the primary mode of evaporative cooling between species of bovids, have found a correlation between the rate of cutaneous moisture loss and the adult size of the animal. This has led to the suggestion that smaller animals eliminate most of their excess heat through the respiratory tract while larger animals eliminate most of their excess heat through cutaneous evaporation.

In conclusion, heat tolerance in the hartebeest is explained primarily by the large proportion of short-wave radiation reflected and heat reradiated from the fur surface and the insulative value of the dense fur coat, all of which combine to reduce the environmental heat load. Unlike the eland, the hartebeest does not seek shade during the period of most intense heat, but remains exposed to the hot sun throughout the day. The proportionately large quantity of water lost through sweating when the eland is exposed to solar radiation helps to explain the shade seeking behaviour of this species. As evaporative heat loss can be shown to vary in proportion to solar intensities, it would be a distinct advantage in the water economy of this species to remain sheltered from the sun during the midday hours (V. A. Finch, in prep.). Nevertheless, when both the eland and the hartebeest are maintained in the sun with free access to water, body temperatures rise only one-half degree centigrade. This indicates that both species are able to remain in thermodynamic equilibrium with a thermal environment of intense radiation.

SUMMARY

Results from these experiments show that coat colour and structure are significant contributing factors in the environmental adaptability of the eland and hartebeest. The lighter coloured coat of the hartebeest reflects 42% of the incident short-wave radiation whereas the darker coloured coat of the eland reflects 22%. Because of the dense coat of the hartebeest, penetrance of radiation through the fur is considered to be small, whereas penetrance of radiation through the thin sparse coat of the eland is considered to be high. Despite differences in coat structure, the quantity of thermal radiation emitted from the fur surface of both species is greater than the thermal radiation absorbed. Therefore, the net flow of long-wave radiation is back to the environment. Primary compensation for the heat load is by the physical process of reradiation. Evaporative heat loss from both species contributes approximately 25% of the total dissipation of the effective radiative heat load. In the eland 78% of the total evaporative heat loss is cutaneous while in the hartebeest 62% is respiratory.

Acknowledgements

My thanks are due to A. M. Harthoorn for introducing me to the fascinating problems of heat stress in East African herbivores and for his consequent invaluable discussion and encouragement. I wish also to express my appreciation to D. Robertshaw, not only for reading the manuscript, but also for his continuous assistance and advice throughout this study. I am further grateful to the East African Wildlife Society, the African Wildlife Leadership Foundation, and the Ministry of Overseas Development, all of whom provided funds for this research.

References

Bennett, J. W. (1964). Thermal insulation of cattle coats. *Anim. Prod.* **5**: 160–166.

Birkebak, R. C. (1966). Heat transfer in biological systems. *Int. Rev. gen. exp. Zool.* **2**: 269–344.

Brody, S. (1945). *Bioenergetics and growth.* New York: Reinhold.

Brunt, D. (1939). *Physical and dynamical meteorology.* London: Cambridge University Press.

Clapperton, J. L., Joyce, J. P., & Blaxter, K. L. (1965). Estimates of the contribution of solar radiation on thermal exchanges of sheep at a latitude of 55° north. *J. agric. Sci. Camb.* **64**: 37–49.

Gates, D. M. (1962). *Energy exchange in the biosphere.* New York: Harper & Row.

Gates, D. M. (1968). Energy exchange between organisms and environment. *Aust. J. Sci.* **31**: 67–74.

Hutchinson, J. & Brown, G. (1969). Penetrance of cattle coats by radiation. *J. appl. Physiol.* **26**: 454–464.

Kelly, C. F., Bond, T. E. & Heitman, H. (1954). The role of thermal radiation in animal ecology. *Ecology* **35**: 562–569.

Macfarlane, W. V., Morris, R. J. H. & Howard, B. (1956). Water economy of tropical Merino sheep. *Nature, Lond.* **178**: 304–305.

Maloiy, G. M. O. & Hopcraft, D. (1971). Thermoregulation and water relations of two East African antelopes: the hartebeest and impala. *Comp. Biochem. Physiol.* **38A**: 525–538.

Porter, W. P. & Gates, D. M. (1969). Thermodynamic equilibria of animals with environment. *Ecol. Monogr.* **39**: 227–244.

Priestley, C. H. B. (1957). The heat balance of sheep standing in the sun. *Aust. J. agric. Res.* **8**: 271–280.

Rhoad, A. O. (1940). Absorption and reflection of solar radiation in relation to coat color in cattle. *Proc. Am. Soc. Anim. Prod.* **33**: 291–293.

Riemerschmid, G. & Elder, J. S. (1945). The absorptivity for solar radiation of different coloured hairy coats of cattle. *Onderstepoort J. vet. Res.* **20**: 223–234.

Robertshaw, D. & Taylor, C. R. (1969). A comparison of sweat gland activity in eight species of East African bovids. *J. Physiol., Lond.* **203**: 135–143.

Stewart, R. E. (1953). Absorption of solar radiation by the hair of cattle. *Agric. Eng.* **34**: 235–238.

Taylor, C. R. & Lyman, P. (1967). A comparative study of environmental physiology of an East African antelope, the eland, and the Hereford steer. *Physiol. Zool.* **40**: 280–295.

Symp. zool. Soc. Lond. (1972) No. 31, 327–344.

CUTANEOUS THERMORECEPTORS

A. IGGO

Department of Veterinary Physiology, Royal (Dick) School of Veterinary Studies, University of Edinburgh, Edinburgh, Scotland

SYNOPSIS

This survey of the properties of thermoreceptors in temperate and tropical species has sought to establish the distinctive properties that enable them to be recognized as a distinctive and separate category of cutaneous receptor. In addition at least four subsets of specific thermoreceptors have been defined—cold receptors, warm receptors (which presumably contribute to both normal temperature sensations and thermoregulation) and hot and cold thermal nociceptors, which would not normally be active at usual skin temperatures. The last subset may well be activated under intense solar radiation.

Lack of information is most conspicuous when we turn to thermoreceptors in the skin of mammals that normally inhabit the tropical deserts. A single example is our ignorance of the temperature sensitivity curves of the thermoreceptors. Available information on primates does not establish any conspicuous differences in thermal range although the cold receptors in particular, appear to be more highly developed in primates with an enhanced sensitivity in the mid-temperature range.

INTRODUCTION

Mammals living in desert or arid environments may be exposed to severe thermal stresses. The skin surface temperatures may rise above 40°C despite sweating which would tend to cool the skin. W. V. Macfarlane (pers. comm.) has recorded skin temperatures as high as 47°C in cattle. Such temperatures are greatly in excess of the normal "neutral" values in temperate conditions—these latter range from 25–35°C. In these rigorous environmental conditions the behaviour of cutaneous thermoreceptors becomes of considerable interest, both from the viewpoint of:

1. sensory physiology, as directly influencing behaviour and
2. thermoregulation.

There is no direct information available for the properties of thermoreceptors in desert-living animals and it is necessary therefore to turn first to the conventional laboratory species (cat, rabbit, dog, rat) in which most of the detailed electrophysiological results have been obtained and then to consider the primates which have been studied more extensively in the last few years. These species (particularly *Rhesus*, *Cercopithecus*, *Saimiri*, *Papio*) all inhabit humid tropical environments though only some extend into the arid tropics.

CUTANEOUS THERMORECEPTORS

The existence of cutaneous thermoreceptors or temperature sensors has been the object of considerable controversy, a consequence of which has been a steady stream of information from several laboratories in the last three decades. The classical work of European histologists and psychophysicists led to the formulation by von Frey and by Goldscheider of the view that four kinds or modalities of cutaneous sensation existed and that each was subserved by a separate set of cutaneous receptors—the cold receptors were Krause's end bulbs (end korperchen) and the warm receptors were Ruffini endings. These, by now classical and widely quoted, attributions have been challenged by the discovery on the one hand, that cold receptors in cat facial skin are not Krause endings (Andres, 1971) but are distinctive unencapsulated enlargements of small myelinated afferent fibres, forming invaginations of the epidermis and on the other hand, by the identification of Ruffini endings as the encapsulated dermal receptors of the SA II mechanoreceptors in cat skin (Iggo, 1968; Chambers, Andres, von Duering & Iggo, 1972). Ruffini endings had previously been proposed as mechanoreceptors in joints (Boyd & Roberts, 1953). Warm receptors have not yet been identified morphologically. Their structure is of considerable theoretical interest since they have non-myelinated afferent fibres in both subprimates (Hensel, Iggo & Witt, 1960; Iggo, 1969; Bessou & Perl, 1969) and primates (Hensel & Iggo, 1971). The structure of specific mammalian cutaneous receptors with non-myelinated afferent fibres is not known with certainty, principally because of the difficulties in recognizing the nerve terminals in electron micrographs (Cauna, 1969).

RECEPTOR FUNCTIONS

The physiological properties of cutaneous thermoreceptors have been defined most exactly by electrophysiological recording from single afferent nerve fibres in anaesthetized animals combined with rigorous quantitative control of skin temperature with thermodes (Hensel & Zotterman, 1951). The general functional properties of cutaneous thermoreceptors were defined by Hensel *et al.* (1960) in a paper on thermoreceptors with non-myelinated afferent fibres in the cat. They are:

1. maintained discharge of impulses at static skin temperatures, the frequency of which is related to skin temperature (static response, Fig. 1),

2. a rise (or fall) of the frequency of discharge during a change of skin temperature (dynamic response)—for cold receptors the frequency

increases during a fall of temperature (Fig. 2) and conversely for warm receptors,

3. insensitivity to non-thermal stimuli, and

4. threshold sensitivity similar to human perceptual thresholds for temperature changes in the skin.

Additional criteria established by later work include

5. small receptive fields, with each afferent fibre supplying only one or two small receptive spots (not greater than 1 mm^2, Iggo, 1969),

6. afferent fibres with conduction velocities less than 20 m/sec, in some species as low as 0·4 m/sec.

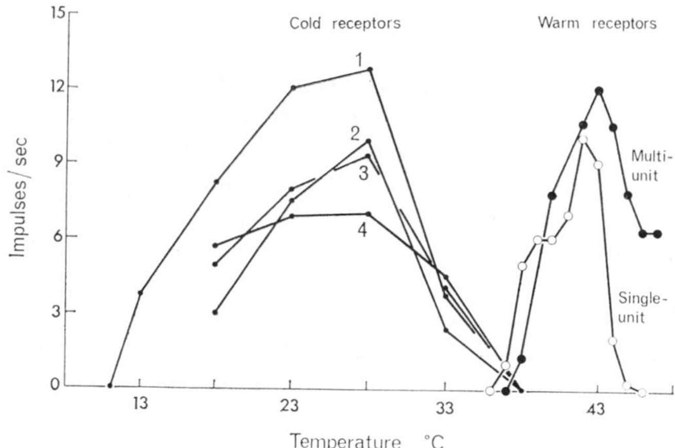

Fig. 1. Static sensitivity curves for "cold" and "warm" thermoreceptors in scrotal skin of the rat. The discharges were recorded from single afferent fibres dissected from the scrotal nerve (from Iggo, 1969).

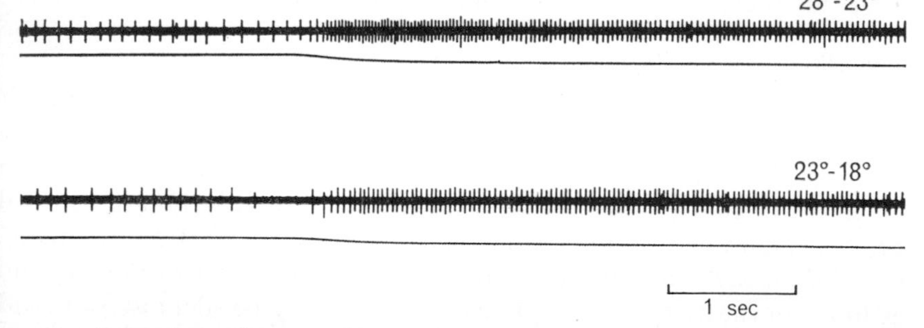

Fig. 2. Discharge from a cold receptor in scrotal skin, recorded from an afferent fibre dissected from the scrotal nerve. In the upper record the skin temperature was changed from a constant 28°C to 23°C as indicated by the lower trace, and in the lower record from 23°C to 18°C (from Iggo, 1969).

These functional characteristics are satisfied by thermoreceptors in all species studied and serve to distinguish the "true" from the so-called "spurious" thermoreceptors (Iggo, 1969). These latter generally turn out to be slowly-adapting mechanoreceptors such as the SA I and SA II receptors (Iggo & Muir, 1969; Chambers *et al.*, 1972). The slowly-adapting units of Hensel & Witt (1959) presumably correspond with SA II units and, although axonal conduction velocities were not measured, can be assigned to the SA II category on other grounds. The lingual T & M units of Poulos & Lende (1970a,b) may be identical with the slowly-adapting tongue units described by Iggo & Leek (1967) but there is insufficient published evidence to make a positive identification.

Static discharge

The static discharge of thermoreceptors can remain at a fixed mean frequency, under constant thermal conditions, for several hours, although such thermal constancy would be unusual in normal free life. Nevertheless, the thermoreceptors have the capacity to respond in a highly characteristic way to the skin temperature, as is clearly seen in Fig. 1, which illustrates the responses of scrotal thermoreceptors. Two important features of the static discharge are evident from this figure:

1. each thermoreceptor has a characteristic curve, with a narrow range of temperatures over which it exhibits peak sensitivity and,
2. two distinct populations are formed—the cold receptors and the warm receptors.

Their peak sensitivities lie on either side of the normal deep body temperature. In Fig. 1, the differential is about 18°C, with the warm fibres peaking above deep body temperature and the cold fibres below neutral skin temperature (taken as 33°C). Minimal "static" thermoreceptor discharge would occur at 35–37°C in the scrotal nerve and on either side there would be predominantly cold or warm fibre activity.

"Dynamic" sensitivities

The "dynamic" sensitivities of the thermoreceptors also exhibit maximal responses over the same range of temperatures as the static discharge, indicating that the information supplied by these units in response to equal increments of temperature is highly non-linear and very dependant on the skin temperature at which the changes are made. In addition, the response range for dynamic discharge extends beyond the limits of the static range. Thus a cold unit may be silent at 40°C and at 38°C but will be excited during a change from 40°C to 38°C. For this reason the absence of activity between 35°C and 37°C in Fig. 1 should not be regarded as establishing exclusive cold/warm receptor activity on either side. If the temperature is changed within this narrow range, then the dynamic response characteristics will lead to simultaneous but opposite changes in the activity of both cold and warm receptors. For example—at a steady 40°C the warm fibres would be active and cold fibres inactive. Changing the temperature to 37°C would lead to a reduction in the frequency of discharge in warm receptors and the appearance of activity in cold units. At a steady 37°C the warm units would once again be active and cold units inactive. The existence of the two sets of thermoreceptors provides a mechanism with a much greater range of responses than a single set could provide, with a corresponding enhancement in the richness of the information available to the central nervous system.

Since the thermoreceptors are widely scattered as individual units on the surface of the body, the question arises whether the individuals respond in an identical manner, with coincident peak sensitivity. Hensel & Wurster (1970) compared published data for several species and also calculated mean values for a sample of 32 units in the infra-orbital nerve of the cat, with receptive fields in the skin of the nose. There is general similarity in response of cold receptors in the rat and cat. Peak sensitivity was at 26–30°C and the maximal rate of discharge was about 8 impulses/sec. There is less information available for the warm receptors, but once again there is general agreement on a maximal static sensitivity at 41–45°C, with a fairly narrow range of individual variability. These results indicate that the two classes of thermo-receptor provide fairly exact information about skin temperature, and that adjacent receptors under uniform skin temperatures would be firing at similar mean frequencies.

A characteristic feature of the thermoreceptors so far described is that the individual units discharge a regular stream of impulses, which change smoothly in frequency when the temperature is altered (Fig. 2). The axonal diameters, assessed by measuring the conduction velocities, are small. The first exact measurements of this kind were made on afferent units in the saphenous nerve (Iggo, 1959; Hensel *et al.*, 1960; Iriuchijima & Zotterman, 1960; Bessou & Perl, 1969) and established that the afferent fibres were non-myelinated (i.e. C fibres). Subsequently it was established for the infra-orbital nerve that some cold units in the dog were myelinated (Iggo, 1969) with maximum diameters of 3μ, and it is probable that tongue cold receptors also have myelinated axons.

Grouped discharge patterns

It was among these latter units that an unusual kind of discharge pattern was first observed (Hensel & Zotterman, 1951; Dodt, 1952)—

the discharges were grouped rather than in a regularly spaced stream. More recently this phenomenon has also been recorded as a consistent feature of cold receptors in the general body skin of primates (Iggo, 1963, 1969), but before considering these, the grouped discharge in subprimates will be described. A proportion of infra-orbital nerve facial cold receptors respond under either static or dynamic conditions with a grouped discharge of impulses, which under static thermal conditions may continue indefinitely (Fig. 3). When the temperature is changed suddenly the grouped discharge pattern may be disrupted, and the bursts of impulses are replaced by a steady stream. If a less severe dynamic thermal stimulus is provided the disorganization of the pattern is less conspicuous. The recent availability of small digital computers has greatly eased the task of analysing this kind of grouped activity and Figs 3 and 4 show typical results, as interval histograms collected "on-line". When results such as these are "plotted" as temperature-sensitivity curves (as in Fig. 1), the maximum sensitivity or peak mean frequency of discharge occurs at 27–28°C as for units with regularly spaced uniform intervals. However, detailed examination of the discharge (Fig. 5) reveals differences in the microstructure firing pattern, related to the skin temperature. The grouped discharge shows least variability at 26°C and 23°C, where regular doublets and triplets occurred respectively, with a low coefficient of variation. At higher and lower temperatures the discharge was less regular and the coefficient of variation was higher. At 29°C doublets were interspersed with single spikes, although the spacing of the groups was fairly regular, whereas at 20°C the discharge continued as doublets but they were less regularly spaced. This greater regularity of the grouped discharge at intermediate temperatures in the range was a consistent feature, as also was the upper limit of three impulses to a group, even when the temperature was changing. Not all dog facial cold units exhibit this grouping of impulses and no explanation for this has yet been found.

The cutaneous thermoreceptors so far described have shown thermal sensitivities which would fit them for the role of receptors for the perception of warm and cold skin. Their activity declines at high and low skin temperatures (i.e. above 45°C and below 15°C). At such skin temperatures discomfort or pain may be experienced and different sets of thermally sensitive afferent units become active—the putative (Fig. 6) thermal nociceptors (Iggo, 1959; Bessou & Perl, 1969; Iggo & Ogawa, 1971). The characteristics of these units—threshold of 42–45°C, and below 20°C respectively—fits them for the role of nociceptors. The high temperature thermal nociceptors would be expected to be active at the high skin temperatures mentioned at the beginning of this article,

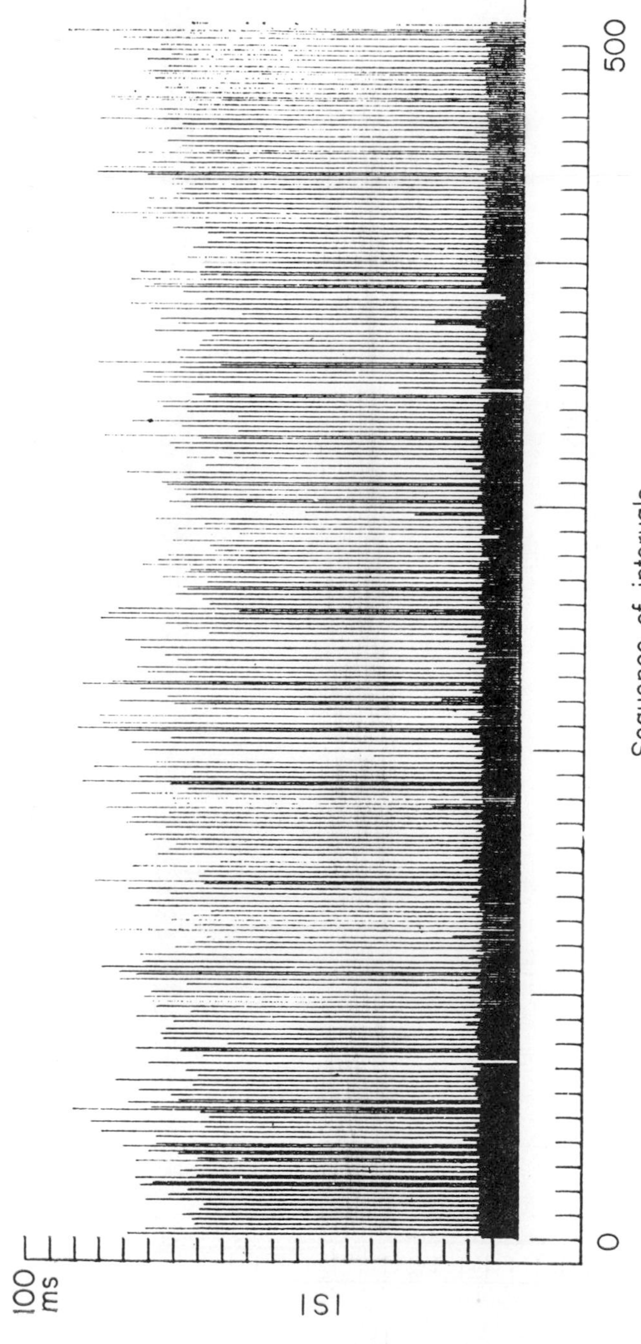

Fig. 3. Sequential impulse interval histogram recorded from a "cold" thermoreceptor unit in the facial skin of a dog (infra-orbital nerve) at a constant skin temperature of 22·3°C. There was a regular succession of short and long intervals in the discharge.

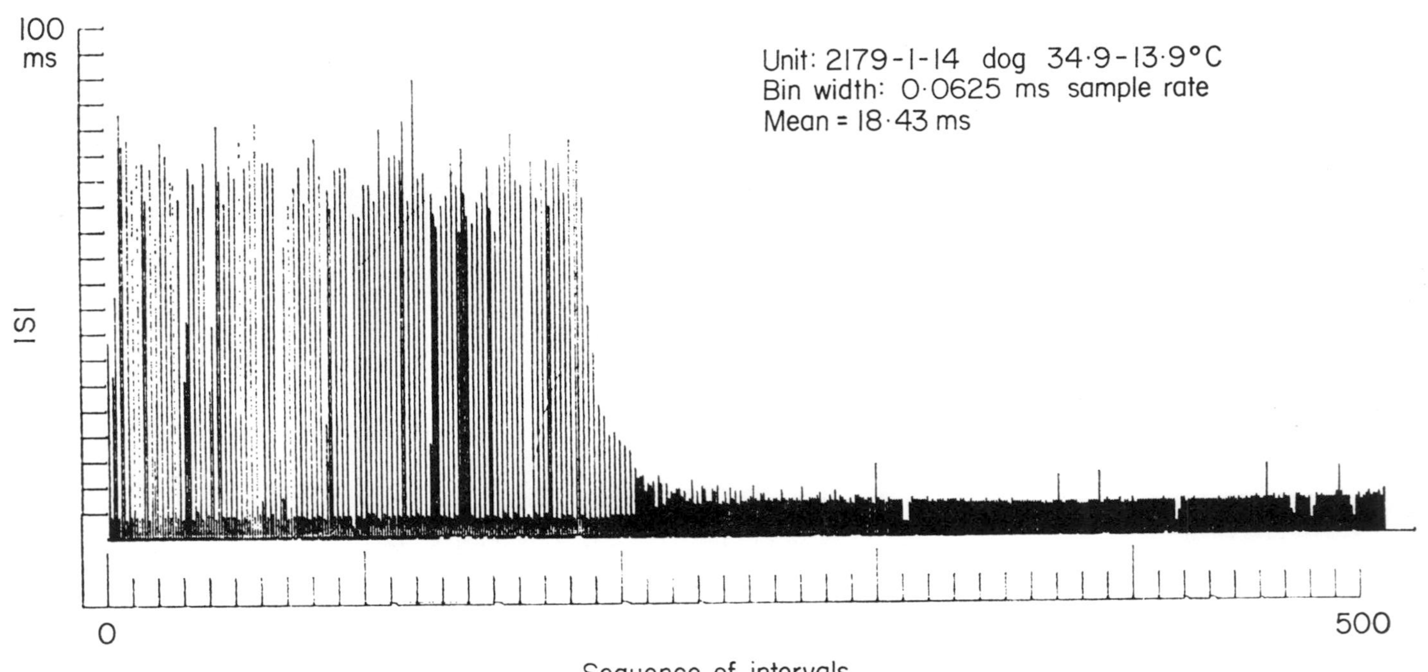

Fig. 4. Sequential impulse interval histogram, as in Fig. 3. The temperature was 34·9°C initially, and was then changed rapidly to 13·9°C. The "cold" thermoreceptor unit of a dog responded with a change in pattern of discharge, the alternate long and short intervals being replaced by a regular stream of short intervals.

although they have not yet been examined in desert non-primate or arid-region species. Their function in thermoregulation is also obscure, and most work in this field seems to assume that the sensitive thermoreceptors make the major contribution. However, since these presumed nociceptors may be active at skin temperatures likely to be experienced

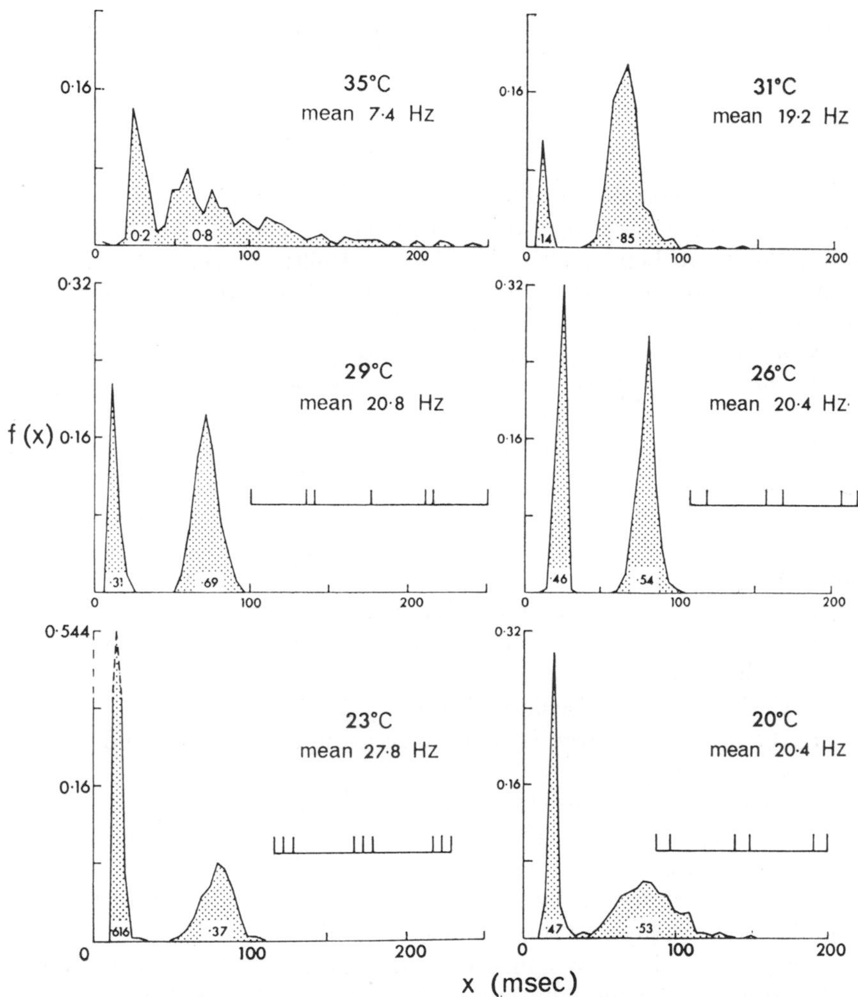

FIG. 5. Interspike interval histograms for the discharge of a "cold" thermoreceptor unit in the facial skin of a dog, at six different constant temperatures. At 29°C, 26°C, 23°C and 20°C the corresponding patterns of discharge are indicated by the inset diagrams. At both high and low temperatures the discharge was less regular than at intermediate temperatures. The mean frequencies of discharge are shown in cyc/sec.

in tropical conditions, their contribution at least to behavioural thermoregulation should not be overlooked.

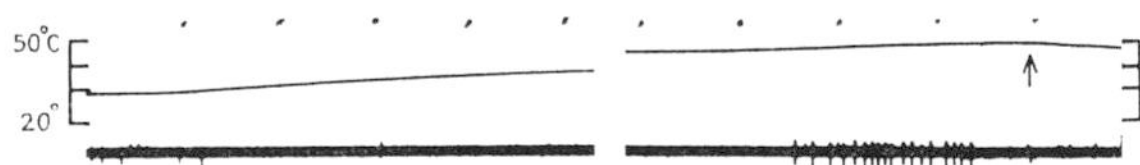

FIG. 6. Response of a "thermal" nociceptor in cat skin, during radiant heating of the skin. A response occurred at about 46°C. The upper trace records the skin temperature (from Iggo, 1959).

Primate cutaneous thermoreceptors

During the last decade there has been increasing attention paid to primate cutaneous sensory mechanisms (Iggo, 1963, 1964, 1969; Perl, 1968; Poulos & Lende, 1970a,b; Hensel, 1969; Hensel & Iggo, 1971; Kenshalo & Gallegos, 1967; Iggo & Ogawa, 1971) and to human skin (Hensel & Boman, 1960; Knibestöl & Vallbo, 1970).

Several distinctive features of primate receptors have been firmly established as a result of this work, but whether they are a consequence of greater specialization or of an adaptation to a tropical environment is not known. The similarities with non-primate species will be considered first. These are:

1. two categories of sensitive thermoreceptor, cold and warm, with static and dynamic sensitivity curves bearing a general similarity to the non-primates and
2. small, usually single, receptive fields for a single unit.

The more striking differences for thermoreceptors on the general body surface are

1. the peak static discharge frequency is higher,
2. the static discharge is invariably grouped over the mid-part of the temperature range,
3. there is a larger maximal number of impulses in a burst,
4. the majority of the cold units examined have myelinated afferent fibres (up to $3\mu m$ diam.),
5. the peak frequency of discharge during dynamic thermal stimulation is as high as 200 impulses/sec.

The general kind of response of cold units in hairy skin of the limbs is shown in Fig. 7 which illustrates the response of a single unit to four thermal stimuli. Each time the temperature was lowered rapidly there was a vigorous response from the cold unit which settled down after about 5 min to the discharges shown at the right. The conspicuous grouping of impulses in the static discharge is clearly seen in these

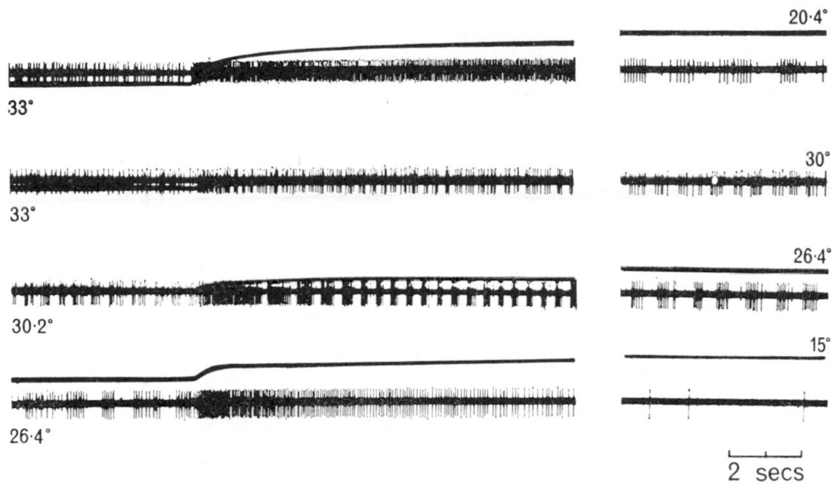

Fig. 7. Monkey "cold" receptor in hairy skin. In each record one trace shows the action potentials in the cold unit and a few smaller action potentials in unrelated units, and the temperature at the thermode/skin interface recorded with a thermistor. Each record was taken after the skin had been at the initial temperature for at least 5 min. The right-hand column of records shows the adapted discharge, at the temperatures indicated (from Iggo, 1969).

records. The static discharge has been examined, using "on-line" interspike interval histogram techniques, by A. Iggo & H. Ogawa (in prep.) and representative results for three units are shown in Fig. 8. The two cold units each carried a strongly grouped discharge at temperatures between 20°C and 30°C, indicated by the bimodal interval histograms whereas at higher and lower temperatures the interspike intervals were more regular in length, generating unimodal histograms. The warm unit, by contrast had a unimodal histogram at all temperatures tested, with peak activity at 44·8°C. The general pattern of cold unit activity for units was examined by pooling the data, for the range 35°C to 20°C with the results shown in Fig. 11. Over this range the pooled mean frequency showed little variation, peaking at 27°C. In earlier experiments (Iggo, 1969) the upper limit of the static sensitivity range was 38–43°C and the lower limit 12–23°C. Groups of impulses first appeared (Fig. 11) at 31°C, and had the effect of sharply increasing the peak frequency of discharge between 32°C and 31°C, although the mean frequency was little altered. At lower temperatures, down to 30°C there was a progressive increase in the number of impulses in each group, to a mean of four at 20°C. The mean frequency of discharge in each group as well as the frequency of groups per second were maximal at

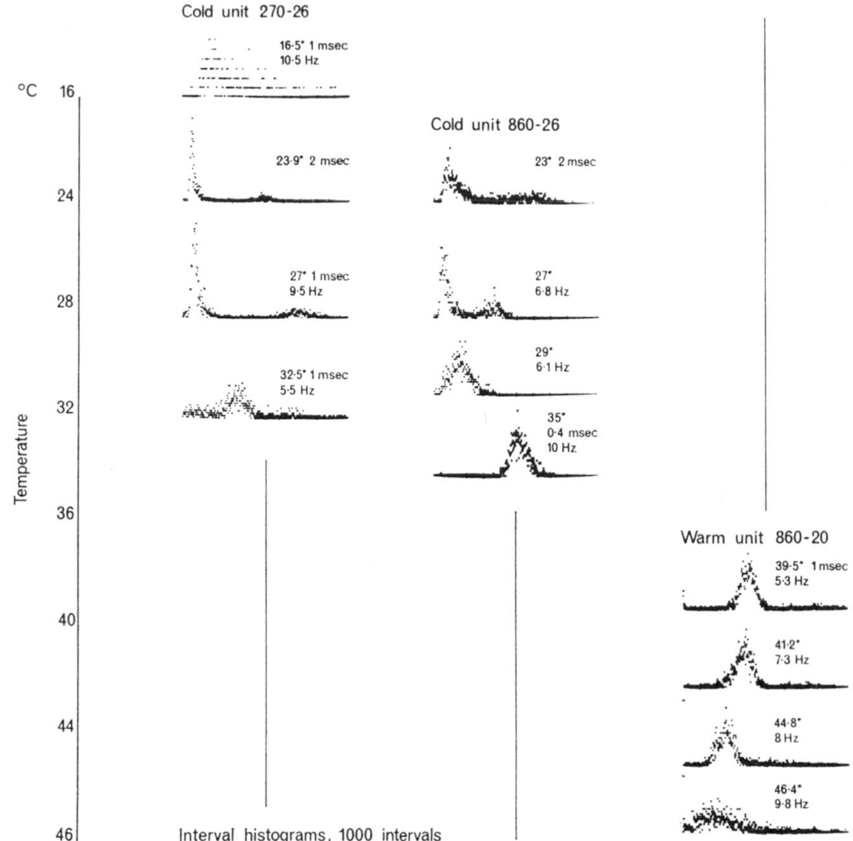

FIG. 8. Interval histograms for three monkey thermoreceptors. Each histogram, recorded under constant thermal conditions at the temperatures indicated, was generated by collecting 1000 impulse intervals. Both the "cold" units had bimodal histograms at intermediate temperatures, whereas the "warm" unit always had unimodal distributions. (From Iggo & Ogawa, 1970, unpubl. obs.)

27–28°C. The grouped character of the discharge thus had a dramatic effect on the information carrying capacity of the cold units as well as introducing a large difference in the cold unit discharge above and below neutral skin temperature.

The pattern of discharge in primate cutaneous cold units was examined in greater detail by Iggo & Iggo (1971), with the results shown in Fig. 10. In these experiments using *Cercopithecus* spp. at the University of Ibadan, Nigeria, the temporal pattern of discharge over the full range of dynamic sensitivity was examined by recording from single colds units dissected from the saphenous nerve while slowly changing the skin temperature from above 40°C to below 18°C at about 0·27°C/sec. The records in Fig. 10 are excerpts from a continuous strip record of the discharge and show the sequential changes in the discharge pattern. Figure 11 shows the changes in three parameters of discharge—in (a) the mean frequency, there is a progressive increase to a peak about

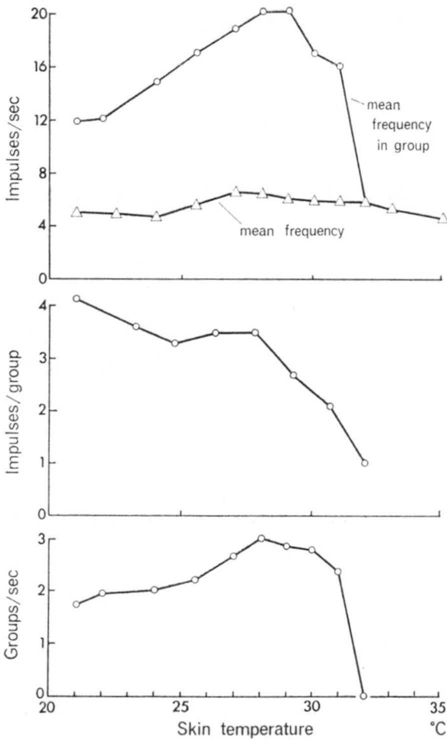

Fig. 9. Static temperature response curves for monkey "cold" units. The data for 19 cold units were pooled and average values are plotted. Groups of impulses were present at skin temperatures below 32°C, as indicated on the abscissa. This figure was prepared from interval histograms. (From Iggo & Ogawa, 1970, unpubl. obs.)

27°C followed by a decline at lower temperatures. The sudden emergence of groups of impulses is shown in (b), at nearly maximal frequency followed by a steep decline until the disappearance of groups just below 24°C. The most striking temperature dependence was shown by the number of impulses in each burst or group of spikes (c), which increased steadily from an average of two at the upper end of the response, to five at the lower end.

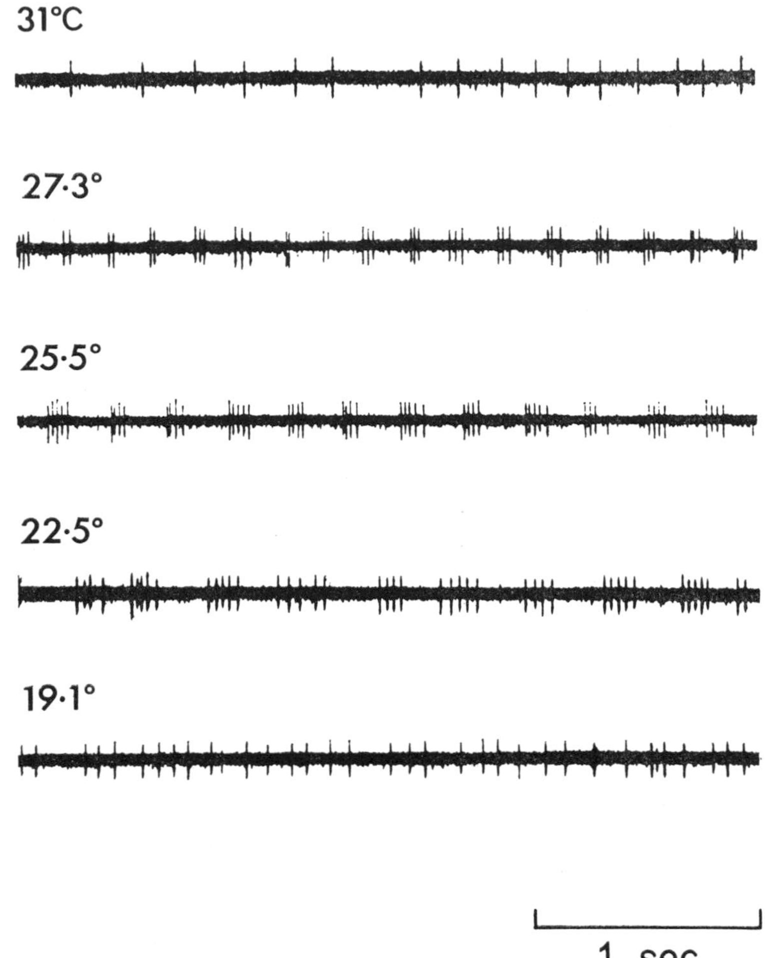

Fig. 10. Discharge in single "cold" thermoreceptor of *Cercopithecus aethiops* during continuous cooling of the skin, from 42°C to 15°C at 0·3°C/sec. The temperature at the left-hand-side refers to the start of each record (from Iggo & Iggo, 1971).

These results suggest that the cutaneous cold receptors are more highly developed than in the non-primate species studied, because:

1. Grouped discharge is present in cold receptors in the general skin surface, as described above, as well as, like the cat and dog, in facial skin where they have been reported in *Saimiri* monkeys by Poulos & Lende (1970a,b) and Poulos (1971), and where the cold receptors are more or less the same as those in the skin of the fore and hind limbs of other primates.

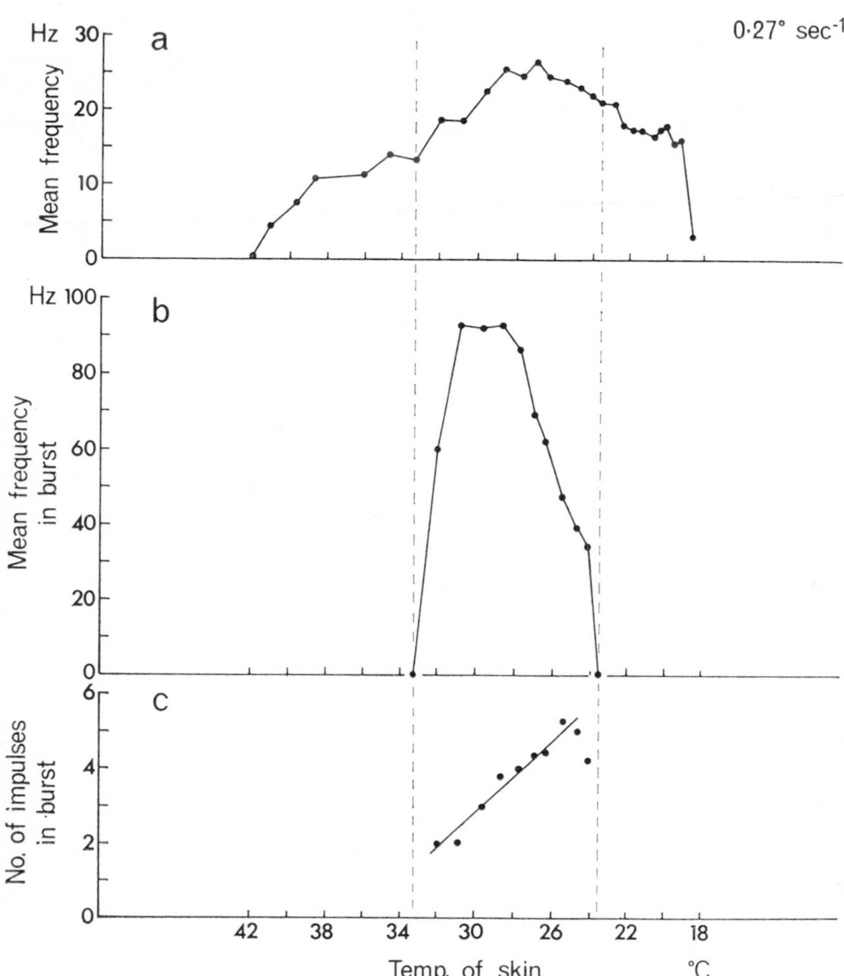

FIG. 11. Plots of the discharge characteristics of a cold unit of *Cercopithecus mona* during continuous cooling of the skin, as in Fig. 10. The upper curve shows the mean frequency of discharge, regardless of the pattern. The middle curve is the mean frequency of discharge within the bursts, which were present between 33°C and 23·5°C and the lower curve shows the number of impulses in a burst, at the indicated temperature (from Iggo & Iggo, 1971).

2. Grouped discharge is more strongly affected by temperature in primates, in particular, such parameters of the grouped discharge as number of impulses/burst and number of bursts/sec. In contrast the facial cold units of the dog illustrated in Figs 4 to 6 although affected by temperature were less variable in response, especially under dynamic conditions.

3. The axons of the cold units in peripheral nerves in the limbs were myelinated (Fig. 12) with the majority of the units lying in the range 3 to 12 m/sec, corresponding to diameters between 1 and 2 μm. The presence of myelin, by increasing both the conduction velocity and

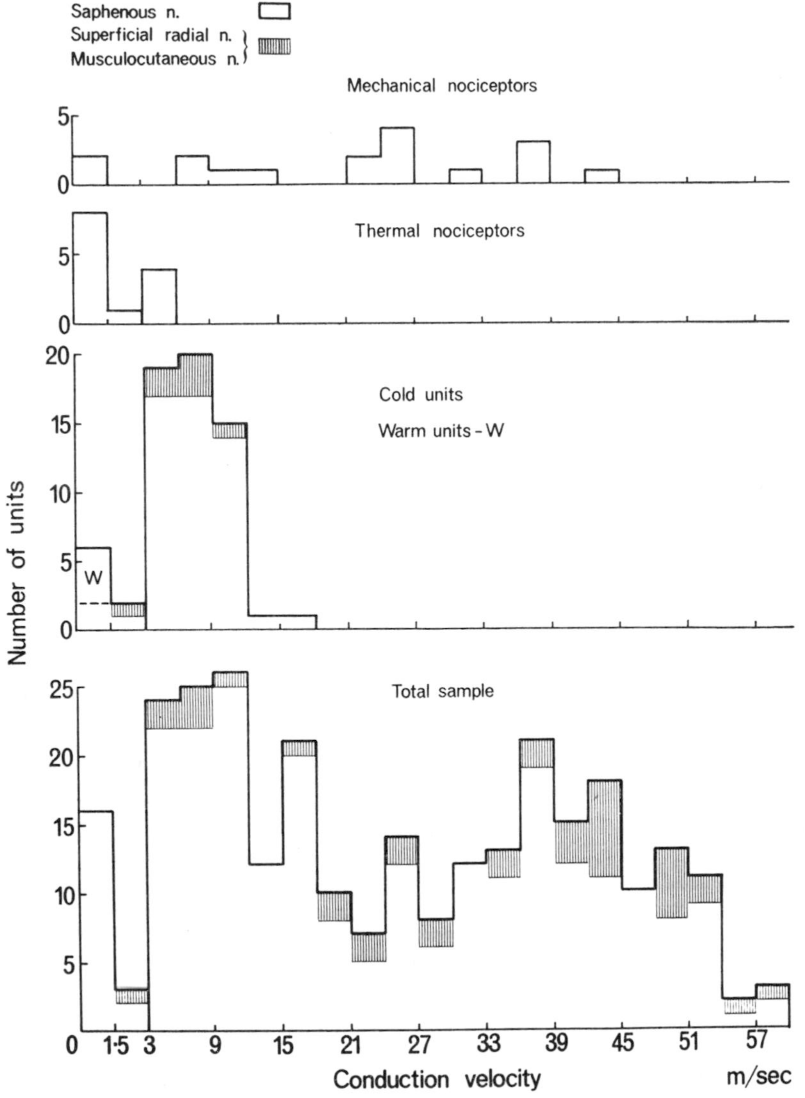

FIG. 12. Conduction velocities of a sample of cutaneous afferent fibres dissected from the saphenous, superficial radial or musculocutaneous nerves of monkeys (*Macacca* spp.). The thermoreceptors all had conduction velocities below 18 m/sec. (From Iggo & Ogawa. 1970, unpubl. obs.).

maximal impulse frequency capacity of the cold unit axons makes possible not only more rapid responses to temperature change but also an increase in information capacity in each channel.

The primates, therefore, can be expected to make more effective use of the environment in which they live. By a curious paradox, the warm units appeared to be less highly developed. As shown in Fig. 8 they do not carry a grouped discharge at any temperature nor, as reported by Hensel & Iggo (1971), do they have rapidly conducting nerve axons. They are capable nevertheless of firing at frequencies as high as 36 sec. There is also an indication from the work of Hensel & Iggo (1971) that there may be two kinds of sensitive warm receptor in primates, one with maximal response at 40–42°C, as in non-primates and the other with a maximum several degrees higher. These latter are distinct from the thermal nociceptors in two ways—the threshold is at least 10°C lower, and some of the primate thermal nociceptors are myelinated (Iggo & Ogawa, 1971).

Acknowledgements

I am grateful to the Leverhulme and Wellcome Trusts for financial support.

References

Andres, K. H. (1971). Structure of cutaneous receptors. *Proc. 25 Int. Physiol. Congr.* **8**: 136–137.

Bessou, P. & Perl, E. R. (1969). Response of cutaneous sensory units with unmyelinated fibers to noxious stimuli. *J. Neurophysiol.* **32**: 1025–1043.

Boyd, I. A. & Roberts, T. D. M. (1953). Proprioceptive discharges from stretch-receptors in the knee-joint of the cat. *J. Physiol.* **122**: 38–58.

Cauna, N. (1969). The fine morphology of the sensory receptor organs in the auricle of the rat. *J. comp. Neurol.* **136**: 81–98.

Chambers, M. R., Andres, K. H., von Duering, M. & Iggo, A. (1972). The structure and function of the slowly adapting Type II receptor in hairy skin. *Q. Jl. exp. Physiol.* (in press).

Dodt, E. (1952). The behaviour of thermoreceptors at low and high temperatures with special reference to Ebbecke's temperature phenomenon. *Acta physiol. scand.* **27**: 295–314.

Hensel, H. (1969). Cutane wärmereceptoren bei primaten. *Pflügers Arch. ges. Physiol.* **313**: 150–152.

Hensel, H. & Boman, K. K. A. (1960). Afferent impulses in cutaneous sensory nerves in human subjects. *J. Neurophysiol.* **23**: 564–578.

Hensel, H. & Iggo, A. (1971). Analysis of cutaneous warm and cold fibres in primates. *Pflügers Arch. ges. Physiol.* **329**: 1–8.

Hensel, H. & Witt, I. (1959). Spatial temperature gradient and thermoreceptor stimulation. *J. Physiol., Lond.* **148**: 180–187.

Hensel, H. & Wurster, R. D. (1970). Static properties of cold receptors in the nasal area of cats. *J. Neurophysiol.* **33**: 271–275.

Hensel, H. & Zotterman, Y. (1951). Quantitative beziehungen zwischen der entladung einzelner kältefasern und der temperatur. *Acta physiol. scand.* **23**: 291–319.

Hensel, H., Iggo, A. & Witt, I. (1960). A quantitative study of sensitive cutaneous thermoreceptors with C afferent fibres. *J. Physiol., Lond.* **153**: 113–126.

Iggo, A. (1959). Cutaneous heat and cold receptors with slowly-conducting (C) afferent fibres. *Q. Jl exp. Physiol.* **44**: 362–370.

Iggo, A. (1963). An electrophysiological analysis of afferent fibres in primate skin. *Acta neuroveg.* **24**: 225–240.

Iggo, A. (1964). Temperature discrimination in the skin. *Nature, Lond.* **204**: 481–483.

Iggo, A. (1968). Electrophysiological and histological studies of cutaneous mechanoreceptors. *The skin senses:* 84–111. Kenshalo, D. R., (ed.). Springfield: C. C. Thomas.

Iggo, A. (1969). Cutaneous thermoreceptors in primates and sub-primates. *J. Physiol., Lond.* **200**: 403–430.

Iggo, A. & Iggo, B. J. (1971). Impulse coding in primate cutaneous thermoreceptors in dynamic thermal conditions. *J. Physiol., Paris* **63**: 287–290.

Iggo, A. & Leek, B. F. (1967). The afferent innervation of the tongue of the sheep. In *Olfaction & Taste* **2**: 493–507. Hayashi, T. (ed.). Oxford: Pergamon Press.

Iggo, A. & Muir, A. R. (1969). The structure and function of a slowly adapting touch corpuscle in hairy skin. *J. Physiol., Lond.* **200**: 763–796.

Iggo, A. & Ogawa, H. (1971). Primate cutaneous thermal nociceptors. *J. Physiol., Lond.* **216**: 77*P*.

Iriuchijima, J. & Zotterman, Y. (1960). Afferent cutaneous C fibres in mammals. *Acta physiol. scand.* **49**: 267–278.

Kenshalo, D. R. & Gallegos, E. S. (1967). Multiple temperature-sensitive spots innervated by single nerve fibers. *Science, N.Y.* **158**: 1064.

Knibestöl, M. & Vallbo, A. B. (1970). Single unit analysis of mechanoreceptor activity from the human glabrous skin. *Acta physiol. scand.* **80**: 178–195.

Perl, E. R. (1968). Myelinated afferent fibres innervating the primate skin and their response to noxious stimuli. *J. Physiol., Lond.* **197**: 593–615.

Poulos, D. A. (1971). Temperature related changes in discharge patterns of squirrel monkey thermoreceptors. In *Research in physiology*. Kao, F. F., Koizumi, K. and Vassalle, M. (eds). Bologna: Aulo Gaggi.

Poulos, D. A. & Lende, R. A. (1970a). Response of trigeminal ganglion neurons to thermal stimulation of oral-facial regions. 1. Steady-state response. *J. Neurophysiol.* **33**: 508–517.

Poulos, D. A. & Lende, R. A. (1970b). Response of trigeminal ganglion neurons to thermal stimulation of oral-facial regions. II. Temperature change response. *J. Neurophysiol.* **33**: 518–526.

Symp. zool. Soc. Lond. (1972) No. 31, 345–356.

EVAPORATIVE TEMPERATURE REGULATION IN DOMESTIC ANIMALS

D. MCEWAN JENKINSON

Department of Physiology, The Hannah Research Institute, Ayr, Scotland

SYNOPSIS

Domestic animals lose heat in hot arid environments principally by evaporating water, through sweating, panting or both. The relative importance of these two avenues of moisture loss varies with the prevailing climatic conditions and is considerably different between species. The horse, donkey, camel and cow depend mainly on sweating although the cow also pants, while the sheep, goat, dog and pig rely much more on respiratory heat loss. The domestic mammals exhibit different patterns of cutaneous moisture loss, which have been tentatively explained on the basis of the relative importance of the secretory and myo-epithelial components of the sweat glands. Sweat gland activity is at least partly under the control of the sympathetic nervous system, but, with the possible exception of the horse, there appears to be a peripheral mechanism acting between nerve endings and the sweat glands (which are not innervated). The efficiency of panting also varies between species, the goat being less efficient than the ox and sheep. Sweating and panting can be produced by thermostimulation of the hypothalamus which appears to be the principal coordinating centre for body temperature regulation. The thermoregulatory reactions of domestic and other animals are, however, greatly affected by behavioural responses and by different combinations of environmental factors which complicate comparisons between species.

INTRODUCTION

Although in hot dry environments domestic mammals exhibit varying degrees of lability of body temperature, the camel having the most labile and the sheep the most stable body temperature, they are all homeotherms. Heat gained from metabolism of food or by radiation from the sun is dissipated by conduction, convection, radiation and by evaporation. As ambient temperature increases, however, the relative importance of Newtonian heat loss declines and the major source of heat dissipation in hot environments is evaporation. In the cow, for example, at an ambient temperature of 15°C, the heat loss by evaporation is only about 18% of the total whereas at 35°C evaporation accounts for about 85% of the total heat loss (J. A. McLean & D. Calvert, unpubl. data).

EVAPORATIVE HEAT LOSS BY PANTING AND SWEATING

The moisture evaporated from domestic mammals in hot arid environments is derived from two main sources

1. the skin, by sweating and to a lesser extent by insensible perspiration and
2. the respiratory tract, by panting.

The relative importance of these two main avenues of heat loss also varies with ambient temperature. The cow in an environment of 15°C loses 54% of its evaporative heat output by respiratory moisture loss but at 35°C, respiratory loss although higher, accounts for only about 36% of the greatly increased total evaporative loss. Other physical factors such as humidity and wind velocity can to a lesser extent also alter the proportion of heat loss from these two sources and physiological factors e.g. hair coat type play a part in modifying the relative output of moisture due to sweating and panting. For example in an ambient temperature of 40°C some 76% of the total evaporative loss from the very young unshorn lamb is by panting while a shorn lamb in the same environment loses only about 54% of its evaporative heat loss by this means (Alexander & Brook, 1960).

In addition to climatic influences and within species variations there are even more marked differences between species in their modes of evaporative response to a hot climate; some rely much more on sweating than others (Fig. 1). The donkey, which does not pant, and the camel, depend almost entirely on sweating for their evaporative cooling in hot environments (Schmidt-Nielsen, 1964; Schmidt-Nielsen, Schmidt-Nielsen, Jarnum & Houpt, 1957). The cow loses about two-thirds of its evaporative heat by sweating in contrast to the sheep which loses only about one-third by this means and relies more on panting. The sweat glands of the pig do not respond to heat (Ingram, 1967) and there is therefore a negligible contribution to total heat loss from skin evaporation which in this instance is apparently purely insensible water loss. Although the pig pants it survives in hot climates mainly by behavioural thermoregulation. By wallowing, a procedure which enables it to evaporate water at a rate comparable to sweating in man, the pig can improve its heat tolerance. By wallowing in mud rather than in water it can sustain a high evaporation rate for more than 2 h (Ingram, 1965). Desert rodents, which are devoid of sweat glands, do not sweat nor do they increase their respiratory rate in response to heat. They can, however, spread saliva over their bodies to assist body temperature control (Hainsworth, 1967) but many such as the kangaroo rat avoid stressful environments by burrowing (Schmidt-Nielsen, 1964). The

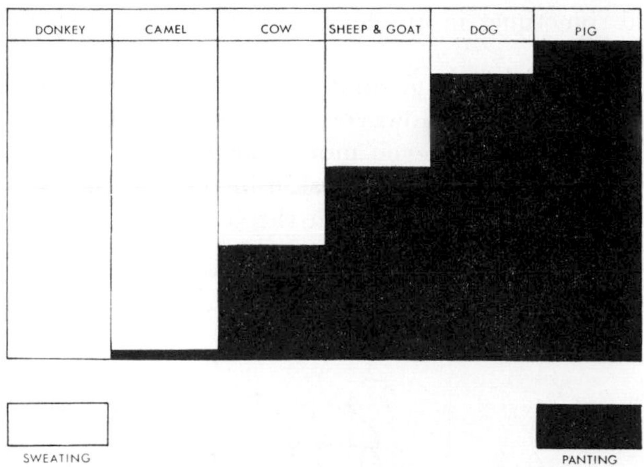

FIG. 1. A diagram illustrating the relative contribution of sweating and panting to evaporative heat loss from different domestic animals in a hot, dry environment. Insensible perspiration and non-panting respiratory heat loss account for a relatively small amount of the total loss under these conditions.

large domestic animals, however, depend largely on sweating and/or panting for body temperature regulation in the heat.

SWEATING IN DOMESTIC MAMMALS

Sweat glands are present in the skin of the buffalo, camel, cat, cow, dog, horse, llama, sheep, goat and pig. These tubular glands consist of a fundus or body and a long straight duct. The fundus wall consists of two layers of epithelium, an inner secretory epithelium, the cells of which are generally flat or cuboidal with round nuclei and an outer myo-epithelium of canoe-shaped cells with oval nuclei. The sweat glands of domestic animals are always associated with a hair follicle as part of what is termed the "hair follicle unit" and open into the hair follicle canal (Jenkinson, 1965). Not all hair follicles, however have an accompanying sweat gland. In the buffalo, cow, horse and pig there is a sweat gland associated with each hair follicle but in the camel, sheep, goat and dog the hairs are grouped and only the large primary hairs have a sweat gland associated with them. In some breeds with a high secondary/primary hair ratio there is therefore, a small number of sweat glands in relation to the dense fine undercoat which mitigates against efficient evaporative heat loss. This is especially true of the sheep the wool of which is hygroscopic and its uptake of water results in an exothermic reaction and sometimes in an elevated skin temperature on sweating (Bligh, 1967).

The density of sweat glands/unit area of skin varies between individuals and between breeds. However, the differences in density between the domestic mammals are even more marked. For example there are only about 20–30 sweat glands/cm^2 skin in the pig compared with 200 in the camel, sheep and goat, 400 in the buffalo (*Bos bulbalis*) and as

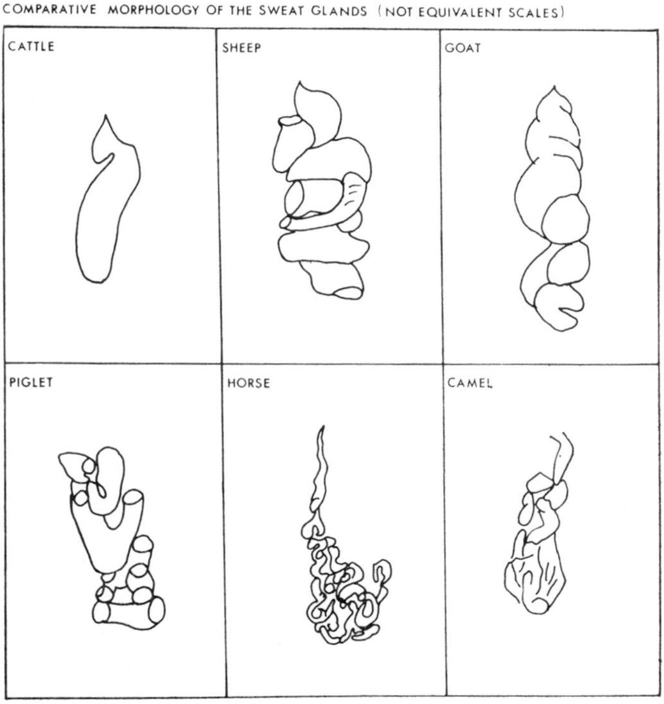

COMPARATIVE MORPHOLOGY OF THE SWEAT GLANDS (NOT EQUIVALENT SCALES)

CATTLE SHEEP GOAT

PIGLET HORSE CAMEL

FIG. 2. A diagram illustrating some of the different shapes of sweat gland found in domestic animals.

many as 2000 in some Zebu cattle. Species differences in the appearance of the sweat gland fundus also occur as can be seen from the examples in Fig. 2. A wide range of sweat gland shape is also found within species as typified by the cow in which three entirely different skin types have been identified (D. McEwan Jenkinson & T. Nay unpubl. data).

Although the differences in sweat gland density and possibly sweat gland shape are of significance in explaining the differences in sweating efficiency observed in the different domestic mammals, the physiological activity of the gland appears to be a more important factor. In the cow the density of sweat glands is similar over the general body surface yet the evaporative loss from the skin is considerably greater on the neck than on the ventral surface of the body (McLean, 1963).

Skin evaporative loss in different domestic species

Different patterns of evaporative loss from the skin reflecting different modes of sweat gland function have been described (Fig. 3). These records have been obtained by study of the moisture loss from skin areas of known dimensions using ventilated capsules. The examples given in Fig. 3 are taken from the work of different authors. On heat exposure, after a short latent period the sheep and goat exhibit discrete discharges of sweat which have been shown to occur synchronously all over the body (Bligh, 1961). In the cow there is a stepwise increase in sweating to a maximum which is then sustained (McLean, 1963). The horse also shows fluctuations in sweat output as sweating increases with heat exposure. These fluctuations are particularly marked in the burro (Bullard, Dill & Yousef, 1970). The camel appears to have a longer latent period prior to sweating than the other domestic animals and exhibits a smooth onset of sweating when it does occur. Bligh (1967) postulated that these different sweating patterns could be explained in terms of the relative importance of the action of the secretory cells and myo-epithelium of the glands. For example, the synchronous discharge pattern of the sheep and goat could be due mainly to myo-epithelial expulsion of the glandular contents, the secretory process being slow and uncontrolled. The stepwise increase in cattle can be considered as being due to myo-epithelial contractions superimposed on a secretory rate rapidly rising to a maximum level, and the smooth rise in sweating of the camel to secretory function with little or no myo-epithelial activity. The sweat gland myo-epithelia of domestic animals tend to have the same diameter/unit gland diameter and if they are involved in sweat output their frequency of contraction would appear to be of greater importance than the relative strength of each contraction (Jenkinson, 1971).

Figure 3 shows that although sweating is sustained in the cow, donkey and camel, the magnitude of response in the sheep and goat declines at each discharge. In the goat after about 1 h no further discharges of sweat occur if the animals are maintained in the hot environment for a further 5 h (Jenkinson & Robertshaw, 1971). This apparent fatigue is not due to a decline in the number of active glands but rather to the rate of expulsion exceeding the rate of sweat production. The inability of the sheep and goat to sustain a high sweat output is reflected in their greater dependence on respiratory heat loss.

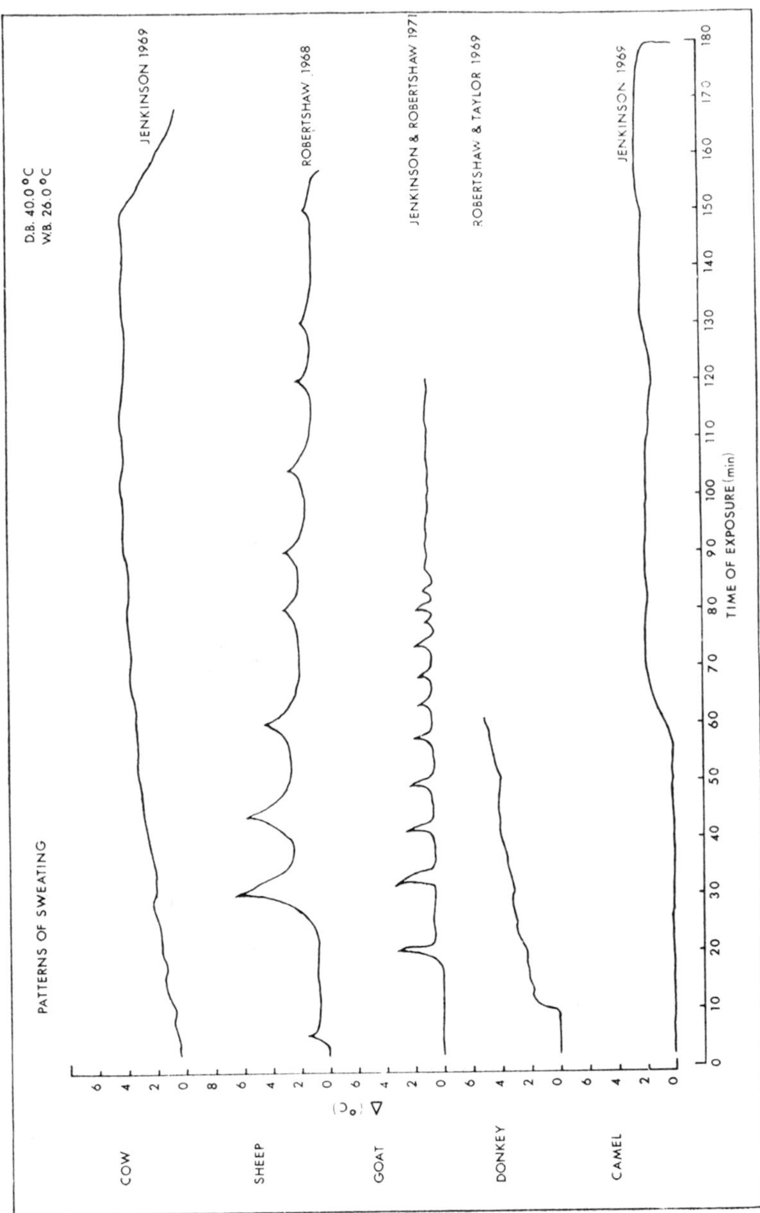

Fig. 3. A diagram compiled from the work of various authors to illustrate the different patterns of cutaneous evaporative loss in domestic species.

The different patterns of cutaneous moisture loss also illustrate the inadvisability of comparing only the sweat output in different species, especially if measured shortly after the onset of sweating. The mean sweat gland secretory rate in the goat, during the phase of sweating, has been estimated at 0·013 μl/h/gland compared with a rate of 0·016 μl/h in the ox (Jenkinson & Robertshaw, 1971). Although the sweat gland output is similar in these two species during sweating, it is clear that the goat does not sustain such an output. The efficiency of sweating therefore depends not only on the amount of sweat produced per unit time but also on the output being sustained over a prolonged period. No direct comparisons of sweat output between species have been made in this review since most of the data on sweating rates have been taken shortly after the onset of sweating, and not at intervals during sudomotor activity. The pattern of sweating output can also be influenced by other factors such as dehydration. On exposure to heat the dehydrated steer exhibits a longer latent period prior to sweating than the hydrated animal. The onset of sweating can be delayed for more than 2 h and the magnitude of response is often less than in hydrated animals (Bianca, 1965).

Control of sweat gland activity

The sweat glands of most of the domestic animals respond to heat (Fig. 4) and therefore play some part in thermoregulation. The pig is a notable exception (Ingram, 1967). In all the species studied to date the sympathetic nervous system has been shown to be involved in the control of sweat gland activity. In the cow, sheep and goat, for example,

Factors involved in the stimulation of sweat gland activity and the control of heat-induced sweating

Species	Response to heat	Pharmacological response		Involvment of sympathetic nervous system	Involvment of adrenal medulla	Sweat gland innervation
		Adrenaline	Acetylcholine			
Equine	+	+	+	+	–	+
Camel	+	+	–	*	*	–
Cow	+	+	–	+	–	–
Sheep	+	+	–	+	–	–
Goat	+	+	–	+	–	–
Dog	+	+	+	+	–	–
Pig	–	+	–	+	*	–

* No evidence traced

FIG. 4. A summary of factors involved in sweat gland stimulation and control. The data are from the work of a number of authors.

sympathectomy greatly reduces heat-induced sweat gland activity (Findlay & Robertshaw, 1965; Robertshaw, 1968) and secretion from the adrenal medulla does not appear to be involved in the controlling mechanism. This is true also of heat-induced sweating in the donkey (Robertshaw & Taylor, 1969) although in this species circulating adrenaline from the adrenal gland plays an active part in exercise-induced sweating. The sweat glands of domestic mammals appear therefore, to be under the control of the sympathetic nervous system. The sweat glands of all the domestic mammals studied to date respond to the hormone adrenaline but only those of the horse and dog respond to acetylcholine. Atropine does not, however, block heat-induced sweating in the horse and the haired skin of the dog (Aoki & Wada, 1951). The cholinergic response of the glands in these species is not apparently part of the controlling mechanism of heat-induced sweating. As can be seen from Fig. 4 only the sweat glands of the horse appear to be innervated (Jenkinson, Sengupta & Blackburn, 1966; Jenkinson & Blackburn, 1967a,b, 1968a,b). In domestic mammals apart perhaps from the horse, there would seem to be a peripheral mechanism possibly humeral in nature, but as yet unknown, acting between the sympathetic nerve endings and the sweat gland. In view of the action of adrenaline on the sweat glands this hormone could conceivably be a transmitter substance and hence attempts have been made to locate stores of catecholamine in the skin. Using a fluorescent microscopical technique Thompson, Robertshaw & Findlay (1969) found dopamine-containing cells in the skin of cattle but these have been shown to be mast cells which are probably not specifically involved in sudomotor activity (Jenkinson, Thompson, Kenny & Pearson, 1970). Due to natural auto-fluorescence of the sweat glands it has not been possible using such techniques to determine whether or not they have their own catecholamine stores. Adrenaline has been found in horse sweat (Brunaud & Pitre, 1945) and catecholamine metabolites have been detected on the skin of cattle. It is possible that adrenaline may be the link between the sympathetic nervous system and the sweat gland but this point has still to be resolved. The nature of the peripheral mechanism and the mode of action of adrenaline on the sweat glands have still to be determined.

PANTING IN DOMESTIC ANIMALS

Apart from the horse and camel, the domestic animals respond to a hot environment by greatly increasing respiratory rate and decreasing tidal volume. The efficiency of the response is not the same in every instance however as can be seen from Fig. 5. This Table, the data for

Comparison of thermally-induced respiratory responses at 40°C

RH :	49 % :	20-30% :	35-45 %
	Change from control conditions		
	Ox	Sheep	Goat
Tr	+0·9°C	+0·5°C	+1·2°C
f	+484 %	+674%	+800%
Vt	-49%	-74%	-32%
Va	+9%	+81%	+246%
$PaCO_2$	-11%	-29%	-41%
Ve	+203 %	+97%	+509 %

FIG. 5. The differences in rectal temperature (*Tr*) and the percentage change in respiratory frequency (*f*), tidal volume (*Vt*), alveolar ventilation (*Va*), partial pressure of carbon dioxide in the arterial blood ($PaCO_2$) and respiratory minute volume (*Ve*) in the ox, sheep and goat at 40°C compared with lower control conditions.

which were obtained from the work of Hales & Findlay (1968a); Hales & Webster (1967) and Heisey, Adams, Hofman & Riegle (1971), illustrates the percentage change in various respiratory parameters in the ox, sheep and goat at 40°C compared with fairly thermoneutral conditions. Although the humidity was not precisely the same for each of the three species studied this does not appreciably affect the values given or invalidate the comparison. The increase in rectal temperature is very small in all three species. However, the goat shows a greater change in respiratory frequency (*f*) and smaller decrease in tidal volume (*Vt*) than the ox and sheep. This results not only in a much greater respiratory minute volume (*Ve*) but also in an increase in alveolar ventilation (*Va*) and lower arterial partial pressure of CO_2 ($PaCO_2$) than in the ox and sheep. In all three species the panting response to heat, although mainly involving evaporative heat exchange in the upper respiratory tract, also involves an increase in alveolar ventilation, the magnitude of which in the goat makes it much more susceptible to respiratory alkalosis. The oxygen cost of panting is relatively low; in the pig for example it is less than 17% of the total at 40°C (Ingram & Legge, 1969). The dog has a higher oxygen cost of panting compared with the ox and sheep and it has been suggested that this may be the result of a higher proportion of inspired air going to the alveoli—a form of breathing which requires more oxygen (Hales & Findlay, 1968b). This may also be true of the goat compared with the ox and sheep and thereby indicate a genuine difference between the efficiency of thermally induced hyperventilation between the domestic species.

In very hot environments the nature of panting may change; respiratory rate falls and tidal volume increases against a background of an increasing ventilation rate. This form of respiration, "second phase breathing", is the last line of defence against extreme conditions for panting animals and results in still greater heat loss but it also induces severe respiratory alkalosis and has a high oxygen cost.

CENTRAL CONTROL OF SWEATING AND PANTING

Sweating, panting and other thermoregulatory responses can be produced by thermostimulation of the skin, spinal cord and hypothalamus and by electrical and pharmacological stimulation of the hypothalamus (Bligh, 1966; Hammel, 1968; Thauer, 1970). The anterior hypothalamus is therefore a temperature sensitive region. It is also, however, the principal coordinating centre for body temperature regulation. This region of the brain appears to be a focal point for afferent information on temperature from other regions such as the skin and spinal cord and is now generally accepted as a regulatory centre. There is still controversy, however, regarding the part the hypothalamus plays, relative to other thermosensitive regions in overall body temperature control (Benzinger, 1969). In domestic animals, however, the evidence to date supports the view of Hammel *et al.* (1963) that heat dissipation and conservation result from coordination by the hypothalamus of information from different thermoreceptors including the skin, nasobucal region (Bligh, 1959) and hypothalamus itself.

Much of the knowledge to date concerning physiological responses of animals to hot environments has been obtained using well-fed, hydrated animals in controlled temperatures. Different combinations of environmental factors modify the basic thermoregulatory reactions, as does dehydration on sweating, thereby complicating comparisons between species. The tolerance of domestic and other animals to hot conditions is also affected by behavioural responses. Some of these environmental influences and animal responses will be dealt with in subsequent chapters of this book.

REFERENCES

Alexander, G. & Brook, A. H. (1960). Loss of heat by evaporation in young lambs. *Nature, Lond.* **185**: 770–771.

Aoki, T. & Wada, M. (1951). Functional activity of the sweat glands in the hairy skin of the dog. *Science, N.Y.* **114**: 123–124.

Benzinger, T. H. (1969). Heat regulation: Homeostasis of central temperature in man. *Physiol. Rev.* **49**: 671–759.

Bianca, W. (1965). Sweating in dehydrated steers. *Res. vet. Sci.* **6**: 33–37.

Bligh, J. (1959). The receptors concerned in the thermal stimulus to panting in the sheep. *J. Physiol., Lond.* **146**: 142–151.

Bligh, J. (1961). The synchronous discharge of apocrine sweat glands of the Welsh Mountain sheep. *Nature, Lond.* **189**: 582–583.

Bligh, J. (1966). The thermosensitivity of the hypothalamus and thermoregulation in mammals. *Biol. Rev.* **41**: 317–367.

Bligh, J. (1967). A thesis concerning the process of secretion and discharge of sweat. *Envir. Res.* **1**: 28–45.

Brunaud, M. & Pitre, J. (1945). Existe-t-il de l'adrénaline dans la suer du Cheval? *Bull. Acad. vet. Fr.* **18**: 339–347.

Bullard, R. W., Dill, D. B. & Yousef, M. K. (1970). Responses of the burro to desert heat stress. *J. appl. Physiol.* **29**: 159–167.

Findlay, J. D. & Robertshaw, D. (1965). The role of the sympatho-adrenal system in the control of sweating in the ox (*Bos taurus*). *J. Physiol., Lond.* **179**: 285–297.

Hainsworth, F. R. (1967). Saliva spreading, activity and body temperature regulation in the rat. *Am. J. Physiol.* **212**: 1288–1292.

Hales, J. R. S. & Findlay, J. D. (1968a). Respiration of the ox: normal values and the effects of exposure to hot environments. *Respir. Physiol.* **4**: 333–352.

Hales, J. R. S. & Findlay, J. D. (1968b). The oxygen cost of thermally-induced and CO_2-induced hyperventilation in the ox. *Respir. Physiol.* **4**: 353–362.

Hales, J. R. S. & Webster, M. E. D. (1967). Respiratory function during thermal tachypnoea in sheep. *J. Physiol., Lond.* **190**: 241–260.

Hammel, H. T. (1968). Regulation of internal body temperature. *A. Rev. Physiol.* **30**: 641–710.

Hammel, H. T., Jackson, D. C., Stolwijk, J. A. J., Hardy, J. D. & Strømme, S. B. (1963). Temperature regulation by hypothalamic proportional control with an adjustable set point. *J. appl. Physiol.* **18**: 1146–1154.

Heisey, S. R., Adams, T., Hofman, W. & Riegle, G. (1971). Thermally induced respiratory responses of the unanaesthetised goat. *Respir. Physiol.* **11**: 145–151.

Ingram, D. L. (1965). Evaporative cooling in the pig. *Nature, Lond.* **207**: 415–416.

Ingram, D. L. (1967). Stimulation of cutaneous glands in the pig. *J. comp. Path.* **77**: 93–98.

Ingram, D. L. & Legge, K. F. (1969). The effect of environmental temperature on respiratory ventilation in the pig. *Respir. Physiol.* **8**: 1–12.

Jenkinson, D. McEwan (1965). The skin of domestic animals. In the *Comparative physiology and pathology of the skin*: 591–608. Rook, A. J. & Walton, G. S., (eds). Oxford: Blackwell Scientific Publications.

Jenkinson, D. McEwan (1969). Sweat gland function in domestic animals. In *The exocrine glands*: 201–221. Botelho, Stella, Y., Brooks, F. P. & Shelley, W. B., (eds). Philadelphia: University of Pennsylvania Press.

Jenkinson, D. McEwan (1971). Myo-epithelial cells of the sweat glands of domestic animals. *Res. vet. Sci.* **12**: 152–155.

Jenkinson, D. McEwan & Blackburn, P. S. (1967a). The distribution of nerves, monoamine oxidase and cholinesterase in the skin of the sheep and goat. *J. Anat.* **101**: 333–341.

Jenkinson, D. McEwan & Blackburn, P. S. (1967b). The distribution of nerves, monamine oxidase and cholinesterase in the skin of the pig. *Res. vet. Sci* **8**: 306–312.

Jenkinson, D. McEwan & Blackburn, P. S. (1968a). The distribution of nerves, monamine oxidase and cholinesterase in the skin of the horse. *Res. vet. Sci.* **9**: 165–169.

Jenkinson, D. McEwan & Blackburn, P. S. (1968b). The distribution of nerves, monoamine oxidase and cholinesterase in the skin of the cat and dog. *Res. vet. Sci.* **9**: 521–528.

Jenkinson, D. McEwan & Robertshaw, D. (1971). Studies on the nature of sweat gland "fatigue" in the goat. *J. Physiol., Lond.* **212**: 455–465.

Jenkinson, D. McEwan, Sengupta, B. P. & Blackburn, P. S. (1966). The distribution of nerves, monoamine oxidase and cholinesterase in the skin of cattle. *J. Anat.* **100**: 593–613.

Jenkinson, D. McEwan, Thompson, G. E., Kenny, J. D. R. & Pearson, J. M. (1970). Histochemical studies on mast cells in cattle skin. *Histochem J.* **2**: 419–424.

McLean, J. A. (1963). The regional distribution of cutaneous moisture vaporization in the Ayrshire calf. *J. agric. Sci. Camb.* **61**: 275–280.

Robertshaw, D. (1968). The pattern and control of sweating in the sheep and goat. *J. Physiol., Lond.* **198**: 531–539.

Robertshaw, D. & Taylor, C. R. (1969). Sweat gland function of the donkey (*Equus asinus*). *J. Physiol., Lond.* **205**: 79–87.

Schmidt-Nielsen, K. (1964). *Desert animals.* Oxford: Oxford University Press.

Schmidt-Nielsen, K., Schmidt-Nielsen, B., Jarnum, S. A. & Houpt, T. R. (1957). Body temperature of the camel and its relation to water economy. *Am. J. Physiol.* **188**: 103–112.

Thauer, R. (1970). Thermosensitivity of the spinal cord. In *Physiological and behavioural temperature regulation*: 472–492. Hardy, J. D., Gagge, A. P. & Stolwijk, J. A. J. (eds). Springfield: C. C. Thomas.

Thompson, G. E., Robertshaw, D. & Findlay, J. D. (1969). Noradrenergic innervation of the arrectores pilorum muscles of the ox (*Bos taurus*). *Can. J. Physiol. Pharmacol.* **47**: 310–311.

Symp. zool. Soc. Lond. (1972) No. 31, 357–369

EVAPORATIVE HEAT LOSS IN HOT ARID ENVIRONMENTS

JOHN BLIGH

ARC Institute of Animal Physiology, Babraham, Cambridge, England

SYNOPSIS

Evaporative heat loss is necessary for the maintenance of homeothermy whenever the thermal gradient from organism to environment precludes the balancing of heat production and heat gain with non-evaporative heat loss. Evaporation may be increased by wallowing, saliva-spreading, panting or sweating. An evolutionary progression from "primitive" behavioural wallowing to the autonomic process of sweating is possible, but the propensity of a species for one evaporative process or another is probably related to the past and present interaction between the species and its *total* environment. This may include, besides heat load, activity level, availability of shelter and of water, and seasonal and nycthemeral variations in meteorological conditions.

General structural and functional differences between species relate to the different total environments, past and present, of each species; evolutionary selection of one mode of evaporative heat loss rather than another may reflect these different influences. For example, the need for supercutaneous insulation against seasonal or nocturnal cold may have retarded the development of cutaneous evaporative heat loss during seasonal or diurnal heat; or the insulation of a supercutaneous coat against solar radiation may be, or have been, more advantageous than a capacity to discharge sweat onto relatively naked skin.

Panting may have advantages over sweating in some environmental conditions because an insulative coat does not interfere with respiration. However, the net effectiveness of panting (energy lost per unit of water evaporated minus the energy expended on forced convection for the evaporation) apparently declines as body size increases, so panting may be relatively ineffective in large animals. For the sustained activity of hunting as in man or of flight from predators as in horses, sweating has distinct advantages over panting. Copious sweating may therefore be related more to the internal heat load of muscular work than to the external heat load.

Mammals also vary in their degrees of thermal stability. Daily or seasonal variations in body temperature, apparently tolerated by some species, may be related to limitations in the availability of food or water. The survival value of the thermolability of some large species of mammals in hot arid environments may be attributable to the resultant conservation of body fluids.

INTRODUCTION

Until relatively recently it was customary to divide the animal kingdom into two distinct groups: the *poikilotherms* which exert no control over body temperature which consequently varies with that of the environment, and the *homeotherms* which control body temperature by physiological means so that it is maintained at a relatively steady level despite quite large variations in ambient temperature.

However, even if those species which enter a state of torpor daily or seasonally are excluded from consideration, mammals cannot be described as homeothermic without a fairly liberal interpretation being placed on the meaning of the word.

If the difference between core and ambient temperature is sufficiently great heat will flow passively down a variable thermal gradient at the same rate as it is being produced in the body. When the difference is insufficient the heat content, and therefore the body temperature, must rise unless the animal can use an evaporative heat loss process to restore the balance between heat production and heat loss. If all mammals were truly homeothermic the ability to tolerate heat stress would depend almost entirely on the ability to lose heat by an evaporative process, and a rise in body temperature would be indicative of the inadequacy of this process to cope with the heat load. Since homeothermy ultimately depends on the evaporation from a body surface of an aqueous fluid which must be replaced, the maintenance of a stable body temperature and the tolerance of hot arid environments might be physiologically incompatible.

Bligh & Harthoorn (1965) showed that even in the absence of extreme heat stress and when water is readily available, the extent of the daily variation in body temperature varies between species (Fig. 1). The sheep referred to in Fig. 1 were a native East African breed on the equator in Uganda but a similar fine control of body temperature was also found in unrestrained Welsh Mountain sheep in Britain (Bligh, Ingram, Keynes & Robinson, 1965) and in the wild Soay sheep which inhabit a small island of the St. Kilda group in the North Atlantic (J. Bligh & S. G. Robinson, unpubl. obs.). Since the sheep starts to pant immediately upon exposure to heat (Bligh, 1959), and can maintain the stability of body temperature by evaporative heat loss when the ambient temperature is equal to or greater than body temperature, there is every reason to assume that the sheep is an obligatory homeotherm whose heat tolerance depends on the availability of water and on the capacity of the animal to lose heat by evaporation.

The camel, at the other end of the spectrum, has a much more variable deep body temperature even when water is readily available. This was first reported by Schmidt-Nielsen, Schmidt-Nielsen, Jarnum & Houpt (1957) who found that the extent of this variation in body temperature increased when the animal was deprived of water. Schmidt-Nielsen *et al.* (1957) have suggested that this increase in daily swing in body temperature when the animal is dehydrated is an adaptive function

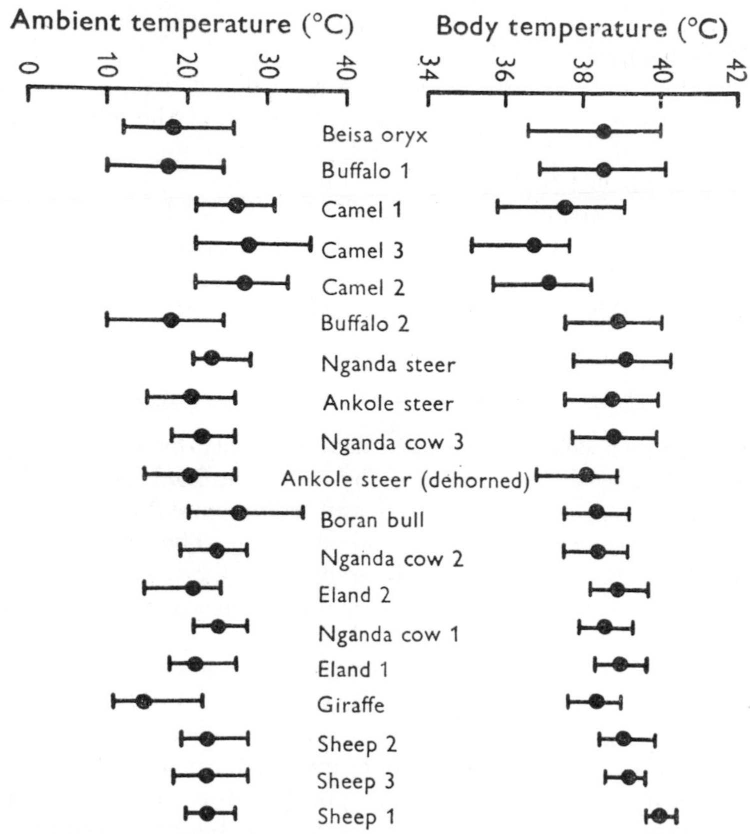

FIG. 1. The extent of the variations in the core temperature of some unrestrained animals recorded continuously during a 24-h period by a radiotelemetric technique. The extent of the variations in ambient temperature during these 24-h periods is also shown (lower series). The filled circles indicate the mean temperatures during the 24-h periods (from Bligh & Harthoorn, 1965).

of an animal which inhabits a hot arid environment, and that this adaptation greatly reduces the evaporative heat loss which would otherwise be needed to stabilize body temperature.

Thus the sheep is tolerant of a hot environment because of its ability to lose enough heat by evaporation from the respiratory tract to maintain thermal stability, while the camel is tolerant of a hot dry environment because it allows its body temperature to rise thus obviating the need for evaporative heat loss and this in turn results in a concomitant conservation of water. These two examples may be near opposite ends of a continuous spectrum of species exhibiting variations both in their degrees of thermostability, and in their use of evaporative heat loss to achieve heat tolerance.

Both time and data are inadequate for a detailed discussion of the relations between these physiological variables and the environmental conditions to which species are best adapted. I can only consider briefly three topics which I find particularly interesting:

1. species variations in the means of losing heat by evaporation;

2. a possible central nervous function concerning thermostability and lability, and

3. the possible need for a more broadly based concept of "heat tolerance".

PROCESSES AND PATTERNS OF EVAPORATIVE HEAT LOSS

In different species evaporative heat loss may be achieved by the behavioural process of wallowing, by the combined autonomic and behavioural processes of salivation and saliva-spreading, and by the autonomic processes of panting and sweating. There has been surprisingly little discussion on this diversity of evaporative processes and of the merits of one process rather than another in a particular ecological situation.

Wallowing in water, urine or mud might seem to be a primitive evaporative process since it does not involve the evolution of specialized secretory organs. However, it may be doubted whether the complexly integrated patterns of neuronal activity involved in behavioural functions are necessarily more primitive than a purely autonomic function which involves considerably less complex relations between stimulus and response. Furthermore, wallowing is used by such species as the pig and the water-buffalo which would not be regarded as "primitive" mammals by other standards.

Saliva-spreading is another so called primitive function, and is used by some marsupial species (Robinson & Morrison, 1957) but there is now some doubt whether the marsupials, in general, deserve to be regarded as primitive thermoregulators. Licking is also used by the rat which neither sweats nor pants (Hainsworth & Stricker, 1970). This species cannot be classified as "primitive" by other criteria, and it must be assumed that there is some particular virtue in this method of evaporative heat loss in relation to the rat's habitat.

Panting seems to be the most general means of losing heat by evaporation. It occurs in contemporary reptiles, birds and mammals and while parallel evolution of the mechanism in these three orders cannot be discounted, its presence in the reptilian progenitors of the birds and mammals is the favoured proposition. Hammel (1968) has indicated that panting probably is the most common means of evaporative heat loss in mammals and that it preceded the evolution of sweating as a thermoregulatory function.

Although sweat glands occur in association with the hair follicles in the majority of the mammalian species that have been examined, including some of the marsupials (Green, 1961; Mann, 1968), there is no ground for assuming that the glands always have a thermoregulatory function. Recent comparative studies of the patterns of discharge of fluid from the skin have shown that the activity of the epitrichial sweat glands varies greatly between species. There is no evidence of any discharge at all in response to heat stress in the pig (Ingram, 1967) or the red deer (K. G. Johnson, G. M. O. Maloiy & J. Bligh unpubl. data). In other species that have been studied (Allen & Bligh, 1969; Robertshaw & Taylor, 1969), the changes in the activity of the epitrichial sweat glands during heat exposure vary widely from species to species. In the sheep there is a small increase in the frequency of the occasional brief discharges of sweat which are of questionable thermoregulatory significance, whereas in the horse, cow and buffalo there is a high rate of maintained sweat discharge.

Thus the current evidence indicates that the activities of the sweat glands may be of thermoregulatory significance only in some species. It seems likely, therefore, that their general occurrence is connected with another earlier and unknown function.

This species variation in the processes of evaporative heat loss probably does not relate simply to the intensity of the heat stress experienced by the species in a tropical environment: naked sweating man has no obvious advantage over the fleece-covered panting sheep. Indeed, when the intensity of solar radiation is high, the advantage seems to be with the sheep. However, adaptation is generally to the total environment, rather than to a single component. Presumably there were some circumstances other than heat stress in which there is survival value in being naked and sweating rather than hair- or fleece-covered and panting.

Panting has some obvious advantages over sweating. While the effectiveness of the skin as an evaporative surface is greater when a hairy covering does not impede air or water vapour movement, the absence of an insulating coat could lead to an excessive heat gain from direct solar radiation, and excessive heat loss by radiation and convection to a cold environment. The efficacy of panting is by contrast, uninfluenced by the extent of the pelage which may insulate the animal against both radiation heat load and the effects of cold. Another advantage of panting over sweating is that substances, especially NaCl, secreted with the evaporative fluid are not lost from the body unless the animal drools (as cattle do during extreme heat stress). There is also the advantage that, except during drooling, there is no wastage of any excess secretion.

Panting is not, however, without its disadvantages. In some circumstances, especially during the sustained exertions of the hunter and hunted there may be a conflict in the use of the respiratory system for both maximum gaseous exchange and maximum evaporative heat loss. Extending this line of thought it is possible that the high rate of sweating in man and horse relates more to their need to lose heat produced during sustained activity than to environmental heat stress *per se*. This suggestion is supported by the observation that the rate of sweating in the horse in response to an intravenous infusion of adrenaline is much greater than that which can be elicited by a high ambient temperature (Allen & Bligh, 1967). However, the relatively high and sustained sweating of cattle and the buffalo is less readily explained in this way.

It is apparent from these comments that while the processes and patterns of evaporative heat loss in different species are currently being observed and reported, the environmental influences both past and present which favour the adoption of one process in preference to another remain largely unexplored.

ADAPTATION TO ARIDITY AND THE AVOIDANCE OF EVAPORATIVE HEAT LOSS

Schmidt-Nielsen *et al.* (1957) were the first to show that the relatively labile body temperatures of the camel and the donkey become even more labile when the animal is dehydrated, and they were also the first to emphasize the advantage of this lability of body temperature in a desert environment. The steady rise in body temperature during diurnal exposure to a high intensity of solar radiation reflects a low rate of evaporative heat loss compared with that which would be necessary to maintain the stability of body temperature. This appears to be a physiological adjustment to aridity which reduces the risk of a disastrous degree of dehydration.

The physiological processes which effect this increased thermolability are unknown, and will probably remain so until more is understood about the nature of the central nervous control of body temperatures. Clearly dehydration exerts some change in the relation between thermal stimulus and thermoregulatory responses which probably involves the functioning of the hypothalamic controller. Possible effects on the thermoregulatory system are expressed diagrammatically in

Fig. 2. There may be no change in the fineness of the degree of control of body temperature which the central nervous thermoregulator seeks to achieve, but dehydration may in some way reduce the effectiveness of the actual processes of evaporative heat loss—perhaps by reducing the rate of fluid secretion onto the evaporative surface. If this were so, the variation in body temperature would be due simply to the reduced capacity of the animal to equate heat production with heat loss (Fig. 2a). Figure 2b illustrates an alternative proposition. The normal 24-h variation in the body temperature which occurs in most mammals has

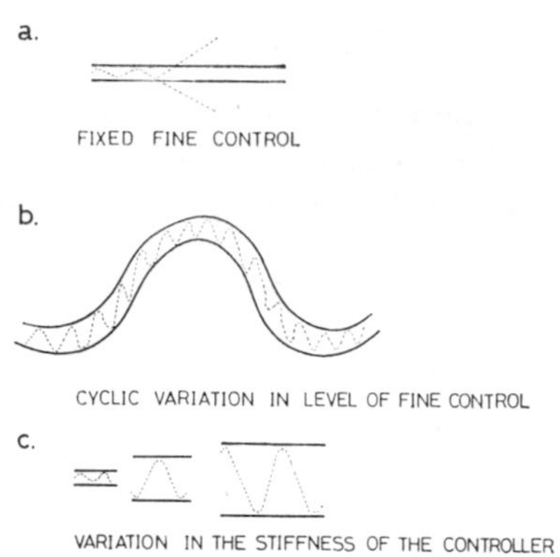

FIG. 2. A diagrammatic representation of the significance that may be attached to variations in body temperature (see text). The dotted lines represent actual core temperature. The solid lines represent the limits within which the thermoregulatory system endeavours to keep core temperature.

been considered to be due to a cyclic shift in the level at which body temperature is being controlled, and the effect of dehydration could be to cause an increase in the extent of this 24-h cyclic shift of the so-called "set-point" of body temperature. If this were so, the rise in body temperature would not result in the activation of the processes of evaporative heat loss so long as body temperature remained close to the rising "set-point". A third possibility is that there are two distinct threshold levels, one for evaporative heat loss, and one for heat production, and that body temperature can vary passively within these two levels. The extent of the 24-h fluctuation in body temperature in different species which, in the studies of Bligh & Harthoorn (1965) was coincident with the fluctuation in ambient temperature, might depend on species differences in the distance between these two threshold levels (Fig. 2c). The distance between these threshold levels may also vary in the one species in different environmental or physiological conditions, and the effect of water deprivation in the camel and donkey may be to raise the threshold for evaporative water loss, and perhaps also lower the threshold for heat production. Evidence of a raised threshold for evaporative heat loss by thermal polypnoea in the dehydrated camel and donkey has been obtained by Maloiy (1971).

Studies on rabbit, cats and dogs of the electrical activity patterns of temperature-sensitive neurones in the region of the hypothalamus concerned in the control of body temperature have permitted the formulation of very tentative proposals concerning the nature of the thresholds for the activation of thermoregulatory effector functions, and how these may be varied.

Five distinct patterns describing the relations between activity and local hypothalamic temperature are illustrated, diagrammatically, in Fig. 3. Some neurones have positive and some negative linear relations, and these are considered to be primary warm-sensors and cold-sensors

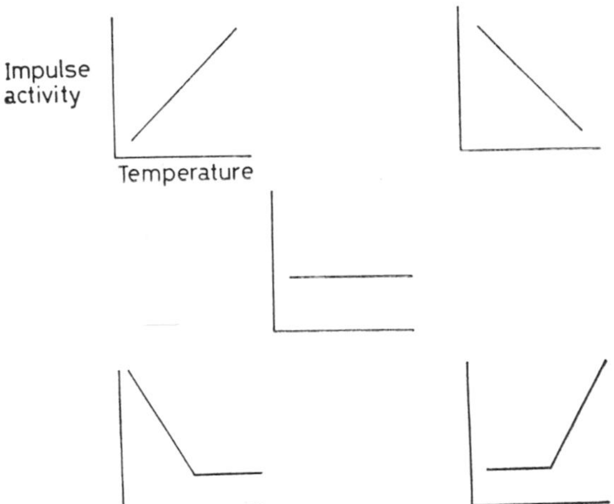

FIG. 3. A diagrammatic representation of the five types of observed relations between local hypothalamic temperature and the electrical activity of single hypothalamic neurones in laboratory species of mammals.

respectively. Other neurones have been found with activities which are virtually unaffected by local changes in hypothalamic temperature. This is a surprising feature since the activity of any neurone might be expected to vary to some extent with temperature, and it has been suggested that these neurones contribute a constant-frequency signal which functions as a reference or "set-point" signal. Those neurones with positive and negative biphasic relations between activity and temperature have been assumed to be interneurones on temperature sensor to thermoregulatory effector pathways. The interpretation placed upon these distinct activity temperature patterns is illustrated in Fig. 4. It is supposed that the set-point signal is in the form of a synaptic inhibitory influence which keeps the interneurone unresponsive to the signals from the primary thermosensor until the activity of the primary sensor is sufficient to overcome the inhibition. In this way there could

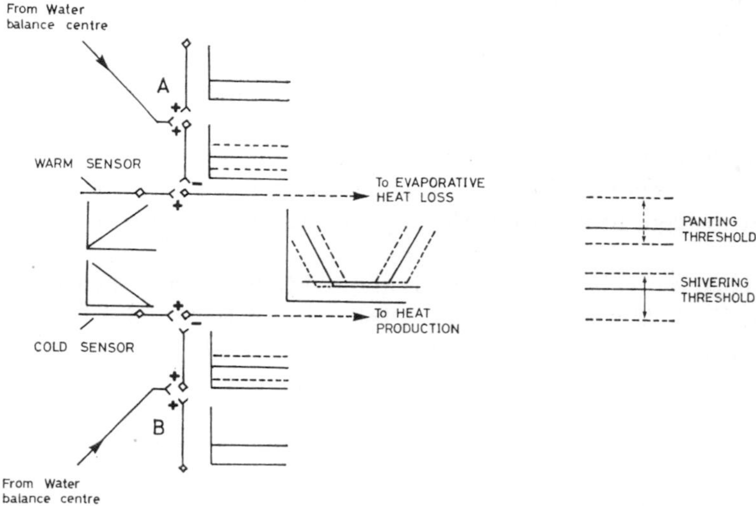

FIG. 4. Suggested relations between the hypothalamic neurones with the different activity/temperature characteristics given in Fig. 3. An inhibitory influence derived from the temperature-insensitive neurones, which act as "threshold-level" or "set-point" signal generators, regulates the relations between the activities of the primary thermosensors and subsequent interneurones. A variation in the intensity of the inhibitory influence might result from neuronal influences acting at synapses "A" and "B". The increased thermolability of the camel during dehydration might be due to excitatory influences derived from the hypothalamic neurone pools concerned in water balance acting at synapse "A", and perhaps also at "B".

be a set-point or critical temperature for sweating or panting, and for shivering.

Numerous studies on laboratory species have shown that if there really is a set-point in temperature regulation, then it is variable in different circumstances. This could be caused by variations in the intensity of the inhibitory influence of the temperature-insensitive neurones resulting from synaptic influences at points "A" and "B" in Fig. 4.

Of course, we do not know that similar units are to be found in the hypothalamic region of the camel, but it requires only a little imagination to suggest that in some species water deprivation, acting via the hypothalamic neurone pools concerned in water balance, might intensify the inhibitory influence as if at synapse "A" in Fig. 4 and thus raise the threshold for evaporative heat loss. This proposition is at least consistent with the observed upward shift in the threshold for thermal polypnoea in the camel and donkey (Maloiy, 1971).

Such an upward shift in the threshold for evaporative heat would not do much to alleviate the risk of dehydration if the heat stress continued for a long time. Once body temperature had risen to the new threshold level for evaporative heat loss, sweating or panting would occur. However, in many tropical arid environments the hot day with a high radiation load on the animal, is followed by a cold night when heat radiates from the animal to the cold night sky. Under these conditions, as Schmidt-Nielsen *et al.* (1957) have pointed out, the animal can afford to store heat during the day because it can shed it during the night.

The lower body temperature is allowed to fall during the cold desert night, the better will be the heat tolerance of the animal to the heat load of the succeeding day. The records of the body temperature of the camel before and after dehydration (Schmidt-Nielsen *et al.*, 1957) indicate that there is a downward shift in the threshold temperature for heat production as well as an upward shift in the threshold temperature for evaporative heat loss. This could be due to an increase in the intensity of the inhibition on the cold-sensors to heat production effector pathways.

If the effect of water deprivation is, indeed, to widen the gap between the threshold temperatures for heat production and evaporative heat loss, then the effect of dehydration on thermoregulation is to increase the range of passive thermolability. This situation should be readily distinguishable from the alternative proposition of an increased 24-h cyclic shift in the set-point level at which body temperature is quite finely controlled. If there is an increased band of passive thermolability, body temperature should follow engineered variations in thermal stress irrespective of the periodicity of these variations. With all the necessary equipment except a camel, I regret that I cannot present the result of this experiment.

HEAT TOLERANCE

The interesting feature of the thermolability of the camel is that this becomes extended under conditions of water deprivation. This indicates that the variability of body temperature control is a dynamic as well as a genetic quality.

In the many studies of the heat tolerance of cattle, it has been assumed that all breeds of this species are obligatory homeotherms and that, when exposed to extremes of heat or cold, they always exercise their thermoregulatory effector functions to the limit in order to maintain the stability of body temperature. Thus an upward movement in core temperature is indicative of the inability of the animal to re-establish a balance between heat production and evaporative heat loss at the normal level of controlled core temperature.

We know that heat tolerance may consist not of a capacity to maintain thermostability in an adverse environment, but of a capacity to tolerate passive variations in body temperature.

The search for greater heat tolerance in a species or breed has largely been aimed at finding individual animals exhibiting an ability to remain thermostable during exposure to heat stress. However, the benefits that thermolability bestows on the camel in hot arid environments could apply equally to cattle. An animal that could browse in the heat of the day instead of seeking shade, and could avoid the loss of water by sweating and panting should be an attractive proposition to the tropical farmer.

The possibility that individual animals within a species may vary in their degrees of passive thermolability, and that heat tolerance may be better related to this than to the ability to sweat or pant and remain thermolabile has been suggested by Schmidt-Nielsen (1964) and Bligh (1970). Chquiloff (1964) has, indeed, reported that the less thermostable native Brazilian cattle prosper better in the heat than do the more thermostable imported European breeds. However, a recent study by Berman (1971) has failed to find any evidence of increased thermolability in cattle during the summer in Israel, and Johnson (1971) has failed to find any great difference in the thermal stability of individual sheep and goats, during short exposures to heat and cold.

Perhaps, after all, this hopeful thought will prove to be barren, but since the studies so far have involved only small numbers of animals, it may be inadvisable for the agricultural physiologist to assume an invariable thermostability in some species, when such marked variations are known to occur between species.

SUMMARY

The maintenance of homeothermy in a hot environment by means of evaporative heat loss, obviously complicates the need to conserve body fluid in order to survive in arid conditions.

Species vary in their degrees of thermolability, in the processes of evaporative heat loss employed during heat stress, and in the ease with which these processes are activated. These species differences may not all be related directly to the thermal components of the environment. Other environmental factors may have influenced the selection of different modes of evaporative heat loss in species which remain equally thermostable in a thermally stressful environment.

Some species which inhabit hot arid environments have relatively labile body temperatures which become even more labile during water deprivation. This is considered to be an adaptation to a situation where the need for water conservation is so great that thermostability has been abandoned. Current views on the neuronal nature of thermoregulatory threshold levels and on the possible influence of dehydration on these thermoregulatory processes are discussed.

The search for heat tolerance in agriculturally important species has been directed towards the selection of animals with the capacity to remain thermostable in adverse climatic conditions. The possibility exists that individual variations in the tolerated degree of passive thermolability may occur within a species and that such variations may be of practical significance.

References

Allen, T. E. & Bligh, J. (1969). A comparative study of the temporal patterns of cutaneous water vapour loss from some domesticated mammals with epitrichial sweat glands. *Comp. Biochem. Physiol.* **31**: 347–363.

Berman, A. (1971). Thermoregulation in intensively lactating cows in near-natural conditions. *J. Physiol., Lond.* **215**: 477–489.

Bligh, J. (1959). The receptors concerned in the thermal stimulus to panting in sheep. *J. Physiol., Lond.* **146**: 142–151.

Bligh, J. (1970). Species differences in the tolerance to meteorological stress, due to differences in function of organisms. *Int. J. Biometeorol.* **4**: 149–156.

Bligh, J. & Harthoorn, A. M. (1965). Continuous radiotelemetric records of the deep body temperature of some unrestrained African mammals under near-natural conditions. *J. Physiol., Lond.* **176**: 145–162.

Bligh, J., Ingram, D. L., Keynes, R. D. & Robinson, S. G. (1965). The deep body temperature of an unrestrained Welsh Mountain sheep recorded by a radiotelemetric technique during a 12-month period. *J. Physiol., Lond.* **176**: 136–144.

Chquiloff, M. A. G. (1964). Estudo comparativo da tolerância de novilhas das raças Gir, Schyz, Jersey, Guernsey e Holandesa P.B., às condições climáticas de Pedro Leopoldo, Minas Gerais. *Archos Esc. Vet. Univ. Minas Gerais* **16**: 19–95.

Green, L. M. A. (1961). Sweat glands in the skin of the Quokka of Western Australia. *Aust. J. exp. Biol.* **39**: 481–486.

Hainsworth, F. R. & Stricker, E. M. (1970). Salivary cooling by rats in the heat. In *Physiological and behavioral temperature regulation*. Hardy, J. D., Gagge, A. P. & Stolwijk, J. A. J. (eds). Springfield, Illinois: Charles C. Thomas.

Hammel, H. T. (1968). Regulation of internal body temperatures. *A. Rev. Physiol.* **30**: 641–710.

Ingram, D. L. (1967). Stimulation of cutaneous glands in the pig. *J. comp. Path.* **77**: 93–98.

Johnson, K. G. (1971). Body temperature lability in sheep and goats during short-term exposures to heat and cold. *J. agric. Sci., Camb.* **77**: 267–272.

Maloiy, G. M. O. (1971). Temperature regulation in the donkey (*Equus asinus*). *Comp. Biochem. Physiol.* **39A**: 403–412.

Mann, S. J. (1968). The tylotrich (hair) follicle of the American Opposum. *Anat. Rec.* **160,** 171–179.

Robertshaw, D. & Taylor, C. R. (1969). A comparison of sweat gland activity in eight species of East African bovids. *J. Physiol., Lond.* **203**: 135–143.

Robinson, K. W. & Morrison, P. R. (1957). The reactions to hot atmospheres of various species of Australian marsupials and placental animals. *J. cell. comp. Physiol.* **49**: 455–478.

Schmidt-Nielsen, K. (1964). *Desert animals: physiological problems of heat and water*. Oxford: Oxford University Press.

Schmidt-Nielsen, K., Schmidt-Nielsen, B., Jarnum, S. A. & Houpt, T. R. (1957). Body temperature of the camel and its relation to water economy. *Am. J. Physiol.* **188**: 103–112.

Symp. zool. Soc. Lond. (1972) No. 31, 371–382.

RECENT ADVANCES IN THE COMPARATIVE PHYSIOLOGY OF DESERT ANIMALS

KNUT SCHMIDT-NIELSEN*

Department of Zoology, Duke University, Durham, North Carolina, U.S.A.

SYNOPSIS

Summarizing remarks, listing selected important highlights of the Symposium, are arranged in synoptic subject categories. Other published contributions are included in order to provide access to some literature sources not extensively discussed elsewhere in this volume.

INTRODUCTION

This paper, which I delivered informally and without a manuscript at the conclusion of the Symposium, is not a literature review, and extensive references are beyond its scope. Its purpose was to summarize and highlight some recent contributions to the comparative physiology of desert animals.

It is always difficult to summarize a field that is in rapid development, for it requires an evaluation not only of the past, but to some extent also of the future. The contributors to this Symposium have provided both. As a group they are responsible for most of the important recent advances in desert physiology, and their articles give excellent reviews and introductions to the research literature. The following synopsis therefore mentions only some of them in conjunction with a few other reports that are of personal interest to me, arranged by abbreviated subject categories.

LOWERED METABOLIC RATE IN DESERT ANIMALS

Sufficient information has now accumulated to conclude that desert animals, on the whole, have lower metabolic rates than closely related species in less arid habitats, as documented, e.g. by J. W. Hudson.

* NIH Research Career Award 1-K6-GM-21,522 and supported by NIH Research Grant HE-02228.

In this connection it is notable that the water turnover rate of mammals, as studied with tritiated water by W. V. Macfarlane, shows a consistent relationship to the metabolic rate. Therefore, water turnover is also correlated with the aridity of the natural habitat of the animals.

A low metabolic rate has at least one advantage in regard to temperature regulation, the internal heat load is reduced, and this presumably will be reflected in a reduced use of water for evaporative temperature regulation. A low metabolic rate also has the obvious consequence that it prolongs the time an animal can live on a given amount of food.

It is interesting that marsupials on the whole have lower metabolic rates than eutherian mammals, as has been demonstrated by T. J. Dawson and by R. E. MacMillen.

TORPOR, HIBERNATION, DORMANCY

It is well known that torpor and hibernation extend the time that an animal can survive on its food reserves. Likewise, an animal with strictly limited water reserves can be expected to survive longer if metabolic rate and use of water is reduced. In this sense torpor can be regarded as a device to stretch time for an animal that is drawing on its water or energy reserves.

An animal that draws on its reserves is in non-steady state. However, torpor can also change the water balance of an animal from non-steady state to a true steady state with positive water balance. This could be due to reduced evaporation associated with a lowered body temperature. Thus, reduced evaporation in dormant rodents has been demonstrated by MacMillen. Also, the Inca dove shows a nightly drop in body temperature which is accompanied by decreased water loss.

On the whole, although it is known that many desert animals undergo periods of torpor, the role of torpor or dormancy in the physiology of desert animals needs more attention that it has received. Both J. W. Hudson and G. A. Bartholomew have contributed information about desert ground squirrels, but it is not clear why one species may aestivate while another in the same habitat may not do so.

DEHYDRATION AND REDUCTION IN METABOLIC RATE

Dehydration (in the sense of a reduction of the water content of the body) has effects on several physiological parameters, one being the metabolic rate, which decreases with increasing dehydration. The analysis is complicated by the fact that metabolic rate is also influenced by body temperature, which changes with state of dehydration, thus indirectly influencing metabolic rate. A computer-aided multiple regression analysis of data on the camel has permitted separation of the direct effects of dehydration on metabolic rate from indirect effects. Decreases in the metabolic rate with dehydration have been observed in a number of East African ungulates by C. R. Taylor. Also A. Shkolnik *et al.* (this symposium, pp 229–242) found a decrease in the metabolic rate in the Beduin goats, when calculated per animal, rather than per unit body weight.

INCREASED BODY TEMPERATURE

An increased body temperature is a widely used strategy which decreases the amount of water used for temperature regulation. In this connection J. Bligh has re-emphasized the dangers of considering a well-maintained body temperature as the sole criterion of heat tolerance. The opposite may well be the case.

The effect of increased body temperature is two-fold. As body temperature is permitted to increase instead of being kept low through evaporation, heat is "stored" in the body and water is saved. Secondly, the increased body temperature reduces the heat load from a hot environment by reducing the temperature gradients, thus reducing evaporation as well. The camel may permit a rise in body temperature of as much as 6°C or 7°C. However, J. Bligh has reported that the sheep do not seem to use this strategy; sheep have an exceptionally constant body temperature with total variations of less than 2°C, even from season to season.

Very high body core temperatures have been observed in East African ungulates by Taylor, in particular in animals with increased heat loads due to activity (running). A very important aspect is that the brain temperature can be maintained several degrees lower than the central arterial blood temperature. The blood to the brain flows through arteries that run through the cavernous sinus, which is filled by relatively cool venous blood draining from the nasal region where evaporation takes place. Thus, the arterial blood supplying the brain is pre-cooled, as demonstrated by M. A. Baker and J. N. Hayward in a number of domestic animals.

The well-established pattern that eutherian mammals maintain a normal body temperature around 38°C, marsupials a few degrees lower, around 35°C to 36°C, and monotremes (e.g. echidna) maintain 30°C, remains puzzling. Many marsupials inhabit the hot, arid interior of Australia, and also the echidna (*Tachyglossus aculeatus*) extends its range to the arid interior. It has been well established that the echidna is not to be considered a "primitive" temperature regulator in the sense that it lacks ability to regulate its body temperature, on the contrary, in the cold it maintains its body temperature very well indeed. More puzzling is the fact that it seems unable to resist heat and succumbs when its body temperature reaches about 37°C.

CONDUCTANCE AT HIGH AMBIENT TEMPERATURE

The North American hares, known as jack rabbits, have extremely large ears. Large ears are characteristic of many other desert animals as well. When air temperature is lower than body temperature, the large ears are effective in dissipating heat to the environment. If the air temperature exceeds body temperature, however, the large surfaces would seem disadvantageous in that they increase the surface by which heat is absorbed. In jack rabbits this disadvantage is counteracted by a three to four-fold decrease in over-all conductance at high temperature, primarily due to vaso-constriction in the ears.

This reduction in over-all conductance is important in reducing external heat loads. According to D. S. Hinds and W. A. Calder (pers. comm.) the *Pyrrhuloxia* and the cardinal, two Arizona birds, may also show reductions in over-all conductance when air temperature exceeds body temperature.

ACTIVITY, EXERCISE AND TEMPERATURE REGULATION

Previously, laboratory studies consisted mostly in imposing external heat loads on animals by increasing air temperature, while investigators neglected internal heat loads caused by activity. More recently, increasing attention has been given to internal heat loads and exercise. This is particularly important because of the effects of exercise on body temperature, which often is found to be elevated, yet well regulated at a level corresponding to the activity level.

The muscular work of the respiratory muscles also produces heat, and in panting animals this heat production will be increased. It has been known for some time that dogs pant at a resonant frequency, which means that the muscular work that goes into maintaining a high respiratory rate is minimized. Thus the internal heat load caused by panting is reduced to a small fraction of what it otherwise would be. E. C. Crawford (pers. comm.) has recently shown that the panting of pigeons also takes place at a resonant frequency.

PANTING

Panting in mammals and birds has been studied for many years. Contributions that clarify associated problems of carbon dioxide and acid base regulation continue to be published. Many animals seem to display two types of panting, a stage I with a relatively high frequency and shallow breathing during which gas exchange remains normal, and a stage II which is slower, deeper, and leads to severe alkalosis. According to J. R. S. Hales and J. Bligh, in the ox the second stage seems to permit greater heat dissipation, but at greater cost.

Interesting changes in respiration frequency, tidal volume, and conspicuously large changes in functional dead space have been observed by Taylor in the wildebeest, which seems able to increase functional dead space by including the large nasal sinuses in the ventilated volume.

G. M. O. Maloiy has shown that the increase in respiratory frequency that takes place in camels and donkeys at high temperature is influenced by the state of hydration of the animal. In dehydrated individuals the increase in respiration frequency occurs at a higher body temperature.

PANTING VERSUS SWEATING

We still lack a clear interpretation of the physiological differences between sweating and panting. On the whole, panting animals are of smaller body size, and at a body weight around 100 kg, sweating becomes the primary avenue for evaporation. In the ox, for example, J. D. Findlay shows that, although the ox pants, cutaneous evaporation accounts for 75% of the total heat loss.

A major difference between panting and sweating is that the panting animal provides its own air flow over the cooling surfaces; the sweating animal must depend on free or external forced convection. It is consistent with this view that man, who presumably evolved as a hunter in steppe and savannah country, is an excellent sweater. If sweating is needed primarily during running, the necessary air flow is thus provided. Likewise, the sweating of large ungulates can be interpreted as suitable for animals that are preyed upon, and therefore may be pursued and need to escape by running. However, this simplified picture is not consistent with the fact that smaller ungulates primarily pant; nor is it supported by the fact that the Cape hunting dog, which hunts in a fashion similar to man by tirelessly running down its prey until it is exhausted, is a panting animal.

There is, of course, no *a priori* reason that a simple and logical interpretation exists which can explain, in teleological or related terms, the relative advantages of sweating and panting.

RESPIRATORY EVAPORATION

When heat stress is absent, it is in the interest of the desert animal to reduce evaporation. Exhaled air is saturated with water vapour, and the respiratory tract is thus a major avenue of water loss. It is therefore of importance that air may be exhaled at temperatures well below body core or lung temperature. This is particularly important in small rodents, which may exhale air at temperatures even lower than that of the inhaled air. For example, a kangaroo rat breathing dry air at 28°C has an exhaled air temperature of below 24°C. The water loss from the respiratory tract may thus be reduced by as much as 85%, relative to what the water loss would be if the air were exhaled saturated at body core temperature (38°C).

The lung air is at body core temperature, and on exhalation the air gives up heat to the walls of the nasal passages. These were cooled by the incoming air during the preceding inhalation. The cooling of the exhaled air is due to simple heat exchange, and is an inevitable result of the geometry of the passageways. Birds have shorter and wider passageways, and the mechanism is therefore less effective but still of considerable importance to the water balance. Also lizards, when their body temperature exceeds the ambient air temperature due to incoming radiation, gain an advantage in water balance by exhalation of air at temperatures below body core.

OVER-ALL HEAT BALANCE

The complete description of the heat balance of an animal under natural conditions is a task of formidable complexity. Virginia Finch has applied to large ungulates the approach used by D. M. Gates for plant communities. The results indicate an amazing agreement between measured parameters and theoretical heat balance.

It now seems that an accurate description can be given in quantitative terms of the relative importance of air temperature, convection, relative humidity, radiation from the environment, and solar radiation. When these parameters are evaluated in relation to the animal's size, shape, orientation to the sun, fur absorptivity, conductance of tissue and fur, rate of evaporation, and metabolic rate, a complete description of heat balance is possible. This accomplishment is impressive, and if generally applicable, it will be a major advance in environmental physiology.

In connection with the interesting presentation by Bligh of his theories for the control mechanisms involved in temperature regulation, it is of importance that the thermal receptors necessary to achieve integration of thermal information have been investigated by A. Iggo. Both peripheral cold receptors and warm receptors have, over a wide temperature range, a proportional response to the deviations from a narrow range of thermoneutrality, thus providing an excellent input to the central control system. The concept of a single "thermostatic" control device has long since been abandoned; the emerging description of body temperature control in terms of control theory promises to give clear and conceptually adequate results.

URINE CONCENTRATION AND WATER LOSS

It has long been known that a high concentrating ability of the mammalian kidney is an important factor in water conservation, in particular in small rodents. MacMillen has recently extended such studies to several Australian mammals, some of which have the highest renal concentrating abilities known.

In larger animals, maximum urine concentrations seem to be less extreme. For example, this is the case with the camel, as reported by Maloiy. If we wish to give a rational explanation for this difference, it can be related to the fact that larger animals, which use water for temperature regulation, stand to gain relatively little by forming a more concentrated urine; the amount of water saved is small compared to the need for evaporation. For the small mammal, the entire water balance depends on an efficient renal mechanism for water conservation.

NON-MAMMALIAN FORMS, BIRDS

In the preceding I have mostly discussed mammals, primarily because more information is available about these than about other desert animals. The principles, however, do in general apply to birds, and to some extent also to poikilothermic animals. I shall briefly mention a few points that may be worth considering.

Many investigations have shown that birds, desert and non-desert species alike, have excellent temperature tolerance and heat regulation. This corrects the previously widely held opinion that birds are less heat tolerant than mammals; a belief based on experiments in which the experimental animals were unable to utilize fully their powers of evaporation.

The high normal body temperature of birds may be considered a biological advantage. As mentioned before, a high body temperature reduces the environmental heat load in hot surroundings. This may be particularly important for small birds, which, as opposed to small mammals, rarely utilize underground burrows as shelter against desert heat. Large birds can, and to some extent do, escape by soaring high in the air where temperatures are lower.

The relationship between panting and gular flutter in birds has been clarified by R. E. Lasiewski, G. A. Bartholomew and their collaborators. Panting refers to breathing movements of thorax and abdomen, while gular flutter refers to rapid movements of the thin floor of the mouth and the upper region of the throat. Panting and gular flutter may or may not occur simultaneously, and if they do, they may or may not be synchronized. The importance of the two mechanisms in temperature regulation is well established, but their relative roles remain uncertain.

The effect of panting on the birds includes development of extreme alkalosis, as reported by Calder. One bird, the ostrich, differs from all other birds that have been studied, it can pant heavily for several hours without showing signs of alkalosis.

REPTILES

The important role of the nasal gland of reptiles in the excretion of monovalent ions (Na, K, Cl) has been carefully studied by J. R. Templeton, who also has considered the importance of excretion of Na and K as urates of low solubility. In this connection it is of interest that D. E. Murrish demonstrated that the colloid osmotic pressure of the blood plasma provides sufficient osmotic force to explain cloacal withdrawal of water from lizard urine, but his studies by no means exclude other cloacal mechanisms that may also be involved in water transport.

It was shown by P. J. Bentley *et al.* that the reptilian integument by no means is impermeable to water, and in most reptiles water loss from the dry integument substantially exceeds the water loss from the moist respiratory tract. There is an ecological correlation, in that the evaporation from the integument is relatively smaller in reptiles from arid habitats, although it may still constitute 70% of the total evaporation. The total magnitude of this evaporation, however, is apparently of no significance in temperature regulation. Otherwise, there have been few, conceptually new findings on reptiles that contribute to the understanding of these animals as successful desert dwellers.

AMPHIBIA

A large number of amphibians have been carefully studied by M. R. Warburg who in this Symposium has reported in detail on his interesting results.

One important, indeed revolutionary, recent finding, merits a detailed discussion. J. P. Loveridge has reported that the Rhodesian frcg, *Chiromantis xerampelina* loses water from the skin very slowly, at a rate comparable to that of reptiles. Furthermore, *Chiromantis* seems to excrete uric acid, rather than urea as all other amphibians have been reported to do.

Loveridge, whose work on the water balance of desert locusts is well known, determined uric acid in *Chiromantis* urine, using the enzymatic method (which should be completely specific for uric acid), and found uric acid to make up 60–70% of the dry weight of the urine.

Three *Chiromantis* were kept in dry air at room temperature for 122, 155 and 183 days. The former two died, but the third survived for the six months, losing weight from 27·10 to 9·14 g (a 67% weight loss). It was rehydrated and fed, and recovered fully. The weight losses in dry air of various frogs and one reptile are shown in (Fig. 1). The results seem extremely convincing.

Conceptually, the most astonishing aspect of this peculiar amphibian is perhaps not the low evaporation, but the uric acid excretion. Uric acid synthesis, when taking place from ammonia derived from amino acid deamination (rather than from purine metabolism) is a rather

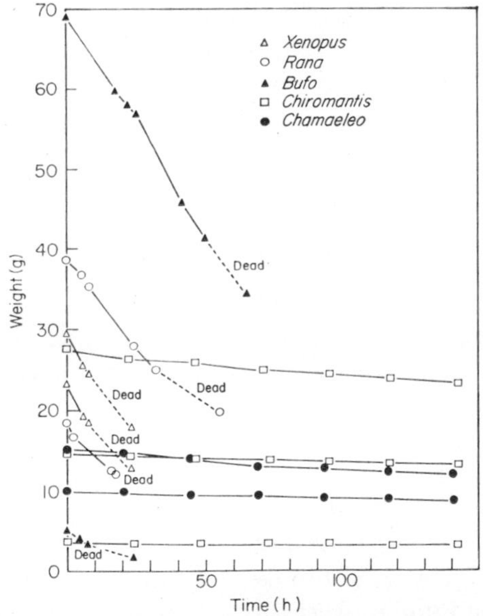

Fig. 1. Weight changes of frogs and lizards at 25°C, 20–28% relative humidity. The frog *Chiromantis* and the lizard *Chamaeleo* lose weight at similar slow rates. The three other amphibians, *Xenopus*, *Rana* and *Bufo*, lose weight rapidly, as is characteristic of moist-skinned amphibians in general. (From Loveridge, 1970.)

complicated synthesis which requires a series of enzymatic steps. Nothing is known about the pathway in these amphibians, but in mammals uric acid biosynthesis requires some six steps involving the use of lysine, glutamine, aspartate, and formate.

The use by an amphibian of the uric acid mode of nitrogen excretion, otherwise characteristic of birds and reptiles, is indeed sensational.

INVERTEBRATES

The water balance of arthropods, especially the desert locust, has been interestingly discussed by J. Shaw and R. H. Stobbart.

Arthropods are in many respects uniquely different from vertebrates, they have a nearly impermeable hard cuticle, and their respiratory system is different. The control of air access to the respiratory system through the spiracles is of profound importance for their water balance. An important mechanism, by now well known, is the so-called discontinuous respiration.

The most spectacular physiological characteristic of arthropods is their ability to absorb water vapour from air far below the saturation point. This mechanism has been well documented in several insects and some other arthropods, but the nature of the mechanism remains essentially unknown. Recent evidence by J. Noble-Nesbitt suggests that the water may be taken up in the rectum, rather than from the general surface of the integument.

The meager information available about the physiology of desert snails requires no further mention: this subject has already been discussed in this Symposium.

SUMMARIZING REMARKS

As I look back over a quarter century of association with the physiology of desert animals, I find that the changes are striking. Early in this period information was obtained only about a few selected species. It was natural, indeed mandatory, that studies were carried out on those animals whose life in the desert seemed most unique. Thus, the ability of rodents to live on dry food without noticeable access to free water, required clarification.

In my mind, the most conspicuous development is that information is now available for a large number of animals, both those that seem spectacular to the human observer, and many others that also survive in deserts in spite of heat and aridity.

It is most important that the increasing amount of reliable information provides material for comparative evaluations. This is indeed one of the most fruitful aspects of comparative physiology, a comparison of the methods and strategies used in coping with the environment often clarifies principles which at first glance are not clear and apparent. Thus, all reliable information that is being accumulated acquires importance in arriving at the fundamental concepts necessary for our understanding of animal life in the desert.

One final word, it is interesting to the physiologist to study what animals do under experimental conditions, this clarifies both how animals respond to certain manipulations and shows what they are able to do under extreme conditions. What is equally important, however, is that field studies are carried out by investigators who have a clear understanding of animal physiology. This approach will be increasingly important in telling what animals really do to cope with conditions in those deserts where they actually live.

References

Much of the information mentioned in these summarizing remarks has been discussed and documented in other articles in this volume. The following brief list provides a few additional references that may give the reader access to further literature sources. I sincerely apologize for failures and oversights, and for my strong personal bias in making this selection.

Baker, M. A. & Hayward, J. N. (1968). The influence of the nasal mucosa and the carotid rete upon hypothalamic temperature in sheep. *J. Physiol., Lond.* **198**: 561–579.

Bartholomew, G. A., Lasiewski, R. C. & Crawford, E. C., Jr. (1968). Patterns of panting and gular flutter in cormorants, pelicans, owls, and doves. *Condor,* **70**: 31–34.

Bentley, P. J. & Schmidt-Nielsen, K. (1966). Cutaneous water loss in reptiles. *Science, N.Y.* **151**: 1547–1549.

Bligh, J., Ingram, D. L., Keynes, R. D. & Robinson, S. G. (1965). The deep body temperature of an unrestrained Welsh mountain sheep recorded by a radiotelemetric technique during a 12-month period. *J. Physiol., Lond.,* **176**: 136–144.

Calder, W. A., Jr. & Schmidt-Nielsen, K. (1966). Evaporative cooling and respiratory alkalosis in the pigeon. *Proc. natn. Acad. Sci. U.S.A.,* **55**: 750–756.

Crawford, E. C., Jr. & Kampe, G. (1971). Resonant panting in pigeons. *Comp. Biochem. Physiol.,* **40A**: 549–552.

Dawson, T. J. & Hulbert, A. J. (1970). Standard metabolism, body temperature, and surface areas of Australian marsupials. *Am. J. Physiol.* **218**: 1233–1238.

Finch, V. A. (1972). Thermoregulation and heat balance of the East African eland and hartebeest. *Am. J. Physiol.,* **222**: 1374–1379.

Gates, D. M. (1962). *Energy Exchange in the Biosphere.* 151 pp. New York: Harper & Row.

Hales, J. R. S. & Findlay, J. D. (1968). Respiration of the ox: normal values and the effects of exposure to hot environments. *Resp. Physiol.*, **4**: 333–352.

Loveridge, J. P. (1970). Observations on nitrogenous excretion and water relations of *Chiromantis xerampelina* (Amphibia, Anura). *Arnoldia*, **5**: 1–6.

MacMillen, R. E. & Nelson, J. E. (1969). Bioenergetics and body size in dasyurid marsupials. *Am. J. Physiol.* **217**: 1246–1251.

MacMillen, R. E. & Trost, C. H. (1967). Nocturnal hypothermia in the Inca dove, *Scardafella inca. Comp. Biochem. Physiol.*, **23**: 243–253.

Murrish, D. E. & Schmidt-Nielsen, K. (1970). Water transport in the cloaca of lizards: active or passive? *Science, N.Y.*, **170**: 324–326.

Nielsen, M. (1970). Heat production and body temperature during rest and work. In: *Physiological and Behavioral Temperature Regulation*, J. D. Hardy, A. P. Gagge & J. A. J. Stolwijk (eds), pp. 205–214. Springfield, Ill.: Charles C. Thomas.

Noble-Nesbitt, J. (1970). Water balance in the firebrat, *Thermobia domestica* (Packard). *J. exp. Biol.*, **52**: 192–300.

Schmidt-Nielsen, K., Crawford, E. C. Jr., Newsome, A. E., Rawson, K. S. & Hammel, H. T. (1967). Metabolic rate of camels: effect of body temperature and dehydration. *Am. J. Physiol.* **212**: 341–346.

Schmidt-Nielsen, K., Dawson, T. J. & Crawford, E. C., Jr. (1966). Temperature regulation in the echidna (*Tachyglossus aculeatus*). *J. cell. comp. Physiol.*, **67**: 63–72.

Schmidt-Nielsen, K., Dawson, T. J., Hammel, H. T., Hinds, D. & Jackson, D. C. (1965). The jack rabbit—a study in desert survival. *Hvalråd. Skr.* **48**: 125–142.

Schmidt-Nielsen, K., Hainsworth, F. R. & Murrish, D. E. (1970). Counter-current heat exchange in the respiratory passages: effect on water and heat balance. *Resp. Physiol.*, **9**: 263–276.

Taylor, C. R. & Lynn, C. P. (1972). Heat storage in running antelopes: independence of brain and body temperatures. *Am. J. Physiol.* **222**: 114–117.

Taylor, C. R., Robertshaw, D. & Hofmann, R. (1969). Thermal panting: a comparison of wildebeest and zebu cattle. *Am. J. Physiol.*, **217**: 907–910.

Taylor, C. R., Schmidt-Nielsen, K., Dmi'el, R. & Fedak, M. (1971). Effect of hyperthermia on heat balance during running in the African hunting dog. *Am. J. Physiol.*, **220**: 823–827.

AUTHOR INDEX

Numbers in italics refer to pages in the References at the end of each article.

R

T

U

V

SUBJECT INDEX

D

L

R